WORLD OF MAN

A LIBRARY OF THEORY AND RESEARCH IN THE HUMAN SCIENCES

Editor: R. D. Laing

The Action–Image of Society

The Action–Image of Society

ON CULTURAL POLITICIZATION

ALFRED WILLENER

Translated from the French
by A. M. Sheridan Smith

TAVISTOCK PUBLICATIONS

This translation first published in 1970
by Tavistock Publications Limited
11 New Fetter Lane, London EC4
Printed in Great Britain
in 12/13 Bembo
by Butler & Tanner Ltd
Frome and London

Illustrations and additional text © Alfred Willener 1970
English translation © Tavistock Publications Limited 1970

A shorter version has been published in French under the title
L'Image-action de la société
by Éditions du Seuil, Paris
© Éditions du Seuil 1970

SBN 422 73320 2 (hardbound)
SBN 422 75050 6 (paperback)

for M.W.

Contents

APPENDICES

Acknowledgements

This work would not have been possible without the cooperation of several people, in particular those who replied to our questions.

I was assisted editorially throughout by Paul Beaud, who was always well informed, efficient, and full of ideas. Chapters 1, 2, 3, 5, and 6 are our joint writing, and Chapter 10 is his own. Pierre Gallissaires helped in the collection of documentary material and wrote Chapters 7 and 8, and one of the appendices. Both of them played a part in shaping the general form of the work in the course of many lively discussions, besides contributing in a more detailed way.

The opinion poll and the recorded interviews were carried out with the aid of Charlotte Busch, Lucy Willener, Michael and Babette Buttgereit, Pierre and Christiane Rolle, Pierre Tripier, and Hermann Jaeger, who also gave help and advice.

Monic Gille, with her constructive attitude, and her sense of order and humour, did much more than the already heavy task of typing all the manuscripts.

A. W.

Paris, April 1969

Introduction to some Conclusions

It was while working with the Edinburgh sociologist Tom Burns on a comparative European project that I had the idea of developing and complementing the study of the problems raised by the curiously solid, widely discussed – and questionable – notion of the image of society, by examining social categories that have been forced to adapt to rapid and constant change.

When the May explosion occurred in France, we realized that it would hardly be reasonable to expect the students to be able to present *an* image of present-day society or a clear vision of the future. We set out to explore the questions raised by this social notion in relation to accelerating and permanent change.

Subsequently, the research developed in rather unexpected ways. It is clear now, with the conclusion written, that the general remarks on literature and the problems concerning this notion of the image of society with which we expected to conclude this study would not really be relevant, any more than hypotheses would be in the introduction – the hypotheses that any self-respecting writer has to formulate as a point of departure. On the basis of the analysis of a short opinion poll carried out by means of a questionnaire (Chapter 2), we came to realize increasingly that the only valid introduction would be the evidence of a student who had actively participated in the events (interview with ND, Chapter 1), which is reproduced practically in full. This interview, recorded in May itself, contains, in fact, most of the themes we developed later.

After some weeks' reflection on our material, it seemed to us that the double juncture between anarchism and Marxism and between politics and culture was probably one of the essential features of the May events, even if it does not exhaust the full range of possible interpretations of a complex phenomenon that comprises aspects of the crisis and evolution of society, of education and social conflicts, and so on. We felt that a kinship existed between May and various other movements, both earlier (Dada, Surrealism) and contemporary (avant-garde movements in jazz, the theatre, and the cinema), and tried to understand, by means of a

xiii

rather special type of exploration, covering all aspects of a particular social world, this current or trend that might be called 'cultural politicization'.

A group discussion with intellectuals who had experienced the events at first hand (Chapter 3) served to illustrate a number of major problems and to outline some of the methods of analysis used. It seemed to us at the time to be essential to study the world inhabited by the different social 'actors', students and intellectuals in particular, from the inside. Such a method, which might be called 'hermeneutic',[1] involves, as we have tried to show in our treatment of the notions of project and projection (Chapter 4), the classification of one's observations within their own frame of reference if their full consequences are to be grasped. We have been helped in this by quotations from authors in the same field, whether or not they were participants in our group discussion.

Taking as a basis texts written by activists, students, and intellectuals, we then tried to describe as fully as possible, but within the limitations of *one* of the main currents of the May Movement, a whole series of stages in their imagination and action, which, since the two notions merge together in practice, we have called 'imaginaction'. The first characteristic of this intersectional, politico-cultural, anarcho-Marxist current is to proceed from a total critique of established society, a critique that is also directed at the established opposition (Chapter 5), to the *affirmation* of a new society that is experienced, here and now, as we ourselves saw, a society that was non-established and intended to remain so (Chapter 6).

As our thinking advanced – the different chapters were developed simultaneously, in relation to one another – we became increasingly conscious of the fact that May seemed, in turn, to explain Dada, Surrealism, Free Jazz, etc. Between the creativity expressed by a number of the participants in May and that of certain non-conformist intellectuals – whose works were hardly read before this spring thaw – or artistic movements that we wished to place in parallel, there exists a homology that presents a problem too vast for us to do more than merely elucidate the data. It is left to other studies, or to an analysis taking this study as its starting-point, to carry the investigation further than we have been able to do at present.

Do these rather obscure movements contain phenomena that are an affirmation of a new society, and not merely of a subculture, or an inverted culture, or a pathology? Are these tendencies, including certain aspects of the May Movement, such as we have presented here, microcosms, a *prototype* that prefigures, if not the society of tomorrow, at least

[1] We shall touch on the epistemological problems in the conclusion.

some of its problems and solutions? Can one speak, with Edgar Morin, of anthropolitics?

What we have come to is not so much a conclusion, an answer to these questions, as a realization that the important thing was not simply to gain a better understanding of May through the parallels we made; what was important was that these parallels could be made at all. Such an approach is the exact opposite of the kind that, from an *a priori* position, declares that 'it was not political'. Political it certainly was, but in a different way.

PART I

The Movement as seen by its Participants

CHAPTER I

The Student in Action

Activists' Accounts

A great many works have already been published that describe, analyse, or interpret the 'events of May', but much remains that is undocumented or unexplained. The brief accounts that follow are, of course, no more than fragments, but they may serve to illustrate aspects of our interpretation that might otherwise suffer from over-abstraction. Their purpose will be to present at the outset a number of the problems examined in later chapters, within the unity of an extended and very 'open' interview. It is, of course, only one example, though one that we consider to be of exceptional quality. In any case, there is no reason why one should not offer an isolated illustration, provided it is relevant; our aim is not, we hasten to add, to produce an overall account of the 'Mouvement de Mai', but to elucidate a new current of practice and ideas. In order to emphasize the diversity of interpretation, and, naturally enough, of insight found among the participants, we shall complement this material with extracts from other interviews. While it is true that a double juncture took place – Marxism/anarchism, politics/culture – all kinds of subtle differences were to be found, of course, and for many individuals one element of the juncture, or one of the junctures, was of particular importance; in addition, there were those who placed themselves completely outside these junctures.

THE INTERVIEW WITH ND

The woman interviewed is twenty-five years old, married, and a third-year student of philosophy and sociology at the Sorbonne. Though not a member of any political party, she has had a certain amount of political experience, mainly in relation to Algeria and Vietnam. She reads

3

newspapers in general, rather than any particular one, and is fairly familiar with the works of Proudhon, Marx, Saint-Simon, Hegel, Fourier, etc. Until May 1968, she paid little attention to political groups within the university, having been put off by the way in which they operated.

She took an active part in the May Movement, and was able, because of her training, to describe it as an observer. Only those passages dealing with the chronological sequence of events have been cut or condensed. The interview took place on 25 May, the day on which negotiations opened in the Rue de Grenelle between the government, the employers' representatives, and the unions, and the day after the important demonstration at the Gare de Lyon that was to end in another night of barricades in Paris and the provinces.[1]

How do you think it all began?

It began quite suddenly. Three weeks ago, no one in the Sorbonne dreamt that such a thing could happen. On the Friday, students were arrested inside the Sorbonne.[2] Actually, I was at a friend's place, revising for my exams. We didn't even put the radio on – it never occurred to us that anything important might happen that would take us away from our work. The events at Nanterre seemed to us to be a really *local* phenomenon . . . That evening, someone came to tell us what was happening. I dashed over to the Quarter and saw rows of police, guns at the ready, guarding the Sorbonne. I said to myself: 'This means war!' Things came to a head quite suddenly. Right from the beginning there was a terrible 'confrontation of forces'. It was no longer a matter of a *flic* walking up and down saying 'Move on!', but the police massed together, guns at the ready, wearing crash-helmets . . .

Was it then that you felt that 'it could happen'?

I felt that something very important had happened. I've always been fairly interested in politics and wanted a change in a society that is absurd for lots of reasons. But in all our talks together, among our friends, no one seemed to know how to get people out onto the streets so that *it could happen*.

And at that point, you began to feel that they were on the streets . . .

No, not that night. I said to myself: 'Look! What's happening?' What I felt was that the Gaullist regime was a police regime, which I already knew anyway. Then I went to the demonstration that was organized on the Monday as

[1] Interview recorded by W.
[2] Friday, 3 May: at the request of the rector, M. Roche, the police intervened to disperse a meeting that was being held in the courtyard of the Sorbonne. The first scuffles took place in the Latin Quarter.

a protest against the arrests.[1] We marched for hours. People were in the streets, watching us. At that time it was all very much a student affair, but the content of the slogans caused a good deal of surprise. I didn't get the impression that there'd been much *mobilization* of people, even of the students – I'd say especially of the students, since they were the people I knew best. It seemed much less emotive. I found a good many students there I wouldn't have thought would have been interested.

How do you explain that things developed the way they did?

There were a lot of people who had been working entirely on one problem, Vietnam, for example, or the Third World . . . It had been quite useful; it made people more aware of world problems, I think. They carried their reasoning to its logical conclusion, though their thought was still coloured by those problems – those of planetary reorganization.

But how did it spread, at that particular time and place?

I don't think this kind of preparation applied to a great many people. What I mean is that it enabled a certain number of people to remain less confined within the problem of a small political organization. It served as a kind of first experience of political practice – it meant that their demands, their slogans, their arguments took on a more real content, were more firmly rooted in the reality of this society. As for the others, I think they were drawn in very rapidly, in the first week, through their experience of what happened on the streets. I think the confrontations with the police revealed more clearly the repressive basis of that society, that police repression was the expression of a more muffled repression that we knew existed elsewhere, quite apart from moments of crisis . . . On the Monday . . . slogans began to be used ('power to the workers') that went well beyond the student problem . . .

Had there been any attempt to reflect on what was happening, any discussion as to the world you wished to create?

No, at that time it was no more than a criticism of Gaullism.

What was it about Gaullism that you criticized?

The fact that it was a government produced by a military *coup d'état*, which, in spite of certain policies accepted by the Communists in the field of foreign affairs, for example, was in fact a repressive government that was carrying out a foreign policy that gave some satisfaction to the Left. Not that I consider the Communists as belonging to the Left. I'll come back to that later . . .

[1] Monday, 6 May: the first great student demonstration in the Latin Quarter and the first large-scale intervention by the police.

The biggest thing I learnt in all this business, and I learnt it right from the beginning, was that the *internal problems of a country* – we were well aware of this, of course – determine the significance of that country's politics to a far greater extent than do external problems, which are merely the super-structure, which collapses as soon as one begins to criticize internal problems . . . We also learnt very quickly that the mode of contestation open to us in this relation of forces, this police state, was violent contestation.

On the Monday, when you saw the first police charges, the first wounded, the first tear-gas victims . . . did you remember anything you had read of similar historic events, in other times and places?

It's very curious, but *everything is new* in such cases. You try to work out what's happening in terms of what you see.

Could you say something about the Friday night . . .[1]

The Friday night was something much more broadly based, that is, there were young workers, there were university teachers – about 50,000 people altogether. The extraordinary thing about it – to us, at least, who were used to peaceful marches from the Bastille to the République, organized by the Party and the CGT[2] – was that everyone took it upon himself to say how such a demonstration should be organized. Obviously, when there are 50,000 people that's no easy matter. But the people belonging to the most strongly represented tendencies explained through hailers how they saw the demonstration, so for once nobody was telling us that we had to choose between the CP demo and the pro-Chinese demo, with all the political implications and limitations on the mode of contestation that such a choice would have involved.

How did people express their approval?

For example, there was this guy saying: 'We'll go this way. They told us to go to Issy-les-Moulineaux, we'll go to Issy-les-Moulineaux.' Then we said to each other, 'He's a pro-Chinese', judging by what he said at the microphone. So people went up to him and asked him why he had said that, and a discussion got going. There was a certain amount of indecision, but people were really discussing among themselves. The exciting thing about that case was that the *decisions* were *discussed*. There were people who explained those decisions out loud so that everyone could hear. Someone had tried to carry his point of view simply by saying 'We'll go this way', but people did not follow him without knowing why.

[1] The night of 10–11 May.
[2] The form traditionally taken by left-wing demonstrations in Paris is that of a march from the Place de la Bastille to the Place de la République. The 'Party' is, of course, the French Communist Party, and the CGT (Confédération Générale du Travail) the Communist-led trade union federation. (Translator's note.)

What were your own feelings, seeing this unusual process at work?

Well, I said to myself: 'Right! Now why did he tell us to go that way?' I went over to him and tried to find out why he wanted to go there. I discussed it with him . . .

Had you any desire to go a different way?

Actually, no. But I'd no particular wish to go to Issy-les-Moulineaux. If we're going to oppose the regime, then we should do it where it hurts most.[1]

Is that what you thought beforehand?

No, one *discovered* it. You see, I'm not as young as most of the students and I had a lot of old reflexes from earlier demonstrations. I was constantly having to stop myself. I understood what was happening, and said to myself, 'Hell, there I go again, reacting in the same old idiotic way!'

For the others, for the younger ones, did it seem quite natural, then, or was it simply a sort of apprenticeship?

It was an apprenticeship for everyone, of whatever generation.

How was the decision taken?

It was, after all, a demonstration to obtain the release of the arrested students, so we decided to march past the Santé prison, the *symbol* of our prison society. When we got to the Santé, people started to shout, 'Free our comrades!' And, suddenly, everyone started arguing, saying that it was just as disgusting for all the others who were in there; that, really, there were people who had been locked up for social reasons that were just as absurd as those for which the students had been arrested in the Sorbonne. People started shouting, 'Free the prisoners!' One always rose to a higher social level. It was very interesting.

Was it quite clear that 'prisoners' meant 'all the prisoners', not just 'our prisoners'?

Yes. I've talked with a lot of guys who've worked in remand homes. Really, the fact of arresting someone is *a failure on the part of society*. Anyway, that's how they see it: a society that has no other way of intervening but by making an arrest – repression, in other words.

Were there any banners declaring allegiance to a party or a union in this demonstration?

What has happened recently is very interesting. The banners referred to people's work. They were *syndicalist* in presentation – but whereas the union claims to be non-political, it's at the work level that political problems arise.

[1] The implication being that Issy-les-Moulineaux, a working-class suburb to the south-west of Paris, was not such a place. (Translator's note.)

7

That's another thing that was disproved by the facts – people came with their union banners, but in fact they were participating more and more in demonstrations of a political nature and the political parties couldn't stand the pace. Because if a party had arrived at that time and tried to impose its organization on a movement that had decided to find its own *internal structure*, it would have been an act of aggression against that movement.

Did people manage to group themselves behind the banners?

They started off like that, but these divisions broke down very quickly.

Right, what happened then? You got to the Latin Quarter and found the police guarding the Sorbonne. What did you decide to do then?

Confronted by *flics* dressed up as they were and in the state they were in, even when there are 50,000 of you . . . Anyway, we didn't know our own limitations and *possibilities*. In fact, it was the *flics* who enabled us to *discover* them, because before our guys didn't know the extent of their own courage.

Who proved the most courageous?

The eighteen-year-old lads. Then, by the Friday, there were the workers. We felt that our problems were all closely connected: qualifications, unemployment, a society in which people couldn't develop properly . . . What's more, those aged between eighteen and twenty have been educated under conditions of terror – the terror of exams, of dates that are always being changed, etc. Those kids have lived through all this in a state of constant anxiety. And then there is the fact that for *that generation* the Communist Party has meant much less than for the others, that the Party's line on peaceful coexistence and negotiation seemed to them little more than a trap. The older ones have known a time when the Party carried more weight, both among the working class and among the young intellectuals. For the young workers the Party was either everything or nothing. The others seemed to think they couldn't do anything without the Party.

How was the decision to occupy the Quarter taken?

We'd already half-surrounded the Sorbonne when people started saying, 'We'll surround it and stay there.' We felt as if we'd been thrown out. Someone said: 'We'll sit until the *flics* move off.' When we started our occupation, there were a lot of guys going around with megaphones, saying: 'Some of us want to sit down and surround the building. *If you want to stay*, do so.' Some people left then, quite a lot in fact. Little by little, things got organized. People sat down in front of 10,000 armed *flics*. It was terribly impressive.

Then the barricades were set up . . .

. . . The younger lads were afraid, and sat down without moving. Things couldn't go on like that. We started getting things to put between the *flics* and us. The barricades began to rise, first one, then sixty of them. It was extraordinary. Sixty barricades, without a fight, just in order to put something between them and us . . . The local people were in the same mood as us. They didn't expect an attack. They came out onto the streets, brought us food, and put their transistors in the windows so that we could hear the news. There was an *extraordinary warmth* everywhere. There were a lot of young workers with us, talking the same language, and saying things like: 'Come here, you'll never do it like that, let me show you.' And everything was done with such a feeling of *joy* . . .

Is it true that the distinctions between teachers, students, and organizations . . . broke down?

Oh, yes! And there were extraordinary opportunities for discussion. In that physical work, which just happened, like that, people got *organized* with great efficiency, while at the same time discussing politics, society, the Gaullist regime. . . . Afterwards, the guys who went to negotiate[1] came back and said: 'They had nothing to offer us.' There was a moment of panic. People were saying: 'They must be crazy. It's impossible! Don't they realize?' Then we started to mount the barricades in a big way . . . It was a *psychological* thing really. There was a real risk of a fight breaking out. Spontaneously, people gathered round the barricades to stop any hot-head flinging a cobblestone at the *flics*. It was vitally important that it should not be *us* who started things. We'd agreed to negotiate. We'd settled in. Again, people were very determined.

A few minutes later the police were ordered to clear the barricades. Mme ND had to take refuge in a room in the Rue Gay-Lussac, where she stayed until morning, hearing 'people who'd been trapped between two barricades shouting and screaming all night'. On Saturday, the 11th, the prime minister, Georges Pompidou, arrived back from an official visit to Afghanistan, and promised that the arrested students would appear before a court of appeal without delay and that the faculties that had been closed would be reopened. On Monday the 13th, the day of the demonstration against repression, which brought together the trade union organizations and the teachers' and students' organizations, the Sorbonne reopened its gates.

[1] About midnight, three university teachers and three students, including Alain Touraine and Daniel Cohn-Bendit, met the rector, M. Roche, inside the Sorbonne to negotiate the freeing of the students arrested on the previous Monday and the evacuation of the Latin Quarter by the police.

The discussions inside the Sorbonne developed rather as they had done during the demos, when they gradually took shape, with people arguing, the crowd passing critical comments, and sometimes people who had never spoken in public *doing so for the first time*. I think it was there, in the demos, that people *learnt how to do what they have done since in the Sorbonne*. They realized their own potentialities. Again, because we had a lot of old reflexes like the relations we had previously had with our usual environment . . .

Did you personally speak more than usual?

In so far as I really took part in what was happening in the streets I learnt a lot of things. I've probably mentioned only a part of what I learnt, because one can't always remember things very clearly. Among those who spoke, there were the professional talkers, people who had not taken much part in things, like the members of the Communist students' organization. They wanted us to disperse straight away. They went around shouting 'Disperse! Disperse!' all the time. They refused to teach people anything, and tried to stop people expressing themselves, hoping to impose their own organization on them. They took advantage of the fact that the Sorbonne was full of people – a captive audience – to shoot their own particular line. *We'd* learnt that it was possible to do things differently. People got up and criticized what they were being told.

What things could be done differently?

It was mainly at the stage of decision-making as developed during the demos . . . especially during the building of the barricades. One way in which the CP has deeply affected the thinking of the older generation is, in my opinion, by saying that 'the *working class* is radically different from other working people', which has allowed it to set itself up as the intermediary and spokesman of the working class. We could see now – we were already more or less aware of the fact – that by sharing the same life, in the same concrete situation, in the same movements, we found ourselves using the *same* arguments, thinking in the *same* way, and criticizing in the *same* way.

There was no longer any need of an intermediary . . .

We came to realize not only that intermediaries were more and more useless, but that they acted as a *brake*. They cut the workers off from other working people, and, in fact, that was probably one of the reasons for the failure of working-class movements in recent years.

Now, what about the assemblies in the Sorbonne?

As I say, we experienced other things, spontaneously. Things were criticized at the level of fundamentals. We heard arguments that were not at all the usual ones. We could back up our arguments with actual experience. This was made much easier by the fact that there were so many people who had been in the same situation and had participated in the same way. We had something to go on. *We weren't just talking in a void,* with all the tension that that usually brings with it. If you found an argument, you became the spokesman for a certain number of people.

Did people understand one another? What kind of language did you use?

Much simpler than usual. The *phraseology* of all the organized groups had disappeared.

At that point, what sort of changes did you envisage, not only in the university, but also in society?

There were things that appeared in the long term and other things that belonged to the immediate struggle, the question of exams, for example. There was a double perspective: if we wanted to continue the strike, it could only apply to the exams, because the lectures had ended – the exams were the only activity we could contest. We had to work, therefore, to persuade people to boycott the exams and then to participate in the struggle. On the other hand, I think we must find a deeper analysis of the problem. The reason why this student movement had a violence that had never previously been known was because these students were not engaged in a struggle concerned only with the student body, with strictly student problems, which would be of very little interest to them once they had left the university. On the contrary, they were engaged in a struggle as *future workers.* As future workers, they began to reflect on the sort of training they were being given at the university. The students in the human sciences played a particularly important role in all this, because psychologists and sociologists are constantly having to stifle their convictions. A psychologist working in industry, for example, has to select people according to the requirements of the boss, and thus becomes an accomplice of the boss. And it was they who made a particular study of the problem, since for them the problem was much more real. If you're studying philosophy, for example, and want to become a teacher, it's not so readily obvious that you're participating in a repressive system.

As you have shown, the method worked out in the demonstrations was adopted in the method of discussion. Was it also adopted as a method for changing society?

Yes.

You're sure I didn't just put the idea into your head?

No, no. That's exactly the point of view I put at our meetings with the workers. Before, we were told: it's either the CP or de Gaulle. In the end, nobody wanted either, which, in my opinion, justified people's passivity. So new methods were needed.

Nobody?

Yes, nobody. Even among the workers. Some time ago, I took part in a study of the CP. We discovered all kinds of anxieties among the workers. When there was no active struggle taking place, there was a kind of excitement over wage differentials, which meant that the Communists were respected, for they do work hard, both as union officials and as shop stewards. The others would say, 'Oh, I just watch the telly', but they've got a bad conscience about it really. At the same time, there was a widespread malaise among the workers brought about by the fact that the CP had never got the mass of workers to participate, but had always channelled them into special forms of education, in which its own role was never questioned. So I think it then became very clear – we already knew this, but it seemed to us rather utopian – that *other kinds of organization* had to be imposed; that such a thing was possible; that, for example, the fact of being on strike, in places where people have the most illuminating experience of their lives, their places of work, enabled them to discover all kinds of things, and ways of doing things.

You speak of imposing other forms of organization. Why impose them, and on whom?

They must be imposed against Gaullism and the CP. I visited strike pickets in factories, with magazines, pamphlets, etc. I talked quite a lot with them. I could see that people have absolutely no illusions as to the success of their wage demands. They know perfectly well that it will all be taken back off them later. On the other hand, they know that if the CP came to power it would be fairly repressive. They daren't *imagine* anything different. We don't have any ready-made solutions. What we have to get people to accept is that they must find their *own* solutions, participate in the elaboration of those solutions.

That's the stage reached, in one way or another, by the students. But do you think it's equally possible for the young workers, say?

Absolutely. During the first few days, people were very much under the control of the CGT. You handed out a pamphlet signed Sorbonne, Action Committee, Committee of Students and Workers – and they'd tear it up. The day before yesterday, I was distributing the newspaper *Combat* – the CGT had forbidden the distribution of *Combat* and the delegates wouldn't touch it. But the younger ones objected. 'This is incredible!' they said. 'If the paper's no good, we'll criticize it. *We're not sheep.* We've got to make up our own minds – think about things.' You see, the reactions are the same. Things are moving at the base. On Sunday, I was out in the surburbs, talking to some young railway workers. They understood perfectly well what happened at the Sorbonne. They were in the demos. They got us to explain our point of view. They wanted organizations that were at the same critical level as those we were creating in the university.

To return to the Sorbonne, how are the work commissions organized?

They weren't organized at once. At first people would say whatever came into their heads – they'd talk about whatever problems they happened to have. We came to realize that a general assembly was rather awkward to handle – handle isn't really the right word – let's say, that we weren't making much progress. So we decided to form *concurrent commissions*, on the basis of different points of view, and to present properly developed arguments, coherently set out, to the general assemblies. Anyone could attend the work of any commission. But there were commissions on workers' control, programmes, etc. People were divided up into groups of about a hundred.

Were there any people who 'stood out' from the broad mass at that time?

Yes, there were some who spoke more than the rest, and who got the support of a section of the students. They had greater facility for public speaking. So we went along to see them, and they discussed with us what they were going to say.

Who kept order? Was there an elected chairman?

We've a chairman who can be *removed at any time*.[1] If he ever tries to manipulate us, we'll ask for his removal, and vote for another.

Who put names forward?

One guy said, 'All right, I don't mind having a go' – which is unusual enough. Generally, no one wants to be chairman. Anyone who says a thing like that is not usually particularly outstanding.

Did you feel that what you proposed for the educational system and for society could be implemented?

Yes. I'd better explain what we did. There's one phenomenon you must bear in mind. The students who went out onto the streets were a minority. From Monday the 13th onwards, after the night of the barricades, all the students arrived who, in the first week, had been revising for their exams. So we held general assemblies on the struggle itself, on the need to boycott the exams until September so as to keep the movement alive, etc. There was an enormous

---

[1] *Révocable à tout instant*: *révocabilité* is one of the key notions of the May Movement and of New Left theory generally. The idea is that elected officers are answerable at all times to those who elected them, and can be removed at any time. (Translator's note.)

13

amount of explaining to do, because everything I'm telling you now I *learnt in the streets*. Those who arrived later were non-political – they had their own methods and didn't want to consider the social problem as a whole.

Can you tell me more about these new methods, this new way of seeing things?

One thing that is quite new is to make people accept that you can oppose things without necessarily having *ready-made solutions*, to make them abandon any preconceptions from the outset. This is of the utmost importance, and something I am myself always emphasizing. Some people said to us, 'You young people, you want to destroy everything. But what's going to become of us? What are we all going to do?' We explained to them why we don't want the old system any more. We presented an analysis of what happened, and then someone said, 'Right, now it's up to *all* of us. The new university concerns you too. You're not going to sun yourselves on a beach while your future is being decided in the Sorbonne.'

Have you considered the future development of education? Have you, for example, discussed the need to adapt curricula to the rapid changes in society?

We haven't discussed the matter in those terms. We have approached it by drawing attention to the fact that, more and more, people are employed for ten or fifteen years and are then completely swamped by the changes that have come about. We also demand that people should spend part of their time gaining practical experience, and that, side by side with this, there should be a continuous process of re-education with a view to keeping people up to date with developments in their field. What we don't want is the practice whereby someone is thrown out of his job at forty after working his guts out for fifteen or twenty years. The idea of a university open to all is not just demagogy. An engineer should be able to work a thirty-hour week and still be able to go back to the university to keep up with the latest knowledge. A university should be a place where knowledge is exchanged, where people would go to get what they need and pass on what they have acquired.

And this led you on to talk of a new type of society . . .

You can't avoid it, when economic pressure is used to implement a certain principle of qualification and a certain policy for curricula. The aim of Gaullism is to create an elite, with everybody else having only an extremely specialized education, without any critical basis. So you see, we were soon led to oppose the efforts of the government.

But didn't you find that just such elitist points of view were expressed?

Unfortunately, yes, and I'm bound to attack the Communists again here. We've had some pretty tough arguments with them – they really have become a reactionary force in the university. If the Communist bureaucracy took over from de Gaulle, it would nationalize industries without radically changing their structures, it would impose its economic directives, and shape the university according to the requirements of those directives. But that shape would not necessarily be what the mass of the people wanted. For example, the aim of the Soviet Union is to achieve, having started at a lower economic level, and in record time, the same standard of living as capitalist society – and by making the same choices.

What were the broad outlines of the new organization to emerge?

I'm not saying that in the university we've already laid the foundation for society as we'd like to see it. But a parallel could be drawn with the new organization of the university: administration by general assemblies, which delegate joint staff–student commissions; intermediate committees between the national level and the general assembly, dealing with a particular problem; the permanent participation of people, etc. I think this would provide a starting-point for discussion. The fact that we are demanding *self-management*[1] as a means of arriving at, contesting, and influencing decisions, not with a view to revolution, but as a means of holding society together – I think that's something we can already take as a basis.

At the time we are speaking of, did the various organized political groups manage to get a hearing, and present their programmes?

No, their programmes are even more reactionary than what they actually do. They're intermediaries. For example, the PSU[2] had its programme, before this movement. Incidentally, I went to a PSU meeting and said, 'Really, the strength of the PSU is that it didn't try to shoot its own line. Anyway, your programme's discredited, and you've nothing more to say. The road to socialism is not via a programme and the election of deputies.' I got the support of 80 per cent of the meeting, which consisted of people from the École nationale d'administration.[3]

By 'shooting its line' you mean presenting a certain type of programme?

That's right. For the Communists it's a mass of claims that can be immediately absorbed (*récupéré*)[4] by the government. This is proved by the fact that the

---

[1] Now the accepted translation of the French *autogestion*. The older term 'workers' control' is both over-narrow in application and indefinite in meaning. (Translator's note.)
[2] Parti Socialiste Unifié, a fusion of a left-wing breakaway faction of the French Socialist Party (SFIO), former members of the Communist Party, and other left-wing groups. (Translator's note.)
[3] One of the *grandes écoles*, autonomous schools within the University of Paris, with a highly competitive entry and corresponding prestige. The École nationale d'administration provides the management and administrative elite in the civil service, the nationalized industries, and, increasingly, in big business. (Translator's note.)
[4] The notion of *récupération* is another key idea of the May Movement. It is used frequently and

15

government accepted them without difficulty. There are other groups, like the Trotskyists, who want to revive Bolshevism. They say, 'This student movement is fine, but you must get organized. Come and join our strike committees. Above all, you must preserve the union – it's the union that will defend your interests.' It's a form of organization that leads the base to abrogate *its right to make its own decisions.* Every voluntarist organization that has tried to impose its own line has sought to find a way of breaking the movement of the base.

What would be the opposite of a voluntarist party?

In so far as this movement will continue to function, a party with a genuine *raison d'être* would be an assembly of people based on common options, who would use the fact that they are together to discuss and develop their arguments. Such a party would be a political commission that would make proposals.

In short, it would be a procedure for developing proposals in common, rather than an apparatus for seizing power?

There'd be no need to seize power. It would get to the *root* of the problem.

Let's go back to the critique of contemporary society. What, apart from its repressive and elitist aspects, of which you have already spoken, are the points you are particularly opposed to?

The *intellectual oppression* that is increasingly affecting people who are pushed into non-vocational jobs, who become more and more specialized. It's a mutilation of people.

Has the way in which you feel these criticisms, or perhaps the number of them, been changed by the recent events?

Everything's become much clearer. For example, before, we used to talk of the consumer society, of distinctions between workers and intellectuals, but it didn't form part of a coherent whole.

What categories would you now use to describe society?

I'd speak of different categories of workers. The student movement is really a movement of young workers, of people who need to study in order to earn a living, and who, at the same time, are conscious of the role they are expected to play in society, and who are perfectly well aware that they will be used

---

in different ways. The basic idea is of being 'taken back', 'absorbed', by the system. Instead of crushing opposition, the system tries first to 'buy it off', to provide it with the status of a 'licensed', and therefore harmless, opposition. In New Left thinking generally, this fate is seen to have befallen not only the 'Social Democratic' Parties, but also the Communist Parties and their corresponding labour organizations. (Translator's note.)

just like the others. More and more, workers are sharing the same fate. People are being *crushed*. And they are coming together to defend themselves collectively. People were stifled. It all came out during these events: the slogans on the walls . . .

Who wrote those slogans? Any particular groups?

I think at first it was pretty spontaneous. Later, people tried to channel them.

Well, how, from a philosophical or sociological point of view, would you define what has just happened? Haven't you, in fact, done something that runs counter to determinism?

I don't think so. Determinism can be turned round. One is the product, and at the same time . . . it can be said that one undergoes a certain impression, that the form of the critique is determined by the oppression.

Yes, but how can one pass on to another level then? Do you define this society of the future simply in terms of a reaction . . . ?

This reaction is the cause of something else. Without this reaction, one couldn't produce what we're producing now.

But would you say that you wish to replace a system of excessive oppression with a system of total spontaneity?

No, I don't think so. There was a system of oppression. The day the Sorbonne was opened, there was spontaneity, joy. In one of the lecture-halls was written, 'Already the 10th day of joy'.

It was an outburst . . .

Yes, but at the same time, there was another determinism. This outburst is under daily threat. Because it is threatened, we must hasten to reply to those threats by inventing something else, in order to confront them.

Have you reached the stage, then, of seeking a kind of essence of man, of man as he 'really' is, outside society, if you like?

No, I don't think so. One is conscious of a certain number of conditionings, and one tries to find forms of society in which those conditionings are chosen. That is to say, for example, that the workers on strike have found a way of meeting each other, because they have expressed a certain number of criticisms about conditionings that people cannot feel from the outside. It's not a question of the essence of man, but of seeking a new organization of society that corresponds to a certain practice. That doesn't mean that we'll reach an ideal social state that is fixed and determined. We'll decide to move more and more towards something.

One last point. Did people talk about their experiences, their personal problems, in these discussions?

Oh, yes! There were lots of small problems that we didn't manage to sort out intellectually. The striking thing is that if people's personal problems found their place more easily in these discussions – because people were less repressed – things were cleared up straight away. The thing that had an enormous effect, I think, was the constant attempt to express things in the most individual way possible, so that everything could start again from scratch.

EXTRACTS FROM OTHER INTERVIEWS

At the end of May and the beginning of June, we recorded six other interviews with people who, like ND, had participated to various degrees in the events.

We met the first of these, a philosophy student aged twenty-four, in the middle of a discussion group in the Sorbonne courtyard. He is a member of 'M 22' (Mouvement du 22 Mars). We shall refer to him simply as Phil. St. Though not actually members of a political group, the next two – both women – were close to a Trotskyist movement, the JCR (Jeunesse Communiste Révolutionnaire), which played a fairly important role, both as a distinct group and by the participation of certain of its members in the creation of M 22; one of them is a young sociology graduate (abbreviation: Sociol. Grad.), the other a research technician and a member of the CGT (Technician). The fourth, who, as we shall see, belongs to an anarchist movement, is a graduate in German (Germ. Grad.). The last two belong to a rather different world. One is a young music graduate of the Paris Conservatoire, and a jazz and pop musician (Musician); the other, a graduate of the School of Oriental Languages (Orient. Langs.), was, at least at first, less involved in the events, because he was already employed in a professional capacity.

These interviews, as I have already said, are not reproduced in full. I have preferred to quote passages that will serve, either as corroboration or as contradiction, to illustrate our first interview. Like the opinion poll that follows, this chapter is intended as an introduction to the various approaches we have chosen to follow in the rest of the book. Together with the documentation we have collected, they are the material on the basis of which we shall try to propose certain hypotheses. We have included them in the book above all to enable the reader to follow the same path as ourselves, that is, proceeding essentially by intuition, to try to distinguish, in the midst of what is not always a very coherent whole, even at the level of the single participant, between the 'old' received ideas and the 'new' ideas that emerged in and from the movement, a sort of dominant tone, rather like the basic colour on which a painter builds up his picture and which we see emerge when we stand back from the canvas.

Certain themes raised in these first two chapters are therefore subsequently abandoned in so far as they do not enter into the composition of this dominant tone.

The beginning of the interview with ND serves as a reminder of the atmosphere that reigned in most French universities at the beginning of the events. Apparently, most students took very little notice of what was happening at Nanterre – the press, and, for that matter, foreign student movements, had little to say about it.

ND stated that she regarded the Nanterre phenomenon as 'really local'. French society, as many observers have remarked, is highly compartmented into socio-professional groups. The same can be said, it seems, of the student world itself, as between different faculties. For those who were not aware of this phenomenon, May provided an illustration:

> For me, it was the most astonishing revelation of the incredibly cellular character of French society (Germ. Grad.).

Even for students as aware of social and political problems as ND, it did not seem possible, until May, that any real contact could be made between the political concerns of the students and those of other politically conscious social groups, let alone those of the 'population' at large:

> . . . in all our talks together, among our friends, no one seemed to know how to get people out into the streets so that *it could happen* (ND).

In the student world, this feeling of powerlessness led either to a complete lack of interest in politics, or to the sectarianism of small groups, approaching problems at 'world level', while fighting among themselves. What we find here is a dispersal of effort that parallels the compartmented character of society.

But it only needed the police to enter the Sorbonne (Friday, 3 May) for hundreds of students, often apparently very divided politically, to come out into the streets on the same side of the fence. This was due quite as much to the polarizing effect produced by the confrontation of a common danger as to a community of interest or analysis.

19

These small political groups are probably unaware of, or underestimate, each other, while at the same time being unaware of what they have in common with many 'ordinary' students.

> I didn't get the impression that there'd been much *mobilization* of people, even of the students – I'd say especially of the students, since they were the people I knew best. It seemed much less emotive. I found a good many students there I wouldn't have thought would have been interested (ND).

To this discovery by the students of their own potential corresponded a discovery of the 'population', of 'the worker' in particular. The most varied opinions have been expressed as to what has been called the fusion, the alliance, or quite simply the first meeting, of two social groups that are normally so separated; we shall return to this problem in due course. A prudent opinion may be quoted here:

> The joining of forces and the dialogue between students and workers remained at the level of mutual discovery (Germ. Grad.).

Apart from this, the active participants discovered or practised for the first time new modes of action. In certain cases, the apprenticeship of these participants took place quite naturally; in others, it required a deconditioning of old habits that were constantly on the point of reasserting themselves:

> I was constantly having to stop myself. I understood what was happening, and said to myself, 'Hell, there I go again, reacting in the same old idiotic way!' (ND)

The first time a new method of decision-making was attempted on a large scale seems to have been at the demonstration at the Place Denfert-Rochereau on 10 May. The process – it could be useful, I think, to illustrate it in detail – was seen in various ways.

For ND – we have read the whole of her description of this process – each group presented its opinion first and each proposal was then discussed by the demonstrators as a whole:

> Someone had tried to carry his point of view simply by saying, 'We'll go this way', but people did not follow him without knowing why (ND).

On the other hand, this is what another demonstrator had to say:

> The human mass just started to move. Being in the middle, I just followed the direction . . . Someone decided where we were going (Technician).

A similar divergence is to be found in the interpretations of the leaders or spokesmen: for some, it was pseudo-democracy, for others, decision-making in common:

This public confrontation was a parody of direct democracy in which only those who possessed a megaphone could make themselves heard (Bensaïd and Weber, 1968, p. 155).

And it was like that, by taking a suggestion from one person and ideas from someone else, that the route was decided on (Mouvement du 22 Mars, 1968, p. 28).

Again, ND reported that, although at the beginning of the demonstration people were grouped behind their banners, 'these divisions broke down very quickly'; whereas another woman we interviewed insisted that the political groups were always present as such during the demonstrations.

In support of ND, who might seem exaggeratedly optimistic, many observers noticed that, at the beginning of the events at least, 'the *phraseology* of all the organized groups had disappeared' (ND).

The vocabulary became a lot less rebarbative, less abstract, at the beginning at least; later, when politics returned, things changed a bit (Germ. Grad.).

The work of the general assemblies or commissions is, of course, just as much the subject of various interpretations and necessarily selective presentations. In view of the extent of the criticisms expressed about the manipulation that was supposed to have taken place, ND's description is welcome. Not that we have any wish to deny the existence of any such manipulative practices, but the work carried out[1] could hardly have been so rich and varied in approach if these practices had been constantly and universally dominant.

In particular, ND refers to the broad outlines of the working methods used: general assemblies prepared in open, concurrent commissions; discussion of the proposals made by these commissions; session chairmen who can be removed at any time; the rejection of prearranged programmes, and so on.

The peculiarity of this situation was that the problems of democracy presented themselves not only in the universities, between students, between small groups and the mass of students, but also between students and other social categories. This is all the more obvious, in that the eternal

[1] Cf., for example, the collection of reports made by the various commissions, *Quelle Université? Quelle Société?* (1968).

question of the necessity and role of elites was often discussed at the level of principles or even of direct action:

> What we have shown in the last few days is that direct democracy is a great method. You have to create meetings in the street, on the spot, where the workers are to be found. You have to go to the factory gates and explain your views (Phil. St.).

As ND also showed, these contacts became perfectly natural once the movement got under way:

> By sharing the same life, in the same concrete situation, in the same movements, we found ourselves using the *same* arguments, thinking in the *same* way, and criticizing in the *same* way (ND).

This position expresses, in other terms, the theme 'we are all workers'.[1]

This egalitarianism might be contrasted with a whole range of elitist positions, from the idea that the intellectuals must 'serve the people' to that which places the people in a passive role, at least initially, and the students or intellectuals in the vanguard, defining society in terms that are supposed to suit the 'people'. I shall be content here to quote two positions that are situated between these poles, while differentiating themselves from what has just been said:

> What do the students represent in terms of numerical and political power in the country? As a class, their role is that of intellectuals, but it's through the workers that everything must happen (Sociol. Grad.).

The same interviewee later explained that in fact the students seemed more conscious than the workers of the need to overthrow not only the Gaullist regime, but also capitalism.

To put it even more clearly, the role of the students was that of educators. They must devote themselves to 'the education of the workers through contact . . . the politicization of the workers in the factories' (Technician). This politicization is all the more necessary because the people, alienated by existing society, and betrayed by their leaders, are incapable even of expressing their own real desires; it is up to those with a greater political consciousness to teach them what they should want in their own interest.[2]

Apart, of course, from the direct practice of egalitarian action imposed

---

[1] A slogan often used in the commissions' reports, and chanted in demonstrations, etc.
[2] Written in these terms, this example may seem something of a caricature. Yet I have heard certain participants in the movement express themselves in this way, though in private, it is true. Such positions would no doubt have been given a poor reception in a general assembly.

by the circumstances of the struggle in the streets, for example, the contacts improvised between students and workers were not without their problems. But even those who believe in these principles and explicitly reject 'vanguardism' recognize these difficulties, in particular as regards communication, the social differences being, for the moment, a reality, at least in the 'normal' appearances of everyday life:

Above all there's the fact that the young workers are very reticent, very suspicious towards intellectuals. There is also the question of finding a common language. Very often we use terms that they find very funny, for example certain words concerning the new forms of action. I remember using the word 'specificity'. They'd criticized us for kicking up a shindy. We explained to them. We told them that there was a specificity of action between students and workers. Because, unlike us, they had to have a discipline, they had to keep the machines in working order, etc. . . . Guffaws all round. I explained that, in the last resort, they'd be wrong to destroy the machines, which were their livelihood, but that we could break up some old-fashioned lecture, that the only way we could stop our machines was by making the lecturers look ridiculous . . . (Phil. St.).

From the new point of view expressed by the tendency represented by M 22, a party would be regarded at most as a political commission.

There'd be no need to seize power. It would get to the root of the problem (ND).

The work of the militant would consist only in arousing discussion:

What we have to get people to accept is that they must find their *own* solutions, participate in the elaboration of those solutions . . . that you can oppose things without necessarily having *ready-made solutions* (ND).

The style of action – to which I shall return in detail in the following chapters, particularly in relation to M 22 – is based on the invention of new solutions.

Take tactics, for instance: all you have to do is make existing structures look ridiculous, and to do that you have to show things up, using irony, for example. When lecturers won't change their working methods, but go on 'lecturing' us, you have to make fun of them, force them into a new dialogue. You have to cause a disruption . . . Workers must disrupt things in a different way, they have to find their own way (Phil. St.).

We see the emergence, then, of a general opposition – such an opposition is, of course, not new – between the advocates of entirely new

23

methods and those who, like the existing parties, hold to the old, tried methods, but are unable to apply them. It is hardly surprising that student opinion reveals less divergence on the subject of such parties: there is obviously a wider degree of agreement at the negative level.

For the philosophy student, the Communist Party and the CGT are 'riddled with bureaucracy', and wish 'to appear inoffensive, to become incorporated in a parliamentary opposition, to come to power with a pro-NATO Left', by acting 'within the limits of legality, within the limits of parliamentarianism'. The position of ND with regard to parties and programmes, which she repeats several times in the course of her interview, is very similar.

> The CP had never got the mass of workers to participate, but had always channelled them into special forms of education, in which its own role was never questioned.

One of the women interviewed, whom I quote as an example of a different attitude to methods from that expressed by ND, makes similar criticisms of the CP and CGT:

> In refusing to the utmost to allow wage claims to become politicized . . . the leaders of both the CGT and the CP are behaving exactly like men of the Right, like any factory boss. They are factory bosses! (Sociol. Grad.)

In attacking what seems to them like a Poujadism of the political machines, which are afraid for their own positions, some of the students differentiate themselves, quite obviously, from what might be called the anti-organizational tendency, as soon as it is a question of strategy and not of a critical analysis. According to them, the present CP must be replaced by a new party that would continue to work with the other organized force, the CGT.

> Leaving the Party (in May) was not an error, but leaving the CGT was (Sociol. Grad.).

This tendency was defended in particular by the Maoists of the Union des Jeunesses Communistes (Marxistes-Léninistes), whose organ, *Servir le peuple*, called for 'the strengthening, on class principles, of the CGT, in spite of traitors and cowards, in order to forge it into an ever more powerful weapon in the struggle of the workers for wellbeing and freedom', while at the same time denouncing the union bureaucrats and the 'revisionist leaders of the French Communist Party'.[1]

[1] Special number of 21 May 1968, p. 6.

The same divergences appear when contacts between students and workers are mentioned. Despite similar general analyses, different opposing tendencies emerge as soon as an attempt is made to define in detail the work that should be carried out by the militant. Speaking of the JCR, one of the women we interviewed said:

> As a group, the JCR don't approve of this rather improvised form of contact at factory gates . . . They want a rigorous analysis . . . of the kind 'we must avoid confusion, approximation, syncretism, etc.', they want rigorous thinking and they know where they're going (Technician).

Rigour of thought and rigour, too, in simple matters of organization.

> You can arrive half an hour late for a meeting of intellectuals. If you do the same for a meeting of workers, there's nobody there to listen to you. Work in industry involves seriousness and regularity. Workers judge an organization as much by its militant seriousness as by its political line (Bensaïd and Weber, op. cit., p. 84).

There is a wide gulf, as we can see, between this conception of serious militantism and that proposed by most of the tendencies in M 22.

> I'd describe our present style of action in terms of Dada, except that Dada had to turn towards the absurd, whereas we must turn towards revolution (Phil. St.).

Obviously closer to this last point of view, in which the ludic element plays an important role, ND describes the atmosphere of joy that reigned, especially among the students, in the assembly and elsewhere, the 'extraordinary warmth' that was to be felt during the building of the barricades, and that many observers also noticed in the occupied factories, despite the obvious gravity of the situation. 'In one of the lecture-halls', she says, 'was written, "Already the 10th day of joy".'

I shall return later to the importance of the 'psychoanalytical' vocabulary used, especially by ND (crushing, mutilation, stifling, etc.), to describe everyday life prior to the events, the greyness of which was all the more striking for the participants in that they were then living so intensely, in a kind of permanent festival.

> It was an explosion of joy and freedom. People did not really believe that they had power in their hands. In the discussions, it was quite unrealistic, utopian, because people talked about doing a whole lot of things which were quite obviously impossible to achieve. It was much more sentimental than

25

anything else, a desire for joy, everyone saying not what he thought was possible, but what he wanted to say (Germ. Grad.).

In an early stage at least this attitude, which was bound up with the sudden lifting of the usual weight of society and its constraints, and with this possibility of dreaming of the reconstruction of the world and of expressing those dreams, was, as the German graduate says, a pure 'desire for joy':

> They expressed themselves on the walls, on paper, everyone being able to write as he wished. It was not necessarily a group inscription; it could be a personal, individual inscription, as, for example, 'We came here to laugh, not to be bored stiff' (Germ. Grad.).

In a secondary stage, though one not separate from the first, joy is no longer its own justification, but is in a dialectical relation with creativity, whose condition and consequence it is, at the level of both direct action and ideas.

Creativity is first of all the ability to develop, to create oneself.[1] What could be affirmed, in the case of those participating in the street fighting, in the 'active' process in which they had precipitated themselves and been precipitated, continued to be affirmed in the meetings of various kinds: the ability to go beyond what, socially, one is, to go beyond what, in normal times, seems possible.

> The discussions inside the Sorbonne developed rather as they had done during the demos, when they gradually took shape, with people arguing, the crowd passing critical comments, and sometimes people who had never spoken in public *doing so for the first time*. I think it was there, in the demos, that people *learnt how to do what they have done since in the Sorbonne*. They realized their own potentialities (ND).

The conversation I had during one demonstration,[2] with an ex-student of oriental languages, turned around oriental methods of self-realization (yoga, judo, etc.). According to him, freedom from various social constraints was not enough to achieve such self-realization:

> The only valid constraints are those one imposes on oneself, with a view to self-realization. I don't even think about external constraints (Orient. Langs.).

There is interdependence, he said, between a personal search, particularly in and through action (in struggle, for example), and the teaching pro-

[1] A theme to be found in the work of E. Fromm (cf., for example, *Man for himself*): before man makes anything, he makes himself.
[2] The demonstration of 24 May, at the Gare de Lyon.

vided by Masters, who are severe in the interests of their disciples, which forms part of a tradition of an initiatory type.

According to some students, the period of pure freedom was followed by one of hesitation and search, then a new type of conditioning.

> One is conscious of a certain number of conditionings, and one tries to find forms of society in which these conditionings are *chosen* (ND).

This accelerated self-development is accompanied, according to others who share the approach of the Japanese language specialist quoted above (Orient. Langs.), by a constant state of 'excitement' (he uses this word very frequently). It seems that many students felt an unparalleled stimulation[1] in May, which might be connected with this phenomenon. The relation between this increased possibility of expression, self-realization and the growth of creative powers – that is, in May, the ability to imagine and to invent a different university and a different society – would seem to be the result of mutual encouragement.

Hitherto, this kind of experience seemed to have been confined to artists. The fact that it was practised in May, partly in imitation of artistic experiments, partly spontaneously, by reinvention, provides a rough, initial definition of the political and cultural *rapprochement* to which I attach particular importance. Just as the philosophy student compared the new style of action with Dada, the German graduate found resemblances between certain discussions in the assembly and the methods of the Surrealists:

> The important thing was to be able to express yourself. Foresight, practicality, etc., were quite secondary. Building the future, yes, but with words and for the sheer pleasure of it. This reminded me of the automatic writing practised by the Surrealists. Here, it was automatic speaking (Germ. Grad.).

It is useful to note here that, although there is some similarity between the experience of life and creation of certain artists and the mode of politico-creative life discovered in May, this obviously does not imply that the students are facing up to the relations now existing between artist and public – relations that play an important role in the very meaning of

---

[1] It must be said that this stimulation had a number of causes, among which ND singles out the danger of the movement being absorbed (*récupéré*), or more simply that of police repression: 'We must hasten to reply to those threats by inventing something else, in order to confront them' (ND). Moreover, the notion of permanent change, which was present throughout May, is probably partly linked with the fear of a decline, which might take place as soon as the Movement seemed to 'run out of steam' – hence the need for perpetual stimulation. Certain observers have identified this, too negatively I think, with a 'forward flight', which could only be a flight from reality and responsibilities.

the work of art. Thus the German graduate recounts a meeting between students and artists in which 'nobody seemed to know what to do or how to do it'. The students had absolutely nothing to offer. The artists had something to offer, but communication between the two was very difficult. For example, the painters said, 'We can give you some pictures to hang up in the Sorbonne, and if they sell you can keep the money for the student movement', but the majority of the students rejected this as paternalistic and individualistic, saying 'that's not what we want at all'.

The similarity, then, would seem to be more with the mode of creation practised by individual and collective improvisation, with the informal, than with the content of works, which, however revolutionary they may be, are taken up by the dealer system of 'bourgeois culture'. This is why there seems to me to be a parallel with the improvisatory experiments of musicians, in the field of jazz and above all in its most recent trend, 'free jazz'. This is how the young musician with whom I spoke in May describes his own experience in this field:

Sometimes I felt an extraordinary feeling of liberation when playing free jazz. We were free to do whatever we liked. I had the tune in my head, then suddenly I'd drop it completely. I no longer wanted to know that I was playing this piece. I was completely alone. I passed from a beat in 3-time to one in 5-time, according to how I happened to feel at the moment. Then everything got started. Later, the whole band played together. We returned home, as it were. Then someone else found an idea and we all worked on it to help him to express it.

To help him, or to complement him?

No, not to complement him, but to sustain him, to urge him on to develop the idea.

Did some of you manage to express yourselves as well as or better than usual?

Better, definitely. For example, Bionda, who likes to study things in advance and be master of his means, wasn't able to express himself normally in the first piece, but after the second piece he joined in. And Thévoz, too, got sounds out of his guitar that he'd never thought of producing before and that became part of the language for that piece. That was the time he took a screwdriver out of his case and played with this screwdriver on his instrument, because he felt that the plectrum was outdated. Another time, when the others had just played a perfectly traditional chorus, I wanted to go off on my own. Then I heard sounds that were complementary with what I was starting to do – it was Serge playing the trumpet with half-valves (a process of

28

altering the sound manually). Gradually, each of us ground out the sound from his instrument in a way that corresponded to the new language we were creating. We felt we had to do something new. We couldn't go on playing a normal chorus after that (Musician).

Here, too, we find the stages – and they are not necessarily chronological – of break, of beginning again, of 'anything goes', of a tendency to isolation which is later surmounted, at least in part, through communication, of the acceptance by all of monologues, which can be either simultaneous or successive, but which move in the same direction, and, lastly, the stage of creating a new language. I shall return later to these stages in relation to the May events.

The practice of constant questioning, which is indispensable to any artist who wishes to remain creative, was also central to the new political ideas, as advocated and experienced for a few weeks by the students and other participants in the May events. It is quite natural, then, that many of them should have no clear view of the future, accepted by all. Far from being regarded as an obstacle, this absence of any fixed programmes or doctrines was, on the contrary, regarded as a *sine qua non* of any fruitful change.

Throughout the remainder of this book we shall try to explore the image as formed in and through action, so it should be enough, in this introductory chapter, to illustrate briefly the often differing points of view expressed on this subject in the interviews.

> What is now absolutely clear, and of secondary importance, is that there is no programme of reconstruction for anything. In the discussions, people were constantly questioning everything, and intend to go on doing so, that is, to arrive at a certain form of permanent contestation, permanent questioning, even of their own formulations. There are only a few basic notions. The principal idea is that people, wherever they are, should themselves take over the running of their own affairs (Sociol. Grad.).

Through trial and error and what, by analogy with music, might be called collective improvisation, a certain consensus emerges, sometimes to the amazement of the participants themselves. For example:

> When a commission meets, anyone can take part. At first, you think you're in the middle of a shouting-match. Ideas are bandied about, and then, in the end, the broad outlines begin to emerge. What you have to aim at is really permanent change. There must be no petrified structures. They must be constantly questioned (Phil. St.).

Just as ND said, towards the end of her interview, all programmes must be renounced, all previously worked out solutions, so that everything can always begin at the base; and so that everything, likewise, can constantly evolve:

> It's not a question of the essence of man, but of seeking a new organization of society that corresponds to a certain practice. That doesn't mean that we'll reach an ideal social state that is fixed and determined. We'll decide to move more and more towards something (ND).

I have already spoken of creativity and self-realization, so I should perhaps also emphasize the subversive character of the 'cultural' experience undergone in that juncture with the political. This point is well expressed in the following passage from the interview with the philosophy student, recorded in the midst of a good deal of coming and going in a corridor in the Sorbonne:

> For us, culture and revolution are the same thing. All culture, true culture, culture that is new, is always contestatory, and if there is no contestation in the streets, one sets up thought in the streets, one sets up culture in the streets. Our revolution must be completely different from those that have been bureaucratized and have tried, in fact, to kill art, to kill contestation.

CHAPTER 2

The 'Average' Student

An Opinion Poll

In May 1968, it was paradoxical, to say the least, to attempt to practise sociology on the basis of a student questionnaire, when French intellectuals of the Latin Quarter approved more than ever before of the summary criticisms of both sociology and questionnaires.[1]

Though personally an advocate of the use of different methods, and sceptical of studies based entirely on questionnaires, I thought that even a limited opinion poll would produce interesting results. What I needed, on the one hand, was to complement, by a technique involving a selection of individuals, what other observers would certainly describe on the basis of analyses of discussions[2] or interpretations of the phenomenon as a whole. And I was very attached to the idea that the imagining of social alternatives and the expression of a great many personal reactions and projects, usually relegated to a state of latency, should be seized while still 'hot', that is, as they were being produced and exteriorized.[3]

The two most characteristic inconveniences of questionnaires were to be inverted. Instead of obtaining facile, lazy answers to closed questions and stereotyped comments on open questions, I met with resistance to and comments on the former and a superabundance of inventive answers to the latter (this expectation was generally verified).

When I read the results of this research, it struck me that although the

---

[1] 'When the last bureaucrat is hanged with the guts of the last sociologist, will we still have problems?' could be read on the walls of the Sorbonne.

[2] It is still too early (December 1968) to judge the work that is being done in this field; the publications that have dealt with the discussions are, so far, the least serious of all the works to have appeared (in particular, the two books devoted to the seizure and occupation of the Odéon theatre); however, a number of sociological teams are at work. I have myself described the general assemblies, the tracts, and the press communiqués concerning middle managers (see Willener *et al.*, 1969).

[3] R. Pagès's plan for 'hot' studies was a great encouragement for me to attempt this present study (see Pagès, 1963).

principal aim of this poll was to convey what an *average* student might reply in the midst of a socially hallucinatory period – most of the respondents had obviously spent most of their time in the occupied faculty buildings – it also helped to *situate* the themes of imagination and change. The replies varied widely and, apart from one or two gaps, embraced the whole spectrum of opinion. Taken together, they produced a coherent picture. Naturally, I had no intention of treating the results as a quantitative classification, the sample being obviously too small ($N = 77$), but it seemed to me that it was well distributed, and produced what was constantly lacking in the necessarily partisan debates, namely, a feeling of a complex *space* of opinion.

It is both necessary and legitimate to study, at this point in time, certain of the *themes* that emerged from the May events. And it is only too obvious that nobody would capture *the* phenomenon in its entirety. The time of the anti-sacrilegious taboos against all questioning has passed. Even if one wishes to avoid – and such has always been my major methodological concern – presupposing, at the level of phenomena, a simple atomism in order to facilitate analysis,[1] one is obliged to make a choice and one must realize that every study is concerned with some particular aspects.

The themes of the social imagination and of permanent change, in relation to earlier sociological studies of images in society, are merely two dimensions to consider among many others in my attempt to understand the explosion and what it suggests for the future. To seek the new forms of images of society – and this is my central objective – involves limiting still further the field of attention.

This poll shows that perhaps one-fifth of the students really imagined a society in permanent change, a society of an entirely new type. Incorporating in their thinking old and new elements, fragments of ideas heard in collective efforts of imagination, passages from a personal reflection that usually remained unexpressed, they produced a sort of experimental collage.

What I have attempted to do in this chapter is to place this type of 'action–image' within a definition of the spectrum of opinion; later, I shall concentrate attention on only *one* avant-garde form.

In earlier studies, questions had been developed with a view to distinguishing between dichotomic and serial views of society (cf. Willener, 1967). Those who tend to see the categories that make up society as few

[1] More than ever, the actor feels that *everything is linked with everything else.*

32

in number, of the 'class' type, and above all in terms of power (that is of the excess power possessed by some), are usually contrasted, on a number of questions, with those who do not have this *discontinuous* view. To envisage a greater number of categories, in a hierarchical order, of the social-ranking type, often in terms of status or income, is tantamount to arranging them on a continuous scale; these serial images usually imply a social distribution not of power – in the absolute sense of those who have it and those who don't – but of relative influence. This is a complex subject that touches on a number of sociological problems – problems that can be dealt with only very briefly, sufficiently to explain the meaning of questions 2 to 5, which were intended to provide an index that would situate the respondents.[1]

In the case of questions 2, 3, and 4, which concern the image of contemporary society, two lists were read to the interviewee for each question: the first (list *a*) attempting not to introduce the notion of class into the description of the country, of an average French city, and of a factory; the second (list *b*), on the other hand, being dichotomized or involving a strong contrast between the terms proposed (in the case of the factory, for example, 'the boss and his collaborators/the workers'). In an auxiliary question, the respondents were able to reject these lists and propose others.[2]

For the sake of convenience I shall call 'dichotomists' those respondents who chose reply *b* three times, and 'gradualists' those who always preferred reply *a*. The others are arranged in 'heterogeneous' combinations. The overall results are shown in *Table 1*.

It should be noted at once that the 'no replies' and the rejections of the lists proposed in the questions are often motivated by a desire to provide an even more clearly dichotomized view ('exploiters and exploited', for example). This was particularly so in the question referring to the 'factory', which explains why I was able to reclassify many 'no replies'; in any case, student opinion had a particularly clear image of the industrialist.

An examination of general trends reveals that, although the two main

---

[1] This operational definition, like all others, is an imperfect one, but it has the merit of existing. Many analyses of the May events try to establish a judgement of *the* May Movement on the basis of an observation of a single group of students; the indices obtained are local ones; the merit of an explicit operational definition is that it may be improved in the course of successive studies; the major problem – 'What, precisely, is measured?' – can be resolved only very gradually. This poll is a pre-study that will be pursued; the material presented here does not make full use of its possibilities.
[2] Cf. the questionnaire (Appendix I) and the identification of the sample (Appendix II).

types of view are equally divided under the heading of 'country', they are unequal on the other two questions: whereas at the 'city' level the proportion of dichotomists falls very sharply below the number of gradualists, the gap is inverted at the 'factory' level. More than half of those interviewed have a dichotomist view of the factory.

These replies make it possible to classify those interviewed and will be used in the course of the analysis.

TABLE I Images of contemporary society $(N = 77)$

Reference of the image	Type of reply			
	Gradualist (a)	Dichotomist (b)	Combined (a/b)	No reply
Country (q.2)	31	32	1	13
City (q.3)	37	21	—	19
Factory (q.4)	30	41	1	5
	Acceptance of the lists			
	Ye	No	Yes/No	No reply
Country (q.2a)	29	29	2	17
City (q.3a)	28	30	1	18
Factory (q.4a)	30	24	—	23

THE PROFESSIONAL WORLD OF THE STUDENT

The next question (5), concerning the university, was more open than the three preceding ones, but of the same type. It involved no alternative, but the interviewee was asked to supply a list of categories and to state whether there were any regroupings of categories on the basis of identification.

In fact, few of the respondents followed this suggestion. Only a small number of replies concerned the opposition between students and staff, sometimes adding that the administration was identified with the state and, more rarely, distinguishing the assistant lecturers and lecturers from the professors. Very few students found a sense of identity ('partial and not very deeply felt', one of them (35:5)[1] remarked) between the staff, beginning with the assistant lecturers, and the students. It should be noted that, despite the very definite accusations made at this time against the teaching staff, there is no mention of collusion between it and the administration. But then, as we shall see later, the more 'militant' of the students interviewed showed little interest in this question; they were concerned about other things.

The responses to this question are particularly interesting when compared with the results obtained from the preceding three questions.

The pure gradualists,[2] moderate in their view of society, are equally so in their judgement of the university. What they deplore most strongly is 'its archaic character, ill adapted to modern needs'; 'too removed from life' (19:5); lacking 'contact with social problems' (23:5). They also criticize the 'bookish' aspect of the teaching, and a reference to the methods of the 'Napoleonic tradition' recurs several times (one of those interviewed quotes the American universities as an example to be followed).

The main demand concerns relations between staff and students, where there seems to be a total absence of communication, except in terms of subordination. 'We are regarded as minors', complains one respondent. 'We should have a voice in the senate' (48:5). Others demand autonomy as a way of escaping from 'dependence on the government'.

If one now takes the diametrically opposite group – the pure dichotomists[3] – one striking thing emerges from the comments as a whole: no solution, even a partial one, is proposed for the crisis in the university; there is no mention of any kind of reform. The dichotomists are not interested in the university. They demolish it in a few ironical formulas: 'it's the greasy pole' (10:5); the 'place where you learn ways of getting at the cheese' (14:5); 'the bastion of the authority of the old' (71:5); 'a nursery where babies suck in bourgeois knowledge' (34:5). The university is regarded by all (at the time this was the subject of a number of debates) as having as its sole function the training of the *cadres* that will enable the system to survive: 'it's where the future *cadres* of the nation are turned out' (56:5); 'a factory for turning out those who will oppress the people, in the service of the ruling class' (58:5); its sole function is 'the training of people who'll exercise a certain authority in the

---

[1] (35:5) denotes respondent 35, question 5.
[2] Those who gave gradualist replies to all three questions concerning country, city, and factory. There were 13 in this category.
[3] Those offering a dichotomist view of country, city, and factory. There were 15 in this category.

established system' (31:5). The last speaker was alone in this group in defining what the aims of a university should be: 'The training of the individual, the utilitarian function of training for a job, an extension of general culture, open to all and not just to a minority.' Few defined categories, as they were asked, except to distinguish between various types of student: there were the 'future bourgeois' and the 'unadaptables' (16:5); the 'aspiring bourgeois' and those who refused to allow themselves to be 'swallowed up' (34:5); 'the malleable, the sheep, content and resigned, the majority' and the minority that is 'not content, but angry' (71:5).

This might be the moment to begin, though not to conclude, a discussion of the origin of dichotomized social views. Is it despair at the character of the university that induces dichotomic views of society, the students becoming all the more sensitive to the discontinuities objectively present in society because the absence of any rapid advance in the democratization of the university makes them unaware of the few openings that are also developing in industrial society? Or is it, on the contrary, a contaminated view of the university? Have objective realities, made more gloomy by the simplifications used in the class struggle, strengthened a dislike for a university, which is, after all, beginning to change?

A comparison of the data suggests, at least, that gloomy views of society are accompanied by a particularly negative attitude towards the university.

So far, I have considered the two extreme groups – the pure gradualists and the pure dichotomists (28 out of 77), but there remain the majority who gave less homogeneous replies. The largest group (26 out of 77) combines a dichotomic view of the factory with other replies (*a* or *b* for country or city).

The group closest to the pure gradualists (country: *b*; city and factory: *a*) provides comments that are above all anti-archaic: 'outmoded structures'; 'feudal stage'; 'training ill adapted to society'; 'closed, compartmental system'; 'gap between staff and students', etc. The same applies to those who chose the dichotomized list only for question 3 (combination *a/b/a*): 'the university hasn't kept pace with developments'; 'the curricula are overloaded and useless'; 'the students have no responsibility'; 'the university lacks autonomy', etc.

I have placed in a separate category those who chose only one dichotomy among the three replies: that concerning the factory. In this category one finds comments of the same type as those just quoted, but one also finds others that are much closer to the 'revolutionary' views of the

36

pure dichotomists: the university is defined as essentially bourgeois, train-ing *cadres*, 'the watchdogs of capitalism'; it's a 'machine for producing degrees'; 'the selection-purification operation' . . .

One feature, then, that is confirmed throughout the analysis of this poll is the relevance of the dichotomic factory-image – a powerful and central indicator.

A later section concerns the professions regarded as being particularly admirable or contemptible (question 8).

Professional *esteem* is restricted to what is really a very limited field. Those professions that student opinion does consider worthy of esteem all lie outside industry. They are medicine, which is mentioned 28 times; teaching, 36 (university and lycée teachers, 15; other teachers, 21); and the artistic professions, 10.[1]

The 'producers' mentioned are producers only in the more noble sense of the term: the scientific and technological professions are mentioned 10 times (and include one 'explorer'); pure scientists, 23 times.

Thereafter the positive replies yield only small numbers, which shows that the scale of values remains very traditional: workers are mentioned 6 times; journalists, 3; farmers, 3; finance (banking, stock exchange), 2; the rest are distributed over single examples (13, including one 'revolu-tionary').

The positive judgements, then, follow very closely the notions of prestige expected of sons of the 'liberal bourgeoisie', with their preference for the liberal or 'humanist' professions; from the idea of the liberal vocations, one passes to that of the professions that 'serve' man, without exploiting him.

Lastly, at the higher intellectual level, pure scientists enjoy considerable prestige, and that of university teachers is not as low as one might have thought – this is confirmed by the low number of negative choices accorded to the teaching profession ('university teacher' mentioned once, and accompanied by the comment: 'if it's a refuge').

Apart from this, the negative choices are more 'conjectural'.[2] The police are mentioned 12 times, to which one might add, as belonging to a similar category of reprobation, private detective agencies (2), the army (9), politicians (8), the bureaucracy (6), and the 'bosses' (9). These various expressions of bitterness add up to 46.

[1] Again out of 77; several positive and negative answers were given by each respondent.
[2] 'Flic, fils de flic et père de flic' is the most telling illustration!

On the whole, the replies are more dispersed here, and refusal to reply or hesitation in doing so is very frequent (found in almost half of the sample, which is most unusual): 'no job is stupid'; 'it's not the profession, but the individual that counts'. Apart from these traditional comments,[1] a number of replies reveal a desire to reply in an overall way: 'all professions are contemptible'; 'those who exploit others, without working themselves'.

In second position are the 'parasites' (speculators, 'middle men'; shop-keepers are placed in this category and are mentioned 11 times) and other

TABLE 2 Career-images $(N = 77)$

Image	Before May	After May
Career as a 'path'	26	15
Career as a 'zig-zag'	22	26
Career as a 'labyrinth'	16	14
No reply	13	22[1]

[1] The 'no replies' are higher on the item 'after May': when in full 'action', many students had no wish to ask themselves this question.

'amoral' types (procurers, prostitutes, murderers – 9). Thereafter the replies are widely distributed: as a contrast with the positive replies, mention should be made of one entry for 'doctor' and, for their curiosity value, two for 'right-wing journalist'.

A few replies mentioned certain 'alienated' trades (conveyor-belt workers, machine-operator, puncher – 5), but nobody mentioned ideological or 'cultural' alienation.

Let us now consider how the student sees his career (question 9): does he see it as a sort of *path* already laid out for him, or will he have to *zig-zag* to some extent before finding the career that suits him, or, again, does he see his future as a *labyrinth* from which he may never escape? Respondents were asked to indicate whether their views had changed in the light of the May events. The results are shown in *Table 2*.

Before the May events, the prospect of their future careers does not seem to have presented any particular problems for a majority of those interviewed. In so far as the 'path' and 'zig-zag' images both involve a

[1] Given in earlier studies.

feeling of security, one can say that 60 per cent of the respondents envisage no major difficulties as far as their careers are concerned. This security is not always desired, of course: many of those who opted for 'path' emphasized that it had to be followed 'whether one likes it or not'.

As seen from the perspective of the May events, the future seems much less assured. Two categories of reply undergo major changes: the assurances of a 'rectilinear' career falls heavily (from 26 to 15), and uncertainty increases proportionately (22 'no replies' as against 13). But it should not be assumed that it is those who were most sure of themselves who are suddenly confronted by the unknown.

TABLE 3 May and the career-image $(N = 77)$

(a) Replies concerning 'before May' images	(b) Replies concerning 'after May' images			
	'Path'	'Zig-zag'	'Labyrinth'	No reply
'Path' (total: 26)	14	7	3	2
'Zig-zag' (total: 22)	—	15	3	4
'Labyrinth' (total: 16)	1	3	8	4
No reply (total: 13)	—	1	—	12

For 49 of the respondents, the May events did not alter the image they had of their professional future (*Table 3*). One respondent who had expressed feelings of anxiety ('labyrinth') considers that the action of the students has enabled him to envisage the future as a path. If one considers that the 'path' and 'zig-zag' replies express greater optimism than the 'labyrinth' replies or the 'no replies', it can be said that the insecurity that May has aroused in some is balanced by the hopes that it has produced in others: 12 of those interviewed moved from 'optimism' to 'pessimism' (replies 'path/labyrinth', 'path/no reply', 'zig-zag/labyrinth', 'zig-zag/ no reply'); 12 others moved in the opposite direction, in so far as the 'path/zig-zag' responses express hopes for greater mobility and less monotony, as the accompanying comments make clear.

As the 'zig-zag' choice was presented in the question in the most attractive form, it is apparent that:

those most optimistic at the beginning (the 'zig-zag' replies in (a)) fall by about a third, 7 of them seeing their future as uncertain ('labyrinth' or 'no reply');

of those who first replied 'path' in (*a*), the 'optimists' ('zig-zag' replies in (*b*)) are more numerous than the 'pessimists';

the majority of those for whom the future was uncertain before the student action do not consider that this action has improved their prospects (for example, out of 13 'no replies' in (*a*), there remain 12 in (*b*)).

Nevertheless, as we noted above, the unchanged replies are in the majority, in spite of the circumstances.[1] For most, then, the student action should affect only the means of entering a profession. At most, May

TABLE 4 Career-images according to age ($N = 69$)[1]

Age-group	'Path' %	'Zig-zag' %	'Labyrinth' %	No reply %
Up to 21 ($N = 31$)				
'before May'	35	30	20	15
'after May'	20	20	30	30
22 and over ($N = 38$)				
'before May'	29	29	24	18
'after May'	16	45	10	29

[1] There were 8 'no replies' with respect to age.

should have an influence on the relative attractiveness of the various professions, some of which, it is hoped, will be 'debureaucratized'. However, it will become apparent, when we consider the interviewees' age, university faculty, or views of society, that this is not a uniform trend.

Let us begin by checking the effect of age (*Table 4*). At first sight, the replies concerning professional prospects 'before May' reveal few differences between the students under 21 and those over; if anything, the feeling of security (path, zig-zag) is slightly higher among the younger interviewees.

As to the effect expected of the May events, they seem to have produced similar repercussions in both age-groups on those who first opted for the 'path to be followed, whether one likes it or not'. May has re-

[1] A very few of those interviewed revealed, in their choice of 'labyrinth', an attraction for adventure ('plunge into the unknown'; 'we'll see'; 'the unknown could be quite fascinating'). Only one envisaged the possibility of pursuing a career in the Movement itself.

duced the number of replies expressing security in noticeably equivalent proportions.

This is not the case with those who were at first less affirmative. Among the younger subjects, 'after May', 6 out of 10 see their future as a labyrinth (30 per cent) or cannot give a reply (30 per cent). Among the older, on the other hand, 6 out of 10 choose one of the first two terms proposed, 'path' or 'zig-zag'.

Age – that is to say, the stage reached in their studies – seems to serve as an index of the hope placed in the student action, or, more particularly,

TABLE 5 Career-images according to faculty[1] $(N = 61)$

Faculty	'Path'	'Zig-zag'	'Labyrinth'	No reply
Arts				
'before May'	11	5	8	6
'after May'	5	12	4	9
Sciences				
'before May'	11	11	5	4
'after May'	8	11	3	9

[1] I have checked that the dichotomists and gradualists in the sample are evenly distributed in the two divisions, as are the two age-groups.

in the new possibilities that the expected success of the May Movement was to open.[1] The more advanced students see it as a greater source of hope.

An analysis of the same series of replies by the index of the factory-image shows that the dichotomists have more confidence in the positive results of the May 'revolution' than have those who preferred a continuous, gradual view of industrial hierarchy.

If we now consider the 'faculties', or rather the two broad divisions that I have made – the Arts and the Sciences[2] – it becomes apparent that the replies of the arts students show greater change as a result of the events than do those of the science students (*Table 5*).

Moreover, the science students explain this stability in their comments, some of which appeal to what they regard as self-evident facts: 'I'm

[1] This is particularly clear among the *lycéens*: 'after May', 5 of them (out of 6) see their future as a labyrinth: 'The Movement', one of them explained, 'has opened up a new world for me – a world I'm throwing myself into without knowing what it contains' (73:9).
[2] The two were almost equally represented in the sample: 30 and 31 of the 77 interviewed, respectively. (I have used the term 'Arts' to cover what the author refers to as 'Lettres' – the academic 'arts' subjects such as French, foreign languages, classics, history, philosophy, etc. – and 'Beaux Arts' – the studies pursued in art schools; the term 'Sciences' here includes medicine. Translator's note.)

studying medicine, so I think I have only one aim – to become a doctor', said one of those whose future seemed completely mapped out, whatever the circumstances might be (28:9); while another, who aspired to greater mobility, declared that such mobility would be a result not so much of the nature of the society in which he would pursue his research in genetics, as of his own development: 'Without wishing to appear boastful,' he said, 'it seems to me that my future will depend above all on change within myself' (49:9). Others, again, make a clear separation between politics and work ('I don't feel that my future has been affected by our action', said a future mathematician who sees his career only as a 'path', 49:9), or express doubts as to the feasibility of the changes brought about by the events: 'The students' action cannot alter their future', said a science student who twice chose the 'zig-zag' alternative (51:9).

Among the academic arts students, those who continue, 'after May', to see their professional future in a rectilinear, foreseeable form, are future teachers. For them, the students' action opens up more attractive prospects than those they had previously envisaged. Although the career of a teacher is 'relatively clear cut, its contents and practice, despite certain guidelines, require a perpetual questioning of assumptions' (59:9). Another, who had promised himself 'to teach for ten years', saw the future only as 'a path laid down', but, he said, after May 'the profession seems to me to be less closed in upon itself and a teaching career will involve more unexpected elements: retraining, the development of new teaching methods, etc. It will provide less moral comfort and security – and that's an excellent thing' (62:9).

Similar aspirations are to be found among the arts students who change their view according to whether they are considering their career before or after the students' action. These aspirations are expressed in the changes to be observed in the three columns in *Table 5*: uncertainty (the 'labyrinth') diminishes by 50 per cent; the certainty of a secure but uneventful career (the 'path') falls even more heavily, but hopes of greater mobility, on the contrary, more than double. These hopes are expressed, for example, in this comment from a history of art student, who abandons a rather unattractive path-like view of the future in favour of one based on the zig-zag: 'Before,' he says, 'our future direction was determined, in a more or less arbitrary way, in the primary school', whereas now 'there will be more interchange between the different branches of study and greater mobility' (31:9).

*   *   *

It must be remembered that the main purpose of these analyses is to open the way to a sharper awareness of the complexity of what, in May, was called *the* student phenomenon, in a completely undifferentiated way. Perhaps the hypotheses suggested by these trends may be developed and tested in later studies, on the basis of larger samples.

SCIENCE FOR WHOM?

In the course of earlier studies of French working-class life, I have noticed a growing tendency to see technologically influenced modes of organization in political terms. It is as if even the most neutral elements, relatively speaking, by the mere fact of their presence in both a concrete situation and a world of social images, were in some way contaminated. This tendency, it seems to me, is more strongly marked in France than in other Western countries. While I have no wish to indulge in disturbing generalizations, it does seem to me that we have here a clue to a phenomenon of non-analytic thought.

To be more precise, there are two aspects, difficult to disentangle, but nevertheless different in nature. On the one hand, contamination is objectively inscribed in the situation. The neutrality of an instrument, in itself a mere product of technology, is never more than relative. The instrument not only serves a purpose: it is introduced, used, and perhaps rendered unusable by someone. And even before that, the conception of the instrument implies an arrangement of tasks, an organization of the work of implementation, etc. On the other hand, contamination is the fact of the definition of the situation, objective in another sense,[1] that is, produced by association with an image of the situation in which – situation and image – it is inscribed.

A question on science (question 10) involved an explanation of this complex: is it true that certain social images are linked with the idea of a contaminated science? First, I shall comment briefly on three broad groups of reply.

The first group are the optimists (23 replies out of 77), some of whom might be called 'pure' optimists, while others express certain reservations.

Among the 'pure' optimists one finds comments like 'science tends to break down social categories' (53:10); or 'science benefits employers, workers, and housewives', which implies, in addition to its reference to

---

[1] What is generally called the subjective is no less objective, at the level of the actor as well as in terms of action.

43

apparently hierarchical categories, an 'industrial' image of society; the housewife is seen in terms of her work situation – using her kitchen gadgets. Sometimes science is seen in terms of a 'broader' role: 'It's the only thing that enables man to make progress, science unites peoples of different countries' (52:10).

But even in the most positive judgements there appears the idea of the strategic use of science, of its exploitation for personal ends by those who 'can': 'Science works towards the progress and happiness of the greatest number . . .; unfortunately, certain categories are still suffering from its effects, especially those who are placed in an unfavourable intellectual or physical situation from birth' (65:10). For others, science 'alleviates certain material problems, it enables us to gain time, but it creates needs and enslaves people to their comfort and thus accentuates the differences between certain strata of the population and prevents the poorest from benefiting from it' (47:10). 'The advantages are not freely at the disposal of all, so the middle and upper classes benefit from it more' (40:10).

These replies contain, if not always the image of a class society, at least a constant reference to inequality of opportunity.

A number of optimists specify that science will play a beneficial role 'in the long term' (36:10). Although 'the better off benefit in the short term, indeed, right away, all social categories benefit from technological and scientific progress' *in the long run*. Although science 'appears to favour the system for a time, in the end it can only hasten its collapse' (54:10).

Obviously, then, the expression of a positive view of science does not, in a great many cases, involve an acceptance of existing society and may very well be accompanied by a desire for its overthrow.

In a number of replies, one finds a desire to distinguish between general types of research, according to the source of their financing. Whereas most comments emphasize the use that is made of science – there are plenty of references to the risk of atomic warfare – and attribute the contamination of science to the context of the social system, some see the contamination in more direct terms: 'It depends on the scientist, if he is financially dependent on the state, science does not benefit everyone' (16:10). 'The system that finances the research benefits' (4:10).

In the second, clearly negative group, the replies express the belief that the principal beneficiary of science is a *section* of the population (26 replies out of 77), for example, 'the employers' (64:10), 'the industrialists' (45:10), 'the so-called bourgeois classes' (72:10), 'the possessors of the means of production' (15:10), 'the capitalists (I don't want to explain why, it would take too long)' (18:10). 'The Holy Trinity of Progress, the washing-machine, the refrigerator, and the television set', says another (13:10), are merely superficial advantages; 'in society as it has existed up to now, only the ruling or privileged classes have benefited from science' (13:10).

A more moderate version of this interpretation, in which the section is not explicitly presented in terms of power (possessors of the means of production and similar terms, such as capitalists, industrialists), but in terms of purchasing power ('the moneyed classes', 67:10), must be placed in a category of its own. 'The present economic system is more geared to the production of goods for individual consumption and it is therefore the more favoured classes that benefit most' (59:10).

In a third group, the replies see the 'system' as the principal beneficiary of science (24 replies out of 77): 'Science benefits the system, and works against everybody – that's my personal, profane opinion', confesses one respondent (68:10). 'Science bores me to death . . .' (68:10). 'Anyway, science is subordinated to the system' (61:10).

Whereas previously the benefiting section was designated in a stereotyped way, with very few variations, these replies are more varied and unexpected.

Some, it is true, express their wonderment in a simple affirmation – 'It's quite clear, it's the system, what more can you say!' (71:10) – but others reflect on the basis of a different society, or one in the process of transformation. 'Technological progress has turned against the working class', one respondent remarks, but 'we are witnessing a revolt of the working class against conditions of exploitation' (2:10). Science is criticized for what it fails to do: 'Whereas everybody should benefit from it, in order to be free and devote himself to pleasure and art', it benefits the 'system' (76:10); 'The scandalous fact is that, for all the means that science has put at our disposal, most people live not much better than in the Middle Ages' (13:10).

The system benefits from science in the following way: through the atom bomb, through 'the power of statistical research', through computers, through the chemical industry being 'in the hands of the state', through space research (22:10). 'In the end, you realize', concludes one reasonably logical reply, 'that technological progress, which makes economic growth possible, does not satisfy the fundamental needs of man and is used above all to maintain and strengthen the system' (37:10).

Lastly, I should like to quote one quite unexpected reply, which forms the extreme point of pessimism: 'Everyone is oppressed by science' (71:10).[1]

An initial analysis showed that the replies could hardly be differentiated along faculty lines. The 'science' students seemed neither more nor less optimistic than the 'arts' students; the most that can be said is that there were more hesitant replies among the first.

A second analysis, in relation to the images of society, yielded results that are sufficiently clear to make them worth presenting, despite the relatively small sample on which they are based.

For a group of 41 respondents (out of 77), with an entirely (a) or partly (b) dichotomic view of society,[2] the beneficiaries of science were seen as the following:

	Everybody	The capitalists	The wealthy	The system
(a)	2	6	3	5
(b)	8	8	3	11
Total[1]	10	14	6	16
(No reply: 1)				

[1] Some respondents mentioned more than one category.

For a group of 30 respondents (out of 77), with an entirely (a) or partly (b) serial view of society,[3] the beneficiaries were seen as:

	Everybody	The capitalists	The wealthy	The system
(a)	7	3	3	3
(b)	5	3	6	4
Total[1]	12	6	9	7
(No reply: 4)				

[1] Some respondents mentioned more than one category.

[1] Three questionnaires contained no answer to this question; in the following presentation, I have included indecisive answers under the heading of 'no reply'.
[2] An entirely dichotomic view (a) is indicated by the choice of three dichotomic lists in questions 2, 3, and 4; a partly dichotomic view (b) by the choice of two or one dichotomic list(s), including that referring to the factory.
[3] An entirely serial view (a) is indicated by the choice of three gradualist lists in questions 2, 3, and 4; a partly serial view (b) by the choice of two or one gradualist list(s), including that referring to the factory.

HOW IS CHANGE TO BE CONCEIVED AND PRODUCED?

So far, I have attempted to describe the student world in terms of the ways in which it sees established society, while paying particular attention to the problems of the university itself. But this opinion poll was designed also to serve as the basis for a preliminary study of the theme of change.

Is society seen as a fixed structure or as a process?

For a majority of 49 subjects out of 77, the *structures* of French society have not fundamentally changed 'in the long term'. Those who believe that a *slow process* of transformation is capable of altering those structures are in a minority (21 out of 77); 7 did not reply to the question (6a).

The explanations express a good deal of pessimism with regard to the ability of society to evolve. Although Gaullism may be regarded as having changed, without specifying in what direction, the methods of government ('only the forms of power have changed'), the *economic* structures, are regarded as rigid and fixed: 'The structures? If you mean the economic structures, no, they haven't changed' (68:6a). 'Nothing has changed . . .' (17:6a).

The most pessimistic even think that the system they are condemning has been strengthened during the past twenty years: 'The structures have become consolidated at the expense of the individual.'

Less categorical are those who see the possibility of certain 'changes of detail within the structures': 'But nothing essential has changed; these slight rearrangements all tend to conceal the class nature that characterizes them' (55:6a).

According to this view, there has been neither change nor evolution of the structures, but a shift in the power relations between the social classes: 'The proportions between the different social groups have evolved . . . certain privileged groups have grown (more *cadres* – middle managers – fewer peasants), the standard of living has improved, thus creating the illusion of a change of structures' (62:6a).

So it is hardly surprising that all those whose views are quoted above are in favour quite simply of an overthrow of those structures. Those who choose the 'structures' reply and also think that an 'overthrow' of them

47

is possible – generally on the basis of a conception of 'fixed' structures – are also those who usually elaborate their replies with comments. Even in the climate of May, the need for a revolution is argued; we are confronted here with the 'base', not the activists or leaders; even for the most radical respondents, the necessity of an overthrow is not self-evident.

Of the 49 who chose the 'structures' reply, 20 believe in the possibility of an overthrow (the question did not speak of 'necessity') and 20 others believe in the possibility of a transformation.[1]

The situation is almost exactly the reverse among those who preferred 'process'.[2] They are less numerous (21 out of 77), and more hesitant. They seek to attenuate their choice by emphasizing, particularly, the *extreme slowness* of the process of transformation.

A few remark that the direction taken by evolution is a negative one: 'It's a slow but steady process towards capitalism;[3] in the long run, the workers are integrated into the existing structures and turn themselves into *petits bourgeois*' (23:6a). Another observes: 'There'll always be class differences; up to now they've been due to the standard of living, in the future culture will be the cause' (48:6a).

It might be concluded that in making this choice the interviewees were thinking not so much of a change in the economic and social structures as of an improvement in living standards. But there are also replies that refer to major transformations: 'What we are witnessing is the growth of middle, technical strata.'

When those who think in terms of 'process' conceive of change, it is only 'in stages', 'like a zig-zag, with moves backward as well as forward'. We are very far, in this sample, from the concept of permanent change.

Only one subject (out of 77!) states that 'a society never stands still' – and he modifies his reply in the next question by stressing the difficulty of change and its relative value.

It is worth noting that the few who did not reply to the question provided prosaic, unhostile comments: 'Several attempts at change have been made, but there are financial difficulties'; or poetico-political ones: 'Nothing is transformed, everything is created' (an art student, who then refused to choose between the possibility of an overthrow or of trans-

[1] An additional 7 believe in overthrow and/or transformation. The remaining 2 were 'no replies'.
[2] Only 6 out of 21 think that an overthrow is possible, whereas 12 want a transformation. There were 3 'no replies'.
[3] Implying 'towards its reinforcement'.

formation, preferring 'the infinite creative possibilities to be found in joy'). Yet another was indignant at the use of the term 'structures' on the ground that 'only the word class corresponds to anything real' (58:6a).

Is change possible by transformation, or only by overthrow?[1]

The replies to this question contain few historical references, and little attempt to justify the choice. This may well be due to the rapid nature of the interview. Among the comments, however, one notes that the system should be overthrown without thought of 'what structures will be put in its place'.

Above all, there is an emphasis on the radical, new aspects of overthrow ('we mustn't copy the USA or the USSR') and on its immediate possibility: 'It's now or never!' (15:6b). 'The possibility has appeared at last; even people as obtuse as I can see it' (71:6b). 'The present movement has created a pre-revolutionary climate which can and must, inevitably, overthrow the regime' (18:6b).

Some, however, wonder whether the moment has not already passed: 'An overthrow? I'd like to think so, but it's only a short-term affair' (34:6b). 'At the university level no doubt. On a broader plane, traditional politics is regaining the upper hand' (16:6b).[2]

In several replies, overthrow is associated with violence, for 'one can no longer believe in the possibility of a transformation – the traditional modes of contestation seem too suspect'. It is the violence that has 'exposed the weaknesses of the government', and, 'imposed and revealed', it has demonstrated the need for change to 'a greater number of people'. 'What happened in May proves that through direct, violent action a social group can threaten the established order and system' (37:6b).

The students interviewed saw this social group as themselves: 'The student movement derives its energy from a body of young people who are not yet materially caught up in the present social system.' A certain mistrust of the non-student world emerges: 'If all the socialist forces were objectively against capitalism and determined to struggle for its destruction, then they'd succeed' (37:6b). More direct is the reference in the following reply: 'The workers are a powerful force, but more difficult to mobilize, since they're dependent on their wages . . . They occupied their factories in imitation of the students when they occupied the faculties.' But

[1] The replies were 27 and 32, respectively, out of 77.
[2] The last two replies were given on 22 May, at a time when the factories and faculties were occupied.

this obstacle might be overcome if 'the students open the way, and communicate their dynamism to all those who are at present victims of an inhuman society', involving 'all workers in the anti-capitalist struggle' (22:6b).

Only one interviewee claimed to be in favour of a non-violent revolution and regretted the means used, 'strikes, riots, demonstrations . . .' (12:6b), which deprived the overthrow of its 'creative' aspect. On the other hand, several were apparently as attracted by such an overthrow as apprehensive of it: 'It's interesting, but disturbing too' (49:6b).

The advantages of an overthrow of structures appeared only briefly in a few replies, but these replies were interesting because they followed quite clearly the direction taken by the open discussions held in May. One states that in order 'to preserve the advantages of an industrial society' it is necessary 'to break with the absurdity of centralization and to create regional autonomy, which alone can make possible at the present time a democratization in depth' (17: 6b). Lastly, two others see this overthrow as no more than 'a new relation between man and the world' (76:6b), as an 'annihilation of the social, but also psychological structures' (56:6b).

As we have seen, those in favour of an overthrow are slightly more numerous than those who chose transformation (32 out of 77, as against 27 out of 77). Among the latter, what emerges from their comments is not so much a justification of transformation as explanations as to why an overthrow is impossible. Reformism was not highly regarded in student quarters: the bad conscience of those in favour of transformation was obvious. Only one, a woman, declared bravely: 'I don't want anarchy! It would be better to preserve the old structures and transform them gradually' (75:6b). Another, more timid, interviewee explained that there had to be changes 'because people were discontent, but they're not too badly off really' (3:6b). These replies were exceptional.

In some of the replies a certain student pride emerges; it was non-student France that prevented the overthrow of the regime: 'France is too conservative' (52:6b); 'After the initial spurt, May '68 turned into a race in which the traditional machinery caught up with us' (63:6b); 'In May '68 only the student vanguard had this awareness, but it didn't get the support of the base. Overthrow was impossible. We must now give this awareness to the working class' (13:6b). It is noticeable that in such statements no attempt is made to differentiate between a vanguard and a student 'base', as if the students as a whole constituted the 'vanguard' and belonged to the 'base' and to the 'working class'.

To be more precise, although *not a single* interviewee thought the over-throw or transformation of the structures to be impossible (the last choice offered in the question), 10 out of 77 did not choose between overthrow and transformation. One interviewee sums up what was probably a fairly widespread opinion when he says that, whether one looks at it from the point of view of 'the heart or reason', 'May' represents the possibility of either an overthrow or a transformation (2:6b).

One interviewee expressed the original view that the structures 'must first be transformed, so as to make it easier to overthrow them, otherwise people won't go along with it' (33:6b); another, more typical, view was that 'an overthrow of the structures of production' must be effected in order to create 'a transformation in the psychology of the individual' (51:6b).

Finally, a particularly interesting reply expresses the view that a gradual transformation is hardly conceivable and that '*a transformation by fits and starts*' would be preferable (54:6b). This sums up, in a clear image, what is perhaps the average opinion of those interviewed. At this point I should like to return to the reply, part of which was quoted above, made by this same student to the question concerning the fixity or evolution of the structures:

> The explanation of May '68, its explosion, is that, because of recent discoveries, a slow, steady change had taken place in people's minds – hence a *change in consciousness* – but that it had been unable to bring about a *change in the structures*; for that to take place, *everything had to collapse* (54:6a).

May seems to be regarded less as a period of revolution than as in some way a normal period 'of violent evolution' (another interviewee uses the expression 'accelerated transformation', 72:6b), corresponding to a need for structural readjustment.

This opinion is implied in much that has been written about the May events. Daniel Cohn-Bendit, for example, says: 'I think we can obtain only successive improvements, of a greater or lesser degree of importance, but these improvements will be won only by revolutionary action.'[1] Elsewhere one often finds this rejection of the reform/revolution dilemma.

Must the agents of change act spontaneously or be organized?

It may seem rather strange that, on the dates on which these questionnaires were filled in, only 6 interviewees out of 77 chose spontaneity alone as

[1] *Le Nouvel Observateur*, 20 May 1968.

the means of achieving change. And even then, some of these added reservations ('spontaneous, non-organized, but which will have to be organized, though the problem of organization may be the main obstacle in the movement').

In fact, only 3 replies give absolute primacy to spontaneity – which is advocated for its own sake and in defiance of the old organized forces of the trade unions and the political parties. 'The prior organization of forces is always accompanied by a political convergence and by the bureaucratic red tape that is bound to be created within the movement' (49:7). 'Change cannot come from the old forces, since they themselves must be changed as a *sine qua non* of change' (68:7). And this reply adds: 'Organization follows change, in the eternal cycle of change, organization, sclerosis, change.'

For these three interviewees, change can come about only after a break, through the exercise of imagination and invention, for 'no pre-established schema, dogma, model, etc. is valid' (71:7). In order to free oneself from those old schemas and to create something radically new, 'action must begin with feeling and not with orders, otherwise no free act is possible' (49:7). 'Change must be based on the spontaneous dynamic of invention' (68:7), and 'it's up to the masses to make their own programmes, in common action, discussion, contestation, criticism, questioning, and invention' (71:7).

The 'organized forces' alternative was even less attractive. Only one interviewee (75:7), who believes that 'a bird in hand is worth two in the bush', thinks that, for some years, it would be wiser to exert pressure on the established forces. To the previous question, she had already declared, 'I don't want anarchy!'

On the other hand, more than a half of those interviewed (45 out of 77) chose the alternative of 'new forces in the process of being organized'. Among the explanations, three kinds of argument can be discerned:

More than a quarter of the interviewees explain their choice of this solution by referring to the failure of the old modes of organization, the 'old *cadres*', who are regarded as being 'too restrictive' (3:7) and capable of bringing about no more than 'apparent changes' (7:7), because, imprisoned within this 'rigid framework', they are 'lacking in imagination'. The new forces will avoid such sclerosis, 'for one gets used to a system' (40:7): 'We must struggle against the inertia of those who are afraid of everything, especially of what will happen in the near future' (41:7).

The actual organization of these forces received scant attention. A few replies, however, are worth singling out. In contrast with present modes of organization, there is an emphasis on the role of the base: the organization must be 'constantly contestable, created by the base and controlled by it' (14:7); 'everyone must participate in the elaboration of new structures' (22:7), on a basis of 'great flexibility' (63:7); the old forces may participate in the movement 'if they accept the need for perpetual adaptation' (23:7).

A second group embraces those who share a particular nostalgia for spontaneity. The spontaneous forces are regarded as indispensable in providing the original 'impulse', but organization is the 'prerequisite of success' (4:7): 'The forces begin spontaneously, then become organized' (9:7). Several express the fear that spontaneity alone might lead the movement to failure: 'Spontaneity is essential at the beginning, but must be organized very soon or it loses its strength' (13:7); 'All revolutions must be spontaneous, but with a tendency to become organized in order to resist the old forces, which are already organized' (18:7); 'Non-organized spontaneous forces are soon incapable of dealing with the situation that they have created and fail to act quickly enough to make the best of that situation' (63:7).

It would seem that for this group alone the fear of being 'bought off' (récupéré) – a theme that was constantly to the fore at the time – tilted the balance in favour of the third alternative proposed in the question.

The last group rejects both the idea of spontaneity and that of the old organizations. 'There is a risk that spontaneity will lead to anarchy, which only brings with it a regression of social progress, but the present organized forces are incapable of freeing themselves of their rigid framework' (47:7). 'Change brought about by the spontaneous forces may well result in anarchy' (64:7); 'No lasting action can be carried out in disorder' (73:7).

Finally, a few of the respondents hesitate before the alternative of 'spontaneous forces' and 'new forces in the process of being organized', and, in comments similar to those quoted above, pose a practical problem: Are young intellectuals capable of believing in priorities; are they already too objectivized and eclectic? One reply sums up particularly well this kind of uncertainty:

> I hesitate between the two, because there are valuable and dangerous sides to both of them. Non-organized spontaneous forces avoid bureaucratization

and sclerosis, but run the risk of inefficiency and failure. The new forces in the process of being organized have a greater chance of success, but run the risk of becoming slow and petrified. What we need, perhaps, is something between the two, but it's yet to be discovered and defined (70:7).

Only three other replies link the idea of 'new forces' and a 'recourse to the old organizations', as a means of reconciling 'heart and reason' (2:7). As one subject puts it (35:7): 'Experience and perhaps moderation' are the necessary adjuncts to the 'rejuvenation' of the organizations.

Lastly, there is a fairly high rate of no replies (14 out of 77), and in the comments an assortment of the various ideas that were in the air at the time. One such idea, that of the *vieille taupe*,[1] is seen by a number of commentators on the May events as accounting for the explosion.[2] According to this view, the 'new forces' are new 'only in so far as it is new for them to come out into the open . . . they have always existed' (56:7).

Then there are the 'extremists' of the revolution, for whom 'change is inevitable and irreversible', and it does not matter 'in what way it evolves' (17:7). 'Organization merely accelerates the process of decay; change can spring only out of the chaos of spontaneity and total confusion' (8:7).[3] Three replies are more 'traditional': one of them defends the CGT, which has been 'betrayed by its leaders', and advises the interviewer, in future, to follow 'the teachings of Comrade Mao Tse-tung' before drawing up a questionnaire.

After this examination of the comments, correctives should be added to the purely numerical breakdown of the replies.[4] Only one heading remained practically unchanged, that concerning the old, organized forces. Some of those interviewed think that these forces can be used as factors of change, not because they represent an efficient machine, but because their numerical strength provides a base whose eyes must be opened.

On the other hand, the party of spontaneity is considerably reinforced by the 'yes, but . . .' of categories III, IV, and V. A new breakdown, on

---

[1] The mole, which burrows for years, then suddenly emerges in the light of day. (Translator's note.)
[2] Cf., in particular, Glucksmann (1968) and Viénet (1968).
[3] This last comment seems so definite that it is difficult to see why the respondent did not choose the alternative of 'spontaneity', unless it was to express a dislike for 'over-reasonable' questionnaires.
[4] Out of 77 questionnaires, the following replies were obtained:

I	Spontaneous forces	6
II	Organized forces	1
III	New forces	45
IV	I & III	8
V	II & III	3
VI	No reply	14

this basis, shows that a little over a third of the interviewees imagine change as a process rather like the following: a long repressed spontaneity that suddenly explodes, followed by the creation of new forces that must be organized, but in a flexible way, so as to avoid, on the one hand, being 'absorbed' (*récupéré*) and defeated by the old organizations, and, on the other, falling into the old errors of bureaucratization and sclerosis.

TABLE 6 Modes of action and organization

	O^1	T^1	OT^1	No reply
REPLIES IN TERMS OF STABLE 'STRUCTURES':				
I Spontaneous forces	2	I	—	—
II Organized forces	—	I	—	—
III New forces	11(*a*)	15(*b*)	2	I
IV I & III	2	—	3	I
V II & III	—	—	2	—
REPLIES IN TERMS OF 'PROCESS':				
I Spontaneous forces	I	I	—	I
II Organized forces	I	—	—	—
III New forces	5(*c*)	8(*d*)	—	I
V II & III	—	—	—	—

O = overthrow; T = transformation; OT = overthrow and/or transformation.
Note: The responses do not total 77 because 'no replies' to questions 6 and 7 are not shown.

If, in concluding this section of the poll dealing with change, we bring together the three aspects already examined, a few regroupings emerge (see *Table 6: (a), (b), (c), (d)*.

(*a*) First, let us consider the relatively numerous 'revolutionary' group (structures/overthrow/new forces). For them, the structures of present-day society are such that it is quite useless to try to transform them from within; for, even if the standard of living has improved, even if people's attitudes have changed, this merely gives 'the illusion of a change of structures' (62:7), which, in fact, 'have been consolidated at the expense of the individual' (14:7). The old organizations are regarded with a good deal of mistrust, not to say hostility: it is they that must be overcome, since they prop up the old system. The role of the students is regarded as being of prime importance. The workers represent a considerable force, but they are much more difficult to mobilize, since they are dependent on bureaucratic organizations. The students, on the other hand, are constantly at the ready, because they are not yet caught up 'materially' (22:6b) in the present social system.

(*b*) A second group, which sets out with a less fixed, less absolute idea of structures and regards their transformation as a possibility, also expects to be based on 'new forces'. The failure to overthrow the system is explained either by economic considerations or by the fact that there does not yet exist a true revolutionary organization. But many are no less certain that a profound change was brought about in people's minds. Some deduce from this that 'the overthrow will come about next time' (63:7).

Spontaneity almost always arouses mitigating comments: it is regarded as 'attractive', and necessary for providing the initial 'impulse', but, on the other hand, it is 'unpredictable and not very constructive' (27:7). It runs the risk either of leading to a regression on the economic plane or of allowing the traditional organizations to swamp the Movement and 'absorb' it. Also, it gains less support than do new forms of organization that might be based on the 'old model', but adapted in such a way as to remove its various 'sclerotic aspects – bureaucracy, lack of imagination, inflexibility' (28:7).

(*c*) The interviewees included in the process/overthrow/new forces category do not differ appreciably from those who chose the structures/overthrow/new forces combination. As we saw earlier, few of those interviewed believe in the possibility of really transforming society. This is particularly true for those who chose the process/overthrow option. In fact, they stress the extreme slowness of the process of transformation (15:6b), its negative aspect (the integration of the workers into the capitalist system, 23:6a), or its irregularity (progress, followed by regression, 16:6b).

(*d*) This category includes the 'moderates' and the 'pessimists' (process/transformation/new forces). For the moderates, the possibility of a gradual transformation of society appears greater than for those in category (*c*): 'a society is never immobile' (7:6a); 'change implies a certain continuation' (64:7). However, this change is difficult to bring about, even at university level. For the pessimists, radical change would be desirable, but May was not the right moment for it, because only a student vanguard wanted it, because France is too conservative, or even because 'the university, being in the possession of the state . . . any attempts at change come up against the administrative barrier' (52:6 and 7).

Lastly, I should like to analyse these tendencies in terms of our indices. Constants emerge in the view of *present-day society* and of *change* (questions 2 to 7). The particularly systematic character of the students' replies is both a help, in the analysis of the results of a relatively small sample, and a characteristic feature of the student world that presents its own basic problems; but I have no wish to labour this point.

Of the 15 pure dichotomists[1] interviewed, 13 think that the structures have not basically changed in the long term, and advocate their overthrow.

The 13 pure gradualists (non-dichotomists)[2] hold less decided opinions. Those who believe that society evolves according to a constant process are more numerous, however. A clear majority speaks not of an overthrow of the structures, but of their transformation (9 replies out of 13).

It would seem, then, that the dichotomists form the 'revolutionary' core of the 77 interviewed. Their number varies little through the series of questions 2 to 7. Their replies are coherent: they see society as a relation of forces in which the stronger prevent any evolution taking place. They deduce from this that the structures must be overthrown. It should be noted that over half of them belong to a political or union organization, whereas this proportion is only one-quarter for all those interviewed.

The non-dichotomists, on the other hand, are much more reformist, but also less systematic in their reasoning. Their ideas are a combination of the 'traditional', not to say conservative, and the 'new'. Ten of them (out of 13) say that they are neither members nor sympathizers of an organization, which is well below the general average; only one expressed a wish to join the National Union of Students (the UNEF) – and he was in the final year of his degree course.

Similar tendencies are to be found among those included under the heading 'heterogeneous combinations', according to whether their view of society is more or less dichotomic.

Thus *Table 6* shows that 22 of the interviewees who replied to all the

[1] According to their images of 'country', 'city', and 'factory' (cf. questions 2, 3, and 4).
[2] Idem.

questions are favourable to the structures/overthrow or structures/overthrow/transformation combination. Comparison with their previous responses shows that 20 of them replied with at least two dichotomies to questions 2, 3, and 4.

The inverse proportion applies for those who chose at least two gradualist lists in these questions. It is among them that the majority of the 'reformists' are to be found. However, one thing should be noted about how these 'reformists' dealt with the question concerning the factory. Of those who chose only one dichotomized list, that concerning the *factory*, a majority replied in terms of *fixed structures*.[1] On the other hand, of those who imagine the factory as a more graduated hierarchy and choose the dichotomic list only in relation to the country or the city, there is a greater proportion of replies in terms of process, as was also the case for the pure non-dichotomists. It is apparent, therefore, that the image of the factory plays a more determining role in an overall view of society and change than does, for example, that of the country as a whole.

If one brings together these tendencies (questions 2 to 7), one can see the emergence of three broad groups of subjects:

1. Dichotomists, who advocate an overthrow of the structures by new forces.

2. Gradualists, who believe in the possibility of an evolution of society and who are in favour of its transformation – 'modernization', one might say – by new forces.

3. A mixed group containing a majority in favour of a transformation of the structures by new forces and whose dichotomic view of the factory is the determining factor in their view of society and of change.

The first group embraces those who, in the language of May, might be called extreme 'Leftists' (about one-fifth of those interviewed). The second (numerically about the same size) embraces the students with more traditional, more conservative views, whose aspirations go little beyond a certain modernist reformism. It would be plausible to relate them to the Centre of the French electorate.

Between these two extremes is a majority of 'undecided', often closer to the second group in their views of present-day society, as can be seen in the quantitative analysis of the questionnaire, but more attracted to the 'ideas of May', as an examination of their comments reveals. In the terms

[1] They form the majority of category (b) in *Table 6* (structures/transformation/new forces).

of the general political vocabulary, this group corresponds to the 'floating vote', which can be more influenced through the imagination.

It would no doubt be easy enough to attribute these 'ideas of May' only to a few leaders, which would reduce the 'average' student entirely to the level of a receptive object. At this stage in our description, another question arises: What were the imaginative predispositions which, in May, were able to find expression, when the average student suddenly found himself expressing publicly what he had felt, but until then had been unable to *put into words*? How much of it was passive imitation, mere conformism, in fact, and, to that extent, how were the leaders able to develop and spread these ideas?

THE IMAGE OF THE NEW SOCIETY

In discussions that have taken place recently throughout the country, an image of a new society has emerged; what features of this new society are important to you personally?

This was our first question. By plunging straight into the subject, on both a general and a personal level, it was intended to influence the direction and expression of the replies as little as possible, while at the same time reducing resistance to the closed questions that were to follow. Apart from a few exceptions (two 'no replies' and some rather thin replies), the overwhelming majority of the students played the game: this was due not only to the 'brainstorming' atmosphere of the May weeks, but also to the fact that the imagination had really seized upon society as a source of deep, personal preoccupations.

Attention was centred on the individual. The replies were oriented by no other frame of reference than a sense of the new. The qualitative analysis presented here must show, above all, the originality of certain formulas, the principal themes around which the content of a new society is expressed. It will show how the 'average' student interprets, invents, and reinvents the thinking of the time. The interviewees were neither leaders nor activists, and often less articulate than those that could be heard in the assemblies. It is true, however, that the students, who were reputed to be sceptical of all opinion polls, would probably not have replied in this style of ideologico-personal improvisation if they had not already been plunged into the bath of collective improvisation provided by the May discussions.

New ideas from traditional sources

It is hardly surprising that 'spontaneous' reflection should come up with certain traditional themes of political thought, above all those of French socialist inspiration.

First, egalitarianism. One student, for example, wanted a society in which 'the concentration of big capital in the hands of one man would be forbidden, in which everyone would have his share of responsibility, in which there would be neither extreme poverty nor extreme wealth, and in which manual labour would no longer be undervalued' (56:1). Different replies used the symbol of money to express the need for a levelling of society (38:1, 42:1, and 6:1).

Certain of the formulas used contain apparently 'new' elements – like the idea that the concentration of capital should be *forbidden* – in the sense that to the individual expressing them the views are quite new, although the views themselves are taken from an old store of ideas.

The breaking down of barriers is a theme that often recurs. Here the sense of the new would seem to belong to a more general awakening than that actually expressed in many of the replies: 'A lot of students, who've probably never lived among working-class people, are now taking an interest in them' (40:1). This last reply, situated half-way between hope and sceptical realism – like many others in this poll – adds, however, 'the opposite doesn't seem to be the case yet'.

'USINES, UNIVERSITÉ, UNION', declared one poster that expressed this same preoccupation. 'It's my earnest wish,' said another interviewee (28:1), 'that the coming together of workers and students that is now beginning to take place may one day be more than a childish dream.' Another speaks of 'pedagogical fusion and slow transmission from one to the other' (64:1) in referring to the elimination of several types of cleavage (between parents and children, staff and students, bosses and workers) which he identifies in a strategic whole. Lastly, one student, who was particularly interested in this subject – judging by the length and complexity of his reply – speaks of breaking down barriers, divisions, and hierarchies.

It goes without saying that the theme of egalitarianism and the breaking down of barriers is also to be found in many of the formulas attacking the present hierarchies: 'There'll be a transition from concentration and centralization to a number of autonomous social centres . . . Contrary to what is happening in the present pyramidal system, it is a question not of overthrowing the pyramid, but of flattening it out' (68:1). Others go so far as to speak of the abolition of the hierarchies, which are seen to be 'too exclusively financial' (28:1), and therefore unjust, a cause of unmerited privilege, etc.

It should be noted, however, that a section of the replies were in favour of developing, rather than revolutionizing, existing society. 'Looked at realistically, this new society is really not very different from society as it is now. It can only be an exaggeration of it, rather like American society' (67:1). Some express even more negative views, even against change altogether: 'Society will remain as it is. I'm against the movement in so far as it aims at changing society. I'm against revolution' (19:1). Another: 'Fringe benefits and wages should be improved' (6:1). And, even in May, in the midst of all the euphoria, there are cynics: one art student, specializing in engraving, did not hesitate to admit that, although many of his friends were in the struggle against bourgeois art and capitalism, he would try and adapt himself to any society: 'society based on capitalism suits me best', the problem being to sell large editions of engravings (7:1).

Nevertheless, a section of the students questioned opted for 'middle-of-the-road' solutions or for highly individualistic ones. Among the former, one finds positions of this type: 'The leaderships of the trade union organizations and the left-wing parties don't seem to accept a fundamental reform of society, *a fortiori* a revolution' (2:1). And this law and economics student, using another Latin phrase even more aptly, continues: 'The fundamental difference between the demands of students and workers presents an acute problem for the students; the majority of them come from a middle-class background and are shocked *a priori* [*sic*] by the wage claims of the workers.' But the search for 'middle-of-the-road' solutions is presented several times, as is the need 'to reject extremes, whatever they may be' (24:1). 'The new society', says another, that imagined by the majority, 'is a sort of mixture of capitalism and socialism' (52:1).

What is perhaps relatively new at this time is that the themes that emerged correspond perfectly with general positions of acceptance, partial rejection, or total rejection of society, and belong to the current of anti-authoritarianism[1] that was one of the basic features of the whole May Movement.

---

[1] Expressions like the following show how fundamental this was: 'rejection of authority', 'desire to participate', 'a long-repressed desire to express oneself', 'a need to think' (11:1).

From liberation to self-determination

This is the libertarian vein, whose intrinsic newness is debatable, but which is exploited publicly, with frankness and enthusiasm, even by the 'uncommitted' student, who often belongs to no very clearly marked subculture.

A number of expressions used here imply that the 'essence' of man is his freedom. 'Man must no longer be a producing animal, but an awakened being, open to joy and to art' (76:1). Whereas some propose 'the abolition of all machine-work' (74:1), others emphasize not only that we no longer want men who are merely 'puppets obeying machines' (55:1), but that, in general, 'society must not have precedence over the individual, it should be simpler and gayer, and no longer oppressive' (61:1). The theme of joy, in fact, is frequently found side by side with that of liberation. And the true abolitionists express themselves in euphoric terms: 'Abolition of slavery, abolition of work, abolition of the family, abolition of the state' (8:1). Which, in other terms, means, 'liberation from inhibitions and repressions' (74:1) and may be accompanied by community or individualist images of a new society.

In the individualist direction one finds references to 'broader inter-personal relationships' (66:1) or to 'more truthful interpersonal relation-ships', expressions that are accompanied by a little sociological construc-tion: 'This will lead to greater ease in communication, which, in turn, will lead to a larger consensus in the organization of society' (65:1).

But we must not forget the cases of the sceptical students. While claim-ing to feel the need for a society without machine-men, these students add, for example: 'To be quite honest, I don't take the idea of a new society very seriously, despite the events' (72:1). For many, the image exists primarily at the level of 'a hope for individual freedom', and what was new for many of the students was simply this 'awareness of new problems and a discovery of discussion' (27:1).

In the direction of new collective solutions, there is a glimpse of a society of 'citizens', in which 'group feeling, for example, the notion of collective work, for the collectivity' would be developed (55:1). Another sees a society, 'in which one lives as a collectivity, in which the group idea predominates and in which the individual feels that he works not for the profit of a few, but for the whole collectivity' (37:1).

This is a very old objective, of course, but again what is new about it here is the 'natural' way in which it rose to the surface, as it were. Several students make the point that it is not a new society that emerged, but 'rather a new image of society. Let us say that perhaps people became aware,[1] rightly or wrongly, that democracy, in France, was no more than a meaningless word.' And this very cautious student adds that there should be no talk of revolution: 'It is simply a refusal to let oneself be led, a desire to participate in the life of the country' (48:1).

In the end, all this boils down to a general insistence on self-determination. For many, this is expressed in terms of the university. But, in fact, it is an overall reflection on relations between the individual and society, 'a society in which men's needs are satisfied and realized, determined by men themselves and not imposed on them, as now' (37:1).

Although it is true that the arguments in favour of liberation often remain in the form of an affirmation of a need or a 'human' right, one also finds a surprising number of replies mentioning various modes of integration; but the nature of the collective life varies above all around the pole of an anarchist-type hyper-federalism.

There is the key expression of a reply already quoted which mentions 'a number of autonomous social centres' (68:1). A cybernanthropic[2] image carries the 'collective' solution to its individualist extreme when one student imagines 'a weekly consultation of the people: everyone would have a telephone at home, connected to a computer; everyone would say what he wanted and IBM would say what was to be done' (34:1).

Others, with less precise ideas, speak simply of a life in society presupposing 'a desire for participation', that is, 'a positive desire to create a more integrated and cohesive society' (20:1). Others, again, outline the proposal made by the Communist Party: 'A people's government, with the union of all the forces of democracy and social progress, on the basis of a common programme' (44:1).

Without ascribing too much importance to quantitative trends based on this poll, it can be said that within these limits the anti-authoritarian trend is dominant. 'In my opinion,' says a moderate student already quoted, 'communism alienates freedom, and the transformations that are

---

[1] Whereas it is fairly obvious that the theme of awareness is strongly stressed, the fact that it is linked with internationalism should be noted: 'A society in which everyone would be aware of himself and of the world and in which everyone would have the right to criticize and to take on responsibility' (17:1). 'The rejection of all narrow-mindedness (social classes, national frontiers)' (69:1).
[2] H. Lefebvre, who coined this term, has produced a robot-portrait of a being that is not a robot, but a man of the modern communication systems, dominated by and dominating cybernetics, the cybernanthrope (cf. Lefebvre, 1967).

taking place, and will take place, must culminate in a liberal society. Liberty does not mean anarchy' (24:1). In some cases, this 'liberal' tendency is carried to the point of a libertarian affirmation.

CREATION CONDITIONED BY PERMANENT CHANGE

We now come to the second and third stages of the process of constructing the new. After the rejection of structures and self-affirmation come the exercise of freedom – creation – and its condition or consequence – the permanence of change.

Once there is 'real freedom, not just formal freedom, that is, a freedom of autonomy, spontaneity, humanity', as one student notes (70:1), 'the result will be an increase of creativity'. We are now in the region of *social invention*.

It is true that although a very large number of comments emphasized the need for creation, very few of the replies revealed any special gift for invention. One finds expressions like the following: 'Priority must be given to the individual and his spontaneity against all forms of oppression' (71:1). 'The dignity of life is related to the maximum development of each individual, whatever his gifts may be' (56:1).

Some are conscious of the fact that the long public discussions, which turned into veritable forums of collective creativity, 'provide the image of a new, theoretical society, but one that has not yet been realized objectively' (63:1).

Many comments go no further than an affirmation of a desire for the participation of all. Creation, then, is not the invention of a new solution, but of a new man:

> Men must be given back their dignity. What's a roadsweeper or an office clerk in life, compared with a doctor? They're nothing. They don't count. Nobody listens to them. We gave them an opportunity of expressing themselves, and even if what they say isn't very interesting, it doesn't matter. People listen to what they have to say and they feel that they are someone (22:1).

It is more than permissiveness that leads to creativity. We have here a theme that has often been ignored in the social field, and one that for some time now has been a major preoccupation of artists, that of the importance of the creative act, quite apart from any considerations of content or finished result.

Because personal creation is traditionally seen as the preserve of artists, the theme of creativity is often linked with cultural phenomena. 'There is a need for an open culture, a culture related to life' (57:1). Another, speaking of liberation, creation, and the priority that 'must be given to the individual and his spontaneity', affirms that the liberation of repressed and dormant instincts and desires is related to 'new possibilities of cultural development' (71:1). To the very many expressions that imply the need for self-determination – 'it's up to each individual himself to choose what concerns him' (14:1) – must be added a solution that seems to relate together participation, adjustment to oneself, and practicable self-expression: 'An extension of cultural activities without the direction of an authority' (51:1). 'Technology at the service of man, for a reduction in working hours and the possibility of culture and human life' (23:1). And this last reply envisages a situation in which 'students work at night in the factories with the workers, while workers spend their evenings at the university', which would bring about a wider understanding 'through education and culture'.

We have become convinced, says another, 'that the only means of social levelling is culture' (36:1). By culture, he does not mean, of course, as is sometimes explicitly stated, 'culture in the present despicable, bourgeois sense'; 'other human possibilities than intellectual ones' must be liberated. The list of these possibilities is a rather colourful one: 'instinctive, sexual, emotional, artistic' (68:1). Later, the same student stresses the importance of the slogan: 'Through the imagination, all is possible.'

Lastly, some replies speak of 'the real and permanent putting into practice of the concept of cultural revolution' (63:1).

Thus the full gamut of the various uses of the concept of culture has been run. From the idea of culture in the literary and artistic sense, we have moved to a use very close to that of cultural anthropology (daily life, even products and the act of producing), and, finally, to the quasi 'Sino-political' use (the violent transformation of the centres of cultural transmission: universities, museums). We have looped the loop. At this phenomenal level, an academic concern for different conceptual usages is irrelevant: a complex social concept pivots on an axis that is common to all three senses. In May, it was more than usually 'natural' and understandable to slide from one of these senses to the others.

We must now turn to what is the condition and logical consequence of an insistence on freedom and creativity, namely, the non-fixity of organizational arrangements, whatever they may be.

At its minimum point, it is the non-fixity of the 'personal'. One student demands 'a society in which membership of a class will no longer be through birth, but through personal ability, which will involve *permanent mobility*' (56:1). But it is also the non-fixity of the structure: many comments condemn 'the fossilized society we've had up to now' (31:1); there is even a transition to a notion more demanding than that of mere mobility, that of the disappearance 'of the workers/cultural classes *hierarchy*, which must not be accepted as inevitable or as some state of nature' (59:1).

It is not a question of mere flexibility, but rather of 'fluxibility'. Apart from such relatively banal expressions as 'permanent struggle for justice' (12:1), 'questioning of all government institutions' (31:1), 'freedom of expression, no censorship' (5:1) – and perhaps even, implicitly, *in* such expressions – there emerges an absolute demand for 'non-rigidity', non-crystallization: 'the disappearance of all permanent privilege, permanent contestation and demystification, involving constant renewal' (60:1).

This new society, which one student baptized 'society of contestation' (4:1), is directly related, by another, to the idea of research:[1] 'The results of literary, psychological, and scientific research would be pooled and all teachers would be compelled to maintain "the spirit of research", which would avoid all sclerosis and lead to an education that was not imposed, but acquired' (54:1).

Finally, a 'society that was not fossilized in its structures would make it possible to avoid the disappointments that are apparent now' (35:1), which brings us, once again, to that ideal of a fusion between personal desires and established solutions. Though it should be added, of course, that no solution could be *established*: every solution would always be subject to constant transformations.

It goes without saying that one of the major difficulties in appreciating 'the events of May '68' will remain the fact that interpretation cannot be assessed by means of quantitative analyses. Anyone may present hypotheses and find sufficient support in directly and qualitatively empirical tests.

This is true for this poll, based as it is on a small sample of students. Its principal justification was to draw attention to the existence of a whole

---

[1] This is the only reply that mentions research. The student in question is female, a classics student and a member of the Jeunesse Communiste de France.

range of opinions, which did not even all belong to the same world, but in which, nevertheless, a certain logical arrangement could be found. We cannot and must not be under any illusions as to the accurate representativity of the analysis from a quantitative point of view: I have simply tried, by cautiously revealing certain tendencies, to sketch a number of plausible hypotheses. The use of the questionnaire method of inquiry, the usual schema of analytical research, involves imperfections that I have not always succeeded in avoiding. We have tried to carry out 'on-the-spot' research, to present certain 'open' questions, to encourage criticism of the way in which the questions were framed, to explore the world of representation through a series of questions, and so to create an instrument of analysis. As with any other method, it would be easy enough to draw up a list of its inconveniences.

I shall conclude with what, in my opinion, is one of the most characteristic tendencies in 'May':[1] the emphasis on the cultural aspects is linked with an image of society in which the dichotomic conception of power is dominant.

In view of the fact, therefore, that opinions of a frequently 'radical' nature were expressed as to the place, the content, and the style of culture – in every sense of the word – I set out to specify what type of student tended most frequently and most plausibly to link it with other themes that were characteristic of the 'revolution'.

It appeared that those students for whom society was more gradualist than dichotomic expressed themselves far less often in explicitly cultural terms. If one counts up all the replies containing a reference to the idea of permanent change, to that of 'liberation', and to a *cultural* aspect of social life, they are distributed as shown in *Table 7*.

One of the things indicated in this classification is the original phenomenon, to which we shall return several times in later chapters, of the juncture of two currents, which, in the interests of simplicity, might be called Marxist and anarchist. Those who have a class view of society, which particularly implies the idea of domination, usually hold to a traditional conception of politics (defined in terms of the 'class struggle', of opposition between political 'organizations', etc.). In May, one finds a 'libertarian' tendency that accords at least as much strategic importance to 'culture' as to organizations, without in any way departing from a political image of society. Although it is difficult to be specific about the content of this politicization – it is just this phenomenon, linked as it is

[1] This abbreviation is used in this book for convenience.

with new images of society, that I wish to explore – its two axes would appear to be permanent change and culture. The content of the latter is certainly very varied, but it tends to give precedence to creation, that is to the *construction* of reality,[1] by the individual or by groups, rather than to adaptation to what is regarded as established reality. And although the rejection of determinism may appear under different forms, the idea of culture is pre-eminent, whether in the sense of the 'daily life' of each individual, or, more generally, of a life-style, art, or the transformation of a civilization, etc.

TABLE 7 Image of the factory and political action

Respondents	N^1	Permanent change	Liberation	Cultural transformation
Dichotomists – factory[2]	41	5	16	14
Gradualists – factory[3]	30	2	9	4

[1] Some of the respondents made more than one reference. Replies containing no such references numbered 16 among the dichotomists and 17 among the gradualists.
[2] All those who chose list (*b*) in the question on the factory.
[3] All those who chose list (*a*) in the question on the factory.

Lastly, it is obviously a fundamental question to know whether the image of a feudal-type factory, with a single, absolute power of domination on the one hand and an equally complete subordination on the other, is a cause or a reflection. Problems of the which-came-first-the-hen-or-the-egg type must be reduced to precise partial problems if there is to be any hope of resolving them.

Generally speaking, it seems to me that the rejection both of traditional politicization and of present-day society has developed in the generation of students involved in May a desire to express themselves as the creators of their own world, individual and collective – self-determination having become the principal axis rather than a mere precondition. The image of society, then, is no longer a representation fixing a precise content, but just this sort of act of creation, an action-image or acted-image through which one sees oneself in the act of creating a new society. The kinship

[1] To use Berger's excellent expression (cf. Berger and Luckmann, 1966).

with those 'art' movements that tend to deny art as a thing apart must therefore be examined.

A section at least of the students at the 'base' are aware that a new 'politicization' has begun. We shall see, in greater detail, how several young intellectuals and then some well-known activists analyse this phenomenon: if they recognize its existence, how they have experienced it, and whether, for them, it should be developed by inventing appropriate methods.

PART II

The Movement as seen by some of its Observers

CHAPTER 3

Interval or Prefiguration?

A Group Discussion

It seemed to me that a discussion on the political and cultural aspects of May would enable us to situate, in the minds of readers who did not live through that period in Paris, or, more specifically, in the Latin Quarter, the juncture that forms the starting-point of this study: cultural politicization.[1] The participants, who met in November 1968, were fairly close to each other, at least from a professional point of view, since, with one exception, they could all be regarded as sociologists (teachers and/or research workers). But, as we shall see, their interpretations of the events were far from identical, though, of course, the spectrum of opinion was far narrower than that to be found among the mass of students.[2]

Two of the participants teach in the sociology department at Nanterre (René Lourau and Pierre Tripier), another in a professional school (R. Linbaum); Pierre Rolle is a research worker at the CNRS[3] and part-time teacher; R. Bonnet is a young architect. They were chosen because each was personally acquainted with at least one other of the participants and could contribute his own style of interpretation. Obviously, I have no intention of sticking labels on them. The problems involved were not always within their usual range of preoccupations, and the comments they made are obviously only a partial and therefore imperfect expression of their personal positions. It is with this express reservation – and their permission – that the following extracts are reproduced, with the names of the speakers added.

[1] The 'group-discussion' method, which was particularly successful in experiments carried out at Frankfurt, seemed to me to provide a perfect complement to the individual-interview method; it was carried out here with 'experts', which was a great help from a technical point of view.

[2] The large amount of published material on May is particularly interesting in this respect, showing as it does how the most varied interpretations can be made of the same, very brief, historical period.

[3] Centre National de la Recherche Scientifique, a state-subsidized organization that provides grants and facilities for a vast range of research projects, individual and collective, in every academic discipline. (Translator's note.)

I have obviously had to cut the transcript of the tape-recording[1] – the four hours of discussion recorded amount to a hundred closely typed pages – but I have not 'arranged' or recomposed the material. Contrary to the impression we had at the time, the line of argument develops as clearly as possible, in a discussion that was in fact even less 'directed' than might be imagined from the text.

We did not prohibit digressions (though they are not reproduced here) or over-long developments of certain points. In consequence, the subject originally proposed did not receive all the attention I could have wished; one of the participants felt frustrated, or at least inhibited, by this fact. On the other hand, problems that I did not regard as being directly related to this study were raised and discussed at length – with the result that other points of view emerged than those to be found in the already published analyses of the events. They certainly enabled me to broaden my own initial views. A double technical problem presented itself – how to select the participants and how to conduct the discussion in a fairly permissive way. After this first experiment, it seems to me that an exploratory discussion of this kind must be non-directive, but that the selection of the members of the group – this is a problem well known to research groups – should be made through a series of discussions, which would serve as a guide for adjusting the composition of the group. In view of the difficulties, it seems to me that the discussion that follows went well beyond what could be reasonably expected of it at a single meeting: it deals with certain of the major themes of 'intellectual' and, of course, 'political' thinking during and about May; it sketches the broad outlines of the juncture between the political and the cultural, and touches on various areas of analysis to which I shall return in later chapters.

Where participants have expounded their positions in greater detail, or more explicitly, in published material, I have quoted from these publications.

THE EXPERIENCE OF A NEW TIME

LINBAUM: What took place in May itself was a sort of interval . . . There was a difference in the rhythm of time, even in the meaning of time. For example, decisions were made in the morning to be implemented that same evening or even . . . 'Where are we going?' Nobody told us, nothing was

---

[1] Digression, repetitions, and two paragraphs that I considered to be too far from the point; a few rephrasings (on the whole, I have retained the conversational style), and a few polemical allusions that hold up the development of the argument.

written down, we had to decide what to do together, then do it straight away . . . So there was a change in real historical time. What happened could not be encompassed in the old conception of time.

Before, society reproduced itself[1] at an increasing, progressive rate. Then suddenly there is a break, and instead of finding themselves in the rhythm in which they normally live, morning, evening, holidays, not holidays, people find themselves in a rhythm in which they have to decide what they're going to do from one minute to the next: 'Shall I or shall I not go to the demon-stration . . .?' There are two problems, I think . . . the problem which, confronted by an event like a revolution, is a mass phenomenon: a radical change in the conditions in which people find themselves, psychologically, and therefore sociologically, in general, there is a different conception of time, a new, very special, purely synchronic time; and whereas, in other conditions, a thing can be reproduced, a certain system is perpetuated, here there is no framework any more.

w: *And what happens, then, in such a period, when they start thinking about what things will be like in the future, in, say, five or ten years?*

LINBAUM: Take the planner, for example. The planners may not have a clear picture of what things will be like at the end of the plan, but I think they all know what the end of the month or the end of the year will be like. We have a clear idea of what our evening will be like at home, watching television, say.

Before, everyone was integrated into the time processes. I came home at seven and I knew that later I would have to go to bed, then get up again next morning to go to work . . . So there is a time that has a fundamental influence over everything I think; I'm not going to dash around any old how, because I know that if I do I'll need more time to recuperate – except, perhaps, for certain artists . . .

w: *Could it be said, then, that it was a 'faceless revolution'?*

LINBAUM: There are two things to distinguish here: first, the quality of time, since people felt it. Personally, I think one of the things that has been most quickly forgotten is that there are moments, as in 1848, or 1789, etc., that is, all those moments when there is a *social break* – we saw the same thing at the time of general mobilization, too – that are special moments. I think there are certain moments that affect society, that disrupt its time. The war, too, per-haps, then, later, everything settles down again, but at first there must be some sort of shake-up, which therefore gives a special value to everything that is said at the time.

[1] 'The conditions of production are also those of reproduction. No society can go on producing, in other words, no society can reproduce, unless it constantly reconverts a part of its products into means of production, or elements of fresh products' (K. Marx, *Capital*, Chapter XIII).

And then there is the face of the revolution: that depends on how you look at it. If you look at it close up, you see images being produced . . . like the images that were produced in May . . . If you step back a bit, you'd see perhaps the discourse before, the discourse after or between the two, and the discourse of the break itself. But what is the discourse of the break, what is the discourse specific to May?

ROLLE: On the whole, I approach the idea of 'images of society' with some caution . . . Of course, an image of society did appear in May, and it had very specific features. The tactics of the Mouvement du 22 Mars were really just that – a sort of new image. What it was saying was: 'We think that the state is of such and such a kind, it cannot allow this sort of thing, it is repressive and it cannot show itself to be any other than that if we do this.' So a sort of social experiment was carried out: they set about creating a certain image of society in people's minds and even distinguishing between people who didn't think alike – it was a very new kind of experimental politics.[1] This image of society is something we lived in – before May. Or, at least, even if one didn't accept it, one lived in it just the same because the whole social system drew you towards it. For example, the remarkable thing was the distinction people made straight away between various equivalents of society: the state, for example, was hardly mentioned. The nation, as distinguished from the state, was something that, in every respect, was less precise before May than after May. What people discovered in May is not something that they have lost since, it's an experience; I think it's something they will keep with them.

LINBAUM: I'd like to add a few words to what I said just now. The problem of the alternative has been presented. The alternative is the comparison between two moments before/after, it's a comparison between two times of reproduction, in the capitalist moment, and in the socialist moment. . .

TRIPIER: If one analyses what occurred at the level of events, there is, of course, M 22 and its strategy, which we have followed very closely. First, the important thing is the concept of repression that is introduced into political life where it did not exist before. One shouts against the repression of the university system, then against the fact that the university system really does practise repression, that is, it uses the *flics* to do its repression for it. But the moment when things took on a new dimension was when Pompidou withdrew, when he did a Thiers; he did not, like Thiers, withdraw to Versailles, he stayed at the Matignon,[2] but he did exactly the same thing. He let things develop. I think that for people who, in the university movement, structured to some extent the way in which things developed, there was already a more

[1] Called the tactic of *exemplary action*; we shall return to it in this chapter, and later in the book.
[2] The Hôtel Matignon, the Prime Minister's residence and office in Paris. (Translator's note.)

or less underground social practice. People who had spent exhausting winter nights arguing and discussing for hours on end, when everyone had the right to express an opinion, when different political tendencies confronted one another, when an attempt was made to construct at the same time an analysis of society and of what would replace it and of how to get there and how the university, etc., etc., all this existed and was functioning before May.

During the first 'sit-in' in the Sorbonne it was those people who, you might say, took the initiative where these practices were concerned – though there was more to the May phenomenon than those practices alone.

Later, what was important was something else, what might be called the reverse side of May: the people at the factory gates.

LINBAUM: On what might be called the ideological plane, May represents a problem both for Marxism and for our society. There is also another phenomenon, that of May as a total phenomenon, which affected the entire population, gave rise to several thousand pages of complaints and grievances and revealed a mass of problems concerning centralization, hierarchization, power in the factories and in the universities . . .

ROLLE: But if you distinguish between two types of problem . . . Do you think that a problem of power in the factory, for example, hierarchization, is a problem independent of the Marxist problematic?

LINBAUM: No, that's not at all what I mean, I think that the essential significance of May is a crisis in Marxist thought, and perhaps even a break in Marxism . . . Indeed, this break necessitates a renewal of theory which will make it possible later to interpret what has happened more precisely. Why did it happen in France? How? etc. . . . So, in my opinion, there is an ideological problem that seems to be universal, namely, the problem of liberalism, of the triumph of the bourgeoisie, things that are not without interest, that are in fact very specific phenomena and that cannot be interpreted by Marxism . . .

ROLLE: I don't know whether we're going off the point, but I protest violently against the word 'universal' . . .

w: *Let's go back to the problem of the 'faceless' phenomenon. What does it mean? Are Marxists and non-Marxists undergoing a crisis in their thinking?*

LOURAU: Personally, I'm quite willing to play the game, that is, to *project* back, to try to rediscover, to re-project what we felt in May. I was wondering what struck me most at the time, and I realized with some consternation that I was unable to recall the essential points that had struck me most and that I later used, that I rationalized, whereas there had been two or three things that had profoundly affected me. What you called just now the discourse of

77

the break – well, I heard it, as we all heard it. The break in the sense in which, on the one hand, I was expecting what happened, and yet, at the same time, was not expecting it at all. What I mean is that it exceeded all my hopes . . . as Mallarmé said of the Eiffel Tower . . .

x:[1] Everyone thought that . . .

LOURAU: Yes, but at the same time those students that one thought one had – was accused of having – taught, influenced, indoctrinated, for a year or two at Nanterre, when they expressed themselves, I had difficulty in recognizing my own work. I understand the abuse of the *vieux schnoques*,[2] who did not recognize themselves at all . . . I myself, a young *schnoque*, took it very hard. Quite a few students made the same remark.

Up till then, we lived in a fairly comfortable world. It really was a tragedy: things happened along predictable lines . . . Rationality . . . The fate of the world bound up with economic growth, raw materials, etc. . . . And then, quite suddenly, there was another discourse, which was much more Surrealist, in Gabel's sense,[3] that is, a total grasp of reality, whereas the specialists of rationality, who had a good deal of difficulty in seeing reality, were swept aside, for a time. About your hypothesis of the transition from the project to projection, I think it's the problem of *exemplary action* you're really talking about. We're really in the sphere of the social imagination and of symbolism, since it's a question of acting apparently without strategy, with tactics decided from one day, one moment, to the next, and without really knowing that it will also be exemplary. And, of course, this is pure creation, the 'society of spectacle'[4] in all its splendour, but this is pure aleatory science.

Whereas up till then we had Leninism or the other political models, which were highly scientific and 'predictional', we are now faced with a new science, 'stochastics': there'll be a lot of mistakes, no one knows where we're going and it'll only be after a certain number of mistakes no doubt, but we don't regard them as errors (since we did not know what we were supposed to be successful in doing, we did not know where we were going), it's only *afterwards* that we can say that a particular action was exemplary, that is, that it acted upon the *social imagination*. It did act, but not in the same way as a picture. A picture acts upon the imagination, or in the sphere of ideas, of ideology. Here one acts upon something *through actions*. We are inside very real, very localized,

[1] Speaker not identifiable from the tape-recording.
[2] A pejorative term: 'old fool'.
[3] 'I shall use, with some slight distortion, the concepts of *Surrealism* and *Subrealism* developed by J. Gabel (in *La Fausse Conscience*, 1962). *Subrealism* is identified totally with the norms, the hierarchies and persons who embody them . . . The *Surrealist* is characterized by a "defect of identification" . . .' (cf. Lourau, 1968a.) This distinction, which does not cut across those of integration/deviance, institutional/anomic, is particularly relevant in the field of our research. It is obviously similar to the instituted/instituting distinction.
[4] I shall come back to this expression, which serves as the title of a work by the Situationist G. Debord, *La Société du spectacle* (1967).

topographical things like the occupation of premises. They are extremely simple actions that might sometimes be mistaken for schoolboy rowdyism. They are too real, too realistic almost.

You know what happened on that night at Nanterre, with the phallic administration building, anyway . . . it wasn't very serious, it was more Surrealist than rational, and it's the coming together of just some small fact like that and something that is there, at the time, something latent in the social imagination, that produces the exemplary action. One of the things that struck me was what made most people, not only the Leninists and the partisans of traditional politics, but also ordinary sensible people, talk of 'those young hooligans like Cohn-Bendit'. They were incapable of taking the thing seriously, it just wasn't worthy of inclusion in the political textbooks.

In other words, I think that when one is speaking, on a very serious, strategic plane, of the whole business in terms of political innovation, one is obliged also to speak of what is new from a general point of view, a political reference that is to be found in the imagination, in communication. After all, McLuhan's dictum that the medium is the message is not really that new. Young people of between twenty and twenty-five have learnt to mistrust the 'signified', in other words, and to shake up the 'signifier' to see what it will come up with.[1]

LINBAUM: To return to this theme of the serious . . . It must be said again, people were not, in the midst of such a break, concerned with being serious and responsible. Again, it's a question of the time relation. To be responsible is to say to oneself, 'Tomorrow I shall be here and will be able to say what I am doing today' . . . I think that what might prove interesting here is the notion of total *immaturity*, where the present dominates time in a radical way.

Before May, people already had images. To take the students, there were Marxists, traditional Trotskyists, and the JCR, and, on the other side, Beatniks, Provos, and Situationists . . . that is, there were two currents, one of which was related to a certain degree of maturity, concerned in fact with the construction of a possible world, and the other, to a certain degree of immaturity, involving the rejection of an impossible world.

On the whole, the Beatniks rejected politics completely and concerned themselves with the problem of hallucination, the sole truth, but that too is an image of the present; whereas, on the other side, there were highly constructed images of the future, concerned with the construction of a new world. We must discover how these groups confronted the events, and how it was that M 22, that is, a non-organization, an anti-organization, got the movement going, made it possible, and carried all the others along with it.

---

[1] Games are situations that make it possible for a number of people to participate simultaneously in a significant scheme of their own lives: cf. McLuhan, *Understanding media*, Chapter 24, 'Games'. The message, I think, is *projected onto* the medium – it is in this sense that the medium is the message.

THE ORGANIZATION OF SPONTANEITY

W: *Was M a 22 non-organization, or an organization of a new type? Moreover, when it's a question of occupying such and such a place, is there one single representation of the meaning of the action? Or was there, quite simply, the possibility of projecting into that action an interpretation that might differ according to the subgroups and according to individuals? I think there are two problems here.*

BONNET: At one meeting, Cohn-Bendit was accused of being a star. This did not result in a split: Cohn-Bendit realized the error he had made, that he had to some extent played the role, shall we say, of the star of M 22. What I mean is that without any organization, any organized traditional structure, each individual was important. It's just that, because of the advice he gave, he might have a little more importance, on condition that the others accepted him, but this doesn't alter the fact that such an individual remains a rank-and-file member of M 22. In a way, *everyone is a rank-and-file* member. But when M 22 'organized' something, well, yes, obviously an action was decided on by a group of individuals . . .

ROLLE: We must be sure what we mean by 'organization'. Organizing really amounts to working together. One shouldn't really say any more than that yet one always implies much more. So, in the sense that people worked together, not necessarily in a permanent way, and not on the basis of a constitution that is supposed to regulate relations between people, if one can abstract from such an organization all that is traditionally associated with the word, then I think it may be called an organization.[1]

LINBAUM: I meant anti-organization in the sense that Cohn-Bendit was opposed to Bensaïd and the JCR, with their greater organization. And only in that sense. I never said that M 22 was nothing at all.

ROLLE: It was an attempt at an experimental politics. That seems to me to transcend the problems of the past. Before, all action was supposed to be dependent on a certain programme, which was worked out *beforehand*. To go back to 'images', it was a concept of society that had to be *imposed* on people, on the basis of which they could be united.

Whereas M 22 was a genuine attempt to carry out a social experiment. That's why a lot of people met in M 22 who really, in terms of their fundamental aspirations, had nothing in common.

[1] It is probably significant that the importation of the Anglo-American use of the word organization (as in the phrase 'organization man') has not been an easy one; the idea of organization, like that of Party or Party apparatus, with its increasing hierarchy of discipline, arouses in France what Trotsky called 'the tragic sense of the organization' (cf. Naville, 1962, p. 88). This is related, it seems to me, to the notorious inability of the French to form a consensus on the degree of spontaneity, voluntary organization, and discipline required in a political unit, hence the all too well-known tendency to divisions, splits, etc.

w: *Are we in agreement with Lourau that this experiment contained much that was random?*

TRIPIER: It seems to me that what we were saying just now about non-reproduction is true of an initial phase and untrue of a second. That is to say that later there was the systematic reproduction of provocation against the police, the barricades . . . and from then on, there was nothing aleatory about it. At Nanterre, we saw Cohn-Bendit, with his charismatic personality and his amiability, succeed, with only a handful of nobodies, in bringing together, on the basis of a certain strategy, groups that were not in agreement, and that were really incapable of agreement, and that will probably never be in agreement again, especially the JCR and the UJCml.[1] I'm not sure how to interpret the end of the events, but I wonder to what extent the fact that Cohn-Bendit and a number of people who had made M 22 possible were no longer there was responsible – perhaps I'm being guilty of creating heroes, but I do wonder if it's not because they weren't there that the whole thing fizzled out.

LINBAUM: We must first realize that there was an element of surprise in May . . . and a surprise that couldn't be repeated. I think that there was an enormous difference in character between the beginning of May and the end of the demonstrations. Towards the end, there was a movement that was guided by nobody, that was losing much of its significance, that set off in all directions at once, because before there had always been a small group[2] that decided the direction to be taken. In the end, all was confusion. I think we must distinguish between the surprise, the novelty, in a sense, the revelation of May, and the possibility of reproducing this over a long period or even of pursuing the same direction.

BONNET: It's no longer essentially a student problem now. One could depend much more on the young workers. We realize now that they want to prove that they can do better.

w: *We've now reached a stage in the discussion when we can take up again something that Tripier mentioned as being essential: the contact between students and workers. The question I should like to go on asking concerns the nature of the 'political'. Was it political in the traditional sense, or a new type of politicization?*

LOURAU: First, I'd like to finish with the problem we were discussing earlier, that of spontaneity and organization. It's a question we should put to M 22. I've had the opportunity of speaking with some of them. It seems that they themselves distinguish between two stages of spontaneity.

In the old sense of the term, which was itself questioned to some extent,

---

[1] Union des Jeunesses Communistes Marxistes-Léninistes or 'Maoists'.
[2] These small groups 'disappeared in the revolutionary ebb, but the flow gave them back the importance they had lost' (Bloch-Michel, 1968, p. 67).

the organization is something that exists. You organize, then all you have to do is await the revolution, like the CP. If organization is understood in this *static* sense, then May was spontaneity, the aleatory, the rejection of structuration. Everybody and nobody was a regular activist. On the other hand, there is a second level, that of *action*, which is still that of organization, but in an active sense . . . something gets organized . . . It isn't X or Y, or a member of the political bureau, who passes orders to the leader of such and such a cell of rank-and-file members. At that stage, although no one is able to define what it is, even those most involved, something other than spontaneity emerges. There is what you call a projection, perhaps only in the short term, but certainly a projection onto possible action, onto immediate aims, which is not a continuation of what went before, and even less of anything that may follow.

It's in terms of the concept of spontaneity that I would distinguish between two stages of organization. The first, at which nothing, in fact, is representable with precision, is the imaginary. At a second stage, according to new forms, something takes place that is as vigorous and as rewarding as action that has been planned long ahead by an army general staff.

I could add an example taken from my own ethnography. The morning after one of the first nights, 10 May, a Saturday, I was in one of the premises where some of the M 22 'gang' – they really are like a gang – had slept . . . About midday or two o'clock in the afternoon, they started waking up; others arrived, half dazed from lack of sleep. And I was very struck to see that as they came in, as they started talking among themselves, I felt as though I was in a coach coming back from a rugby match. It is fantastic – the return home after a rugby match; you are a bit tired and you analyse the match. It is a time of great socialization. When you set off you say nothing; you are tense, and talk of tactics or of tricks to be played on your opponents. Afterwards, you conduct a truly social analysis of the match, as they did of that night of the barricades. And what struck me, in both the form and the content of those exchanges, was how little they had to do with politics. The astonishing thing was that what interested them were the little incidents that arose from their own practice, their relations with each other in the gang, and as boys and girls – for sexual problems were not divorced from politics, even during the night of the barricades, of course. It should be noted, moreover, that the couples had been regrouped in the previous few days. I realized this during the night I had been blockaded in the Rue Gay-Lussac until eight in the morning, seeing my students – boys and girls. In fact, that's what they were talking about more than anything else at two o'clock next day. Analysing the situation, some of them said, for example, that the girls who had been most engaged in the struggle were those who were with a guy, or who had recently taken up with a guy. You know, things like that. And that's the kind of thing that was

82

being said during the two or three hours people were getting up in that gang of M 22 kids.

There again, either we're at the antipodes of politics, or it's a new way of seeing politics, as something that is not at all separated from life, but a life-style.

LINBAUM: At the time of the May events, when nobody gave anybody orders, when, at each moment, one had to decide what one was to do the next moment, there was no *mediation*. This means that, in the end, one can speak of each political actor of that time as of Louis XV and his mistresses. Louis XV's love affairs *were* politics. Now everybody's love affairs are politics.

ROLLE: I think at this point we should see what Marx has to say about classes, otherwise I fear we shall end up merely myth-making. Marx never defined classes as Joseph Stalin was later to do, that is, as states. Marx defined classes around problems. There are passages in which he says 'there are three classes', and others, 'there are five classes'. This means that in each case the classes are centred on different problems. I think that to see things in terms of class alliances is to remain within old concepts, when, in fact, a certain number of professions do not belong to the same class as the others. Some of the old barriers have disappeared now.

All the same we should ask ourselves why, if it is not the only cause, the students' revolt found an echo in the factories. In a way, a factory worker is first of all a student, with problems that are not so different, at a different level, from those to be found in the university. First, he is stuck in a dead-end job; then he has to get his CAP[1] and pick up a so-called 'overall' knowledge, but nothing of much practical use. It's a system he knows only too well: he has teachers, with whom, of course, he cannot argue and who are often very bad teachers, and he takes exams where the number of passes is fixed in advance. Then he enters a factory, where, again, he is subjected to constraint. I really can't see what's so very different between this situation and the other (the university). The fact that the students revolt, and that this finds an echo in the factories, means that the problems brought out into the open by the students were also industrial problems. It was a question not of establishing an alliance between classes, but of *recognizing* a *fusion* between hitherto differentiated social categories.

w: *Could you be more specific?*

ROLLE: Authority, exploitation, these problems are really indistinguishable. The aim of socialism is the ending of the authoritarian division of labour. In my opinion, this is what one saw, what one began to see, appearing in May.

[1] Certificat d'aptitude professionelle.

KNOWLEDGE, AUTHORITY, AND COMMUNICATION

LOURAU: I think there's another point in respect of which one may not be able to speak of fusion, but at any rate of objectively similar problems.

I was very struck, when speaking to workers at the Péchiney factory this summer, by their preoccupation with the problem of authority: authority and knowledge. It is obvious that, in 1968, knowledge is on a quite different plane in the factory and the university: in one case it is linked with earning one's living, in the other it is not. In the name of knowledge, status differentiation, division of social labour, so-called technology, forms of authority that were once justified are being maintained.

The particular example I'm thinking of is that of the Péchiney workers, who, during their month-long strike, kept the factory going (the aluminium furnaces in the Lacq complex). As usual, during a strike, they had to keep them in operation or all the furnaces would have been ruined. They kept them going on their own, without the managers and foremen, and they reorganized everything. They obviously didn't know everything that the engineers and foremen had been learning for ten years. When there was something they didn't know, they called in foremen who were not on strike – but only to offer advice on a particular point. There might be some tap in the furnaces that they daren't touch for fear of blowing the whole thing up.

Second, they operated the furnaces in such a way that every bar of aluminium produced had a defect. Unlike in other strikes where, in the end, they hardly affected production at all, they sabotaged the whole lot, but in such a way that they proved that they, the workers, could produce the stuff themselves. They showed how the *relation to knowledge* in a factory could be completely altered. And they didn't hesitate to say so to the foremen and managers when the strike was over, in June. They told them, in particular, that, prior to May, the factory had been like a church, with an altar, with people in front of the altar, and the faithful, that is, themselves, the workers, behind. And that the May strike had made it possible to overthrow the altar. One is reminded, I think, of the lecture, the professorial lecture, in the problem of education. They are analogies. I would not go so far as to speak, like you, of fusion, but I think that the analogies are gradually becoming apparent all the same.

ROLLE: I would say, all the same, that, in general, something has happened in those professions requiring higher technical knowledge. The former students – I meet quite a few – are unemployed, or, if they're not unemployed, are doing work that has no connection with what their parents expected them to do when they went down from university. There, too, are laws that have reached a certain number of professions that once seemed to enjoy a permanently privileged position: this is the basis of an *objective fusion*.

TRIPIER: Fusion, alliance . . . I don't know. I was struck by the difference in *language* between students and workers, and this is why I think that an alliance is the most one can achieve . . . There's still an enormous social distance.

w: *I'd like to return to one of the questions that come to mind concerning this 'knowledge as capital' of which so much is being said at present. Put in polemical terms: is there a students/future managers/capitalists sort of Poujadism of knowledge? Are they seeking the support of other classes in order to defend their own interests?*[1]

LINBAUM: In a way, that may be true in content. We made a distinction earlier between 'the heart and the head', and this is very interesting because what do we mean by the head? If we pose desire and knowledge as fundamental terms, knowledge is the detour that leads to the satisfaction of desire. According to Marx, the problem is that theory plays the role of detour in relation to pre-Marxist utopian positions, that is to say, that on the one hand they expressed desires and, on the other, remarked that reality was otherwise and said 'property is theft', thus morally condemning contemporary society, but without mediating through knowledge. Marx does that too – 'alienation, alienation' – until the point comes when he inverts the term. In the sense that, if some change must be made in society, it must take place within the determinism of history itself and therefore by means of knowledge. In other words, I think there is a transition from *immaturity* to *maturity*. Immaturity might be defined as a sort of non-mediation of desire, whereas maturity is determined as a mediation of desire through knowledge.

BONNET: I'm not going to speak of all the discussions that have taken place in the factories, in which really there was no dialogue, because whenever they were asked questions the men would systematically give funny answers. I'm talking about the union activist, say . . . With the rank-and-file worker, you could discuss things in the factory. What he'd often say was, 'Yes, but you see, for us, the CGT activist . . . when you've got problems about wages or some argument or other – he's always there to defend us.' The fellow who said that was himself a member of the CGT and for him the union meant more than just being a card-carrying member. A fellow who didn't have a CGT or any other union card put things quite differently. He merely said: 'When we've got something we want to say, we're just told to shut up!' They realized themselves that even *among themselves* no dialogue was possible . . .

w: *But when they said, for example, 'We want this or that', they were indicating in a certain way an ideal reality. It was the same with the students, everyone said what he*

[1] 'The student rising is the first expression of the new themes and new class conflicts of our society. The essential point is not the accumulation of profit, but the accumulation of knowledge . . . The students are their own vanguard' (Touraine, in Labro, 1968, pp. 46 and 47).

wanted, the kind of university, the kind of society he wanted. Didn't this provide them with a common ground?

BONNET: I think it did. This is connected in a way with what we were saying just now about Poujadism, etc. . . . . It's an argument that has been taken up by the CGT in a number of factories. They tried hard to put that one over, but it must be realized that the form of society demanded by these so-called 'student Poujadists' was such that student Poujadism was impossible. It would have been possible if the revolution had succeeded and brought in a structure of a French CP Marxist type, say Marxist-Leninist, as in the USSR, that is, a party dictatorship. But that's not at all what was being demanded by the majority of students, workers, and others.

LINBAUM: Yes, it's in just those terms that the problem really presents itself at the level of Marxist theory. Because, in the end, May was an example of successful group action. The groups confronted the question of revolution alone and unaided. In other words, May was primarily a phenomenon that poses the problem of what revolution can be, in particular at the Marxist level.

ROLLE: I should like to remark that although it was difficult to talk to the workers – and there were, after all, several difficulties – that doesn't mean that these difficulties were of an absolutely different kind from those that workers met with in *talking to each other*. Up to now, they had been provided with a certain number of common notions by a practice that they were beginning to reject, that is to say, that of the CP and the CGT. In fact, it was through the mediation of the Party and CGT that they spoke, or rather didn't speak, since there was no need for them to speak to each other. In May, they discovered the need for communication in a movement in which they were caught up, but they found that it was extremely difficult to speak among themselves.

THE PROBLEM OF DECELLULIZATION

w: *I should like to reformulate a general question: To what extent was there, in May and June, merely a 'reaction' against the established order and a tendency to imagine what is not yet established as the opposite of what is? And to what extent, on the contrary, was there 'action' rather than reaction, that is, a project that defined, in a positive way, the desired alternative?*

LOURAU: It seems to me that although the CP emerged as the 'villain', as the reference-point of all one disliked, it was right to complain because there is an anti-communism that is easy enough to stir up, which has an objective basis in France. But apart from that, the CP served as a projection: it was the Rorschach of the other groups. Through it, they imagined everything that the

Left must not be, everything that a revolutionary organization can be, everything that socialism must be. The CP appeared as the bizarroid of the test. I think this was not so much as the CP itself, but because it and other political and union organizations were too similar to and too identified with the modes of organization of other institutions. They have set up within themselves exactly the same things as are to be found in the Church, the state, and in economic or cultural institutions. So it was a critique of what a revolutionary party should not be that was made during May. People realized that those institutions – which should be *counter-institutions* – were no different from the others. They were no longer listened to. The means used, their structures, the structures of communication, all that comes under the term *bureaucracy*, were practically the same as those of the civil institutions. The leaders and even the rank-and-file members of the CP, for example, identified with their institutions at least as much as with socialist projects. The CP has a structure that is based more and more on that of the great institutions, which are also intended to 'hold', in every sense of the word – to hold their members in check and to stop them getting too restless.

BONNET: It's an interesting fact that an idea launched by M 22 was taken up by everybody, even by organizations that had the same structure as the CP. They felt they were discovering something. I've always been against bourgeois anti-communism – all the same . . .

W: *I'd like to put in a word here. You say 'bourgeois anti-communism'. People have also talked of 'bourgeois spontaneity'. If you leave people to act spontaneously, is all that they are capable of a spontaneity so marked by the system that they never attain real spontaneity?*

LINBAUM: I think one of the most significant expressions in May was 'crapules staliniennes' ('filthy Stalinists').[1] It is really one of the key expressions. In fact, there were two: bourgeois society and filthy Stalinists. In other words, there were two modes of attack: an attack against society as it is and another against those who claimed a monopoly of the revolution and who, manifestly, did not use it. Another thing we must remember about May is its place in a historical period. It's not simply an isolated moment, but it has its place in history: ten years after de-Stalinization, several decades after the formulation of Marx's theories, after the 1917 revolution, etc.

TRIPIER: I'd like to add a reservation here . . . I think one should always distrust people's explicit language and even explicit action. And in relation to the CP as the 'reference-point of all one disliked', I'm still wondering about the question of union or alliance: to what extent was the explicit

[1] An expression used in a number of pamphlets and slogans, and applied by D. Cohn-Bendit to the leaders of the CP and CGT at the time of the procession of union members and students on 13 May.

language against the Party the non-acceptance of a certain form of institution that will always be the form adopted by the institutions of the working-class movement? Aren't we reacting – and I include myself – as petit-bourgeois?

w: *Has anyone else anything to say about this? No? Then let's move on to something that is very close to the notion of division of labour that was mentioned as a theme. Lefebvre calls this 'non-reduction':[1] not to specialize to the limit, not to divide labour, not to speak of a problem in an analytical way, not to separate work, politics, and private life . . . This is what Lourau was referring to, not to separate love and politics. This is a problem that we meet again in the cultural sphere – in the theatre, one is trying not to separate politics, private life, etc. It's the Living Theatre's Paradise now – not later, a paradise that can be expressed in relation to time. Fusionism, if you like.*

LOURAU: Since you mention it, the Living Theatre came to Nanterre in November 1967, two or three days after the end of the first strike – which was when the whole process began, even if it was a reformist strike, and when people began to come out into the open, the future leaders especially.

The Living Theatre had a great success that night: most of the students who were there, including those who took part in the strike, the sociologists, etc., booed it for its more 'fusionist' aspects, its simultaneous trance elements. It even got to the point at which Dany, who was not yet Cohn-Bendit, but the folksy little fellow with his little band of anarchists, simulated the actors' simulation of a trance by spreading like a carpet over the audience below. He too had got up on to the platform of a lecture-hall and rolled around. The actors didn't particularly like this. I talked with J.-J. Lebel a few days later. Lebel was in the company at the time and was one of those who simulated a trance and were carried, stiff with catalepsy, onto the stage. I said to him: 'The Living Theatre has understood nothing of what is happening at Nanterre. It's come here as if to a provincial theatre, without taking any account of the context, the context of the strike' – which, it's true, had not yet taken on its later, more ludic character, but which, all the same, had given rise to a good deal of expressivity. 'It's come here', I said, 'and is carrying on as if it's bringing Art to an audience of old ladies! And that's not the context at all – that's why the audience reacted as it did.' Lebel was very surprised and said that the Living Theatre had no idea what was going on at Nanterre at the time . . . usually, it's very sensitive to that sort of thing. If they had known, then, of course, things would have turned out quite differently. Anyway, how I see this incident is that this desire to stick to life, to try to unite representation and politics, in particular, came later, at Avignon and Geneva.[2] Before, it had

[1] 'To reduce is not only to simplify, schematize, dogmatize, order. It is also to arrest and fix, to change the totality into a part and yet to claim that it is the totality . . .' (Lefebvre, 1968, concerning the concept of reduction to be found in Marcuse, who, it seems, has not developed it sufficiently explicitly).
[2] Lebel, in *Procès du festival d'Avignon*, 1968, quotes from several texts used by the Living Theatre,

completely failed, because it had not realized the *Surreality* that reigned at Nanterre at the time, and that had been *eminently political.*

My own conclusion from all this is that what one finds in the Living Theatre is much more an ideology of fusion, of participation – which, in fact, is to be found in any 'groupist' ideology, in particular in the Club Méditerranée or group dynamics – than any real analysis of the context in which they claim to immerse their representations in order to deny all separation between private life, public life, politics, and theatre . . .

LINBAUM: In reviving the pre-May protest movements, the Living Theatre belonged to the mode of *immaturity*, with the Beatniks and that kind of thing. Marx said that to realize our desires we need a detour, which is action, revolution – meanwhile, I must suppress my desire . . .

THE BREAK AND ITS SOURCES

w: *When you say immaturity, do you mean that for a revolution to succeed, taking into account the established system and the forces present, strong organizations – workers' organizations – are needed? What can the new methods of the 'French-style cultural revolution' achieve?*

LINBAUM: I'm afraid I don't like the question at all. It forgets one thing: history. Nothing has the same meaning at all times. Anarchism, for example, does not mean the same thing before Marx, during Marx's lifetime, just after it, and now. If one doesn't place oneself within the historical period, one deprives oneself of the possibility of understanding.

It was not an immaturity like Taoism, the search for the void, any void. It was the void of something, there was something to void, without any doubt at all, that was probably the CP, its monopoly of revolution, of Marxist ideology, or the Soviet Union in its monopoly of the alternative. So the problem can be presented in this way: the immaturity in question has a history, it emerges at a particular moment. Taking the four terms of the May discourse – criticism, spontaneity, imagination, joy – if immaturity is founded upon desire, then it denies time. In that case, criticism becomes, as for the pre-Marxists, *moral* criticism. Spontaneity is contact with the present. Why? Because it is in the present that one can resume contact with one's desire, and joy is a proof of the existence of desire in the present moment, it's the justification for what one does, it's a proof of non-ideology, since ideology can be a *degraded* form of knowledge.[1]

---

showing that the company considered that, in the summer of 1968, at Avignon, 'the time had come' to break with established society more completely – publicly and politically – than they had done in the past.

[1] The following distinction attenuates, but does not entirely remove, the pejorative character of the notion of immaturity:

Non-degraded maturity was able to transform its immediate desire into a *mediated* desire, through

ROLLE: I'd like to point out that the term *spontaneity* is a bureaucrat's term. What does it mean? The bureaucrat, sitting at his desk, sees people who are not doing the same and calls it spontaneity. In May, no one spoke of spontaneity, except in the sense of using language that one thought might be acceptable. One spoke rather of *imagination*. I think the difference is an important one: imagination is for the guy who lives it, who is in touch with the situation; spontaneity is a concept that has meaning only for the bureaucrat, as something in opposition to him.

In fact, this element of opposition to bureaucracy was not as important as people often seem to think now. For a time, people behaved *as if the CP didn't exist*. In the factories, this happened. I'm not saying they succeeded (the CP was there). But they were successful up to a point. The CP began to disintegrate. The man who had to be liquidated, and really was liquidated in May, was Lenin. I don't mean Lenin as a historical personage, of course, but Lenin as a model. Leninism is dead, and this may enable us to re-read Marx with different eyes.

TRIPIER: To return to your question, I wonder to what extent this sort of unity of being *qua* political being can be produced only in periods of break. The period prior to that of 'war communism' in the USSR was such a period. It's during extremely short periods, when really *everything seems possible*, perhaps even at the Liberation of France, or in 1936 . . .

LOURAU: Yes, one remembers Marceau Pivert's words, 'everything is possible'.[1]

TRIPIER: At times like that even sexual repression is swept away. I wonder if it's not an effect of the break.

What interests me are the *forces of break*. In other words, what are the analyses, the slogans, the visions that make such breaks possible. One really must study the *Situationists* about this. Indeed, Cohn-Bendit recognizes this throughout: on the one hand, it's the Situationists and perhaps, on the other, *Socialisme ou Barbarie*[2] that were the forces of break.

W: *It's conceivable that these forces prepared the ground for the break, rather as Épistémon [1968] says that the Rogers school has had an influence in France. The*

knowledge. The central element of this ideology is the value of aim; time is that of transcendence, realization, accomplishment. *Degraded* maturity has lost or distended its links with that which is beyond ideology, namely desire and knowledge (Linbaum, 1968, p. 36).
[1] Marceau Pivert was a revolutionary socialist leader who played an important role during the Popular Front period. It was to him that Maurice Thorez, the Communist Party leader, addressed the words that were to be taken up again in May, 'everything is not possible . . . you must know how to end a strike'.
[2] 'Organ of criticism and revolutionary orientation', an extreme left-wing review (1949–63), run by a group whose composition has changed fairly often and which consisted originally of activists who were opposed to the various Trotskyist movements.

ground might have been prepared through the Situationists, a certain form of Surrealism, perhaps, too, certain films. There are all kinds of influences that made possible a break, which was later more directly caused by a conjunction of several factors.

What I think it would be interesting to discuss now is how certain cultural phenomena prefigured certain methods of break or action. Take the collage, for example. I think there was something very curious about this for a French rationalist mind: many students put into their speeches elements from different schools of thought and somehow stuck them together. These elements, which had been gathered from widely different sources, then took on a new meaning.

BONNET: No, I don't agree. I find that in May, in all the meetings, even small gatherings of five or six individuals, one could see absolutely no difference between before and after. What I mean, for example, is that the various Trotskyist groups were still using the same arguments; when they took up a vaguely anarchist argument, it somehow didn't suit them, you could tell they didn't really believe it.

W: *Perhaps these groups were more particularly concerned with coherence? How did the others react?*

BONNET: They might seem the most coherent, but in any case, if they could be coherent, it was precisely because they were contributing nothing that was essentially new. Those that listened to them were also more or less sympathetic; there was no change, no break in their audience.

LINBAUM: Yes, and if we want to speak of a break, we must decide, a break of what? There was a break at the ideological level, and what is anti-ideology if not science on the one hand and desire on the other?

W: *Some people have spoken of a revival of archaic themes. I think there's an interesting problem there: Were relatively old arguments or ways of thought revived, but placed in a new discourse, and therefore redefined?*

ROLLE: I don't really see what can be meant by a return to old ideas. All right, there was a lot of talk about workers' councils; that's one idea that's not exactly a new one. The communism of the councils was opposed by Lenin. Whether it's old or not, revived or still alive, I don't know. As to the influence of the Situationists, I know a little about that and I don't think they had any influence at all.

TRIPIER: Ah, but there are elements in the Nanterre business that can be explained only by reference to them . . .

ROLLE: At Nanterre, of course, Cohn-Bendit, for example . . .

TRIPIER: But not just Cohn-Bendit! When Edgar Morin was barracked they were there . . .

LOURAU: . . . All that was in connection with *Arguments*.[1] But it's curious that kids of twenty or twenty-two should already possess this revolutionary tradition, a tradition of enemies and alliances. It certainly astonished the teaching staff. As did the fact that the students were analysing Rosa Luxemburg, etc. When Morin came to replace Lefebvre, who had gone to Japan for a few weeks, he was booed and jeered. Morin! The friend of the young, a specialist in young people's affairs, etc. I think *Arguments* had a lot to do with it.

There was an even more serious break in May: those who called themselves the *Enragés-Situationnistes*, people who wanted to join, or rather (because you can't join just like that), who wanted to be *centred* on the Situationists, wanted desperately to be accepted by Debord, Vaneigem,[2] and the others. They carried their polemics against the *Arguments* group to an extraordinary point. For them the 'reference-point of all one disliked' was no longer the CP, but the 1956–62 revisionists, since *Arguments* had ceased in 1962, so there were only six years. They threw big bags of shit at Axelos's door, threatened Lefebvre physically, etc. Whatever one thinks of the objective importance of *Arguments*, of *Socialisme ou Barbarie*, etc., they were all part of the reference-point. I think there was a genuine desire for a break, even if, in reality, these things had nourished it. People like Dany and others had read the main articles in *Arguments* on social classes, and the principal numbers of *S ou B*. But they used them to find something else, and that too tended to become negative, whereas in fact it was very close to them. Things had got to the stage of criticizing critical criticism.

ROLLE: I agree, but all the same there was a social movement of great importance and it assumed quite new forms. A connection with *S ou B* really can't explain the success of a certain number of ideas. Now, of course, the *S ou B* people can hardly contain themselves . . .

LOURAU: Self-management has been talked about, and very seriously too, for the past fifteen years. Now everyone's talking about self-management. So one can say all the same that there's a certain continuity, that, before May '68, apart from a few groups of teachers, of whom I was one, who were in touch with *S ou B* and who played an important role; and then, at another level, there is the general social situation.

ROLLE: But this social situation cannot be found directly in the facts. One sees it if one offers an interpretation of it. And two interpretations of it are possible. We set out earlier with the *fusion* or *confusion* of different spheres in the activity of some people. But we must find out whether it's an attitude of mind that has been induced or whether, in fact, it corresponds to something

[1] A review whose contributors are intellectuals from the 'human sciences', adopting an equally critical attitude to the human sciences and to society, that is to capitalist and socialist experiments. The editorial committee includes E. Morin, K. Axelos, and J. Duvignaud.
[2] Well-known Situationists, who were regarded as leaders.

. . . whether it's a new social awareness. I think that's the important thing: to find out whether people wanted to live a certain mixed style of life, and reconstitute a personality that had been dislocated by society . . . or whether, on the contrary, it's a question of new needs and not of a personality divided from all eternity.

And this brings us back once more to the problem of the political, which is no longer merely an activity based on the state; politics is no longer merely that . . .

w: *Let's go back to the rather provocative expression used just now about spontaneity being only bourgeois.*

LINBAUM: Yes, in fact I wanted to take up this notion of desire, of the image one has of desire, of the fact that desire is the contrary of ideology as well as of knowledge. The notion of disalienation does play a role in Marxism, since it's the break between the young and the old Marx, and, in fact, before the May events, there were two tendencies in French Marxism: that of Lefebvre and that of Althusser, the first deriving from the young Marx, 'there isn't time, man must be disalienated, I have to examine everyday life and things are not going at all well, people are bored, they have refrigerators', etc., the second dropping the notion of desire. People had forgotten how to speak of desire since Stalinism. Desire had to be repressed in order to make revolution. Althusser is Marxism as theory of society, but that aspect is also to be found in Marx himself.

w: *What about the insistence, in May, on imagination and enjoyment?*

TRIPIER: This isn't contradictory. When someone says 'the more I make revolution, the more I enjoy love', he has at last reached the point where knowledge is no longer necessary, where desire can operate in its pure state.

LINBAUM: There were no more factories, no more state. What were people to do? They were *forced* to imagine something. There was no longer anyone there to tell them what they were to desire.

w: *And no one to tell them not to . . .*

LINBAUM: Ah, yes, *they* were dead: the factories were on strike, the state was on its knees, frightened, waiting . . .

LOURAU: The teaching staff had gone off to Perpignan to get on with their research . . .

REVOCABILITY[1]

ROLLE: This is all very circumstantial. There is something very important that we have not mentioned: the idea of *equality*. One noticed something

[1] Cf. footnote, p. 13 above.

very remarkable in the discussions: people could actually admit, 'I don't know'! One doesn't usually hear many intellectuals say that. But I heard quite a few say it. And it was not regarded as placing you in a position of inferiority . . . this was very important from the point of view of freeing speech.

LINBAUM: Exactly! What one particularly noticed in May was the ability – contrary to Stalinism – to express a desire in a simple form, for example, liberty, internationalism, disalienation . . .

X: But that's not simple at all! (*Laughter.*)

LINBAUM: . . . No, by 'simple' I mean that people felt this desire directly, expressed it directly, and did not say how it could be achieved. They simply said, 'I want this . . . '

BONNET: But it *had* been achieved, there was no point in saying *how* it could be achieved!

LINBAUM: No, it had been achieved, *for the time being* . . .

ROLLE: We must begin with the forms it took, in the factories, or, rather, with the idea one had of it. One can't say whether it existed already or whether it appeared for the first time, but the idea was 'everyone is important'. For example, in the case of a particular form of the division of labour: 'I'm in a subordinate position, but it's precisely this division of labour that must be questioned.' The fact is that the small-scale attempts to set up, not exactly workers' councils, but some form of self-management, are linked directly with this problem. It's very important. People met in their workshops and said: 'We cannot accept that a particular job should be this or that. The whole thing must be redefined.' That was understandable in a revolutionary situation, even if it obviously had no future in our society.

BONNET: And these strikes were the expression of an absolutely new form. The lads came to realize *of their own accord* that they had to have workers' councils. It happened spontaneously.

W: *Can it be said that these councils exercised authority, that they replaced the management that was no longer there?*

ROLLE: The most elaborate system, which was initiated by the CFDT[1] and which slipped immediately out of their control, was the one set up at the CSF (Compagnie Générale de Télégraphie sans fil) in Brest. They immediately seized on the definition of jobs. The equality principle doesn't work inside a factory.

---

[1] Confédération française démocratique du Travail, the largest non-Communist labour organization, and the second largest organization after the Communist-led CGT.

W: *Yes, then how was this new idea of revocability introduced?*

ROLLE: To begin with, I don't think the idea of revocability is that new. Not only were there traditions, but this revocability already existed. Only it was controlled. It now meant: the power of the council, the group, the mass, and nothing but the expression of the power of the group . . .

TRIPIER: I'd like to tell you about an incident at Nanterre to show how ambiguous the whole thing was. Confronted by this slogan of revocability, Crozier went to the students and said: 'As I see it, the professor is a professor because, among his peers, he is regarded . . .' At that point, Crozier was scared stiff of being revoked. But the interesting thing, as Crozier was speaking, the students were tapping their foreheads and saying, 'What's he talking about?' They knew perfectly well that they wouldn't get the power to revoke him. Either Crozier was just acting, or he took them seriously. In fact, the students were much more realistic than he was. They knew that Crozier would stay on and they couldn't understand why he was putting on this sort of show, talking about revocation in this way.

ROLLE: Perhaps, but although he wasn't revoked directly by the assembly and by 'student power', he in fact left this autumn – and that's not entirely coincidental . . . It was only in May that this problem of the revocability of staff was continually being discussed. You've attended staff meetings and I've attended quite a few. They know very well how it's going to end.

LOURAU: We must be more precise. When the students say, 'We don't want Crozier!', they're talking like Omar[1] when he said on 20 May, 'Let's go and take over the Élysée tonight. The Gaullists are such cretins, we could take over the Élysée tonight!' It's on a ludic, deliberately unserious, plane . . .

ROLLE: But there is an element of seriousness there, because, in fact, nothing can happen in the university until the present power structure is changed. Only in this way will a political process get started.

W: *Let's move on to the second problem – 'scuttling'.*[2] *When the new leaders realize that the others are giving them too much authority, do they abandon posts?*

BONNET: There's an old anarchist principle that when an individual has seized power, even if he starts off loaded with good intentions, he ends up no better than the others. I know of no exception to the rule. So the important thing is not to give an individual the opportunity of scuttling, but to scuttle *him* if he starts going off the rails.

---

[1] A popular student activist at Nanterre.

[2] *Sabordage:* another key notion of the May Movement, etc. The image is of scuttling a ship. When the leader of a group shows signs of exerting undue influence, or the group shows signs of excessive dependence upon him, he should step down himself or be demoted to the 'ranks'. The full range of meanings emerges in the course of the discussion. (Translator's note.)

w: *In a society like ours, where people are so used to being told what to do, isn't it the duty of the new leader to 'scuttle' himself? Did that happen?*

BONNET: No, I don't think so . . .

TRIPIER: When Cohn-Bendit left France, I wondered to what extent he had taken over the role of Dutschke. You know that Dutschke, at the time he was almost assassinated, had in fact 'scuttled' himself. He had decided to be the standard-bearer of the SDS,[1] but to give up any power he had within the SDS. I talked to Dany about it at the time and I wondered if he didn't feel obliged to follow Dutschke's example.

LOURAU: There is a fact that should be mentioned here – and the same applied to Dany. At the time that he was nearly assassinated and was about to 'scuttle' himself, Dutschke was about to be revoked anyway and his position was being violently contested within the SDS. We should add that Dany was in the same situation.

BONNET: Cohn-Bendit scuttled himself because he was told: 'If you go back to the ranks, it's all up.' But he didn't realize this himself, not at first. They almost came to blows about it on one occasion . . .

FROM THE 'TABULA RASA' TO CONSTRUCTION

w: *Perhaps we can now ask ourselves to what extent such periods are simply transitory – a means of making a clean sweep, a tabula rasa, a getting rid of old fetters – and to what extent they try to be a cultural parallel.*

When confronted with so-called free forms, like free jazz, for example, one wonders whether it is not primarily a demolition job or whether it is the beginning of something new. And this brings us back to the problem that was raised briefly at the beginning of this discussion – is it a project or an object of projection? There are people who, when confronted with free jazz, have said: 'It's an expression of the revolt of the American Negro in its most violent political form.' Others have said: 'No, on the contrary, it's much closer to the whites than anything that's gone before.'

LINBAUM: You see how important it is whether you take a thing in its historical context or in eternity. When things are 'absorbed' and assimilated by society, they may survive as such. But when they arrive on the scene, they arrive as a 'stage' in a discussion. Dada existed. Dada was 'absorbed' to a large extent, but that doesn't mean that it did not have meaning in its own time. Albert Ayler[2] represents a moment, a stage, in the discussion about music. A movement of struggle – which doesn't mean that an attempt won't be made

---

[1] Sozialistischer Deutscher Studentenbund, the German Socialist Students' League.
[2] A free jazz musician.

to absorb it, later. They might even go so far as to put it in a museum. And we'll be all the more pleased to recognize ourselves in something that dared to challenge Western culture.

I think these relations between cultures are very much of a 'master and slave' kind. The artist struggles against the ideology of the moment and is absorbed.

BONNET: Apart from the fact that the artist is often reactionary and bourgeois, he tries to impose his painting on others.

W: *In architecture, for example, what has happened this spring?*

BONNET: May certainly didn't disturb architecture, except in the sense that for a month architects felt that their order was being threatened. Apart from that, architecture with a capital A hasn't been affected at all.

W: *But what did you learn, personally, at the time, in terms of architecture?*

BONNET: Nothing. I was pleased that a lot of people were thinking, like me, of something other than architecture. But the profession itself was never for a moment brought into question. What I learnt was essentially human. For example, when the workers tried to run the building firms, they wanted to do something positive. The contractors thought that there'd be no more architects in France. The contractors and engineers (who are completely in the hands of the firms) have thought for a long time that the architect would be abolished. So they, too, thought of self-managing the building industry. Obviously, whereas the worker thought this in order to produce at lower cost, by abolishing profit, the contractor thought the exact opposite, namely, abolish the architect as 'the builder's policeman' and put up gerry-built monstrosities for much more profit.

ROLLE: Contrary to what you have said, I find it very interesting what the architects did. And in relation to this I'd like to come back to the theme of the division of labour. The architect has the know-how and the contractor has the money – so there's always the possibility of friction. The problem of the division of labour is usually solved by the use of subordination. Collaboration is the very thing that is not possible.

What happened at the Beaux-Arts is very simple. There are the reactionaries, who want the prestige of art for the sake of Art, and those who want to preserve their prestige by taking over the know-how of the technologist. I think we can generalize here: student problems were not specifically student problems.

W: *What was specifically a student situation was being more open to change, to different possibilities. Later, in their new professional situation, the students will meet the problem of barriers, 'functional' problems let us say, or the problems of 'maturity', to use a term that came up earlier on. What was new in the activities of the imagination may well be abandoned very quickly.*

TRIPIER: There's a lot to be said about 'the unthinkable in society', about the possibility of the *collective worker*, to take up one of Marx's neglected terms, as the unit of self-management.

W: *What was said about this during May? Can one speak of self-management, not only of factories, but of society as a whole?*

ROLLE: I don't know whether self-management was talked about in the old sense used by *S ou B* and others. People talked about a 'seizure of power'. In the end, when faced with a hostile state whose very foundations must be transformed, people seize power . . .

W: *Yes, and how do they represent to themselves the functioning of a different society, with the introduction of self-management?*

LOURAU: What I'd like to say above all is the way that I personally dream of that. It's rather different from the reflections I'm usually capable of making, it's not at all theoretical, though the two are connected . . .

As to the *collective worker*, I don't think the term does present a contradiction in fact. The collective worker was invented by capitalism; cooperation is produced by capital. And this has provided a foundation for a great many utopias that could not have been conceived at an earlier date.

The contradiction I would like to speak about lies in the fact that, on the one hand, capitalism requires cooperation, requires the collective worker, and yet, at the same time, is constantly creating hierarchies and differences of power, money, etc. According to the anarchist utopia of self-management, it would be possible to extract from capitalism this good bit, this good fruit, namely, the idea of the collective, pluri-disciplinary worker, working in transparent collaboration with others, and in one stroke, by occupying the Stock Exchange and the Ministry of this or that, put an end to capitalism itself. In fact, the two things are closely linked. It is capitalism that has produced cooperation and the very idea of the collective worker. For self-management to be conceivable, we must constantly remember that it will have to be something more than Fourier's utopian images or the present-day, utopian-anarchist images of self-management. If placed in a socialist frame of reference, self-management presupposes the disappearance of capital. So one cannot even think in terms of self-management; one has to dream of it. One has to dream, at the same time, of the end of all the hierarchies of knowledge and power in the factory, which I spoke about earlier, and also of the end of the production principle, the reality principle.[1]

[1] Cf. Lourau's article in *Combat* (5 June 1968):

The problem is that of a new, unheard-of redistribution of the technological and social division

BONNET: I don't agree. For me, self-management is such a natural thing that dreaming about it presents no problems at all . . .

LOURAU: Natural? In your job, in your everyday life?

BONNET: No, of course not. Not in my everyday life.

LOURAU: At the imaginative level . . .

BONNET: In any case, it's something we can think about, now, and would be easy to realize.

W: *Let's move on. Did the students, during those weeks and perhaps without knowing it – which would leave room both for the imagination and for determinism – did they make any kinds of plan for the society of the future, as if they were its architects?*

BONNET: The problem didn't arise like that at all . . . There's an example I wanted to give just now: the old architecture of Greece or the Middle Ages has nothing in common with that of today. If you wanted to build a cathedral, you called in an architect. But the architect didn't draw up plans for the masses of the building, which were then built accordingly. *The realization often had very little to do with the plans.* The masons also had ideas and above all much more initiative, and therefore a greater possibility of intervening. There was a general idea of a cathedral. Everyone knew a lot about everyone else's trade. There was a mixture of skills. From the Renaissance onwards, when techno-logical skill took on a quite different significance, and when politically, too, there was a new structure, the bourgeoisie increased in importance in relation to the nobility. *Technocrats* came into prominence. At the Renaissance the need was created for architects in the modern sense.

W: *Perhaps we should say whether the sociologist has a plan. How would he con-struct the society of the future, if that is what he wants to do?*

ROLLE: It's not self-evident that the 'sociologist' is, strictly speaking, a sociologist yet. So far, preoccupations of this kind have been successfully kept out of sociology. There's been a crisis in sociology for some time now. As a body of knowledge about society, sociology presupposes an unconscious

---

of labour. These two types of division must no longer be analysed in terms of capital, as a superior legitimacy, but in terms of 'living labour', of the 'collective worker', as the only legitimacy.

In an article dating from April 1967, Lourau deals with all the aspects of self-management dis-cussed in May:

We must learn to think of self-management, not as the poetry of politics and critical thought, but as an analysis of a sick society and as the system of reference for a society of the future that will not totally sacrifice desire to the needs of an alienating and alienated society (1967, p. 77).

The above intervention in the discussion could be interpreted as the result of a sceptical attitude only if the speaker refrained from dreaming, or rejected it as a solution, that is, rejected construction on the basis of the *tabula rasa*, which does not appear to be the case.

99

society. In a way, the sociologist finds it very difficult to conceive of a society that is conscious of itself. As I see it, the problem of the sociologist is therefore to envisage his own disappearance.

LINBAUM: Or to envisage the disappearance of society as it exists today.

W: *Presuming that we agree that the sociologist cannot be content to study the functioning of present-day society in its most visible structures, what is he to do then?*

TRIPIER: There was this meeting on projects for the construction of the society of the future held recently near Les Halles; a sociologist started to speak . . .

LOURAU: He delivered a sort of sermon on the society of the future, humanism, man and culture, the individual adventure of man confronting his destiny, etc.

LINBAUM: There's a rather amusing ambiguity here – that of sociology as a university discipline in France. So far, it has taken little note of practical applications, only of theory. The function of the university was a cultural one. Since France was deprived of a role as a great economic power, it was natural that the university should be full of intellectuals, and that French sociologists should also be intellectuals. That's one factor.

On the other hand, society was developing on the economic plane. So the need was felt for a sort of sociologist, a doctor of society, who can diagnose or cure certain concrete problems.

MEANING AS 'EXPERIENCED IN' AND 'GIVEN TO' THE MOVEMENT

W: *Could we, to conclude, come back to the interpretation of May? Is it up to the sociologist to 'give' this 'revolution without a face' a meaning?*

LINBAUM: What does 'having a face' mean for a revolution? This is Aron's old trick, and he'll still be right at this level.[1] The problem of finding a face is itself a problem of authority. Does one have to ask a majority for permission to give a meaning to a movement?

A phenomenon appears in the midst of twenty or so people – it's a sort of happening. Everyone sees it in his own way. Each way is phenomenologically

[1] E. Morin appears to have been the first to use this term:

Everything took place (between 12 and 21 May) as if politics had become paralysed, as if the country had, at the same time, become apolitical and embarked on a revolution. What suddenly emerged was a revolution without a face and, at the moment of writing, I don't know whether it will be transformed by derivation or confiscation before recognizing its face (Morin, 1968b, p. 67).

Whereas Morin uses a negative term to express a state of affairs that he sees rather from a positive point of view, R. Aron, in a book that is to some extent a reply, sees it from a negative point of view: '. . . the critical function becomes nihilism when it denounces society as a whole, without representing an alternative society, when it preaches the cult of violence' (Aron, 1968, p. 136).

true. The police enter the Sorbonne – a lot of things happen . . . In fact, it's just what Aron says about the outbreak of the First World War: 'a diplomatic failure, followed by a certain number of things'. At that level, one can say: 'There have been different points of view on the question. It hasn't been resolved.' Then one tries to see the problem from the point of view of a certain theory of social formation, of history, of ideology, of class relations, and a face will emerge . . . There's a revolution when a problem spills over rather than when there's a solution to it. I think that in present-day France, and for years ahead, a revolution is impossible . . .

BONNET: Careful, we've heard that one before . . .

LINBAUM: I think the surprise element of May no longer exists. What is needed is a theory that will enable what is being repressed to assert itself and to take the path, if not of Leninism, at least of something of the kind, and to face up to the powerful domination of an organization. To overthrow that power, you need a theory. While there is no such theory, I can't see a revolution succeeding.

BONNET: I think the revolution is possible all the time. And May was a typically anarchist event. Nothing can prove that the revolution can break out in six months. But, that's exactly . . .

ROLLE: What amuses me is that whenever one is talking about May one always comes back to what will happen after May, and my interpretation of May is to be found there. There are always two views: one tends to see things in terms of a psycho-sociological process, whatever form it takes; the other says that a certain number of problems appeared in May, problems that concern us now, but that we had been unaware of before and that appeared as a result of a social movement.

TRIPIER: It's rather like 'What's to be done in Latin America after Castro?' It seems to me that if, in the analysis based on the concepts of 'union' or 'alliance', one of the terms is correct, then what will happen is either a form of union or a form of alliance, the liquidation of the CP or its radical transformation.

LINBAUM: Psycho-sociology is only a way of placing a magnifying glass over things, like the break in the history of ideology: both have a *meaning* in relation to a *historical* period.

ROLLE: I was speaking of the theory of theory . . .

W: *Is theory lagging behind practice?*

LINBAUM: No, I don't think so. There's a certain history, a state of theory and practice that correspond to that history. History begins very largely with

Marx, with this problem of changing society through action, with 1917, and with everything that has been thought about 1917, about the possibility of making a revolution.

ROLLE: It's very amusing to see Bonnet, who represents anarchism here, thinking that the problems can still be conceived in these terms. While you, who, if I may say so, represent accident, are according this extraordinary importance to Marx. I'm a Marxist too, but I seem to remember that Marx altered his *Capital* in accordance with the political struggles of the time (for example in the United States, where he was quite unknown incidentally). The course of history would not have been altered if Marx had died in his cradle.

LOURAU: This isn't prophecy, but apophecy!

LINBAUM: In fact, when one says Marx, or when one says Cohn-Bendit, it's not a question of personalities. Personality is nothing. It's never an individual, but always society, or the world, or history that expresses itself. Marx is an individual who expresses the world. He is part of the world. And if he wasn't part of it, then a part of it would be missing. And what's the meaning of a world part of which is missing?

w: *In a way, it's the problem of the 'savage'. Is there any other alternative to a sociology of function (of the established structures) and a critical sociology? Can one attain something that lies outside negation? Can one practise a sociology of 'positivity'? In fact, it seems to me that certain elements in May were moving towards the 'savage', the non-socialized, non-culture . . .*

LINBAUM: We must distinguish between, on the one hand, the 'savage' in the sense of natural, unconnected with historical time, and, on the other, the savage in the utopian sense.

w: *Yes, how important are intellectuals as producers of utopias, or images of the future, or models to be followed? Do they play a role or is everything already inscribed in an objective determinism?*

ROLLE: If one is saying that the intellectual as such has no proper function *in* the revolutionary process, then, yes, I agree. But I'm not saying that one will arrive at objectives simply through the facts themselves. That would be tantamount to saying that the intellectual was alone in possessing a subjectivity, which would be rather extraordinary.

LINBAUM: I'm not entirely in agreement there. One can say from a certain point of view that everything is determined, and, second, that the actors do not regard themselves at all as such. One is acted upon, and Marx was acted upon like anyone else. But that's not the problem.

ROLLE: I should like to say that it is not for technical reasons, but for fundamental reasons, that we sociologists know nothing. Take May as an example:
people started to place themselves in a different situation and to think quite
differently. It was quite striking: it may have been predictable, but it was
obvious enough. A worker friend of mine sent his wife out to work in order
to buy a car. In May, he remarked, just like that, in passing, how absurd the
idea of a private car was. This doesn't mean that when I see him next he won't
want to show me what a marvellous car he's got. It has a meaning in his
present life. In May it had none. So I would say, then, that the main thing is not
what people think. I'm well aware that in saying this I might give the impression of falling into objectivism, but that's not so.

To return to the image of society: I wonder whether, in the last resort, it
isn't often a confused image, in which people project, *extend*, a number of their
behaviour patterns. This image of society may be transformed very quickly,
in a way that is quite unintelligible if one confines one's attention to that society
itself. It is transformed by virtue of the situation in which people find themselves, the reactions they are made to experience . . .

W: *The general field that interests me in this discussion is that of the development of
the image, which, of course, derives from, but is not entirely defined by, the society
and the historical period.*

LINBAUM: It wasn't a *reflection*, since it concerned a crisis within ideology
itself. Even if the economic crisis was in some ways the immediate cause, it
was not the essence of the phenomenon, since the whole social movement
took place at the level of ideology, which had its own development.

Break (*rupture*) plays a role in Althusser's interpretation of Marxism. An
example of such a break is to be found in the case of the research scientist who
suddenly finds what he has been looking for. The admission of ignorance
often occurs at the stage of the search for knowledge, when one is confronted
by the void, before it is found. There is a before and an after, and between
the two a state of latency. After a break, one might say that there is a state of
latency in which something profound is in fact expressed. A sort of thought
that tries (it's quite definitely also the process of the research scientist) to free
itself from everything that is already established as a body of knowledge, as the
language of knowledge. If one fails to free oneself from this, one can no
longer imagine. Two thinkers in history, Nietzsche and Heraclitus – both
very violent – confronted this problem . . . Indeed, it was Nietszche, with
Marx and Mao, who was most quoted on the walls: he speaks of imagination,
of making things present, 'one must always carry within one a chaos in order
to be able to bring a dancing star into the world'.

TRIPIER: There's a problem all the same. You say 'it's a break within Marxism, a break within ideology', then you speak of Nietzsche. Where's your chronology, then? Is it in May, or is it with the appearance of Nietzsche?

LINBAUM: You said yourself just now that there were *anars* before May. The problem, then, is that of the coincidence of a given discourse and its sudden importance in a particular set of circumstances. You might say that every discourse is propagated at every period and that what changes is the response it gets.

TRIPIER: In 1848, the anarchist discourse got a bigger response than the Marxist one. In fact, the Marxist discourse didn't exist yet. I can't see that there's any break.

LINBAUM: But don't you see? There is! In fact, if there's such a thing as a dialectical movement, it's a movement between two poles: for example, dualism and monism. It's an old story. If there's a break, it's because there was a struggle between antagonisms that are always present. There's nothing new under the sun and in a way the same thing never occurs twice.

An interlude, an accident, a prefiguration of the future? I should like to know the reactions of readers, analysing this discussion or the events themselves.

The idea that, in May, the 'real' problems found expression beyond anything that could be observed, even among the young people themselves, may lead to two equally interesting conclusions. On the one hand, these problems are those of the 'institutor' who discovers himself, or at least thinks he discovers himself, in the conditions of a complete reinvention of society. On the other hand, certain problems, if not necessarily their solutions, have a specific chronology. They are already very much with us, and will be increasingly so in the future.

To say that, in a certain way, May prefigures the future touches, it seems to me, on both aspects at once. The problems of the society of the future are the 'modern' concerns of contemporary society, their solution is dependent both on a particular form of society and on the imaginative invention of the future.

CHAPTER 4

Projects and Projections

The discussion reproduced in the preceding chapter has enabled me to develop further my original view: at the beginning of the discussion, I presented my subject as an exploration of the project/projection alternative and reintroduced this theme in the course of the discussion.

The notion of project was introduced into France by Sartre (1960).[1] It was developed and used by A. Touraine (1965) in particular, but it has gained a lot of adherents. Challenging Marxists (but not Marxism), and certain forms of structuralism with their tendency to mechanistic determinism, Sartre insisted on the need to think of man as man-*agent*, and not only as man-*object* (op. cit., p. 110). We must rediscover the existential project, man in the social world, and follow him 'in his *praxis*, or, if you prefer, in the *project* that propels him towards social possibilities on the basis of a particular situation' (p. 111). Touraine writes:

> If the approach of the sociologist cannot be that proposed by J.–P. Sartre, it must be aware of this effort to unite the social situation and the individual existence. The individual must be regarded as a social actor, defined by his status and his roles, or as an operator combining elements that follow certain laws, or as an individual *subject*, defined in particular by his experience of work (Touraine, 1965, p. 53).

Although the notion of project has been used in various ways, even by Touraine himself – his writing can be as confused as it is brilliant and original – it has always seemed to me to combine in a most convenient way the ideas of the *plan* of a subject, the *depassing*[2] of a 'given' situation,

---

[1] *Critique de la raison dialectique:* cf. Chapter III, 'Question de méthode'.

[2] I cannot do better than quote a footnote of Dr David Cooper from his *Psychiatry and anti-psychiatry* (1967, p. 5):

> To depass: a transliteration of the French term *dépasser* as used by J.–P. Sartre in *Critique de la raison dialectique* (1960). It should be understood in the sense of Hegel's *aufheben*, i.e. movement beyond the existing state of affairs to a further state, or synthesis, which conserves the earlier state in a modified form in a new totalization.

The alternative translations are either too inadequate and clumsy ('to go beyond', 'the going beyond')

and the partial *knowledge* of that situation, from the point of view of a social actor or an individual.

It is of little concern to us here that Touraine now says that he is no longer interested in the notion[1] he has done so much to make fashionable in France. 'My intention', he wrote, 'is to show that the orientations of action, the creation of "values", far from imposing a sociology of interiority may and must be studied "in action".' In particular, this would lead one to examine 'the meaning of a relation between the subject and object of one's action' (op. cit., p. 54). This definition of the intentions of a particular sociology accords perfectly with my thinking on the subject of our group discussion, even though there is no question of excluding from the field of analysis the notion of *interaction* – the relation between the various actors – an area of analysis generally excluded from 'actionalist' sociology. In May, more than ever before, the actors themselves *lived* their relationship as *subjects* confronting an *object* of action, without considering at every moment their present relation to established society or always their interactions with other social actors.[2]

If one brings together the idea that there are *projects* and the idea of a plan or programme of action, and if *projection* is conceived as a subjective interpretation of action in the midst of that action, the conclusion of our group conversation would seem to be that, in May, project and projection are not separable, and not really in opposition. I should now like to reorder some of the points made in our discussion, which shows, among other things, that projects and programmes are no more exclusively *objective*, in themselves, than projections are purely *subjective*, or psychological. The project/projection alternative, in so far as it implied that a project or programme is more 'serious', must, in the end, be rejected.

We should break off at this point to define the framework of the exploration pursued in this study. This is more than a rite of professional caution: to draw up a new schema of social organization is easy enough compared with the need to understand a socio-historical phenomenon; it is also much more than the psycho-sociological study of an isolated 'organization', in so far as the prototype that emerges has a meaning for

---

or loaded with the wrong associations ('to transcend', 'transcendence' – which, in any case, is vertical rather than horizontal in implication). (Translator's note.)

[1] During a conversation (December 1968).

[2] This may be why Touraine (1968) now insists above all on the need for the sociologist to construct a meaning for action that transcends the one that the actors were themselves creating.

the future and contains clues to problems that are present in society today. On the one hand, what was observed during those historical days applied only to *certain* events and *certain* participants – I am not claiming that the action–image of society, as I shall call it, was to be found in every exteriorization (in the streets, in the assemblies or commissions). It constitutes, perhaps, one of the most original aspects of the Movement; it certainly does not express the whole of its essence or complexity. On the other hand, and even if the resumption of 'normal' life in France in the autumn made May look like an *interlude*, it would be difficult not to think that certain of the forms of life that appeared *prefigure* the society of the future, or at least what that society might, in part, become, once its development has been 'unblocked', that is, defined by others than those who are at present in the 'instituted' positions of power. This hypothesis implies that it was not just any schema of social organization that was tried out, but a form of life in society linked with problems that are of the present day and that are potentially the problems of the future (rapid and permanent change, segmentation, decision-making, etc.).

From the beginning of the discussion it appeared that on the subject of projections three starting-points should be considered: the social actor acting, of course, but also the actors who, in a sense, are indirect and who are 'the situation' (Society, History) and the theories, the sources of meaning.

Let us call *object* a political action in its concrete aspects – the occupation of a particular place (a university, a factory, a street) or a demonstration – and let us see how the creation of meaning implies, in fact, all these sources, the projection not always being initiated by the social actors, in the personalized sense of the word.

THE MEN–AGENTS OF PROJECTION

It is normal to think of individuals as sources of meaning. Individuals or active groups, in particular, project a meaning onto an object. Whether their usual image of society is influenced by action, or even constructed in the course of action, the meaning of the projection becomes part of a world of representations.

The *prototype* of the *action–image*[1] may be presented in the form of three variants. It is these that I shall try to deal with in this study.

[1] From the idea of 'action–painting', by analogy with the *itinerary* followed by the brush, which traces the *gesture* of the painter, and with the expression 'impressed' upon the canvas in the course

1. *Divergent aleatory projections.* In the least favourable case, the projections of the various demonstrators remain largely secret and *divergent*. These divergences may not be corrected, for the speed of the action or the domination of minorities prevents a process of explanation and explicitation from taking place. The divergences cannot even be expressed non-verbally – by a choice of variants in action – because of the domination exercised by minorities and their networks. Once action is 'lived' and its process developed, a meaning appears, but it is not shared by the participants. In so far as the meaning given to the *object*, before and during action, not only differs, but cannot be corrected, the divergences concerning its implications for the future are shown to be enormous.

In this first variant the tendency to projection is contrary to the idea of a common project. The participants' hopes for and ideas about the future differ so widely that one cannot but conclude that the conjunction of their projections upon the object is based on a misunderstanding. The action may have attained its objective. The result is a truly *aleatory* action–image, in the sense that the conjunction of divergent opinions was built up, and imposed, by minorities, through the acceptance of a misunderstanding, and through the situation.

In contrast with this first type, which has given rise to a good deal of superficial comment, are two more favourable cases.

2. *Convergent projections of negation.* In the second case, a minimum of discussion reveals first a simple common object – a negation. The projections that are added as the discussion develops – emerging partly during the action itself – converge more and more, but the final consensus is concerned above all with what is to be rejected, excluded, attacked, etc. These analyses are not, strictly speaking, the same as those upon which various projections that are no longer secret, or repressed by minorities, are directed. The common elements assume greater importance than the divergence as a result of the practice provided by the action. An adjustment is made between the various opinions. The divergences concern mainly the construction of the future.

3. *Parallel projections of affirmation.* In the course of longer, and above all less specialized discussions, *different*, but parallel, projections are expressed.

---

of the gesture. The experiments in mural painting undertaken by *series* of students and above all the *group* activity involved in the making of posters (from the point of view both of political content and of aesthetic form) are interesting as experiments in collective creation. For an account of the mural paintings, see Dejacques (1968).

A consensus emerges not so much on a precise content as on a way of proceeding: to live the action and the life of the present in the same style. Negation and affirmation are confused here, which dispenses with the need for a phased programme or a precise representation of the society of the future. This representation is put into practice at once: project and projection are merged. The future is conceived as a state to be developed through a process of growth, of permanent change, implying various meeting-points between individuals, groups, and social units – temporary alliances, one might say. The divergences, which are not denied, become specific ways of living the same schema (of the consensus), of, let us say, a pluralist organization, in rapid and constant change.

In particular, these three variants have in common a virtual absence of written programmes,[1] the growth of an action–image in the course of a continuous development, the difficulty of presenting this action–image rationally – which is due particularly to its character as meaning expressed in action – and the fact that action succeeds in producing, temporarily at least, unity among divided participants, who remain more or less divided through the action. The object, as I called it, is empty to begin with – it must be projected upon – but as it is 'acted out', the form of the process sends back the projections that were directed upon it. Action is therefore the exteriorization (*Vergegenständlichung*) of a meaning. Although it is not made explicit and precise *a priori* in variants 2 and 3 – as it may be, more or less overtly, in variant 1 (by minorities) – the meaning cannot be called 'aleatory', simply because it emerges through a process of growth in which all, or most, take part.

Let us pause for a moment at this initial, and obviously incomplete, formulation. The distinctions proposed are, of course, only analytic – the event itself completely overlaps the prototype, and the precise appreciation of the various aspects that have been separated here is no easy matter. In any case, the prototype does not exist in a vacuum.

PROJECTION FROM THE OUTSIDE

Through individuals, the *context* (Society, History) or *social theories*, in turn, project a meaning onto an object. They are also sources of projects.

The group discussion showed that in this respect we expressed ourselves

[1] With the exception of a few slogans and perhaps graffiti or posters – simple formulas – that are also objects of projection. Pamphlets and magazines may appear, but they tend to express distinct areas of interpretation.

in a rather different vocabulary. However, it might be useful to consider context and theory – the various forms of Marxism – in precisely the same terms. It is important today, when faced with the intellectual fashion for abstract systems of *men-objects*, to recall a simple truth: neither the context nor theories can exist without the men who perceive it and conceive them. Society and theories are also, of course, objective realities (independently of the views held of them by certain social categories, the middle classes for example), but they are necessarily interpreted by someone or some people – in a period of crisis, one might say by all. A projection then takes place, from the context and from theory, onto the external 'event', the interpretation that creates it being based on something that exists prior to the action to which a meaning is given.

There is no doubt that the students' interpretation, notably of Marx (usually through versions, themselves interpretative, of the writings of his youth or maturity), projected a meaning onto their action.[1] Although this common denominator did not make it possible to draw up a common list of demands, we must not be misled by this absence of an explicit programme. On the one hand, a formalized vision would not have precluded various interpretations of the formulations used – just as there are various forms of Marxism – and, on the other hand, an underlying projection, common to all on a good many points, probably did exist (abolition of private property, the class struggle, the industrial capitalists as a symbol of exploitation). Again, it must be remembered how strong were the (typically French) tendencies to 'totalization' – a point at which we should pause for a moment in a logico-Byzantine parenthesis.

I mentioned earlier (in a note on Lefebvre) the characteristic rejection of many students of *reduction*, which is often tantamount to a rejection of all analytical method. Through a justified fear of losing the meaning of the *whole*, they refuse to consider the relation between a part *a* and a part *b*. They are only too aware of the differences of meaning that emerge from *a*, *b*, *c*, and *d* according to whether *e* or *f* is added, or both, and refuse to believe that a minimum programme is possible. The traditional idea of political platforms appears to them to be a dangerous masquerade. Agreement may be reached on *a*, *b*, *c*, and *d*, but the discussions may still break down in the end because agreement cannot be reached on *e* and *f*. A few divergent elements, or even a single one, are enough to give a *different* meaning to a number of convergent elements.

[1] In a later chapter I quote from more recent writers who *seem* to have inspired the students to a particular degree.

There follows from this an immense politico-methodological contradiction: for although one kind of reduction, analyticism, has been
avoided, another becomes all the more probable, not to say inevitable,
in action, namely, interpretative reduction. Certain notions will be extended to produce a sort of interpretative monism, either of a modal
kind (on points of agreement, for example notions of repression and
absorption (*récupération*), in the ultra-comprehensive sense), or of a divergent kind (around a point of major divergence also chosen as a general
axis of interpretation, the bureaucracy, for example).

In the case of meaning projected onto the event by the socio-historical
context, for example student movements in other countries, the Gaullist
regime, advances or delays in industrial modernization, the development
of neo-capitalism, or the tendencies of the state to technologized organization, there is no doubt that here too its origin is to be found in the social
interpretations of these realities. In any case, they are too divergent not
to be subject to selection. As my intention is neither to provide a complete
account of May nor to study the origins of behaviour of which I am
attempting to construct the prototype, I must admit to one *a priori* in my
approach. I place particular importance on two axes: the *acceleration* and
extent of change, and *telecracy*[1] (anti-authoritarianism, anti-centralism,
dehierarchization).

One might mention here two aspects of the relation between a revolutionary action and the society in and against which it takes place. The
meaning projected onto the action by those in positions of power in the
established society, such as it is at a particular moment in time, always
tends to fall wide of the mark, in so far as it fails to relate to the society
that is not yet established and that wishes to be instituted. The alternative
is to project the meaning of the most advanced aims of the established
society onto the revolutionary action, which is then seen as a rival in the
business of constructing the future. This tendency is less frequent and is
seen, like the first, as an attempt at 'absorption' (*récupération*); indeed, the
revolutionaries regard it as more dangerous than the most conservative
interpretation.

A number of different approaches were touched on in the discussion
reproduced above. Quite obviously, they cannot all be pursued here. And
the elements, whether factual data or interpretation of those data, must be

---

[1] Government at a distance, a term used by Stück (1968), in an article in which he interprets May
as an anti-authoritarian movement.

ordered in terms of my own mode of analysis. For this reason, we shall proceed through three successive stages involving the relation between the individual and the social actor, the relation between the collective actor and his 'partners' (in the various meanings of the word), and the tendencies towards a sort of synthesis.

Regrouped in this way, the elements that I have kept from the group discussion (complemented by passages drawn from the publications of the participants) will enable us to define our field of exploration: that of the parallel between the cultural and political modes of living.

THE OVERTHROW OF THE RHYTHM OF LIFE

The discussion began with various reflections on the notion of *time*. This notion was discussed on several occasions. It would be useful, it seems to me, to relate it to that of desire, since both, in fact, appear in the field that concerns the life of the individual just as much as the life of man as 'social actor' (dependent on an economic and social system). In view of this, I have left to one side the problems of the historical interpretation of 'time'.

To say that the May explosion produced a 'break' in the rhythm of social life is to draw attention, on the one hand, to the *speed* of the transformation in forms of conduct or social images and, on the other, to the reversal of the relation between – let us say, in the interests of simplicity – the established society and the individual.

Although it is true that the social forms of life are never entirely stagnant, changes are not normally very perceptible. In May, a considerable acceleration of the speed of transformation gave many of the participants in the Movement the impression of a telescoped 'apprenticeship'. The experience of music would seem to indicate that the more the rhythm accelerates, the more the expression – whether joyful or tragic – is intensified.

The fact of acceleration alone, quite apart from the positive or negative appreciation of what is taking place, tends to produce an emotional shock. 'Openings' not only emerge, but seem to be necessary. In, or faced with, this state of accelerated 'free-wheeling', everything becomes more intensely passionate: you push the wheel or attempt to brake it, in a state of profound involvement.

Among those who are pushing the wheel, the usual rhythm of desire and its satisfaction breaks down. Periods in which there is an acceleration of satisfaction – in terms of pleasurable and varied activities, experienced simultaneously or in rapid succession – are followed by almost inactive, fairly long, slack periods. In May, one noticed an alternation between phases of extreme acceleration, pursued to the point of exhaustion, and phases of extreme relaxation, of discussion and the building up of strength. Whereas, in the first kind of phase, the activity of the demonstration, the explanations, and the decision-making followed each other very rapidly, in the second, the discussions seemed interminable, slow, infinitely 'open', lacking in any kind of direction.

The relation between desire and realization, its usual rhythm having broken down, is in fact reversed. Normally, in a modern industrial society, the realization of a desire is postponed until later – 'deferred gratification' – and therefore preceded by an adaptation of the individual to his duties as an actor in an economic or social system, unless he tries to reject such a submission, at the risk of being punished for his non-conformity. There is established, then, an *adaptation* of the expression of desire in terms of what is attainable in a given situation, and a rhythm between the postponement and the realization of satisfaction.

This rhythm and the constraints that the individual sees imposed upon him by his social position do vary, of course, in a hierarchized society. What should be remembered here – and this brings us back to the maturity/immaturity opposition that was mentioned in our discussion – is that in an explosive, liberating period a double process tends to take place: whereas the rhythm becomes de-stabilized, alternately accelerating and decelerating, postponement becomes the consequence of satisfaction and not its precondition, and the expression of the desires one wishes to satisfy no longer takes place *restrictively*, but *prospectively* (in terms of what one wishes to attain, and not in terms of what seems possible).[1]

The change of perspective is clear enough. It is no longer a question of thinking about the imperfections of an economic and social system that is to be *transformed*, in order to give fuller realization to as yet unsatisfied desires, but of rebuilding this system on the basis of an immediate acceptance of desires, the economic and social solutions emerging later and not being taken up and discussed as starting-points. This is a politics of the maximum,[2] whose only weakness is that it might lead to failure.

But the problem must also be presented in another way, passing from the level of the requirements and difficulties of the 'institutor' in his

---

[1] 'I take my desires for reality, for I believe in the reality of my desires' (a common inscription).
[2] Another famous inscription in May – 'Demand the impossible' – may be understood in this sense or as the expression of just such a need for a change of perspective.

relations with the 'instituted' to that of new social dimensions, the problems of the future.

Is it still legitimate, in societies of ever more rapid change, to characterize maturity by the ability to *defer* the realization of desires and by the search for *lasting* solutions?[1]

In the negative hypothesis, the suggested distinction[2] between *non-degraded maturity*, which has been able 'to transform its immediate desire into a mediated desire, through knowledge', and *degraded maturity*, which has very largely lost contact with desire, must be supplemented by another. In the perspective of a non-established society, which is never settled, but is in a state of rapid change, or in a revolutionary period, maturity is defined by the search for solutions that are always provisional and by the non-postponement of the satisfaction of desires – though the relation between the individual and the social actor (and therefore the economic and social system) also gives place to a critical distinction: it would not be enough to promote what until now has been called immaturity (or even more provocatively 'irresponsibility') to the status of a new-style *maturity*; a distinction must still be made between behaviour that is capable of establishing a new society, at least at a certain level, and that which is not ('degrading' now in relation to the social life that is to be established).

We must be content merely to initiate thought on this subject. To separate direct collective action (of the type envisaged by the large political and labour organizations) and indirect individual action (the transformation of people's minds) is no longer enough. In both, there is a tendency to defer the satisfaction of desires. To this is now added a new category of behaviour that refuses to defer satisfaction: on the one hand, that which envisages *directly* the replacement of the present society by a new one and, on the other hand, that which is absorbed into new behaviour, its project of transforming and rebuilding society *indirectly* having lost contact with society, in particular through its ghetto-type life.

If the May phenomenon is highly complex, and embraces both of these tendencies,[3] it seems to me that the following hypothesis is justified: an attitude has emerged that presents desires – hence the 'cultural' life in the 'everyday' sense of the word (way of life, of creating) – and permanent

---

[1] 'Maturity gives importance only to what is lasting . . .' (Linbaum, 1968, p. 38).
[2] Ibid.; cf. note quoted in preceding chapter (pp. 89–90).
[3] The tendency to reason within the Sorbonne ghetto was remarked on in the course of our discussion (the *pieds-noirs* section of the students reasoning sometimes like the French in Algeria once did, speaking as if their attitude was really going to determine the whole of French society).

change as the primary aims of collective, *direct*, and *spontaneous* action; they express the 'modern' needs both of present-day society and of the society to be 'instituted'. This attitude has existed side by side with, or mingled with, behaviour that is strictly enclosed within the present, without any more distant aims. Whereas in the case of certain individuals this was accompanied by a hope that their way of life would be adopted by other individuals or social groups – by imitation – others were entirely wrapped up in the present moment.

We cannot pursue this line of approach any further here,[1] but it should be noted that if my reversal has taken place, as regards time and desire, we would be justified in assuming that the means and aims of social action have also undergone a complete change. Normally, social action obtains satisfaction by right of conquest; it is a *means*. It would seem that the immediate satisfaction of needs has now become the *means* by which an aim is achieved: henceforth, the aim of social action is to defend what has already been acquired.

Carried to its logical conclusion, this schema may seem forced and exaggerated, although different features of the May phenomenon – and not all, or even the majority, as I have said – correspond to it quite clearly. The quotations which, in the next chapter, I shall arrange in a sort of model view, should confirm this point.

THE PARADOX OF THE ORGANIZATION

How was the problem of the relation to others and therefore to the organization presented? One of the speakers in the discussion suggested that the notion of organization denoted simply 'knowing how to work together'. If the word spontaneity expresses a bureaucrat's notion, fear of the word organization certainly characterizes the anti-bureaucrat. Let us carry the schema of the 'logic of May' beyond simple terms and consider the problem in terms of *work* situations, leaving political or cultural 'work' until later.

So long as we do not call the company or corporation as a whole an 'organization' – as a number of American sociologists do – the industrial situation provides an excellent field for thought. More perhaps than other disciplines, industrial sociology poses similar problems, as far as the organization is concerned, to those confronting the observer of 'industrial

[1] Let us hope that the tape-recordings, films, and written accounts made in May will be studied by the ethnographers.

societies' as a whole. In particular, this is due to the meeting, in industry, of different, generally opposed, social worlds.

On the organization of work, P. Rolle wrote (1962): 'By this term one generally means the totality of formal rules that determine the material conditions of work.' And he specifies that he intends, personally, to use this term only to describe 'the structuration of work data by an *act* that establishes, according to its own laws, an economic division of labour' (p. 34). This amounts to saying (p. 35) that the organization of the workshop is also the work of the resistances and initiatives of the workers, which are just as much *decisions* as those of the organizer – a fact that is often overlooked.

In other words, if the organization is a necessary technique of cooperation, it is also, and necessarily, the battleground of the social struggles that take place both within the factory and outside it. The following paradox should also be considered: the organization, which, at a particular moment, if not over a fairly long period, characterizes the *functioning* of a production unit, is both a compromise, resulting from the balance of social forces present, and a plan, imposed by those who occupy the positions of power; the fact that this plan was conceived with a view to the relative strength of the partners, and possibly amended accordingly, does not alter the fact that it is a complex piece of political bargaining that is then imposed by a minority.

The first characteristic of the thought whose broad outlines we are trying to sketch is the collective self-determination of the way of working together, as united partners. The bargaining between social forces would not take place therefore on the basis of a pre-established plan, but 'in the process' of its emergence; there would no longer be an informal organization in relation to a formal organization, but a 'working organization', to use Tom Burns's excellent term.

This brings us, of course, into the realm of 'super-reality'. One can think about the division of labour as it should be, but it would be more difficult – accepting, for the moment, that it would be practicable in a new population – to conceive of it in relation to the 'sub-reality' (contemporary reality identified with people).

A second characteristic of the solutions conceived seems to be that they presuppose a *tabula rasa* at the level of concepts anterior to reality. It is in this respect that the relation with 'others' – to the non-revolutionaries – creates a problem. But for the political current with which we are now dealing, this is not a relevant problem.

The recalcitrant partners and, first of all, the whole 'system' that characterizes the present state of this industrial world can be eliminated or
neutralized. They can be *ignored*: the first and absolute requirement if one
is to win and avoid contamination.

In view of the importance of the discussion among the *cadres* (middle
management), who were more or less in revolt in May, we can now
approach things in greater detail. The *cadres* have always been socially
ambivalent.[1] Above all, they have learnt to be adaptable. If one ignores
their 'boss' characteristics, they can be converted to new forms of cooperation, once the old forms have been removed. Certainly, industrial
production requires skills, and the position that the *cadres* would attain
might, even in a self-managed enterprise, enable them to abuse their
'technocratic' position and to form a new management elite. But this
social category could, or so the argument goes, be absorbed (*récupéré*)
and checked.[2]

For other 'partners', the tactic of ignoring what is established would
lead to its elimination. To 'pretend that the CP does not exist' is not far
removed from the slogan, 'The boss needs you, you do not need him.'
Lastly, the 'white-collar' workers ('collar-and-tie proletarians', the old
expressions recur) would hardly present any problem. The usual ideological schemas are combined, therefore, with the tactic that consists of
ignoring, in order to weaken, the established 'system'.

In the discussion, one of the participants said that one could only *dream*
about self-management, and quoted 'functional requirements', economic
ones in particular, that would make it very difficult to introduce. One
should not conclude from the rational scepticism expressed in that remark
that the speaker regards self-management as unrealizable. The same
R. Lourau wrote of the conclusions reached at a socialist conference at
Grenoble (a year before May '68):

> . . . The distorted and very questionable model of self-management that the
> conference denounced, only to attain, implicitly, the theory or at least the
> *theoretical project* of self-management, is simply the *image* that they themselves
> make of it (Lourau, 1967, p. 69).

Whether one calls a movement like that of M 22 an organization,
a non-organization, or an anti-organization[3] is partly a quarrel over

---

[1] Or rather, plurivalent. But what we are concerned with here is the discussion concerning their
dual status as 'watchdogs of capitalism' and as wage-earners.
[2] It will be noticed that the concept of *récupération* may also be used with reference to new situations.
[3] 'It is, in fact, an anti-organization' (Linbaum, 1968, p. 35).

terminology, but it touches on the problem of the effective realization of new social forms.

A newspaper article written by Lourau 'in the heat of the moment' tries to show that self-management is indeed realizable, in forms that can be deduced from direct experience:

> We do not seem to notice what is happening under our very eyes, namely, that self-management is already with us. Not only in this or that timid declaration by the workers at Donges or somewhere, but in the reality of the social relations in the course of transformation. When the students occupy the Sorbonne and establish rational modes of organization, such as the crèche for students' children; when workers occupy their factories, their offices or their shops, establishing forms of organization that are based on old forms or are entirely new, and prove that it is they and they alone who make the machine work, they are *projecting* into a near or distant future the idea that responsibilities and creative initiative belong not to those who possess the capital, but to those who directly produce social activity. It is not yet the self-management of production . . . but it is the self-management of contestation . . . (Lourau, 1968b).

This is, indeed, the achievement of the activity of *projection* that I mentioned above. Realized in unexpected forms, the action–image is projected in turn onto the future, once it has been built up in the process of action and projection. It illustrates 'possibilities'.

The tactic, based on the general (or generalized) strike, which consists of ignoring enemy or as yet unconverted partners, sets out on the task of social construction by means of self-management. This would be implemented almost automatically in all enterprises at once, and would thus render the whole of the old 'system' incapable of being restored. Lastly, this immediate extension would not only be geographic, but would lead to a radical redefinition of social life as a whole, since every form of life in common would now be run on self-management lines.

This extension would hardly of itself involve problems of organization. It would be realized as the rediscovery of a natural state, once the structures of social domination were put out of action. According to this conception, the only problem of organization to be recognized as such is that of *coordination* between this multitude of units of production and of life. This, too, would be solved in practice, since the functioning of the units does not presuppose the coordination that is eventually achieved. This, again, involves a reversal of perspectives, since the functioning of the parts and their interrelations will constitute the functioning of the whole – it is, to revive a word that is seldom used these days, an anti-totalitarianism.

There remains the problem of 'output', of 'productivity'. How, at the local level, can one encourage production and keep to a production programme? The answer would be that there would be no imposed programme, but only objectives that the self-managed unit would fix for itself; that no constraint would now be necessary to attain them, except that exercised by the majority of the general assemblies over the minority; that the productive effort itself would be considerably reduced when enthusiasm in the creation of the conditions of production and the free distribution of the products created completely transformed what would no longer be 'labour' in the traditional sense.

One could say that relations with others would be considerably simplified by the creation of smaller local units; and, because organization would become a simplified schema (self-management, with such rules as constant revocability, the periodic renewal of the 'councils', and the rejection of *a priori* plans), it would, at most, be what the day-to-day functioning would have required. Not a plan, but the itinerary followed by 'lived' action. And this functioning would exclude any 'routinization', since no schema would ever be able *to establish itself*, in view of the diversity of local experiences, with man defining the organization, through his way of creating and living, and not the reverse.

SOCIOCULTURAL POLITICIZATION

To reject, and then to ignore, the separations between decision-makers and executants, in 'politics' just as much as in work, was one of the aims of the participants of May. To this should be added a rejection of all division between those who create culture, in the artistic sense, and those who consume it. This double abolition of frontiers of subordination brings the political and the cultural more closely together, the latter approximating more and more to culture in the sense of 'daily life', and makes possible the synthesis of two preoccupations, that of oneself and that of others.

The observer who attempts to discover the logic of a particular current of action in May cannot therefore think in the usual terms of 'politics', or he will come to regard this current as simply absurd – which amounts to seeing it as a desperate, purely expressive (Parsonian vocabulary), negative action, which, in my opinion, it was not, as I hope to show.

Traditionally, the political sphere has been defined by the idea of the state, government, parliament, political parties, and even, perhaps, political associations, so that a tendency to 'depoliticization' is interpreted as a lack of interest in the political sphere proper on the part of a whole section of the French population.[1] But for some years now, the political strength of the unions, whether or not they claim to be unconnected with any party, has been on the increase and is becoming increasingly apparent (at particular times, such as the Algerian crisis, for instance), a phenomenon that is beginning to be recognized.

Various remarks made by speakers in our discussion emphasized the importance of union politicization in the May crisis – with *work* clearly assuming the role of an axis, or even a reference, in moments of insecurity. This is to be found both in the logic of 'industrial' societies and in that of the current we are now studying, whose insistence on the importance of the 'local plan' recentres interest, as far removed as possible from excessively centralizing influences, on the places of work. The only form of delegation which, at a supra-local level, may still be acceptable to some is the union organization. This organization seems to them to be all the more legitimate in that the internal functioning of the union presupposes a federalist structure, which is the starting-point of the self-managed local groups.

Nevertheless, this form of politicization is still based on delegation. A sort of crisis of awareness, individual or collective (students), to which some of the activists have referred – in the sense of 'we are all, objectively, proletarians' – certainly seems to have been preferred by a large section of the student population to any politicization through organizations. What we are confronted with here, then, is a politicization of the 'social'. Some young workers and some at least of the students would appear to suffer in the same way from the inadequacy of teaching programmes, the authoritarian relations between staff and students, etc., and both could communicate directly, without mediation, without any kind of transposition, into more abstract programmes, of similar basic requirements, even without intermediaries, through direct action. The 'fusion' would not even have to be explained – it would be more *normal* than the separation imposed by stratification, to use a word that is no longer current, but that expresses very well certain notions I do not wish to pursue at this point.

Even at this stage, one can explicitate the logic of the solution that is

[1] Cf., for example, Vedel (1962).

supposed to resolve the antinomy of concentration on oneself and relations with others. In so far as the student examines his own social
condition and sees that he is 'objectively' a proletarian (proletaroid intelli-
gentsia, to use Weber's term), he becomes aware of the need to make
contact with other proletarians. Political solutions will then be imposed
on both, in the course of a contact that will reveal their strength and the
points of view that they *naturally* have in common, which can lead only
to the same project of transforming society.

To this fusionism of class is added another, some of whose features were
described by speakers in our discussion. The abolition of the dichotomy
between decision-makers and executants, both in work and in politics,
also suppresses the spirit of specialization, and even the idea that a problem can be discussed in isolation, that is within the framework of reference
fixed *a priori*. The rejection of the *a priori*, which I touched on above, is
obviously to be found again at this stage. The non-specificity of problems
has, as consequence and origin, this desire for the retotalization of man –
a theme that was also mentioned in the discussion.

What we find, then, is a second major characteristic, one more central
to the current we are studying here than union politicization is: namely,
the *politicization of oneself*, since man is both the objective to be attained
(a 'fragmented' individual is merely a sub-man) and the source of political
strength. The more politics works towards the retotalization of man, the
more intense it becomes; and the more successful it is in its aim, the more
the desire to pursue that action increases.

From this point of view, all aspects of life – including sexual relations,
as was mentioned in the discussion – would be constantly connected with
'political' decisions. The fusion between spheres that are usually separated
is regarded not only as natural, but as a source of political strength. All
emotion, since it involves the whole person, will play a greater role in this
political 'work', conceived as creation of self and of society. And there is
no boundary to cross from this activity of creation to culture. One is
there. Art will pass into daily life, daily life will become an 'art of life',
and civilization will be transformed. In subsequent chapters I shall return
to the illustration of this current, which summarized in this way seems far
too abstract. We shall see how the wall inscriptions, in particular, combined a Dada-like, Surrealistic invention with daily political practice, how
certain attempts at improvised action resemble practices already well
known in some jazz circles, and how much certain experiments in the
theatre exemplify this fusion.

Here one might extend one of the criticisms levelled against the Living Theatre's lack of preparation. One of the speakers in the discussion suggested that the company had hardly analysed the situation at Nanterre before playing there. Its fusionism – which implies the complete super-imposition of all problems, aesthetic, political, and personal – did not, apparently, lead it to seek a greater understanding of the environment.

This is another important characteristic of the self/others/society relation. This form of self-involvement was perhaps more pronounced in this company – indeed, the company's self-criticism, in the months following May, shows an awareness of the limitations of a sectarian life. But it would seem also to have been prevalent among a whole category of students in May. The analysis of 'outside' society does not go with a tactic that tries to weaken by ignoring. In my own experience, it was strictly speaking 'indecent', for example, to raise the problem of the precise numerical strength or composition of 'the' working class. Yet the tactical value of a knowledge of the environment could hardly be doubted. The reason was that only auto-politicization could fully free immediate action, by dissolving the inhibitions that an analysis of the environment would inevitably have introduced, in the form of doubts and even a mass of arguments against a certain way of acting, in particular through a consideration of the boomerang effects that were increasingly apparent towards the end of the 'events', but were predictable much earlier. 'Dysfunctions', to use a term from American sociology, are such only as long as a certain system holds out. This was no doubt the gamble that was being taken, and it went side by side with the conviction that the system could collapse.

There remains the logic of non-compromise, which also tends away from an analysis of the environment. A desire not to know society empirically is a normal attitude for someone who wishes to rebuild that society all over again. It is an attitude that is accompanied fairly often by faith in a theory that will seize, in all its purity, the essence of a society – the consequent 'analysis', which is really a definitive 'synthesis', is then impervious to any experimental verification.

The considerable importance of the action–image is a result of the doubts experienced by many of those who participated in action; that, at least, is one interpretative hypothesis. They cling to certain forms of Marxism as much perhaps for what they represent, in their eyes, as a source of legitimacy as for their coherence, but they use these forms above all as a weapon in criticism. They have an insufficient knowledge of the society around them, and in a confused sort of way they are aware of this; since they scarcely trust the methods of the social sciences, they have recourse to knowledge acquired directly in the course of action, to the developed image of society that one *is* oneself, for oneself, in direct action.

In the following chapters I intend to retrace in greater detail the wealth of solutions I have just outlined in a somewhat abstract, but I hope systematic, framework. The group discussion stopped short of even an introductory, let alone a complete, treatment of imagination and of the juncture of the political and the cultural. This is hardly surprising. Though not particularly 'orthodox', the various speakers in the discussion remained respectful towards one axiom that is nevertheless a highly con-troversial one for some Marxists: namely, the supremacy of the infra-structure. To politicize the cultural, to calculate or merely to experience the cultural in a strategic way, even according to new conceptions that define culture at the level of daily life, will always, in their view, remain secondary, not to say artificial. Thus the anarcho-Marxists, who ex-perienced with great intensity the affirmative, let us say 'festive', side – I shall return to this aspect later – of the last days of May, shifted their emphasis from the first to the second term of the juncture, once the 'interlude' had come to an end. It is therefore difficult to reconstruct various central aspects of May through the medium of subsequent descrip-tions. Since it is my view that the 'model' lived and experienced in that period *prefigures* important characteristics and problems of society in the future, I shall now attempt to clarify the image of society as it was expressed by certain people before, and by others during or immediately after, this period.

After all, the terms 'interlude' and 'prefiguration' are not really ex-clusive: an interlude could prefigure the act that is to follow, if the audience climbed up onto the stage and stayed there, or, at least, expressed its wish to do so.

PART III

The Movement as seen by some of its Theoreticians

CHAPTER 5

The Image of Established Society

INTRODUCTION

In the months leading up to the May events, the French universities may have seemed particularly calm and studious to university authorities in some other countries. The agitation that was an almost permanent feature of certain American, German, Japanese, or Italian universities seems to have had no equivalent in France. In any case, the surprise caused by the apparent suddenness, the scope and depth, of the crisis was very considerable.

Yet long before this crisis there were warning-signs, almost unknown to the general public – before May, it was no exaggeration to speak of the universities as a closed world – which indicated the existence of a ferment that was to reach its peak in 1968. The first manifestation of this latent agitation was what is known as the 'Strasbourg Scandal'. In May 1966, a group of extremist students succeeded in getting themselves elected to the leadership of the Association Fédérative Générale des Étudiants de Strasbourg (AFGES), by taking advantage of the low membership of the French national students' union (UNEF) in that university. In an attempt to shake their fellow-students out of their political lethargy, the members of the new committee made contact with an organization that, until then, was practically unknown, the Situationist International (SI), with a view to collaborating on a pamphlet – of which I shall have more to say later – entitled: *De la misère en milieu étudiant, considérée sous ses aspects économique, politique, psychologique, sexuel et notamment intellectuel, et de quelques moyens pour y remédier* ('The wretched state of the student, considered in its economic, political, psychological, sexual and particularly intellectual aspects, and some ways of remedying it'). This violent pamphlet, which was ultimately the work of Mustapha Khayati, a member of the SI, and which attacked, without exception, all the parties and all the unions, whether national or purely student organizations, and spared nothing in established society, was distributed at the beginning of the new academic year in November 1966. At the same time, the AFGES committee announced that it intended quite simply to hold a general assembly and get the Association dissolved.

The resulting scandal and agitation were such that a series of actions was brought against the organizers of the movement, both at university level (one of the committee members was expelled from the university) and at legal level, since the pamphlet had been printed and distributed at the expense of the AFGES.

At the time, it seemed a rather local affair. But it was evidence of a desire on the part of a small group of students to break definitively with the legalistic practices of established organizations. Moreover, when reprinted in 1967, *De la misère en milieu étudiant* . . . was to bring to the attention of a vast university public the views of the Situationist International, whose influence, it seems to me, has been considerably under-estimated by commentators on the May events.[1] Not, of course, that their physical participation was very considerable – they are few in number, and intend to remain so. On the other hand, a good many of their ideas and methods were later to be found at Nanterre.

According to E. Brau (1968), the Situationist International is the product of a number of different movements, originally of a literary and artistic kind: one branch goes from Dada to Lettrism and the other from the 'Movement for an Imaginist Bauhaus', the aim of which was 'the search for an integral revolutionary cultural behaviour' (Brau, 1968, p. 58), to the COBRA movement, the Experimental Artists' International, a group of Danish, Dutch, and Belgian printers who wanted 'to escape from the sterile game of gratuitous aesthetics'.[2]

The creation of the SI goes back to July 1957, to a meeting of delegates from the Movement for an Imaginist Bauhaus, the Lettrist International (a dissident faction of the Lettrist group whose ambitions did not go beyond the literary sphere), and the Psycho-Geographical Committee of London.[3]

I shall return later to the detailed ideas of this group. For the moment

---

[1] It should be said that, sparing nothing and nobody, the *Situationists* devote a good deal of their activity to virulent attacks on those who are closest to their own thinking, and have thus alienated a good many intellectuals who would otherwise be sympathetic to their views.
[2] Ibid., p. 59. The name COBRA derives from the first letters of Copenhagen, Brussels, and Amsterdam.
[3] 'Psycho-geography: the study of the precise effects of the geographical environment, whether consciously controlled or not, acting directly on the emotional behaviour of individuals' (Brau, 1968, p. 168).

I should like simply to quote a few definitions provided by its own members in the August 1964 number of their review *Internationale situationniste*.

Why the word 'Situationist'?

> Since the individual is defined by his situation, he wants the power to create situations worthy of his desire. With this in view, poetry (communication as the achievement of a language in situation), the appropriation of nature, and complete social liberation must merge together and be realized.

The SI does not wish to be a political movement in the traditional sense, but rather the centre of a 'new, coherent critique of the society that is developing *now*, from a revolutionary point of view'. The emphasis on the need to adapt the critique to the development of society implies a rejection of ideological Bibles. The Situationists call themselves Marxists, 'though Marx said, "I am not a Marxist" ', and quote Fourier as readily as Lautréamont, Sade, Artaud, Reich, Diderot, or the Marx Brothers, provided they can be embraced by their own overall critique. The SI is 'against all "transitory programmes" and refers to a permanent revolution in daily life'.[1]

Since it wishes to be no more than a centre of reflection – and, as such, foresees its own immediate dissolution in revolution – and of coherent, total criticism, the SI has never tried to expand numerically. On the contrary, any 'deviation' from its basic principles is immediately answered by expulsion. This rigour, or sectarianism, is practised as much within the group as in its relations with the outside world. For the Situationists, the enemies of our enemies are not necessarily our friends, quite the reverse. Its most violent polemics have been directed against such groups as *Arguments* and *Socialisme ou Barbarie* (cf. the group discussion above).

The principal expositions of the theses of the Situationist International are to be found in G. Debord's *La Société du spectacle* (1967), in R. Vaneigem's *Traité de savoir-vivre à l'usage des jeunes générations* (1968), in various tracts and pamphlets, and in the review already mentioned.

---

[1] Before falling foul of them, Henri Lefebvre, then a professor at Strasbourg, was and is still very close to the Situationists – or they to him – influenced as they are by his critiques of daily life and being the first to take up the slogan 'change life'. He was later to reproach them with having turned this critique into dogmatism:

> ... they do not offer a concrete utopia, but an abstract utopia. Do they really believe that one fine day or one decisive evening people are going to look at one another and say: 'Enough! Enough of work and boredom! Let's put an end to it!' and that they will enter the age of endless festivity, in the creation of situations? Though it happened once, on 18 March 1871, at dawn, this combination of circumstances will not be repeated (Lefebvre, 1967, p. 195).

I shall speak later of another medium of propaganda used by the Situationists: comic strips, either original ones or old ones with different texts.

It is not my intention to produce a historical account of the crisis that culminated in May. The Nanterre story is better known than the 'Strasbourg Scandal' and has been described at length in numerous books and articles. I will merely give a brief synopsis of its main incidents.

From March 1967 onwards, the 'campus' at Nanterre was the scene of constant incidents. The agitation, which soon entered the realm of folklore, seems at the time to have had fairly limited objectives: the right of the boys to circulate freely in the girls' hostels and vice versa. The affair concluded with action being taken against twenty-nine students, not all of whom appear to have taken part in the demonstrations, but who were well known for their political activities. There was talk of 'black lists', which, the following year, helped to mobilize a large section of the student population.

At the beginning of the new academic year in 1967, things were far from calm. In November, a strike led to the setting up of staff–student commissions. It can be said that at this time the agitation was still largely the work of individuals, mainly anarchists, and small groups of Trotskyists and Marxist–Leninists – the UNEF had only a weak following at Nanterre – and usually originated in the sociology department.

The year 1968 was marked by a series of incidents of increasing gravity: in January, D. Cohn-Bendit accused the Minister of Youth and Sport, F. Missoffe, who had come to open a new swimming pool, of ignoring sexual problems in a recent White Paper on Youth. No action was taken against the speaker, but the incident helped to sustain a state of unrest which, from strikes and meetings to disciplinary action and the closing of the faculty, led to the bringing of eight students before the University Council and to the entry of the police into the Sorbonne to disperse a demonstration against repression.

One date in this process of escalation has remained famous, that of 22 March, when 150 students met for part of the night in the administrative building. The tract that they drew up there is rather confused, denouncing indiscriminately repression, black lists, the cybernetization of society, etc. Its importance lies not in its content, but in the fact, extremely rare in a country like France, that a group of young activists with divergent opinions should forget, temporarily at least, what separates them, in order to unite around what they have in common: a shared desire to break with traditional practices. 'We did not set out with ideas in search of action', comments A. Touraine, a professor at Nanterre. 'We set out from a sort of immediate practice, which took on meaning and turned into action as we went along' (see Labro, 1968, p. 44).

All they were doing was trying to develop the methods that had been used for some months by those whom the press had nicknamed the *enragés*. Interrupting lectures, boycotting lecturers whom they considered to be reactionary, using humour or, if necessary, scandal, more readily than political argument, they tried to break down the barrier of passivity and lack of interest that the small, organized groups had failed to break with all the weight of their theories.

I shall not attempt in this chapter to give a full account of the complexity and composition of the 'Movement of 22 March'.[1] Indeed, it would be extremely difficult to do so since, apart from a few interviews and the book by D. and G. Cohn-Bendit, most of the Movement's writings are anonymous, and therefore any reference to an author's previous allegiance or to any 'intellectual master' that might make it possible to attach any kind of label to him is precluded. To a very large degree, and even though this may have been temporary on the part of certain tendencies, which later suppressed their autonomy, ideological sectionalisms were eradicated within M 22 in the interests of practice and its immediate analysis. It is this aspect I should like to emphasize, while not forgetting that, whether he liked it or not, D. Cohn-Bendit played the role if not of leader, at least of leader of opinion in the Movement. The meeting of a group of students determined to act and a 'personality', whom we know to have been influenced by both Marxism and anarchism, gave M 22 a particular 'flavour' and a significance that went beyond what it would have had simply as an agitation 'commando unit'.

In view of the success enjoyed in student circles by the methods and the course of action advocated by this tendency, it seemed to me that I should devote some attention to what I shall call the 'young anarchists', not on account of their age, but on account of the groups to which they belong. The past fifteen years have seen in France a proliferation of the dissident factions of the highly traditional Fédération anarchiste, the bastion of libertarian humanists and Marxophobes. This interest is all

[1] Its creation was the work of anarchists, Trotskyists (mainly from the JCR – Jeunesse Communiste Révolutionnaire – a faction of activists who had left or been expelled from the orthodox Union des Étudiants Communistes when, during the presidential election of 1966, the French Communist Party supported the candidature of F. Mitterand), and individuals, some of whom were clearly influenced by the Situationists.

the more justified in that everyone remarked during the events how active the new anarchist–communist tendencies were, especially in demonstrations, barricades, and occupations.

They are more difficult to pin down than the Situationists, whose taste for expounding critical theory they do not share, and they did not enjoy the same 'publicity' during the crisis as M 22. However, they do share with M 22 the same rejection of *a priori* ideologies, and a desire to free themselves from both Bibles and anathemas, to form their own convictions, adopting from different sources whatever seems to them best suited to present circumstances.

With one or two exceptions (the JAC, Jeunesse Anarchiste Communiste, for example), they are not very organized, and function more as research groups, and on the editorial boards of reviews like *Noir et Rouge*, than as political movements in the usual sense. In what follows I shall not try, therefore, to distinguish them formally other than by reference to these reviews. Some of their members played an active part in M 22. But, as I explained above, I shall not try to distinguish the purely anarchist contribution to that Movement, though it was obviously an important one, especially in the conception of the so-called 'exemplary action', an amalgam of anarchist direct action and Marxist *praxis*.

Lastly, it should also be remembered – and the group of tendencies of which I have just spoken itself made frequent reference to the fact – that at the social, and also at the university level, the atmosphere was a good deal less calm in the weeks and months leading up to May than sometimes appeared.

On several occasions, in different provincial cities – in Caen, Redon, Nantes, the important Rhodiaceta industrial group, etc. – wild-cat strikes broke out that took the unions completely by surprise. These movements, which sometimes became very violent (especially in the west, where the strikers fought with the police), lead one to think that, parallel with what has taken place among the students, a new way of conceiving action has emerged among the workers, particularly among the young workers. Many members of the small groups believe that it was this coming together that enabled the crisis to attain its sudden importance. The lack of precision in the information that we have concerning the strikes, and the often too partisan character of that information, have so far precluded a correct study of them.[1]

*   *   *

[1] A number of sociological studies are now being made on this subject (in particular, by S. Mallet).

It can justly be said that much of the thought of the participants in May was based on utopias or on old social or cultural experiences. It is difficult, in this case, to judge to what extent particular complexes of ideas or practices were imported ready made, or whether only certain elements were borrowed, then assembled – or 'stuck' in a collage – with other elements, of diverse origin, and finally interpreted in a new way so as to form truly new complexes. It seems to me that the students have relived certain old themes, but that their thinking is original.

Certain authors or participants, whose books, articles, or interviews I read only *after* the initial period, sometimes acted, as I have already said in the case of D. Cohn-Bendit, as leaders. It is obviously not because they insisted repeatedly, and not without a certain element of coquetry, that they never *intended* playing such a role, that, in the end, they made no notable contribution to the structuring of what seemed non-structured, namely, the way of living this French-style cultural revolution.

If it is true, as I think it is, that May can be characterized by a juncture between Marxism and anarchism, on the one hand, and between politics and culture, on the other, there can obviously be no doubt that the ingredients of this new 'mixture' – the old 'mixtures' having been vigorously rejected – are to be found in very variable proportions.

Since my aim is not to present every tendency, but only those that I have so far mentioned, nor to do justice to the exact relation of each to the Movement – which would be impossible anyway – it would be useful, I think, by following an intuitive method, to build up a sort of new *modal type* of anarcho-Marxist and politico-cultural thinking. This having been established, these three currents – Situationists, young anarchists, and, partly overlapping both, the Movement of 22 March – were the actors on whom I wish to focus attention.

To be precise, I do not intend, even in the case of these tendencies, to reproduce in an exhaustive and analytic way what unites them, separates them, or, more usually, characterizes them. At most this could only be done in the case of the Situationists, M 22 being by definition a 'union' of forces, and the anarchists rejecting any tendency to generalization and some of them refusing even to express a point of view.

To sketch this modal type of a current that I have called 'new' – newness being produced above all by the meeting of a series of elements not usually in configuration, and by the fact that a dream is here *concretized*[1]

[1] E. Morin (1968b, p. 80) speaks of a 'lived concrete utopia'.

– in order to build up an image both of the old and the new society, seemed to me to be an interesting and necessary task.

Whether it is true that a Movement that has sprung from the depths of society expresses, together with the demands of the individuals who form it, a sort of diagnosis of the present and future problems of society, whether it is in crisis or in evolution, I shall leave to the reader to decide for himself. In any case, as I have said already, I shall not be content with a purely psychosocial study. The new current of action and imagination – of 'imaginaction', in fact, to unite in one word what is indistinguishable in reality – is there, in all its complexity, to remind us very forcefully that 'local' problems are linked with the existence of a certain form of society.

THE UNIVERSITY AND SCIENCE

I shall not insist on the most general criticisms, which primarily concern the inadequate basis of recruitment of the French universities, the most spectacular aspect of which is still the virtual absence of students from working-class backgrounds.[1] In fact, one meets with this argument in every student discussion in France. Similarly, criticism of the proper functioning of the universities is fairly widespread and is not confined to the three tendencies that I am examining here, though in this respect their criticisms are relatively more subtle than usual. An attempt to discern, in the functioning of the universities, the class specificity not only of the lecturers' 'views' and their position in the hierarchy, but also of the nature of a 'university education', is probably less widespread.

The style of the criticism levelled at the university, as, indeed, at Science, may vary however, and it may well be worth beginning this analysis with a few illustrations. They belong to a field that appears to be purely separate from society, namely, the analysis of that society.

It is interesting, first of all, to note that they are discussing the university from the point of view of the student and his future role in the 'social system' and not merely from that of his situation in the 'university system'.

The originality of the criticism formulated by the Situationists, then

---

[1] According to the texts (pamphlets, articles, and books on May), the references to the percentages of working-class students in the universities differ. The uncertainty about the exact figure is of little importance; in any case the proportion is infinitesimal compared with the proportion of manual workers in the population as a whole. See, on this subject, the book by Bourdieu and Passeron, *Les Héritiers* (1967 edn), which also deals with the categories of lower-paid office workers and of rural workers, which are likewise considerably under-represented.

largely taken up by the activists of M 22, is – and this is paralleled by their interest in the *actor* – in the violence with which the student himself is attacked. This attitude was to be found during May in innumerable pamphlets and writings, often of Situationist inspiration, like the one published just prior to the events by the 'Committee of public safety of the vandalists' of Bordeaux, which ended, 'Étudiants, vous êtes des cons impuissants'.[1]

The expression *De la misère en milieu étudiant*, which serves as the title of the pamphlet mentioned earlier, contains therefore very little sympathy for the student. This pamphlet attacks not only the university and society, but also those who are their consenting, and apparently satisfied, victims, which indicates a combative, and not a pessimistic attitude, with its implication that beyond mere denunciation there is a possibility of transformation.

It should be noted here that the members of M 22, among others, have no illusions as to the motives of the students, at least of the majority of them, who took part in this attempt at transformation. For them, student demands, even when they take such a radical turn as in May, often remain categorized and tainted with Poujadism. They seem to be motivated more by a fear of failure, insecurity, uncertainty in their future prospects, an anticipated refusal to accept a job they regard as inferior to the qualifications they have acquired or expect to acquire, than by a genuine desire to overthrow the social and economic system. The contempt, not to say cynicism, shown by both M 22 and the Situationists in this respect is obviously related to their contempt for the society that produces this kind of behaviour – a crucial and embarrassing problem for those who, as we shall see, advocate 'scuttling' potential leaders, non-bureaucracy, etc. This is linked to the ambiguity of the student in established society as it is conceived by the leaders of opinion in these groups. But one should point out that there is also a hope in their criticism of today's students: if one criticizes them,[2] it is because it would be possible to transform man, either by forming him in a new

---

[1] Quoted by R. Viénet (1968, p. 292).

[2] This criticism, which is sometimes close to provocation, is often related to a tactic of manipulation that the authors openly admit. 'The student', say D. and G. Cohn-Bendit, 'still has quite a lot of freedom, but he also has a certain irresponsibility.' It is enough to 'exploit this freedom/irresponsibility phase' to train the student mass in action through the 'police repression/student mobilization dialectic' (D. and G. Cohn-Bendit, 1968, p. 48).

N.B. Less well known than his brother Daniel, Gabriel Cohn-Bendit, a thirty-two-year-old German teacher in a French provincial lycée and co-author of this work, played, at one remove, a far from negligible role in May, since his younger brother has declared several times that he owed part of his anarchist ideas to him.

society, or by allowing him in some way to 'emerge' as he is in his state of nature.

Nevertheless, the activists of M 22 agree, to some extent, with A. Touraine when he says 'the students are the advance-guard of themselves'.[1] They are defending, in advance, their future interests. In the society that is being created, the possessors of valuable skills are looking after their future. D. Cohn-Bendit and J.-P. Duteuil do not deny this: on the contrary, their attitude is more severe:

> ... the students who revolt also do so in order to preserve the privileges of the bourgeoisie that they are temporarily losing in the transformation of society, in the transition from competitive capitalism to monopoly capitalism.[2]

In the new type of economic system into which France, according to Cohn-Bendit and Duteuil, is now entering, which is a centralized capitalism, a state capitalism like Russian socialism, the students will be merely *cadres* (and most of them, as Cohn-Bendit points out, middle *cadres*), cogs in the wheel, to use a term that recurs constantly in discussions and writings about May.

Being only a cog is synonymous here not only with having no future, but – in a vocabulary that is typical of these groups and particularly of the Situationists – of mutilation. In a great many of the pamphlets, declarations, and inscriptions of May, one finds analogies in terms of physical mutilation: man in our society is 'crushed', 'castrated', 'blinded', etc. They revive the rather traditional theme of proletarianization ('the increasing modernization of capitalism involves the proletarianization of an ever greater section of the population' – Viénet, 1968, p. 129) and link it with epithets of alienation or submission rather than with epithets of an economic order, based on the idea of the creativity of the individual. *The emphasis is more on the actor than on the system.* Thus one could see, on many walls in Paris, paragraphs from Proudhon's famous formula in *Idée générale de la Révolution au XIXe siècle* ('To be governed is to be watched, inspected, spied on, directed, legislated, regimented, penned, indoctrinated . . .'): 'Refuse to be registered, classified, oppressed, requisitioned, preached at, counted, hemmed in, indoctrinated, Sarcellized, sermonized, bludgeoned, telemanipulated, gassed . . .'.[3] On a broader

---

[1] Quoted in Labro (1968, p. 47).
[2] Quoted in Hervé Bourges (1968).
[3] Inscriptions on the walls of the Odéon. Sarcelles is a modern suburb regarded as a prime example of inhuman urbanization.

plane, involving *sociological analysis*, there appears another vocabulary that was used a great deal in the literature of May; it uses such words as compartmentalization, separation, fragmentation, etc.

Apart from criticism of the most immediate aspects of 'the wretched state of the student' – in particular, financial and sexual difficulties in a university and society that do practically nothing to resolve these age-old problems of youth, who are regarded as not yet having officially 'entered' industrial society – there is, in the very passivity and acceptance, the expression of a fundamental wretchedness: the student does not determine the university and, parallel with this fact, does not determine the type of society in which he wishes to live. In order to understand the contempt with which the activists of M 22 and the Situationists treat the student, we must return to this notion of *proletarianization*. To be a proletarian, in the sense in which they use the term, is to have no possibility of self-determination and *to be conscious* of the fact.[1] All the criticism of the student is based, in short, on the fact that the student has not in general attained this consciousness. On the contrary, he interiorizes the norms that enslave him, both in his strictly university life and as regards his future. 'The student', say D. and G. Cohn-Bendit, 'is passive, because he interiorizes the norms and demands of the university structures' (1968, p. 56). Contrary to the affirmation that was so often made in May by the students, and not only by the most radical of them ('We are all workers'), the majority, according to this analysis, are not in fact proletarians. At most, one might say, this slogan is justified in so far as a 'worker' is precisely a cog in a work system predetermined by the boss, but not in the sense of a worker conscious of his alienation.

The Situationists carry this argument even further and extend it to every aspect of the student's life:

> At a time when art is dead, [the student] remains the most faithful patron of the theatres and cinema clubs and the most avid consumer of its corpse, frozen, wrapped in cellophane and distributed in supermarkets for the housewives of the abundant society.[2]

[1] 'A proletarian has no power over the use of his life and knows it' (*De la misère en milieu étudiant* . . ., p. 31).
[2] *De la misère en milieu étudiant*, p. 9. This phenomenon of frenzied 'cultural consumption' by students has been noted by P. Bourdieu and A. Darbel:

> If entry to the university sets off in most students a sort of cultural bulimia, and marks (among other things) entry to the cultured class, that is, access to the right and – which amounts to the same thing – duty to acquire culture, it is also because the incitement to cultural practice exerted by the reference groups is, in this case, particularly strong (Bourdieu and Darbel, 1966, p. 62).

One finds in the student the same passivity, extended this time to society and culture – in the various senses of the term – through his taste for spectacle. He is a *spectator*.

The same 'consumptionist' attitude – the mere ingurgitation of a 'spectacle' presented by others – is found again, according to this criticism, in the student's attitude to knowledge. *Science* is made by others and for others than the student, either as such or as a future member of the society to come. He listens, records, reproduces, without being able to act either on the direction taken by research or on its implications.

'Neutral science is phoney', said a wall inscription discovered in the Science Faculty building. Side by side with critical arguments, which are relatively well known in intellectual circles, concerning the use of skills and simple techniques (applied psychology, work-study, etc.) in the interests of established society, enabling it to function more efficiently and therefore consolidating it, or concerning the military use of the results of research in physics (ideas that were taken up by D. and G. Cohn-Bendit, 1968, pp. 46–47), the characteristic style of the criticism made by M 22 lies in the approximation to the Situationist idea of the society of spectacle.

Passivity, non-participation: the same themes recur in the discussions that took place both in the studies committees and in the general assemblies. In May, the students were to declare not only 'Nous sommes tous des travailleurs', but also 'Nous sommes tous des chercheurs'.[1] The 'teacher/taught' relation, to avoid terms such as *professeur* that are necessarily regarded as authoritarian – the Weberian distinction between authority (legitimated power) and domination pure and simple is no longer in circulation – will be replaced by a notion of relation between advanced research scientists and student research scientists, each having a role to play in a process of permanent research.

For the Situationists, who also make this criticism of science in general and such disciplines as sociology in particular, the argument is carried to its ultimate conclusion: all science is necessarily contaminated in an economic system characterized by the possessors/dispossessed dichotomy.

This formula, which is shared by the young anarchists, is interesting in that it goes beyond the single dimension that is to be found in the more traditional opposition of possessors/possessed (those who have and those who have not),[2] the latter being reduced to the state of objects, which means that one is really interested only in power. Hence the term 'dis-

[1] With its double implication of 'research scientist' and 'seeker'. (Translator's note.)
[2] Cf. Willener (1957).

possessed' refers to production and the ability to create. The fundamental alienation of work is that man is dispossessed of the object that he produces by his activity, whatever it may be,[1] and – what is more original, relative to the concept, used in particular by the left-wing parties, of surplus value (the *product* of work) – of the *ability* to create or simply the mere *fact* of creating. The emphasis shifts from the old Marx to the young Marx. Using a traditional vocabulary, they revive the notions of productive and unproductive, but in relation to creation and not in relation to the functioning of a system. It is not only the finished object that no longer belongs to the man who produces it, but also the action that he performs in order to produce it when the tool that he uses does not belong to him – tool, in the widest sense of the term, having no intrinsic value:

> . . . appropriated by a master, a boss, a planning commission, a managerial organization, the tool changes in meaning, it deviates towards other extensions the actions of the man that uses it. What is true for the tool is true for every mediation (Vaneigem, 1968, p. 97).

If, again, it seems that a definite priority is given to the individual, to the actor, both the Situationists and the anarchists nevertheless value *science for itself*. Although at present it is contaminated, turned away from its true direction by the use to which it is put in established society, it would, in another system, be beneficial, fruitful, and liberating. Thus, for the Situationists, cybernetics could acquire the power of a panacea, outside the present system in which, on the contrary, it may well become the instrument of the ultimate stage of enslavement:[2]

> . . . if seized from its masters, cybernetics could liberate human groups from work and from social alienation. The project of Charles Fourier is just this, at a period when utopia was still possible. But from Fourier to the cyberneticians, who control the operational organization of technology, there is the distance from freedom to slavery (Vaneigem, op. cit., p. 84).

We shall return to the sociological interest of this theme. In particular, Pierre Naville, in *Vers l'automatisme social?* (1963), has devoted a good

---

[1] Any sociologist familiar with the writings of A. Touraine, in particular *Sociologie de l'action*, will notice that we have here the two axioms of his thinking, the relation of man to the creative act and the wish to control the use to which the product is put.

[2] This problem of the use of cybernetics recurs frequently in the writings of the Situationists. One of their *bêtes noires* is A. Moles, a former military specialist of cybernetics, who, towards the end of his career, became interested in the problems of social interaction and taught at Strasbourg. In October 1966 (cf. Bulletin No. 11 of the *Internationale situationniste*, p. 25), he was one of the first victims of the new methods of contestation initiated by the students, who pursued him with volleys of tomatoes.

deal of, to my mind, valuable thought to what is now known as the cybernetic utopia. An automatized society would make possible a very considerable *autonomy of the parts*, since the system would be capable of adaptation. This is the opposite view of the bureaucratic view, which is totalitarian, the whole determining the parts, exclusively, the opposite being quite impossible.

THE ESTABLISHED COUNTER-SOCIETY

The critique of the 'counter-society' – the opposition parties, the unions – which has become no less *established* than society itself, is one of the principal ideas, both at the level of theory and at the level of action, common to all three of the tendencies with which we are concerned here. There is no longer any need to emphasize its importance, in view of the virulence of the attacks launched against it in May (it gave rise to a mass of slogans, from the famous 'Crapules staliniennes' ('filthy Stalinists') to 'Élections, pièges à cons' ('elections are traps for idiots') and 'Les syndicats sont des bordels' ('the unions are brothels')), and of the fact that a good half of the post-May activist literature is devoted to the denunciation of what it is agreed to call 'the successive acts of treason perpetuated by the bureaucratic organizations' (D. and G. Cohn-Bendit, to go no further, devote most of their book (1968) to these organizations).

As I said at the beginning of this chapter, the first real attack on the traditional forms of politicization and unionism in the student world was launched in Strasbourg in 1966. Against the background of a critique of ideology and bureaucracy, we see the emergence for the first time of an attack on the 'spectacle' that the political life of our societies would seem to represent.

Perhaps at this point we should define this notion of spectacle, which is the peculiar invention of the Situationists and which was widely adopted later. According to the definitions provided by Guy Debord:

> The entire life of societies in which modern conditions of production reign appears as an immense accumulation of *spectacles*. Everything that was experienced directly has been distanced in a representation (1967, Chapter 1, p. 9, thesis 1).

The 'completed separation', the title of this chapter, is the remoteness of real, profound life, in particular political life – a false, superficial reality – a mere image that has become an end in itself. This, in a way, is the argument, in its extreme form, which serves as a basis for all criticism of bureaucracy as an alienated phenomenon in relation to the ends for which it was created and in relation to the objectives expressed in the system of ideas and values proclaimed in ideology. Debord, however, goes further than this traditional argument:

> The specialization of the images is to be found again, in a perfected form, in the world of the automatized image, in which the liar has lied to himself. Spectacle in general, as the concrete inversion of life, is the autonomous movement of the non-living (thesis 2).[1]

What is being criticized, then, is not only the content of the images – that is, the justificatory ideology of an established society – which is still relatively traditional, but the very fact implied in the existence of images:

> Spectacle is not a collection of images, but a social relation between people, mediated through images (thesis 4).

Such a notion is to be found, in M 22 and among the young anarchists, in the constant use of the idea of *récupération* (absorption). The latter say:

> A distinction must be made between, on the one hand, what we think and do, and on the other, *what the bourgeoisie does with what we think*, the way in which the bourgeoisie has an interest in presenting our ethic and our acts of contestation. The bourgeoisie wants to turn our action into merchandise[2] in order to kill it, to turn us into mere reflections. We are reduced to the state of *images* so that we can be absorbed the more easily. But we have learnt to smash the presses.[3]

We see the reappearance, in the idea of the printing press (a few lines later castration is mentioned), of the reference to physical mutilation, which is reminiscent, in another context, of the phrase 'crushing of people' used by the philosophy student (ND) in our earlier interview. Whether in relation to daily life, work, or political activity, there is an almost obsessional idea of the powerlessness of man, perpetually

---

[1] One of the most widespread slogans in May – it would be quite useless to attempt to locate its origin – was: 'Culture is the inversion of life.'

[2] A reference to the many different books and films, before and after May, in which anarchism is presented as rather 'trendy'.

[3] 'Les Idées de l'anarchie étudiante', an interview that appeared in *Magazine littéraire*, No. 19, p. 26. This article contains some interesting information on the juncture between anarchism and Marxism, from a 'modern' point of view:

> In 1917 the Marxist response was the Bolshevik Party, but we are no longer in 1917 . . . and Marxism itself shows us that a group structure is no longer valid an hour after its creation. A truth at moment X in history is no longer true at moment Y (p. 27).

As we shall see later it is Leninism, and Leninism only, that is in dispute here.

manipulated, in this case by the mass media, through images. In so far as these images are mirrors, society 'reflects' only what suits it of the action of the 'opposition' when this opposition is not itself 'the mirror of the bourgeoisie' in power, as is, according to these same young anarchists, the Communist Party.

It is interesting to note here that a large number of books and articles, written both before and after May, refer to McLuhan, or express ideas very similar to his. The article quoted shows the importance of this influence, though it is far from being as crucial as that of Marcuse in his treatment of the same type of phenomena.

How can one smash the mirror? How, in other words, can one avoid absorption? The activists of M 22, reviving an argument that was used notably in relation to Surrealism, which has long been recognized, one might say, by 'official culture', declare:

> We know that there is no gesture so radical that ideology will not try to absorb it. Culture is formed by absorbing revolutionary creativity and using it as a justification of the order for which it tries to gain acceptance. The contestation of culture must be done in such a way that culture cannot absorb the contestation and use it as a new form for its lies.
>
> All cultural contents[1] may be absorbed by the established order. What cannot be absorbed is the violence with which they are expressed . . . Violence cannot be absorbed by the established order because violence is the negation of order.[2]

This leads quite naturally to the criticism of all established opposition, whether party or union (or, in France, of all attitudes labelled vaguely 'Leftist'), not only in the *rejection of all ideology* – which is seen, again, as images – or of *bureaucracy*, that is, of the alienation of an organization from its original aims, but also in the means used (parliamentarianism, isolated wage demands), and in the non-recourse to violence. For a party to be revolutionary – the word 'revolution' appears in the constitutions of several French political parties – is a contradiction in so far as it is recognized by the established order, by the very fact that it is legal, and is therefore compromised, above all when it seems to be playing according to the rules, accepting the *status quo*, even when it claims to be pur-

---

[1] Obviously used here in the broadest sense of the products of any creative activity, including the political.
[2] *Bulletin du Mouvement du 22 Mars*, quoted in *Au joli Mai*, No. 1, p. 48. N.B. The phrase 'there is no gesture so radical that ideology will not try to absorb it' is taken from a cartoon made in 1967 by R. Vaneigem (text) and A. Bertrand (illustrations). Later, I shall come back both to the technique of the Situationist 'comic strips' and to the widespread practice, in M 22 and among the young anarchists, of using quotations without any indication of their origin.

suing objectives fundamentally different from the objectives of that order. It becomes in turn an institution, a constituent part of the state, an *established* force.

In simpler terms, one might say that the unions, whether of students or workers, like the political parties, are conceived at best as ineffective organizations that give the broad mass at the base the illusion of being able to express itself (preferably, the members would be allowed to discuss decisions, but their opinions would not be taken seriously at the top), which really gives them a unique integrating role. This, according to the Situationists, is particularly clear in the case of the students:

> The student (more than other social categories) is content to be politicized. Only he is unaware that he is participating in the modern world through the same *spectacle* (*De la misère en milieu étudiant* . . ., p. 11).

Whereas the unions and the parties should work for the emancipation of the working class, they have become

> mere regulators of the system, the property of leaders who work for their own emancipation and find a status within the ruling class of a society that they never think of challenging (ibid., p. 25).

This criticism of the pseudo-revolutionary opposition extends, as far as those inspired by Marxist–Leninism are concerned, to a general accusation of the bureaucratic nature of certain present-day established forms of socialism:

> Where they have been able to seize power – in the most backward countries, such as Russia – it was only to reproduce the Stalinist model of counter-revolutionary totalitarianism. Elsewhere, they are the static and necessary complement to the self-regulation of bureaucratized capitalism (ibid.).

Although they often place themselves on the plane of the *actor* and not on that of *systems*, the Situationists, for example, also end up speaking of individuals as mere toys – which does not, however, bring them any closer to other 'bureaucratic' views of reality, in so far as they formulate those views in order to criticize them. It is true that an ambiguity remains. In according so much importance to the homeostatic abilities of the systems that almost always succeed in 'absorbing' opposition, is one not over-estimating their coherence? But the 'situation' has often been presented in this way:

> A universally dominant social model, which tends to totalitarian self-regulation, is only apparently combated by false contestations that are permanently

played out on its own terrain, illusions, which, on the contrary, reinforce that model (ibid., p. 26).

This is so, then, on the one hand, because the self-regulation of a fairly flexible and omnipresent system reintegrates the traditional forms of action, thus rendering the unions and parties inoperant, and because, on the other hand, these forms of action themselves express this system.[1]

The criticism, in other words, goes well beyond the rejection of an ideology and a bureaucratic organization that have become alienated from the primary aim of the masses at the base. It attributes to the unions and parties a role, conscious or indirect, of domestication:

> In modern capitalist society, the unions are neither a degenerate working-class organization, nor a revolutionary organization betrayed by their bureaucratized leaders, but a mechanism for integrating the proletariat into the system of exploitation (Viénet, 1968, p. 151).

Although the criticism of bureaucracy bears, as it traditionally does, more on the organization's interest in its own survival and its own functioning, at the national level, it does not spare the small, student, political groups, the *groupuscules*, to use the pejorative terminology – a term, however, that has been taken up, despite its originally sarcastic use at the hands of their opponents, and adopted by the groups themselves.[2]

In fact, one should not exaggerate the cohesion of the student movement, which was united only on the major issues and especially during the 'ascendant' period of the events. Indeed, even during the first few days of May, divergences appeared, as, for example, when the FER (Fédération des Étudiants Révolutionnaires), a Trotskyist movement, refused to participate in the first 'night of the barricades'. Even though, for example, M 22 shared a number of activities with UNEF,[3] its leading spirits always remained highly critical of that organization, even in the midst of the action:

> UNEF is now nothing but a national committee with an apparatus, though it has acquired a real audience and could still build up its movement again. We have always criticized it for representing the bourgeoisie, for its demands

---

[1] 'The unions, the CP . . . play an objective role in reflecting and integrating into the system' (Mouvement du 22 Mars, 1968, p. 37).
[2] There was no loss of humour in May: the students readily adopted all the pejorative terms applied to them.
[3] Union Nationale des Étudiants de France, the largest student union, which is 'Leftist' only in the traditional terminology.

are conceived within a bourgeois framework, with no other aim than the adaptation of the students and of education to a system that remains capitalist.[1]

The smaller student political groups, which are generally orthodox Communist (Union des Étudiants Communistes) or Marxist–Leninist, were criticized both for their ideology, their reference to an existing model of socialist bureaucracy, and for their dogmatic, systematic character.

There is nothing paradoxical, for these small, radical opposition groups, in criticizing the already established character of certain other small groups, who are often close to themselves. For M 22, all 'terminological peculiarities . . . that serve as rigid, unchanging perceptions of reality, and as a means of distinguishing one group from another and not as an instrument of scientific analysis'[2] should be open to question.

In other words, their desire to create a stable identity, rather than a desire to act on established society in a way that is adapted to the transformations of that society, would explain how these methods of analysis become a means of establishing the group, an end in themselves, and, finally, the identity itself.

One can see in this reasoning, as also in several other arguments noted above, this desire to return to the sources – the fundamental directions, the social objectives to be pursued. This search characterized many discussions in May and went side by side with a great aversion to all the traditional methods of organization, which were regarded as necessarily vitiated. This, too, is an important feature of the image of society as the established counter-society.

Apart from these considerations of bureaucratic alienation, criticism is directed more fundamentally, not against Marxism itself, but rather against the Marxist–Leninist conception of the seizure of power, of the transition to socialist society. For M 22, if not for the Situationists, and certainly for the anarchists, any idea of a revolutionary vanguard is to be

---

[1] D. Cohn-Bendit and J.-P. Duteuil, in Bourges (1968, p. 61). This interview took place at the end of May, that is, in the middle of the crisis.

[2] *Bulletin du Mouvement du 22 Mars*, quoted in Zegel (1968, p. 29). One might note that this sentence was quoted in full and with no reference to its origin by D. and G. Cohn-Bendit (1968) and in the anarchist–communist review *Noir et Rouge*, No. 72, p. 11. As I have already remarked, one finds a great many such quotations, without reference to their authors, in the writings of these movements. The Situationists have even erected this practice into a principle – their pamphlets, reviews, and other writings may be 'freely reproduced, translated or adapted, even without reference to their origin'. Apart from a simple desire to aid the spread of their ideas, there is here a more general clue to a new conception of culture. Thus the authors of the manifesto *Nous sommes en marche* (Censier Action Committee) recommend their readers to correct it and to become authors themselves.

rejected; any organization, defined in the abstract, is suspected of re-creating its own hierarchical structure on the old model and of repro-ducing that model in its activity. Thus the revolutionary movement can tolerate neither prophets nor guides. Prophets, because

> even the best-intentioned denunciator will himself reintroduce authority into relations and in turn be denounced. Only action can settle, as was done in the past, this kind of problem ... It is always the masses in action who forge their educators, who educate those who organize their own history and not the contrary (Mouvement du 22 Mars, 1968, p. 56).

Guides, because 'the power instinct' drives them to 'restore the authority relations of the condemned social order' (ibid.).

Not only, and contrary to what the Trotskyists, in particular, believe, should there be no vanguard, and therefore no *a priori* knowledge to impart to, let alone impose on, the people, but, even in the course of action, there should be no separation between the mass and the instigators of the movement. This conception explains, for example, the importance attached to the problem of information: those who possess it must not try to build up a position of strength, therefore an elite position, by abusing the privilege of knowledge. The idea that it is not good to tell the people the whole truth is dangerous; it provides a justification for holding back information and spreading political cynicism; everyone must be capable of understanding and interpreting:

> In a few weeks of struggle certain members have become veritable refrigera-tors: all the information they collect – this activity occupies their whole day – disappears. They store it away like hoarders in the economic crises of the past, in order to exchange it for the tyrannical pleasure of exercising power ... They take pleasure in their comrades' thirst for knowledge, in their anxiety at being deprived of that knowledge. And they distribute this knowledge drop by drop, playing with others' desire.[1]

These characteristics, which are typically anarchist, will necessarily be linked with what I shall say of these groups' methods of action.

Apart from a desire to act as instigators, the Situationists, who have a more rigid conception of revolutionary organization than M 22 and the young anarchists, have also condemned *a priori* solutions based on ideo-logy, particularly centralist notions. In their pamphlet *De la misère en milieu étudiant* ... they attack 'revolutionarist' ideology and the inability to understand the problems of the modern world, attributable mainly to

[1] *Tribune du 22 Mars*, 18 June 1968, quoted in Mouvement du 22 Mars (1968, p. 54).

the 'Stalino-Trotskyists', while at the same time keeping their distance from 'semi-libertarian and non-directive organization [which] threatens at any moment to fall into the ideology of "group dynamics" or into the closed world of the sect'.[1]

THE CONSUMPTION OF SOCIETY

The term 'consumer society', which was also at the centre of many of the discussions in May, can be reversed: to say that men are reduced to the state of consumers in neo-capitalist society amounts to presenting them as mere 'objects'. They consume passively. Carried to its conclusion, the idea can mean that they consume present-day society, rather than attempt – or are able to attempt as subjects – to build or at least to form or de-form that society.

Contrary to certain puritanical views, consumption is obviously more than the satisfaction of pleasure, or even enjoyment. It is the function of the 'article of consumption' that is being denatured: 'Consumer goods tend to have no practical value. Their nature is to be consumable at all costs' (Vaneigem, 1968, p. 68). The same notion reappears in a *Bulletin du Mouvement du 22 Mars*: 'The articles produced no longer have any practical value, but only a commercial value.'[2]

The subject of commercial advertising, and the attitudes it implies, or even exposes only too visibly, is a favourite target of the criticism of present-day society, especially in relation to the pseudo-freedom that consists in being able constantly to consume a great deal of a great variety of things, the consuming act of 'conspicuous consumption' having become more important than the practical use of the bought article, or even the pleasure of living without buying.

One of the most frequently repeated slogans in May was that our world, in exchange for the guarantee of not dying of hunger, offers only the prospect of dying of boredom (the words are Vaneigem's). Not only does the emphasis on quantity – society of abundance – imply a lowering of the quality of the articles, but also a lowering of the quality of con-sumption, of the pleasure taken in it. The notion of passivity, linked with that of quantity, is still implied here, since the consumption of quality demands a greater degree of active behaviour.

[1] Op. cit., pp. 20–24. This is not the place to enter the labyrinth of subtleties to be found in the criticism or representations of the micro-political world of the small groups, vital as these subtleties obviously are for that world.
[2] Quoted in *Au joli Mai*, No. 1, p. 46.

This area of critical concerns in May certainly belongs to an old discipline, known in Germany, for example, as *Kulturkritik*. The essence of this criticism, it seems to me, is contained in the slogan 'Plutôt la vie': a return to a sort of spontaneist, vitalist fundamentalism. This is not the myth of the 'noble savage', but the fact of speaking about and later of practising the 'savage' life.

The juncture between politics and culture, parallel with what has already been said of the student and the university, finds its meaning here: the *superficial* and *passive* character of consumption particularly strikes the critical imagination of intellectuals in relation to cultural 'goods'.

Vaneigem – who occupies a key position as important as that of McLuhan and less well known than that of Marcuse, who has often been presented as the pope of the cultural criticism carried out in May, whereas in fact he was practically unknown to the students and to the French public – has written a book which, at the level of literary production, is itself a prototype of 'imaginaction', of action through an imaginative criticism directed towards a 'depassment' that seems practicable. In any case, reading probably played only a very minor role. These authors are more in the nature of precursors of what many students discovered directly, without their help; on the other hand, they do enable us to present the problems that they themselves, like the students, identified, each in his own way.

One of the main points that recurs in most of the arguments concerning both the 'cultural' and the 'political' is not unconnected with this insistence on the imagination and on 'depassment', since it concerns the notion of 'absorption'. This is obviously also linked with the conception of a revolution of society, depending on culture, in the sense of creativity, non-passivity. If consumed culture does not produce radical change, it is because it is no more alive than the society in which it is produced. We saw above by what process, according to M 22, society could break any form of cultural contestation by absorbing it into its own system of cultural values. The aim of this absorption is always the 'general organization' of passivity. The desire for accelerating change in cultural 'fashions' serves, as Vaneigem says, as an antidote to the desire for change:

> What the producers of happenings, Pop Art, and sociodramas are now doing is concealing passivity by renewing the forms of spectacle participation and the variety of the stereotypes (Vaneigem, 1968, p. 132).

As we have seen, the analyses always seek to combine theoretical renewal with the need for fundamental transformation. In this respect, they are opposed to what an ex-member of the CGT has called the 'voluntarist subjectivism' of that organization, a principle according to which a *theory*, valid for all time, must *determine* the action – voluntary, that is enunciated by the members of a party, or at least by their leaders – by inspiring and guiding the 'movements of a mass' that would of itself be incapable of recognizing the content of an analysis, and thus of producing this action.[1]

But, as we shall see later, this does not prevent the new methods of action imagined by a certain number of intellectuals and students from being, in a sense, a new form of voluntarism, based on a representation that wishes to be more aware, more objective, regarding present-day reality.

MANIPULATION BY NORMS

Another general feature that we should now add to our sketch of established society, as seen by the groups with which we are concerned, is the fragile character of the present social equilibrium. The leaders, that is, in fact, the owning class or its allies, are constantly obliged to correct the partial disturbances to the equilibrium, to repress threats, to adjust the methods of domination. I shall quote here a passage from a particularly interesting Situationist text, which brings together the whole series of problems that constantly crop up around the themes of change, structures, and absorption:

A class riven by contradictions, the bourgeoisie bases its domination on the transformation of the world, but refuses to transform itself. It is a movement that wishes to escape from movement. In the unitary regime, the image of the immutable contained movement. In the compartmented regime, the movement will strive to reproduce the immutable . . . The bourgeoisie in power tolerates only empty, abstract change, cut off from the whole. It's a partial change and a compartmented change. But the habit of change is subversive in its very principle. For change is the imperative that dominates the consumer society (Vaneigem, 1968, p. 151).

[1] A. Barjonet, a specialist in economic questions at the Centre d'Études Économiques et Sociales of the CGT, resigned on 23 May 1968, explaining his disagreement with the views of French Communist economists who 'neglect in fact the scientific analysis of the concrete facts' (Barjonet, 1968a, p. 17) and reveal 'a complete lack of interest in the structural changes that are taking place in society in general and in the working class in particular, paying scant attention to the discoveries that are transforming the productive forces, and through them, the whole mode of production' (Barjonet, 1968b, p. 103).

This play on the different meanings of 'movement' is not without purpose: it is both the movement of a class that has a policy and pursues it, despite its heterogeneity, and movement in the sense of change – the class that refuses to transform itself being a pastmaster in adaptation to changes, which it manages to digest, as it were, to get absorbed by the 'system' in which it manages to maintain its dominant position. Here, therefore, it is the general dimension and appreciation of change that are central.

To express the dual character of subtle adaptation to change and maintenance of the essentials of the system, René Lourau, an assistant lecturer in sociology at Nanterre, used (in an article published one year before May) the term inspired by Surrealist ideas of 'soft cement' (*ciment mou*). Of a certain technocratic attitude towards change, he writes:

> It is enough to inject some solid cement into the foundations of present-day society, while arranging, as often as circumstances allow, a certain tension, articulation, and flexibility, for society as a whole to have the illusion of change, even of revolution (Lourau, 1967, p. 70).

This is what he calls the 'soft cement strategy'.

Whether the managers are possessors of capital or possessors of knowledge – like technocrats who base their power on the 'capital of knowhow' – these structures seem both immutable and changing. The link between the structure's ability to adapt and its ability to maintain itself can be seen in the notion of compartmentalization. The desire to adapt is motivated by the need for the system to obtain the participation of the wage-earners.

> In view of the level reached by the concentration of capital, its degree of rationalization and automation, the society of exploitation finds it difficult to function without the participation of the workers. Decisions are taken at such a high level, and work is so compartmented, that the immediate producer cannot grasp the meaning of directives that are worked out without consulting him and without reference to the modalities of their practical application; in short, he no longer understands the meaning of his work. So he tends to detach himself completely from it, whereas the actual structure of the enterprise (the distance between managers and managed) requires the executant to 'participate' if the system worked out by the managers is to function properly.[1]

[1] *Noir et Rouge* (Cahiers d'études anarchistes-communistes), No. 72, p. 25. (Special issue: 'La Grève généralisée en France, mai–juin 1968'.)

When the role of that ever-increasing body of intermediaries, the 'middle managers' (*cadres*), is discussed, it is not for any share they may have in decision-making, but because they are seen as 'collaborators' of the bosses (or, to give the provocative term used so readily by the students, as 'watchdogs' of capitalism).

Those other intermediaries, the unions, are also seen as allies of the system, whether they like it or not. We have seen the kind of criticism that has been levelled at the union bureaucracy, but an obviously anti-state tendency emerges more particularly from the analyses of the young anarchists. In one of their pamphlets, we read:

> Capital will integrate the labour movement into its system or it will perish. This necessary participation, for Capital, of the workers in their own exploitation is achieved, of course, through the integration of the unions in the state machine, thus turning them into mere consultative bodies, concerned with the application by the masses of the directives of neo-capitalism . . . The class struggle then becomes, as Aron would say, a mere stimulus enabling the capitalist economy to rationalize itself.[1]

Once again we have here the idea of the fragility of the system ('it will perish'), the need for participation, and the criticism of state-technocratic solutions, as opposed to those that mark only the technocratic aspects within the great industrial organizations.

Although it is true that the view of society as a whole remains dichotomic – those with power and those without – the notion of coercion was extended a good deal in May. Many written analyses and many discussions still refer, of course, to capitalism with the knife between its teeth, its violent, subjugating methods being readily illustrated in sackings, the presence of private police in the factories, etc.[2] But the originality of certain analyses – examples will be found particularly among those groups with which we are dealing in this chapter – lies in the extension of this 'violence' to any kind of management, even in a subtle form, as long as the *norms* have not been chosen explicitly and with full awareness of the consequences by the mass of workers. The managers are now trying to encourage, if not to create, *adhesion*:

> The more the imperatives of consumption dominate the imperatives of production, the more government by constraint is replaced by government by seduction (Vaneigem, 1968, p. 169).

[1] *Perspectives anarchistes–communistes*, 'Bulletin de recherche sur l'autogestion', p. 9 (1968).
[2] These subjects provide the main material of *Action*, a magazine founded in May by UNEF, the action committees, and SNEsup (Syndicat national de l'enseignement supérieur, the university teachers' union).

Like the accusations rejected by the students in such slogans as 'Your order is disorder', those directed against acts of violence are rejected by reference to concealed 'violence' (which it would be more accurate to call *manipulation*, a successful attempt to make B, without knowing it, do what A forces him to do, knowing that he must conceal his real intentions).

The emphasis on the possibilities to be found in consciousness is linked with the notion of subjection to a system of norms, or rather to the interiorization of the norms on which the system is at present increasingly based.

> If economic laws appear to become natural laws, of a particular kind, it is because their power rests entirely on the lack of consciousness of those who take part in them (*De la misère en milieu étudiant* . . ., p. 30).

> The bourgeoisie inculcates ideas into the young, then it can do what it likes with them. It is much more effective to convince people that it is wrong to oppose one's boss than to use the police to defend the boss (G. Cohn-Bendit, 1968, p. 19).

The attack on the use of the fabricated consensus extends from the representation of a fundamental manipulation by the 'managers' to that of auto-manipulation.

> Cultural ideology, in economic society . . . is to convince people of the moral legitimacy of the work to which they have been destined . . . whether it is the Christian ideology, with the value it places on the most humble tasks, or the Stakhanovist ideology, with its heroes of voluntary work, or that of the 'great society' everywhere, the role of ideology is the same: to lie about the nature of work in order to make it more acceptable.[1]

> The last chance of the leaders is to make everyone the *organizer* of his own passivity (Vaneigem, 1968, p. 98).

In this context, too, the phenomenon of consciousness is frequently emphasized. The supposed solidity of the structures is seen, at least at local level – one thinks of both the factories and the universities – as an illusion:

> The power of a dean is typical of the auto-power of a bureaucratic organization. If recognized, it is all-powerful; if ignored, it is powerless to act (D. and G. Cohn-Bendit, 1968, p. 133).

This idea, which was first applied by the students, became widespread in May: similar arguments appeared, notably during the strikes by *cadres*,

[1] *Bulletin du Mouvement du 22 Mars*, quoted in *Au joli Mai*, No. 1, p. 46.

engineers, or technicians, about their own position in relation to the power of the bosses, which depended entirely on the importance, even the legitimacy, that was attributed to it.

This interiorization of the norms (similarly, the term 'interiorization of repression' has often been used)[1] extends well beyond the power relations in the factories and universities. Some people affirmed this before May, others discovered it during the events:

> Morally, the alienation is such that even when the Odéon [the theatre] had been opened [that is occupied], the workers stayed outside; the most interesting meetings took place in the square in front of the theatre and not inside. There were lots of people who wouldn't have dared to go in, because there remained the moral respect for the institution that was still there (Mouvement du 22 Mars, 1968, p. 64).

In certain of these arguments – and this was also true of the public discussions – we see the reappearance, then, of an identification of the system of industrial and social norms with the idea of 'culture' – common enough in the social sciences, but nowhere to be found in the traditions of the oppositional thought of the French Left.

THE FUNDAMENTAL CRITICISM

It goes without saying that in the image of a total society that emerges from the few features I have noted – which, of course, are far from doing justice to the diversity to be found both in the writings and in the brainstorming feats of public oratory – is already implicit to a considerable degree the need for a revolution, as *total* as society itself.

> The subjection and enslavement of wage-earners, especially those of an ideological, and therefore interiorized kind, must be neither condemned, which serves no purpose, nor deplored, which engenders a moralizing attitude, nor accepted, which leads to inaction, but combated by conscious, active minorities, adapting strategy to the attempts of the system to extend its domination to all aspects of daily life (D. and G. Cohn-Bendit, 1968, p. 121).

I shall not spend time on the traditional argument: all reforms are always absorbed, hence the need for a radical, total overthrow, which alone would deserve the appellation revolutionary. All the 'Leftist' groups would accept this, though not all would mean the same thing by it. The formulation one meets more especially in the groups with which I am

[1] A very common wall slogan said: 'Kill the *flic* who slumbers within you.'

dealing here is often more radical still. It is concerned with 'civilization' and 'culture', and really functions at an anthropological level.

> It is the whole civilization that is in question, for when such an obvious gap appears between, on the one hand, the mechanisms of organization in general, which overwhelms us with the frantic increase in consumption that is turning us into pleasure-loving animals, and, on the other, the participation of our consciousness, our initiative, our will, everything on which our dignity is based, the imbalance can only throw us towards a new form of the general disappearance of what constitutes our humanity.[1]

It is not difficult to find, in such publications as *Arcane* (the organ of the Jeunesse Anarchiste Communiste, which is intended for, and written principally by, students in lycées), radical demands like the following:

> Criticism, then, will be total and erected into an ideology that is autonomous of the criticized, by the really concrete root provided for the criticizing material [sic] by the *praxis*. A methodology is therefore the immediate corollary of this process of thought. In order to avoid falling into partial contestations, and therefore of being revolutionary only in form, the total criticism must accept this methodology just as it accepts a problematic. The incoherence of the criticism is the basis of the coherence of the repression.[2]

This type of demand, with its 'scientist' jargon, contains, in addition to a desire for a criticism that would be uncontaminated by existing society – that would be something more than its negation, its inversion – a search for theoretical coherence that is fairly rare among practising anarchists. It should be noted that the *Arcane* group is close to the Situationists, who share this approach.

I will now quote from another article in the same publication (it is worth observing that, at least until May, the young anarchists did not express themselves in writing as readily as the other groups) that throws a little light on the adjective 'revolutionary' in relation to everyday, cultural life:

> If the infrastructure can be changed only by collective revolutionary action, the superstructure can be changed only by individual revolutionary action. In the immense stupidity brought about by the system of survival,[3] individuals

---

[1] *Cahiers de l'humanisme libertaire* (monthly review of sociological studies), May–June 1968, p. 5, which, as is apparent in the passage, is representative not of the movement of 'young anarchists', but rather of an old, orthodox anarchist tendency.
[2] *Arcane*, No. 2, p. 12 (Summer 1968 – this duplicated magazine appears irregularly and undated).
[3] In the Situationist vocabulary: 'Survival is life, reduced to economic imperatives. Survival today, then, is life reduced to the consumable' (Vaneigem, 1968, p. 161).

identify the act of consciousness, the revolutionary struggle, with the subjective act of creativity . . . (*Arcane*, No. 3, p. 7).

Lastly, let us remember that 'unitary criticism' and 'total overthrow of perspectives', which are also Situationist terms, always recur – total as this criticism is in relation to civilization, history,[1] or culture, in the sense of superstructure – at the level of daily life, that is, of the individual, and not in considerations of new 'systems' that would replace the established systems. This is the fundamental aim that should be adopted by revolutionary organizations:

> Such an organization presents a unitary criticism of the world or is nothing. By unitary criticism, we mean an overall criticism, directed against every geographical zone where the various socio-economic forms of separate power have been established, and also against every aspect of life.[2]

Scepticism with regard to systems links up, of course, with the general theme of anti-bureaucracy. Before turning to the methods of action – a field in which the innovations seem more marked than in the particular subtleties to be found in the preceding analyses – let us recall a sentence from the author I have already quoted so much, a sentence that was transformed from a text published by a traditional publisher into a slogan that appeared on innumerable walls and was widely discussed:

> Those who speak of revolution and class struggles without referring explicitly to daily life, without understanding the subversive element in sex and the positive element in the rejection of constraints, have a corpse in their mouths (Vaneigem, 1968, p. 19).

COUNTER-MANIPULATION: DISTORTION[3]

Before examining the methods of action proper by which the groups with which we are concerned intend to bring about this total revolution – methods that are fairly original, but occupy an important place in the abundant literature about May, at least in that produced by the students, whose reluctance to represent either present-day or future society is well known – I should like first to describe one of the characteristic practices that appeared before, during, and above all after, the events, namely, *distortion*.

---

[1] 'Our last chance to unmake history . . .' (Vaneigem, 1968, p. 95).
[2] Minimum definition of revolutionary organizations, 7th Conference of the Situationist International, quoted in *Revue de l'Internationale situationniste*, No. 11, p. 54.
[3] *Détournement*: another key term. No English word is an exact equivalent. The idea is of turning something away from its true or original purpose. (Translator's note.)

Distortion, which was adopted and widely used first by the Situationists – especially, though not exclusively, in strip cartoons – consists in adding to a drawing, for example, certain words or phrases that distort the original meaning. Strategically placed, often simple elements, a few words, part of another cartoon, etc., may, according to the psychological laws of total perception, redefine the original meaning. The effect is further enhanced by the presence of a certain amount of black humour that both amuses and shocks the reader. The added elements express the thought of the counter-manipulators not only through the words used – a slogan, a highly philosophico-political sentence – but also through the subtle interaction between the sentence, often chosen to contrast heavily with the original, and the supposedly alienated perception of the usual reader of the cartoon.[1] In the most interesting, average case, there are four characters, then: the reader, who is used to the original; the propa- gandist manipulator, who urges the reader to believe, for example, in the advertising for a product, or an idea; the counter-manipulator, who has produced the distorting collage; and, lastly, in a more abstract way, the corrected version that is presented to the reader, which incorporates the struggle between the meaning of the original and the disturbing element that remodels it.

The two basic laws of distortion, according to the Situationists, are the loss of importance, to the extent of losing its original meaning, of each distorted autonomous element; and, at the same time, the organization of another totality of meaning that confers on each element its new significance.[2]

At first sight, this method might appear as an attempt to undermine certain values through ridicule. But it often involves more than that. In fact, it may alter the overall meaning of a *totality* of elements, even though it sometimes concerns only certain of the elements (for example: the model posing in an advertisement may not personally be included in the criticism directed at the economic system that uses advertising).

In so far as an addition alters the overall meaning of the whole, the elements previously present are in a way 'absorbed', even though trans- formed.

[1] An example of these two aspects is to be found in a distorted cartoon by H. Tonka, entitled 'Fiction of alienated contestation' (published in June 1968), which, in advance, ironically describes the situation after May and the forms that the absorption of the revolution would take. The author puts into the mouth of an American policeman (p. 2), obviously cut out of some detective-story comic strip, the words: 'The dialectical totality of the "critical" university has found a new structure that our structuralists were unaware of.'
[2] G. Debord, *Revue de l'Internationale situationniste*, No. 3.

Distortion is a game based on the ability to devalue. Everything in the cultural past must be 'reinvested' or disappear.[1]

It is probably no accident that it was Jorn, the painter, a member of the COBRA group and one of the founders of the Situationist International, who provided this definition. Collage techniques, whereby existing elements are used and transformed by their new context, are well known in the plastic arts. They do not necessarily involve material destruction, but the restructuring of the meaning, the re-use of what exists.

A certain ambiguity may remain, depending on the individual case, and it may strengthen or weaken the impact of the technique.

There is a specific power in distortion, which is obviously due to the enrichment of most of the terms by the coexistence within them of their old and new meanings – their dual basis.[2]

If the new meaning dominates or at least disturbs the meaning usually perceived by the reader of the original, the desired aim is achieved. It may involve a sudden awareness, an invitation to reflection, to doubt, or at least to participation in the game that will produce a certain detachment from the thing criticized.

The use of images involving an element of sexual attraction as contexts for 'critical' or merely polemical slogans is only one 'distortion' of advertising techniques, in the service of a view of society that actually abhors advertising as a vain and dangerous spectacle.

When the new meaning is in competition with original elements of a more or less agreeable kind – apart from the manipulation of them – there may be ambiguity: the new and old meanings can, at most, coexist.

This practicable and cheap technique of counter-manipulation is all the more effective in that it is placed in the context of an event, a production, etc., that already possess an audience.[3] Although certain student activists, in M 22 and among the young anarchists, were aware both of Situationist theory and of the methods of the SDS, it is permissible to think that the blossoming of the practice of distorting posters and of the use of slogan words taken from the enemy can be explained as much by a logic inherent in such widely known manipulations as advertising as by mere imitation.

[1] A. Jorn, quoted by Vaneigem, 1968, p. 276.
[2] G. Debord, quoted in Brau (1968, pp. 83–84).
[3] One might say, for example, that the students of the SDS practically distorted the reception of the Shah of Persia in Berlin, in order to present before public opinion positions to which public opinion would not otherwise have given much attention.

The playful attitude implied by the method – especially in a culture like that of France, in which there is a very widespread use of puns – would seem to produce a detachment not only from what is being criticized, but even from the content of the criticism and from the critic himself.

> In short, distortion is the most elementary expression of creativity. Subjective fantasy distorts the world. People distort, like M. Jourdain speaking prose and James Joyce writing *Ulysses*; that is, spontaneously, or with considerable reflection . . . Distortion popularizes another use, it invents a higher use in which subjectivity will manipulate to its own advantage what is sold to be manipulated against it (Vaneigem, 1968, pp. 276 and 277).

This play of redefinition and reflection on the potential diversity of interpretations of reality would seem, in fact, to provide promising material for disalienation, to be rich in representations of the future and generally liberating.

Naturally, as became apparent in May, this form of counter-manipulation is itself open to the same technique. A number of posters produced by the students were distorted, by the addition of corrections (playing on the fear of disorder, of totalitarianism, etc.) or of symbols of the enemy (the Gaullist cross of Lorraine after the slogan 'We shall overcome . . .'). The continued practice of distortion by the students, after May, as it can be seen in particular on advertisements in *métro* stations, shows that it is an especially practicable method for the opposition in periods when the established order is dominant.[1]

But there have been cases of striking workers spontaneously using distortion techniques, like the workers of a large heavy lorry plant who rearranged the letters of the firm's name, 'BERLIET', into 'LIBERTÉ'.

In its most ambitious sense, however, distortion can go further. As understood by Vaneigem, it can be said that it goes as far as the 'overthrow of attitudes' that revolution must be. In the following chapter, I shall examine this idea, which belonged initially to the Situationists and which was popularized in May by the wall writings: to change life is to change its *mode d'emploi*, the way it is used.

The politico-cultural tendency that I have described up to now in terms of its image of established society agrees on the need to prevent a new society from becoming established. A new established system, of whatever kind, would in fact force 'men-objects' to adapt to it. In so far

---

[1] The Situationists themselves recognize the limitations of distortion: 'This type of uncoordinated action cannot achieve lasting changes, but can usefully accentuate the sudden awareness that will come about' (Viénet, 1967, p. 33).

as distortion paves the way for what might be called a 'retortion' (*retournement*, a turning round, or turning back) – man beginning to demand existence as a subject, in a society that would adapt to him and not the contrary – this method has more far-reaching implications.

CHAPTER 6

The Non-established Society

In speaking of May, the separation of the action itself and its aims is, of course, a dubious one. It is precisely such a distinction that is being challenged – as I stated in the formulation of the problem – when the representation of the society of the future is contained, more than ever, in the conception of the processes that must lead to the establishment of that society. Though, of course, the term 'establishment' is an inadequate one – as is the very idea of an *a priori* representation – since permanent change was one of the principal axioms of that 'imaginaction', the contraction that I am proposing for what were undoubtedly the two key words of May, 'imagination' and 'action'. 'My knowledge of the world', writes Vaneigem (1968, p. 98), 'exists validly only in the moment when I am transforming it.' Although it was not formulated so clearly by those who put it into practice, this conviction, it seems to me, was nevertheless one of the bases of the May Movement: it is in the moment, in action, that the imagination functioned most authentically.

Indeed, in the tendency with which we are dealing here, there is an avowed wish to be free from the taint of the messianic spirit. The revolution is not conceived as an event that will bear fruit in twenty or a hundred years' time, but at once: this is the theme expressed by the anarchists of the Living Theatre group in the title of one of their productions, *Paradise now*, which was performed at Avignon in the summer of 1968. Cohn-Bendit is in agreement with the Situationists on this when he states forcefully and ironically that 'sacrifice is counter-revolutionary and is the result of a Stalino–Judaeo–Christian humanism'. 'Not *for* others, but with others,' he says in conclusion, 'you make the revolution for yourself, here and now' (D. and G. Cohn-Bendit, 1968, pp. 130 and 270).

Here we have another basic conviction of this tendency, a conviction diametrically opposed to the ultimately authoritarian attitude of those

160

who hope to change man by a new *system*: it is man, who, by becoming himself again, will create the system in which he wishes to live.

If I am keeping until the end of this chapter the few most general key ideas, it is in the interests of clarity. As we shall see, they are few in number and somewhat diffuse, which is understandable in the context of conceptions concerned above all with man, rather than with a system, and intended to define a field of action that is as open as possible. I shall now examine the *methods* of action, which constitute a whole battery of weapons in the hands of a new opposition that intends to preside over the *transition* from the *old* to the *new* society.

I have no wish here to go into the origins of this imaginaction, but I should like to mention a few of the characteristics of two forms of revolt against society that have caught the attention of the Situationists and the Movement of 22 March: the *blousons noirs*[1] and the Provos, whose methods foreshadowed, to a certain extent, those used in May.[2] As Cohn-Bendit notes, the *blousons noirs* reflected

> not the eternal revolt of youth, but a new youth of revolt, expressed by the young because they felt most acutely the profound crisis of modern society. They are perfect products of that society and hesitate between two possibilities, that of integrating themselves in it totally and unreservedly, and that of rejecting it totally and violently (D. and G. Cohn-Bendit, 1968, p. 26).

> At the simplest level, the *blousons noirs*, in every country, express most violently the refusal to conform (*De la misère en milieu étudiant . . .*, p. 17).

But this refusal has its limits. The revolt of the *blousons noirs* leads rapidly to nihilism, 'because it offers no way out (*perspective de dépassement*)' (D. and G. Cohn-Bendit, 1968). They reject normal integration, that is, work, but they 'accept the goods' created for them, in order to absorb them (*De la misère en milieu étudiant . . .*). They come together, in their subculture, in conditions of misery that 'inevitably recreate hierarchy in the gang' (ibid.).

The views of the Situationists on the Provos are more positive, up to a certain point. On the one hand, they admit that the Provos have invented 'a new type of contestation', and thus created the possibility of a new 'way out' (*dépassement*) of the present situation. On the other hand,

---

[1] Literally 'black jackets', from the black leather jackets that are (were?) the most distinctive part of their uniform. They correspond, roughly, to what were known in Britain as 'Rockers'. (Translator's note.)

[2] Any attempt to deal with the origins of all these movements would obviously have to be concerned with student action in the United States, Japan, Germany, Italy, etc.

however, they criticize them for having stopped short on their way. To what they stigmatize as 'the last reformism produced by capitalism – that of daily life' (ibid., p. 18), they oppose the need for a revolution on that level, which implies that it is not enough that a group should isolate itself and lead a subculture life under the protection of the dominant society. It is obvious that parallels could be drawn here with the 'hippies'.

> In order to provide themselves with a base, their leaders have invented the ridiculous ideology of provotariat . . . which, according to them, is intended to oppose the supposed passivity and *embourgeoisement* of the proletariat, a custard-tart in the faces of all the cretins of the century (ibid., p. 18).

We get a glimpse here of the problem raised earlier (in the course of our group discussion) of the relation between this form of revolt and 'the motive force of capitalist society' – the working class, 'its mortal danger' (ibid.).

THE 'UNBLOCKING' OF PASSIVITY

The idea of student provocation is usually placed at the beginning of a whole process, the first step in an escalation – a well-known spiral – also called 'the vicious circle of provocation-repression'. Thereafter, nothing is said about the circumstances that explain why such a process is set in motion. It should first be said that the initial acts of violence that call for repression are already seen as *responses* to equally 'violent' constraints. Exteriorized, visible violence is provoked, the provocation being the violence of a repressive situation, a less visible, but no less real, form of constraint. To avoid verbal confusion here, this form of 'violence' might be called 'potential violence'.

Let us go back to the situation in the university – and to the analysis of the interiorization of norms, which would explain the usual passivity of students.

> To speak of repression in the case of an institution possessing no 'physical' repressive power, such as a university, may seem paradoxical. This repression is part of the very functioning of the institution, its structure, which makes the student passive, because he interiorizes its norms and requirements . . . This passivity kills all real desire and all creative spirit, the expressions of a non-alienated life. In such a case, provocation will be aimed at revealing everything that is sacrificed, or postponed, during the period of studies (D. and G. Cohn-Bendit, 1968, p. 57).

In the initial acts of violence, the aim, therefore, is not only to lead the mass in a movement of solidarity, but to encourage the development of creative activity and to reveal the repressive character of the system in which one usually has to live. This second aspect is one of the axes around which action is imagined.

As the action of a small body of agitators showed at Nanterre, the process may be initiated by a minority.

> The actions carried out accelerated a crisis of awareness in some people: it was not so much 'provocation' as an attempt to force the latent authoritarianism to come out into the open . . . by showing the true face of the 'dialogues' proposed (*Noir et Rouge*, No. 72, p. 11).

This activity should replace – and one remembers the criticisms directed at an ideology that can remain at the level of mere verbal expression – ineffectual discussion:

> We have explained our views on the meaning of provocation, which is aimed only at revealing, in practice, the true nature of Power, not merely by theoretical analysis and criticism, which power accepts (D. and G. Cohn-Bendit, 1968, p. 182).

Thus, for M 22, the entry of the police on the university premises at Nanterre proved the accusation that the Dean was in collusion with the police: 'Things became clear, concrete, instead of remaining at the level of verbal affirmations' (Mouvement du 22 Mars, 1968, p. 14).

In other words, action becomes effective at the level of the extension of self-awareness and of the demonstration that will lead to its own development.

This mode of action was developed beyond these first attempts and became the main tool of the May Movement, at least at the beginning. In the terminology mentioned earlier, it has been given the name of *exemplary action.*

> The exemplary action consists, instead of intervening in an overall way, in acting in a much more concentrated way on exemplary objectives, on a few key objectives that will play a determining role in the continuation of the struggle.[1]

Whereas methods of this type, identified with M 22, have been criticized by other student groups,[2] or by outsiders, as an activism that compensates

---

[1] *Tribune du 22 Mars*, quoted in *Partisans*, No. 42, p. 218.
[2] For example, by the Jeunesse Communiste Révolutionnaire (JCR), some of whose members,

for an absence of theory, and as leading to incoherent action, its advocates, on the other hand, declare that the non-programmed character of this activity was inevitable and, moreover, that it definitely did lead to a common end.

> The Movement of 22 March has no political programme, no political blue-print for the future; it has only, over the next three or four days, a certain grip, an analysis of what is happening and work directly linked to this analysis for next week, in very concrete situations . . . before, things weren't ar-ranged even from one day to the next, we just did things, without any pre-meditation whatsoever, we discussed, there was a certain prevailing atmo-sphere, then we acted, and that's all there was to it (Mouvement du 22 Mars, 1968, p. 70).

The reply to the above criticisms is that, for the small groups in question, coherence and order, that is, organization, would be only a substitute intended to fill 'the absence of real concrete action' (*Partisans*, No. 42, p. 217).

Moving from the idea of 'unblocking' (*déblocage*) passivity to that of 'unlocking' (*déverrouillage*), these actions are intended to make explicit the pseudo-legal character of the juridical rules or norms – which are seen as ideological – that usually hold back the initiative of the opposition.

We must, say the activists of M 22, smash 'a lock that is recognized tacitly, not a legal lock' (Mouvement du 22 Mars, 1968, p. 60). In addition to its revelatory character, the exemplary action, from the beginning, has a dynamic role. It makes possible both 'the uncovering of, the search for situations during which the repressive *cadres* will act as such' (*Analyses et Documents*, No. 155, p. 25), and the transformation of the 'relation of forces in a concrete case, on a precise point', which is seen 'as a funda-mental, irreversible change' (Mouvement du 22 Mars, 1968, p. 61). There then takes place an 'opening on the unknown, which, at that moment, becomes transmissible' (ibid.), which must encourage the pursuit and extension of action.

Thus, on the afterwards famous date of 22 March 1968, the *concrete object* was the seizure of the Senate Council Chamber at Nanterre, which was situated at the top of a tall building that dominated the campus and

---

however, claim to have been 'co-founders' of the Movement. Of M 22, D. Bensaïd and H. Weber write:

> Feeling that all political debate is a threat to its survival, it has kept activism, by a process of elimination, as the only common denominator of the heterogeneous individuals that compose it, and the theoretical basis of this activism, the cult of spontaneity, as its ideology (Bensaïd and Weber, 1968, p. 221).

which, according to Épistémon, the students themselves called 'an intolerable phallic symbol of the authority that oppresses us' (Épistémon, 1968, p. 48). And it is probably no accident, apart from the image suggested by the shape of the building in question, that a vocabulary of a psychoanalytical type is, *as seems to have been the case throughout May*, so often resorted to.[1]

This same author, who is a professor of social psychology at Nanterre, continues:

At the time of this occupation of the administrative buildings, there took place a double psychological phenomenon that can astonish only those who are unaware of the *power of symbols* in collective enterprises. The university authorities, paralysed by the dispossession of the symbol of their power, decided, in collaboration with the Prefecture of Police, to postpone until 2.30 a.m. the intervention of the police and the evacuation of the tower block. Meanwhile, the members of the four small political groups, who, until then, had been in opposition to each other, about eighty individuals in all, underwent a mutation of attitudes in this place that incarnated the supreme power of the professors. In occupying their physical place, they also assumed their symbolic role (Épistémon, 1968, p. 48).

This notion of *symbolism* seems to have remained present in many minds during May, at least during the period when the events were building up to a climax. In the eyes of many observers, the occupation of the Sorbonne played, on a larger scale, the same role as a symbolic object. To express this phenomenon, the sociologist Edgar Morin uses the term 'Sorbonne-Potemkin' (1968a, p. 22), and R. Viénet speaks of the Sorbonne as 'a lighthouse for workers throughout the country' (1968, p. 74).

Among other things, the action appears therefore to have been at the same time a sort of cathartic act, an object of projection – as I shall show later, when I sketch again the modal form of the prototype of action-image – and a meeting-place, outside doctrinal dissensions and differences of interest, that made possible the fusion between various political tendencies. These aspects are obviously difficult to separate concretely, just as the stimulation of consciousness and the dynamization of action through

---

[1] If a juncture exists between Marxism and anarchism, politics and culture, one might also add – with as much justification, especially in the case of M 22 – the idea of a juncture between Marxism and psychoanalysis. Thus Wilhelm Reich, who was little known in France, was rediscovered, first by the Situationists, who quote him frequently, then by a wider student public. Lectures were arranged at Nanterre about his work, and, from 1967 onwards, a pamphlet reproducing one of his manifestos on 'sexual chaos' circulated at the Cité Universitaire.

action, which involves a whole apprenticeship for those who act, whether they are the 'base' and must therefore express themselves, or the 'leaders', who must feel, in a way, what must be allowed or encouraged to emerge.

> Apprenticeship in action is a phenomenon of primary importance for the analysis and continuation of the Movement. We must stop ourselves taking only the apparent and circumstantial in our reconstruction of social reality. The complexity of life and survival in modern society, the problems they present, and the frustrations they arouse, relegate to a secondary place the profound aspirations that are expressed only in periods of crisis and total break (D. and G. Cohn-Bendit, 1968, p. 62).

This passage would explain the rejection of ideology and *a priori* programmes. Such programmes are thought to be based on a superficial view of needs, the real needs usually being repressed and finding expression only in 'exceptional' periods; the criticism that is often levelled at the type of action that tries to grasp these needs in the course of the action itself during such periods falls wide of the mark: if action is in advance of theory, this is no disadvantage, on the contrary, according to M 22, it is one of the reasons for the vitality and legitimacy of the Movement, whose strength is a result of 'the proliferation of tendencies and the advance of practice over theory'.[1]

Another, no less important, aspect of the exemplary action, according to its defenders, is its role in the stage-by-stage *extension of the struggle*: one moves from one initial objective in the action to a higher level. This is one of the aspects to be found in the interview with ND (reproduced above): from a protest against the incarceration of fellow-students, the demonstrators moved on, as they passed the prison, to the idea of freeing all the prisoners.

> If one were to give a perfectly concrete definition of the exemplary action, at the level of an act, and not in terms of a situation, there would be a danger of creating a mythology out of certain actions (Mouvement du 22 Mars, 1968, p. 68).

Action should therefore be regarded as exemplary only after the event, which distinguishes it from the slogan (ibid., p. 69). Thus, according to M 22, the first barricades were exemplary: they were built, not for their defensive effectiveness, which was fairly low, but as 'a collective action in which everyone worked and gave proof of extraordinary imagination' (ibid., p. 68). Subsequent actions were less exemplary, or not at all, since,

[1] *Bulletin du Mouvement du 22 Mars*, quoted in Zegel (1968, p. 30).

once it had been proved that it was possible to erect barricades in the streets, they were no more than 'defensive instruments in the hands of the demonstrators against police charges and not offensive instruments for destroying the bourgeois state' (ibid.).

'Every conquest must be usable, must become a springboard for later action . . .' (ibid., p. 54). The imagination displayed during the first barricades was therefore interesting in so far as it revealed the strength of the demonstrators both to themselves and to society, and in so far as it led to a 'depassment'.

> Our action is linked to a concrete analysis of the situation that makes possible a 'depassment' of the action in the very course of its development.[1]

If there is a deepening of the action of the students themselves, there is also a 'depassment' in the sense of an extension of the struggle to other social categories, which then organize themselves according to the same process. Extension, then *coordination*: it goes without saying that one might discuss here the traditional problem of the 'only valid form of organization' that the anarchists recognize. Speaking of the various actions of workers during the strikes (the typographers' censorship or refusal to print newspapers that they regarded as too pro-government or too right-wing; the organization of food supplies for the strikers by agricultural workers, etc.), some anarchist-communists wrote:

> Thus the extent and severity of the strike, which disorganized the capitalist economy on which we all live, forced certain workers to organize, out of solidarity, on different bases. In doing so, one saw that they attacked: the press, as it exists at present, that is, controlled by the ruling class; the organization of the factories, carried out by members of the ruling class; the distribution of foodstuffs, which is distorted in the interests of the ruling class (*Noir et Rouge*, Supplement 1 to No. 41, p. 3).

The phenomenon of the depassment from one level (*palier*) of society to another – to borrow an expression from G. Gurvitch – and from one social category to another, deepening and extending, may be linked together:

> This phenomenon of depassment, from mere occupation of the factory to an organization of the economic life beginning with the base, is self-management (ibid.).

One would thus arrive, without having imposed anything, but suggested at most, at the *final stage* of the Movement. The following passage

[1] 'Les Idées de l'anarchie étudiante'. Interview in *Magazine littéraire*, No. 19, p. 27.

also reminds one that the absence of doctrine would have the advantage of changes of direction on course, which, difficult, if not impossible, to impose as a basis of action, would impose themselves, by a process of radicalization, as it developed:

> There has always been a gap, in the working-class struggle, between the vigour of the action and the initial demands. But sometimes the success of the action, the dynamism of the Movement may alter, on the way, the nature of the demands. A strike that begins with a partial conquest in view may be transformed into an insurrectional movement.[1]

Lastly, it should be repeated that this process originates in *self-awareness* on the part of the participants and then becomes a phenomenon of *apprenticeship*:

> Through these discussions and actions, the Movement becomes aware that its aspirations lead to a radical contestation of society.[2]

> Speech having been suddenly freed in Paris, people must first of all express themselves. People say confused, vague, often uninteresting things, because they have been said over and over again, but this enables them, after saying all these things, to ask themselves the question: 'So what?' (D. Cohn-Bendit, op. cit.).

The public discussions, then, especially those at the Sorbonne, provided an opportunity for the population to become aware of the problems raised, whereas the 'exemplary actions' provided a didactic spectacle of a less direct kind. For M 22, all action should be directed towards this end if it is to avoid becoming mere *repetition*, which is regarded as a retreat because it blunts the dynamic of this growing awareness. For example, D. Cohn-Bendit explains that the Movement was stopped on the night of 24 May by the disciplinary bodies of UNEF and the PSU (Parti Socialiste Unifié), which prevented the seizure of the Ministries of Finance and Justice, and by the leaders of the JCR, who demanded a withdrawal of the demonstration to the Latin Quarter, 'whereas we had at last broken the mythical attraction of the Sorbonne':

> For us, the seizure of the Ministries and public buildings had as its aim not to install in power the representatives of the working class by taking over the state apparatus, but to arouse, in the whole population, an awareness of the fact that this state apparatus no longer counted for anything, that it no longer

---

[1] D. Cohn-Bendit, interview with J.-P. Sartre, in *Le Nouvel Observateur*, 20 May 1968.
[2] Tract du comité d'action du VIᵉ arrondissement (Mouvement du 22 Mars).

had any power, and that from now on everything had to be reconstructed on new bases (D. and G. Cohn-Bendit, 1968, p. 75).

The most enthusiastic adherents of this view speak of the greater deepening and extension of awareness and imagination:

> It was the workers, at the base, who, responding to the deficiencies of their organizations, took decisions, and it was the first time such a thing occurred in France. For a time, the working class rediscovered its own thought, and even, in some cases, practised its own modes of struggle.[1]

And it should be said that these deficiencies, which have been pointed out so often, in the established organizations of the opposition – as, indeed, of the intellectuals – are not regarded, according to this view of things, as disadvantages; quite the contrary:

> There is no other revolutionary truth but that of the masses, even if a handful of political thinkers may work out a correct revolutionary line for the entire proletariat . . . It cannot be authentically revolutionary, for it is received passively by the masses and does not correspond to an effective act of consciousness on the part of those masses . . . Consciousness cannot be attained for others.[2]

But this consciousness, as we shall see, is not in contradiction with an action initiated by a minority: on the contrary, it would be a result of observing and understanding that action:

> . . . The action of the masses is always in advance of the consciousness they have of that action, and . . . the role of the revolutionary organization is primarily to place itself ahead of that action and to provoke it, and, secondarily, to make the masses conscious of their action (*Arcane*, No. 3, p. 11).

INVITATION TO THE FESTIVITIES

For the groups we are considering here, to place oneself ahead of the action of the masses does not mean playing the traditional role of revolutionary vanguard, in the generally accepted sense, contrary to what a good many other small groups seem to think (one of which, the JCR, called its newspaper precisely *La Nouvelle Avant-garde*). This new or revised version of the role of minorities is defined, principally by the Movement of 22 March, in the phrase: initiate, not direct.

[1] 'Les Idées de l'anarchie étudiante'. Interview in *Magazine littéraire*, No. 19, p. 28.
[2] *Perspectives anarchistes–communistes*, 'Bulletin de recherche sur l'autogestion', p. 5 (published in Summer 1968; written, according to the authors, before May).

We must abandon the theory of the 'directing vanguard' in favour of the much simpler and much more honest one of the active minority that plays the role of a *permanent agitator*, urging the rest to act without claiming to direct them.[1]

The anarchist groups also oppose what they call the Jacobin–Leninist tradition of 'a minority organized like an army and destined to seize power'. They contrast this with

> a minority that provokes events and leaves the masses to take them from there. Its purpose is not to impose its authority on society, but to enable it to move (G. Cohn-Bendit, 1968, p. 18).

The direction to be followed will emerge of itself from the action of the masses, as the masses begin to act in an autonomous manner:

> Our aim is to help, from our position within the Movement, to push events down their natural slope (*Noir et Rouge*, No. 72, p. 33).

Lastly, the notion of 'scuttling' – which is to be found in all three movements – is the culmination of this reasoning: the initial minority must fade away, leave the stage as soon as the play has really got under way. The Situationists seem to have carried this logic furthest; for them, their organization 'played a definite role as a detonator' in only one field: 'that of a centre of total criticism' (Brau, 1968, p. 165). Once the process had begun, its members continued to act only as individuals, for example in the 'Committee of Occupation of the Sorbonne' and the 'Council for the Maintenance of Occupations'. Others saw a need for the minority to merge with the mass as soon as possible:

> The minority is the first stage; then, a depassment takes place and the minority is drowned in the Movement. It must disappear in the mass and be reconstituted according to new modes of contestation.[2]

The absence of a directing role implies, for a minority, that it will confine itself to producing an analysis – a developing one, of course – of the situation, in order to learn the true objectives of the Movement as a whole, and of the group itself:

> We really derive our teaching from the experience of others and from what we experience ourselves (G. Cohn-Bendit, 1968, p. 19).

[1] D. Cohn-Bendit, *Le Nouvel Observateur*, 20 May 1968.
[2] 'Les Idées de l'anarchie étudiante', *Magazine littéraire*, No. 19, p. 28. One sees here also the anarchist idea (or practice) of the permanent minority.

This merging into the mass of the people seems all the more natural in that one of the major themes in the thinking of these groups is the fusion of the various aspects of life, which is expressed notably in the term 'decompartmentalization' (*décloisonnement*). This may be understood in the sense of 'dehierarchization':

> The pyramid had melted like a sugar loaf in the May sunshine. People talked to each other, they understood one another at once. There were no more intellectuals, no more workers, only revolutionaries discussing everywhere, generalizing a communication from which only 'proletarianist' intellectuals, or other would-be organizers, felt excluded. In this context, the word 'comrade' found its true meaning once again, it really marked the end of all separation between people (Viénet, 1968, p. 136).

Thus the problem of the fusion with the working class is resolved very simply, not by identification with the worker – as in the 'proletarianism' of certain groups[1] – but by the disappearance of barriers on all sides:

> The division between 'vanguard' and 'mass' . . . can lead only to a new division in society. The answer is formulated only in the struggle of the wage-earners. It is not conscious and formulated as a demand: it is action itself (D. and G. Cohn-Bendit, 1968, p. 115).

These views of action and of relations with the masses are naturally applied, or, at least, professed, within the minority groups themselves. This brings us back to the notion of 'scuttling' mentioned above, which is a central theme of every anti-authoritarian view:

> Every temporary leadership (or leadership that sets out by declaring itself to be temporary) can have no other aim than lasting as long as possible (*Arcane*, No. 2, p. 16).

The phrase made fashionable by D. Cohn-Bendit – 'I'm only a loudspeaker', not a leader – is merely an expression of this traditional anarchist theme.

> It's not the leaders who make history. They are leaders because they express at a particular moment what the group wants. Otherwise, they dominate.

---

[1] This 'proletarianism' is denounced even by organizations as far removed from the anarchist tendency as the JCR as:

> the abdication of the student Movement before the archetypal proletarian, each worker being regarded as the individual bearer of class consciousness. This reasoning has its slogan, 'serve the people', and its logic: it was by being faithful to it that the UJCml (Union des Jeunesses Communistes Marxistes-Léninistes – the Maoists) denounced the Movement of 22 March in one of their pamphlets as 'a 100 per cent reactionary movement' (Bensaïd and Weber, 1968, p. 92).

It's the truth of the moment that creates the leaders of the moment (G. Cohn-Bendit, 1968, p. 19).

This obviously presupposes a permanent adjustment of reflection and action. True anarchism is 'to question, and to question oneself' (*Noir et Rouge*, No. 41–42, p. 2).

Again, it is a question of practising in the group, at the level of action, the principles one defends on a broader level, that of society itself. One must smash the attitude implanted in everyone of submission to and respect for authority:

> If you lead people, they place faith in you. This corrupts you. If you say or do something good, then people lean on you and say, 'He's okay – he'll do' . . . What we propose is very difficult for people to understand. They think that someone somewhere makes decisions on their behalf, someone leads them, and they also firmly believe that there has to be a central structure of authority. Our problem is to prove they are wrong. There does not have to be an order as we know it now.[1]

In the expression that is now commonly used (as in the interview with ND, for example), the revolutionary organization must refrain from 'shooting its line' (*vendre sa salade*):

> The revolutionary movement of the future must abolish, within itself, everything that tends to reproduce the alienated products of the mercantile system . . . Such an organization must put before everything else the radical criticism of everything on which the society it is combating is based, namely: mercantile production, ideology under all its disguises, the state and the divisions that it imposes (*De la misère en milieu étudiant* . . ., pp. 27–28).

This refusal to fall, in one way or another, into acceptance of authority or systems in which decision-making is monopolized, centralized, is paralleled, of course, by the search for solutions involving self-government. Far from envisaging the end of all organization, the advocates of such positions believe in the ability of the masses to organize themselves. The organization of the Soviets in 1905, the Kronstadt Commune, the Spanish experiments in libertarianism (Catalonia 1936–37, etc.), the growth of self-management in Algerian agriculture, are some of the examples cited to support their case.

A policy of aggressive intolerance of the traditional workers' and students' 'organizations' is a natural accompaniment to this view. Thus,

---

[1] Interview with D. Cohn-Bendit, *Sunday Times*, 16 June 1968, reproduced in Labro (1968, pp. 35–36). One of the May slogans said: 'You demand self-management? Start with self-ownership.'

in May, activists of M 22 tried to break up the processions organized by the National Union of Students in order to let the demonstrations organize themselves and not simply follow the directives of the students' disciplinary body. Carried to its logical conclusion, this reasoning amounts to an apologia of disorder as the only condition that will enable each individual to express his own creative possibilities:

> We must avoid creating an organization and defining a programme straight away, which would have an inevitably paralysing effect. The Movement's only chance lies in just that disorder that allows people to speak freely and that can lead to a certain form of self-organization.[1]

We see here the reappearance of that fundamental belief in the virtues of 'festivity', in which, once all authoritarian pressures have been removed, everyone rediscovers a sort of *joie de vivre* that has been lost in both individual and community life.

The most superficial observer could hardly fail to see in May, in the Sorbonne and even in the streets, not exactly a festive spirit – the expression most commonly used, but more suited perhaps to the annual festivities of certain political parties – but rather an atmosphere of joy, of liberation, of creative research, that was both serious and relaxed. Rather than any political motives, it is this character of explosive exteriorization, which often assumed incongruous forms, even 'indecent' ones for anyone who was too much an outsider, that explains a good many of the hostile opinions about the Movement. In fact, the critical vocabulary included in particular terms like 'happening', 'letting go', 'showing off', etc.[2]

So great was the desire for self-expression that some of the assemblies, in particular the one in the Odéon theatre, were in session night and day, and some of the participants had to be given injections of sedatives so that they would get a minimum of rest, while others insisted on continuing their discussions until they were mentally and emotionally exhausted. Very soon, slogans appeared on the walls, declaring: 'Comrades, five hours' sleep out of twenty-four are indispensable: we're depending on you for the revolution.'[3]

---

[1] D. Cohn-Bendit, *Le Nouvel Observateur*, 20 May 1968.

[2] Once 'order' had been restored, these opinions could be expressed freely. In his book on the incidents that disturbed the Avignon drama festival in the summer of 1968, J.-J. Lebel has collected some of the terms used against the actors of the Living Theatre and the 'contesters' in general: 'Freudians' (a local deputy), 'beggars, filthy ragamuffins of all kinds, villains of every hue and uncertain nationality, ill-fed gangs, chanting obscenities, beasts of both sexes . . .' (letter from a reader of the newspaper *Le Méridional*). Cf. Lebel (1968).

[3] Entrance of the Odéon. Another slogan demanded a reasonable limitation of the number of weekly barricades. Another said simply, 'Dream', though no doubt in a different sense.

One also found on the walls many of the expressions used before May by the Situationists to describe this state of festivity:

> Proletarian revolutions will be festivals or they will not be, for the life they herald will itself be created in festivity. Play is the ultimate rationality of this festival, living without boredom and enjoying without limitation are the only rules that will be recognized (*De la misère en milieu étudiant . . .*, p. 32).

But, according to R. Vaneigem, pleasure in itself is not the only rationality of this play. It is also indispensable in the process of deconditioning, 'depassing' inhibitions.

> The shock of freedom works miracles. Nothing can resist it, whether it is mental illness, remorse, guilt, the feeling of powerlessness, or the brutalization that is created by the state environment. When a water-pipe burst in Pavlov's laboratory, none of the dogs that survived the flood retained the least trace of its long conditioning (Vaneigem, 1968, pp. 281–282).[1]

This living 'utopia', experienced at first hand, would seem, then, to allow the effective realization of a life lived in accordance with one's deepest desires and, according to its advocates and practitioners, would be capable of resolving, through practice, the problem mentioned earlier (cf. the group discussion) of spontaneity. Contrary to what is said by the critics of these experiments, once individuals are freed, and join in this festivity, they are no longer alienated by norms foreign to themselves.[2] This can be explained not only by the fact that more authentic tendencies rise to the surface, but also by the fact that total alienation must bring about, in some way, an equally total disalienation.

> By fragmenting and multiplying the vexations, one will arrive sooner or later at the atom of unlivable reality, suddenly freeing a nuclear energy that one was no longer aware of beneath so much passivity and dreary resignation (Vaneigem, 1968, p. 30).

It should be noted here that many other commentaries on these phenomena of liberation make use of analogies and a vocabulary drawn from modern science.[3] The most frequently used image to describe the May Movement is undoubtedly that of an explosion.

---

[1] Épistémon (1968, p. 56) speaks of collective catharsis, and some specialists have said that they know cases of people whose psychological disturbances, introversion, shyness, etc., disappeared during May.

[2] Later we shall see how the 'spontaneists' replied, after May, to those who used the failure of the revolution as a refutation of these arguments.

[3] K. E. Boulding (1956) drew attention to the importance of scientific analogies – watch, thermostat, etc. – in representations of society.

The revolt was born spontaneously, by a chain reaction of students . . . and all great initiatives have a spontaneous origin (Morin, 1968a, p. 19).

When fragmented to extremity, refusal recreates, contradictorily, the conditions for a general refusal. How is the new revolutionary collectivity to be created? By a chain explosion from subjectivity to subjectivity (Vaneigem, 1968, p. 170).

Parallel with the arguments concerning 'order' – the students spoke of society in normal times in terms of 'established disorder' – a similar argument resolves the problem of the revolutionary cohesion of the masses: they are divided as soon as minorities take over the leadership, but remain united as long as they organize themselves in accordance with their own creativity. This creativity leads necessarily to the establishment of a consensus. The role of the organization is then only that of interpreter of spontaneity:

> Interpretation is certainly of a collective psychoanalytic type, that is, it brings about the emergence, the interpretation, of this or that schema, in the words of the workers, for example, the occupation of the factories (Mouvement du 22 Mars, 1968, p. 99).

The outburst of analysis, of 'wild sociology', gives young intellectuals, therefore, especially 'committed' sociologists, an opportunity of playing their proper social role.[1]

The festival, always an end *and* a means, encourages this creativity in a number of ways. Among the fashionable key words, the idea of the 'ludic' (from the Latin, *ludus*, a game) indicates that various combinations may be tried out and alternatives suggested, in a process of cross-fertilization. The game is already found at the level of the acceleration of the apprenticeship process, in a period of enthusiasm, as much in the personal activity of each participant as in the mutual help given by the different members of the group to each other (cf., for example, the passage in the interview with ND concerning the 'work' done in common during the night of the barricades) and in the invention of new methods of cooperation.[2]

---

[1] The blossoming of spontaneous sociologies of various types could be observed in many of the assemblies – I myself witnessed the same phenomenon among *cadres* in industry. In fact, a distinction should be made between 'spontaneous' sociology and 'wild' sociology, according to the latter a role not only as interpreter, but also as stimulator, as 'awakener by shock'. For a similar distinction – 'wild psychoanalysis' – cf. Épistémon (1968, pp. 34–35).
[2] I do not intend here to examine the notion of 'solidarity', one of the basic principles of all the anarchist tendencies.

Fourier remarked that it would take workmen several hours' work to build a barricade that the rioters erected in a few minutes. The disappearance of forced work coincided necessarily (in May) with the free course of creativity in every field: slogans, language, behaviour, tactics, combat techniques, agitation, songs, posters and strip cartoons (Viénet, 1968, p. 142).

To these examples should be added the solutions proposed, concerning, in particular, the conception of a new mode of the acquisition and transmission of knowledge.[1] It would be a mistake to think that these creative sessions were purely gratuitous and led nowhere. One finds, in the experiments in collective work – such as the conception and production of posters, which have since become widely known, in the studio of the École des Beaux-Arts – examples of activities of this kind that were successfully launched in May and continued later. Various groups of students also worked out a collective preparation for the examinations that some of them, after the electoral victory of the Gaullist regime, were forced into taking in the autumn.[2]

While speaking of these new means of action, we should not underestimate the importance of humour, which, in this period, constantly played a role as sacrilegious celebration and as a stimulation to awareness. At certain moments, too, it served simply as a psychological safety-valve. At the end of a session, after difficult or confused discussion, or simply in order to give free rein to an individual mood (impatience, irritation, fatigue . . .), the participants sometimes declared a period of 'nonsense' in which they would make incoherent speeches, imitate animal noises, etc. More generally, this humour was often the expression of a distance established between themselves and not only the social or intellectual positions they were criticizing – an attitude of desacralization[3] – but also the work they were doing – an attitude of preventive self-desacralization. There is no doubt, too, that in certain circumstances it expressed the nihilistic attitude of at least part of the audience.

The transition from the initial explosion, from the liberating shock, to the permanent festival, and, in short, to the self-management of life and

[1] The numerous theses – which are partly contradictory, and admitted to be such – formulated by the *Nous sommes en marche* group of the Action Committee of the Censier annexe of the Sorbonne are evidence of the extraordinary fertility of thought on this subject (cf. *Quelle Université? Quelle Société?* (1968), in which these texts were published).
[2] I know of the case of one professor who, no doubt to revenge himself for having been strongly criticized in May, increased the study programme to the maximum and so arranged the examination that questions had to be answered on the entire programme, which had not previously been the practice. The students countered this measure by dividing up the subjects to be studied and practising mutual teaching within the group.
[3] 'Le sacré, voilà l'ennemi' (The sacred, that is the enemy) – a slogan on the faculty walls at Nanterre.

work, presents no problems to those who hold the views outlined here. It takes place so quickly that during such a period of improvisation repressed desires rise to the surface and produce, as it were automatically, by simultaneous emergence, a natural reinvention – or rather, the *discovery* of what was only latent – of schemas of community life, such as self-management.

> It is the unconscious aspiration of the working class to become owners of the means of production (Mouvement du 22 Mars, 1968, p. 99).

> Only the current that carries off banalities is new (Vaneigem, 1968, p. 7).

These evident facts – or banalities – must therefore be imposed naturally as soon as other solutions and the weight of established structures can no longer be maintained by force. When the moment came, therefore, there would be nothing else to work out but methods by which the state and opposing organizations could be deprived of their strength.

THE APPROPRIATION OF POWER

The ideas examined here exclude, of course, any seizure of power on the basis of known models, even Bolshevik ones. Some observers have gone so far as to wonder whether this seizure of power was even considered in May. Could it be, then, that the forms assumed by so-called revolutionary activities are purely apolitical?

This is not the place to take up the discussion on the various connotations of the notion of 'politicization'. The method advocated by this current of thought is aimed not at the seizure of power (in the traditional sense, hence the accusation of apoliticism), but rather at the appropriation of power by the masses, that is, its restoration to those who should be its legitimate holders and from whom all so-called political power tries to withhold it. The positions of the three tendencies on the way in which the 'festival' and self-management should be lived are sufficient indication of how a new form of daily life, of working life, should be established. By extension, it might be said that the notion of 'dual power' that we are about to examine is just that, seen in the application of self-management to the whole of the old political and administrative organization.[1] From the initial contestation, one would pass to the

---

[1] It goes without saying that one finds no strategic theory of revolution, in the 'military' sense of the term, in the writings of these three groups. The need for arms, for a certain form of guerrilla activity, is not excluded of course. But such a possibility is seen rather as a means of defending positions acquired in the establishment of dual power than as an offensive means, in the sense of the armed conquest of the centres of power.

accepted collapse of the established structures, then to an absence of structures, that is, to a flexible process of self-management. A member of M 22 wrote:

> At the time, it seemed to me that we were intoxicated by a very schematic image of what the seizure of power could be, by confining it in fact to the seizure of central power (*Tribune du 22 Mars*, 21 June 1968).

This desire to free oneself from all pre-established theory, which we have already observed several times in relation to other subjects, is also to be found among the young anarchists:

> The Trotskyists have an *a priori* scenario: . . . they want to do a remake of the 1917 revolution instead of inventing forms of struggle that correspond to present-day needs. It's at the level of mental structure that they are not revolutionary. What they need is a good dose of Artaud.[1]

All the effort of analysis and imagination is directed on the seizure of the social nerve-centres rather than of the central power, by acting as if the institutionalized sources of power no longer existed. In the spring of 1968, this reasoning was facilitated, of course, by the fact that the various political bodies – the state or the parties – or private bodies – the bosses confronted by a large competent management – no longer seemed in fact to exercise real power. There, too, one finds the anarchists' idea, which was put into practice in May, that it is not the 'political' that counts but the 'social', that revolution occurs not at party level but in the organization of work, of the economy, hence their insistence on the importance of syndicalism and the criticism of apoliticism directed at them by the Communists.

> Only the organs of political life were ignored, as on the day when 40,000 students marched past the National Assembly, where the deputies were in session, without even giving them a hostile shout. The unions, the parties, all the organs that keep the workers in check were swept aside and emptied of all real power (*Noir et Rouge*, No. 72, p. 3).[2]

We find here the idea that all bureaucratized power is really no more than a self-power that is held up only by the submission of those who are dependent on it, who recognize it. The disdain with which it is

[1] 'Les Idées de l'anarchie étudiante', *Magazine littéraire*, No. 19, p. 29.
[2] Viénet (1968, p. 210) also notes this aspect of the Movement and observes that 'for the first time in France, the state was ignored'. He adds, however, that this was not enough to bring about its fall, in view of the lack of 'a sufficiently clear sense of direction'. We shall examine later the various explanations given by the movements in question for the relative failure of May.

treated soon leaves its mark on a public opinion that usually admires the powerful but soon becomes disillusioned when the powerful are shown to be incapable of reacting. And how can one react when one is not directly attacked?

This policy of 'dual power' can and must be applied to every sector of activity: 'critical' universities functioning as self-organizations, without any reference to established structures, factories functioning without management, possibly even without middle management (*cadres*), etc. The student press in May provided detailed descriptions of the direct distribution of food from the producers to the strikers through improvised but effective circuits, thus short-circuiting the usual commercial middlemen.

> It is this establishment of a dual power, which, in dismantling it, deprives the central power of its role as a repressive unifier, that seems to me to be the most important revolutionary task, rather than the drawing up of military plans for a general insurrection (*Tribune du 22 Mars*, 21 June 1968).

At this point I should like to make a brief parenthesis. Such a view of the seizure of power seems to exclude the use of violent methods to eliminate the old structures. But for the tendency described here violence is necessary at certain stages in the struggle. At the outset it is the indispensable means of revealing the latent violence through which all power is exercised. It is one of the factors in achieving awareness.

> During the moment of struggle, inherent in a revolutionary period, terrorism may be understood only as a means of propaganda through action. The implementation of a total criticism by the proletariat must be the logical result of the terrorist act (*Arcane*, No. 3, p. 3).

Thus, to quote only one example, the looting of department stores is advocated by the Situationists as a means of getting round the commercial system. At a higher level, violence is necessary not only for the attainment of awareness, but also as self-defence in the struggle against absorption:

> A lot of people believed that an economics of violence was possible, that is, that one could pass from the occupation of the factories as they are, to dual power, to direct self-management in the factories. It's not possible . . .

A certain degree of violence is inevitable if the old structures are to be smashed 'at the mental level as well as at the real social level in the factories, in production, and in society' (Mouvement du 22 Mars, 1968, p. 72).

From the establishment of workers' control in the factories, one would thus pass, by a process of extension, of *dépassement*, which, again, would give rise to self-awareness (the collapse of all structures), to the idea of the generalized self-management of society.

On 22 May 1968, the 'Council for the Maintenance of Occupations', which included some well-known Situationists, saw that it would soon have to get the railways and printing-works working again, and requisition and distribute food, etc., for the needs of the struggle, and concluded:

It is in such a practical process that a consciousness of the profound will of the proletariat can be felt, the class consciousness that seizes on history and realizes for all the workers the domination of every aspect of their own lives.[1]

The provocation of a political crisis and a crisis of consciousness, the occupation of certain key posts, the consolidation of the paralysis of the state by the spread of strikes: these three stages were achieved in May. The final stage, which begins with the restarting of the factories and ends with the normal functioning of the whole economy minus the usual bosses, began to become a reality in only a few very rare cases. The novelty of the method suggested, and partly put into practice, consisted not only in short-circuiting these bosses, but also in opposing those who may have tried to take their places:

In Eastern Europe, the bureaucracy of bourgeois power has been replaced by a bureaucracy of the Communist Party posing as the leader of the working class: the problem of power has not been solved, but shifted.[2]

This explains the distrust shown to all 'vanguards', since what was at issue was only the setting up of self-government by the 'base', direct democracy, in both the universities and the factories. What was needed, say the Situationists, was the revival of the slogan 'all power to the Soviets', 'but without the Bolsheviks' ulterior motives':

The proletariat can throw itself into the *game* of revolution only to gain a *whole* world, otherwise it is nothing. The only form of its power, *generalized self-management*, cannot be shared with any other forces. Because it is the objective dissolution of all power, it can tolerate no limitation . . . (*De la misère en milieu étudiant* . . ., p. 29).

It might be thought that this appropriation of power, made possible by its abdication, could be helped by the fact that society, through an

[1] Pamphlet reproduced by Viénet (1968, p. 281).
[2] O. Castro, an M 22 activist, in a discussion on Radio Luxembourg, 17 May 1968, quoted in Bourges (1968, p. 81).

evolution linked with progress, has shifted the key posts towards work requiring a *high degree of technical skill* – which explains the 'movement' among the technicians, which was so important in May. Of course, there is very little reference, in studies made prior to the crisis, to this erosion of the real power of the bosses occupying non-technical posts. The active participation of middle management in the strike – in some cases, it was they who initiated it – made it possible, in numerous discussions, to envisage the possibilities of self-management in France with considerable optimism, and later led certain groups to modify somewhat their contempt for the 'watchdogs of capitalism'. Some of these groups – particularly, as we shall see, M 22[1] – even go so far as to think that, in view of the increasing 'proletarianization' of those who were previously mere auxiliaries of the capitalist class, and, parallel with this, in view of their growing importance in the economy, the middle managers and technicians will in future play an indispensable role in the development of the May Movement.

Apart from this, did the failure of the Movement affect the convictions of those whose ideas I have tried to describe? From a reading of their reflections on the events, it would not appear so.[2] Some of them, of course, had their faith in the virtues of shock liberation, of instant deconditioning, somewhat shaken:

> This active strike failed not only because of repression , but also because of the interiorization of repression. Thus, when the workers were put into contact with the small agricultural producers, the workers had at their disposal lorries with full tanks that belonged to their bosses, and they daren't use them.[3]

Is the interiorization of repression, or simply the interiorization of norms, and particularly those concerning ownership – which, in 'leftist' thinking, amounts to the same thing – enough to explain the failure of the Movement? It is not my aim here to provide a precise estimate of the extent to which the appropriation of power was hampered by a lack of confidence in the solutions that had been proposed or were being worked out to take its place, or by pessimism as to the chances of success, or by a fear of 'repression' (sackings, demotions, etc.) in the event of failure. But it is obvious that such a problem exists.

---

[1] D. and G. Cohn-Bendit, too, have supported the view of J.-M. Coudray, who wrote (1968, p. 116): 'In May 1968, in France, the industrial proletariat was not the revolutionary vanguard, but the heavy rearguard.'
[2] However, one may discern in the thinking of some activists, who had been advocates of the theory of active minorities, a trend towards 'vanguardism'.
[3] 'Les Idées de l'anarchie étudiante', *Magazine littéraire*, No. 19, p. 29.

However, repression on the part of 'established society' is not the only cause postulated by the spokesmen quoted here. The failure of the last phase of the process described above is also attributed to union and political bureaucracy – the established counter-society – which was not entirely incapacitated, but, on the contrary, tried to take over the position of the authorities. This is an unacceptable solution, for

> Any attempt to interfere with the influence of the masses on the decision-making of the central organs of society will soon find expression in disagreements and conflicts between two tendencies: self-management tendencies in the 'base' cells and statist tendencies in the organs of central management, which in turn will give rise to a number of social conflicts and lead, in all probability, to the temporary victory of the statist faction over the self-management faction.[1]

If the Capital–State alliance finally won the day, the responsibility lies with the unions and the French Communist Party. The commentators are quite unambiguous on this point:

> If the contestatory Movement of May now seems to have ended in failure, this is ... above all because the unions, and particularly the CGT, have either long since given up the role that they should play, or have never played it (*Arcane*, No. 3, p. 4).

This widespread argument – and not only in the tendency we are studying here – is sometimes supplemented by a deeper explanation, which recalls the role of theory as being always in advance of the consciousness of the people:

> Far too few people possessed a coherent theory of revolution, and its communication to the masses had to overcome extremely unfavourable conditions: in addition, there was the spectacular power of the information media possessed by the existing order, the counter-revolutionary bureaucracies, which had been unmasked by far too few people (Viénet, 1968, p. 211).

Going beyond the simple affirmation of the repression exercised by the state and 'its objective allies', to borrow a phrase used by the French Communists in respect of the Leftists, then turned against the Communists by Leftists, some commentators have tried to study the mechanism of repression and its effects on the masses:

[1] D. Bilandzic, *Gestion de l'économie Yougoslave* (1967), quoted in *Perspectives anarchistes-communistes* (1968, pp. 30–31).

Kept in relative ignorance by the state and by the union bureaucrats, there is, among the mass of wage-earners, a feeling of powerlessness and incompetence that makes them accept the power hierarchy (D. and G. Cohn-Bendit, 1968, p. 125).

By pointing out a similarity of interest on the part of the present leaders of industry and those of the parties and unions to underestimate the abilities of the wage-earners and to make them believe this low judgement of them, this traditionally anarchist argument suggests not only that an unrecognized potential ability could be developed, but that, even at their present level, their abilities could be placed at the service of all. Ignorance of this potential, on the part of the interested parties themselves, could be attributed as much to the policy of the unions, which, implicitly or explicitly, present the situation as unchanging and unchangeable, as to the methods of integration practised by the employers.

Here, one might say, the wheel has come full circle: once triggered off by the students, the Movement spread into industry, through, initially, the young workers and technicians, before becoming general. Then, the falling off of active strikes prevented the general appropriation of power in industry and the country, when the impetus of the Movement came up against the imaginary walls built by established authority. It is now, therefore, up to the students, availing themselves of their 'knowledge', to intervene and break down, in both industry and society as a whole, the barrier erected by the carefully maintained confusion between knowledge and power, between purely technical needs and the essentially 'political' field, that is, the social relations that 'determine the conditions of production and the distribution of profits' (*Perspectives anarchistes–communistes*, 1968, p. 19).

> Since the students possess part of the knowledge that is dispensed to them as future leaders, and since they reject this status, they may effectively *distort* knowledge, that is, diffuse it by making it transparent . . . One must recognize to what extent workers are obsessed by and respectful of knowledge if one is to realize how necessary it is to demystify it (D. and G. Cohn-Bendit, 1968, p. 125).

THE PERMANENT UTOPIA

In the first two chapters of this book, we examined the image that the participants in the action made of the future of the Movement and of the possible transformation of society, and saw to what extent that image was an open one. Indeed, many of the participants insisted on the need 'to make people accept that you can oppose things without necessarily having ready-made solutions'.[1] This new state of mind was perhaps both the strength and the weakness of May. For those at the centre of the Movement, it represented an opening onto hitherto unknown possibilities. For those who remained outside, this opening became uncertainty, the 'fear of the void' that was expressed in the eternal question, 'But what are you going to put in its place?'

The tendency we are examining here, however, cannot be defined entirely in the negative, by its criticism of existing society. In the pamphlets published by the anarchist–Marxists, one finds, for example, detailed studies of present-day experiments in self-management and sustained thinking on what might be done in a country like France – a subject that has also been treated by the Situationists in their journal.

I shall not embark on a lengthy exposition of the arguments advanced in favour of self-management and of the refutation of the traditional criticisms of it.[2] The main points of this controversy are well known and of relatively long date, even if they have followed the development of the conditions of production. Self-management must be considered here above all, in the term often used by the Situationists, as a 'minimum definition' of the society of the future, as the basis of its development.

What form would this development take? As I have said already, the originality of this tendency is that the revolutionary process – though this term does not really fit the present view – is inseparable from the solution advocated. Thus a broad outline of that solution could be discerned in the modes of action practised in May. It would be preferable to replace the notion of the revolutionary process, which, because of historical associations, is too easily associated with the idea of the conquest of central power and the establishment of a new order, with that of *the establishment of permanent change*: in fact, it is on this central requirement, combined with more traditional elements that have long been associated with the anarchists, that the image of the new society is based.

In earlier pages (and in the conclusion of this chapter) it is easy to recognize a good many ideas that have been borrowed from various authors, past and present. A number of close comparisons could be made

[1] Cf. the interview with ND, Chapter 1.
[2] Nor shall I pay much attention to the often very 'literary' descriptions of the life of the society of the future given by certain representatives of this tendency; I shall confine myself here to providing a brief synthesis of the broad outlines of that society as seen by all three of the groups under examination.

between the tendency examined here and the works of such authors as Henri Lefebvre, Marshall McLuhan, or Herbert Marcuse, to mention only a few. I did not consider it useful, each time such a parallel could be drawn, to draw attention to the fact. There are two main reasons for this.

The first is that it seems to me that any 'thinker' could claim to have inspired a Movement like that of May. Whatever similarities can be found, and however striking they may be, it is my view that such descriptions before the event could only have been prefigurations and not influences in themselves.

The second reason is that, although one can certainly find, in the texts I have quoted from, a great many borrowings from parallel sources, these elements have been placed in a new context and have largely changed their meaning, just as each element in a collage loses its original meaning and finds another within the context of the whole work. It is this collage, this composite but new mode, that I wish to describe.

Self-management and permanent change, I have said, are the twin poles of the solution for the future that was both tried out in May – which is what E. Morin meant when he spoke of the living experience of a concrete utopia – and offered as the method of overthrowing established society and the means of preventing the establishment of a new repressive society, by a process of constant *dépassement*, a state of 'permanent utopia'.

An approximate and partial image of this solution might be provided by a description of the way of life practised by certain anarchist groups who attempt to reproduce on a smaller scale, in small sub-societies, the schema of social organization that they would like to see become general.[1] It seems that the groups with which we are dealing here have gone a long way towards putting their principles and theories into practice among their own members, though without having any illusions as to the possibilities, outside a revolutionary context, of extending these experiments by imitation. Some young activists wrote of the Living Theatre, for example:

> It's a floating island of anarchy. Until the basic structures of the capitalist economy are destroyed, the solutions advocated by such micro-societies can be only partial ones – nevertheless, they are exemplary ones, because they represent a break with the ideology of the ruling class.[2]

[1] Indeed, it is interesting to note that this type of experiment in communal living seems to be on the increase in Europe (the best-known examples being those in Berlin) and in America.
[2] 'Les Idées de l'anarchie étudiante', *Magazine littéraire*, No. 19, p. 26.

The spread of this type of organization in small, autonomous social units – the fragmentation of society being the remedy for the present fragmentation of the individual – is seen as the indispensable condition for the re-establishment of communication. The theme of decompartmentalization, which was an inexhaustible subject of discussion in May, is paralleled by the desire to reconstitute the 'total' man within these micro-societies. Sociological analyses of France have shown that bureaucratic forms of organization and the importance of hierarchization produce a separation of individuals, who do not communicate between groups of different status and even very little within the same group, in view of the division between the working life and the private life.[1] It is understandable that an anti-bureaucratic and anti-authoritarian tendency should place so much emphasis on the need for dehierarchization and decompartmentalization.

It is in this context that the idea of the abolition of the gap between intellectual and manual work, between management and labour, should be seen.[2] But this desire for recomposition extends much further, to every aspect of life; in particular, any separation of work and leisure should be abolished, since, ultimately, these terms would lose all meaning in a world based on creation. And since creation would no longer be separated from life,[3] the problem of 'culture' as a field reserved for 'artists' or 'cultured' amateurs would also be resolved. To regard work as a process involving at the same time imagination, decision, execution, and also interpretation – in order to give it its meaning within the social context – amounts to a realization of this general recomposition.

> Far from being 'utopian', the suppression of work is the primary condition of the effective *dépassement* of the mercantile society, of the abolition – in the daily life of each individual – of the separation between 'free time' and 'work time', the complementary sectors of an alienated life, in which the internal contradiction in goods between their use-value and their exchange-value is projected to infinity. And it is only beyond this opposition that men will be able to turn their life's work into an object of their will and consciousness, and to see themselves in a world that they themselves have created (*De la misère en milieu étudiant . . .*, pp. 30–31).

Only self-management, the government of workers' councils 'in which practical theory supervises itself and watches its action' (Debord, 1967,

---

[1] Cf. M. Crozier's study, *The bureaucratic phenomenon*.
[2] I am not excluding other modes of analysis, on the basis of class interest, for example.
[3] On the problem of the liberation of man from the burden of work, see Naville (1957).

p. 176), would make possible the realization both of this decompart-mentalization between men and of the conditions necessary for a type of direct production. The revolutionary project, then, contains two recon-ciliations:

the man-creator, once again in direct relation to the object he produces, by the suppression of the private ownership of the means of production; the self-aware man, who no longer produces in order to satisfy his needs,

but to satisfy his need to create (*Perspectives anarchistes–communistes*, 1968, pp. 13–14).

The setting up of 'communes' and production units – and, of course, teaching and research units, for we must not forget the importance accorded in discussions to the problem of replacing the present educational system – would lead to a sort of hyper-federalism, a 'from bottom to top' movement, which would constitute what a government by the people – to avoid the association of the term 'people's government' – should be.[1] The problems of the relations between the units would be resolved by solutions involving coordination, not centralization. This coordination, however, should be extremely flexible in order to prevent any dictatorship of a majority over minorities, which would enjoy equal rights, and any encroachment of one unit upon the domain of another:

For the representativity to be real, it must be limited to a decision and be immediately revocable. I do not see why, even in a socialist regime, a grocer in Strasbourg or a peasant in Gers should decide on a change of structures in the shipyards at Saint-Nazaire. It's up to those who work in the shipyards to say what they want and how they intend to live (G. Cohn-Bendit, 1968, p. 18).

The originality of this tendency, then, would seem to be, once again, the primacy accorded to everyday life.[2] It is a new *use* of modern technology that is being demanded, one that will make it possible – without its being necessary to 'smash' all the structures of production and communication, but rather by deflecting them, giving them another aim, another meaning – to abolish the dictatorship of work over man, to free him, to free him for other activities:

We must go beyond the notion of economics as the supreme value and ultimate aim of every society, go beyond the imperialism of the notion of

---

[1] Much of the argument of this last paragraph has been borrowed from a contribution made by the social psychologist R. Pagès in an assembly of research workers held in May.
[2] This is particularly so in the case of the Situationists, who, for this reason, are very interested in the problems of urbanism.

economics and give economic production as a whole, in our future society, a humbler place in the scale of human activities, replace the totalitarianism of our economy over our daily life by a preponderance of daily life over the economy.[1]

For some, like the Situationists, the present development of technology offers man, in a reversal of the situation that is now leading to his enslavement, an unprecedented opportunity for self-realization by appropriating 'the untold wealth of the bourgeois world' (*De la misère en milieu étudiant . . .*, p. 31):

> Today, when automation and cybernetics, if applied in man's interest, would make possible the construction of the dream of the old masters and of the slaves of all time, there is nothing but a socially formless magma in which confusion mingles, in each individual, derisory fragments of masters and slaves. But it is from this realm of equivalences that the new masters, the masters without slaves, will spring (Vaneigem, 1968, p. 214).

It should be noted here that the position of a certain type of 'French-style socialism', strongly tainted with anarchism, has been criticized for representing a backward movement in the development of labour to the artisanal stage, or, at least, a regression from the point of view of production and living standards. These criticisms are certainly not without foundation, in so far as the advocates of such solutions have scarcely described in detail the economic and social organization in which self-management and hyper-federalism would operate. But it is no less true that a return to the artisanal stage and to 'naturo-feudal' life, practised in France by some groups, which call themselves anarchist, but which are really mystico-artistic at most (Raymond Duncan and his followers, for example), was never advocated in May, except by a few isolated individuals in search of an outlet for their neuroses.

It would certainly be easy, among the thousands of propositions that emerged from the work of the various student commissions, to find a great many elements that might be called archaic, in the present meaning of the term. This is often a consequence of the desire to question everything, to start from scratch again in order to rebuild society according to a different model. While many of these texts, despite a certain confusion, are very rich in ideas – such as the pamphlet *Nous sommes en marche*, issued by the Censier Action Committee – others have an almost comic concern to propagate 'banalities', to borrow the term sometimes used by

[1] *Bulletin du Mouvement du 22 Mars*, quoted in *Au joli Mai*, No. 1, p. 46.

their authors to describe their own writings. But the Movement generally went beyond this stage towards the search for a better use of the achievements of modern civilization. Thus, after a period in which science was subject to summary accusation, its role in the society of the future was the subject of lengthy debate. The opinion poll (cf. Chapter 2) taken in May among students of different disciplines revealed the great prestige in which the research scientist is held, in spite of the criticisms levelled at the results of his work.

At this point in time, it is easy for certain triumphant commentators to see in the 'return to order' and the Gaullist successes in the elections proof of the failure of the May Movement, of revolution in the traditional economic and social sense, by reducing the situation to the success of a majority, of 'common sense', over a minority of individuals who tried to impose such a revolution on the basis of imaginary needs.

In fact – such, at least, is one of my conclusions – the revolutionary attempt in May was more successful than might appear. Problems that were usually concealed were brought out into the open, discussed, and taken up by a whole body of opinion – numerically small, but situated perhaps at the centre of society's problems. The fact that it did not succeed in bringing about an immediate change in society, or an immediate solution of all the problems raised, cannot be attributed to a basic weakness, but to one of tactics.

Non-established society – in the sense of a form of social organization that rejects all fixity, believes that society should be adapted to the individual rather than the reverse, and advocates permanent change, a day-to-day 'utopia' – has shown what it is capable of. It is now, in a sense, what it wished to be: non-established. This is a rhetorical defence it is true, but in so far as it is admitted that it is not possible for a revolution to be successful through a military-type seizure of the positions of power without incurring the risk of reconstituting the kind of society that one wishes to suppress, the experience of May did not stop on the night of the second round of the elections. This new, 'revolutionary' way of life may not have spread in the way that its proponents hoped. After the initial violent thrust, it ceased to gain ground. But it may well have survived in a subterranean, or 'cultural', form, through the students, through the *lycéens* – whose role in the Movement was as important as it was surprising, and who have shown and are still showing a potential for mobilization and an interest in the problems raised by the Movement that would have been difficult to imagine before May – and through numerous artists and intellectuals, for whom this period coincided with their own self-questioning as to their past role in society, and for many others too.

It could be objected that this aspect betrays the elitist character of a revolt that might appear to be the work of a privileged minority. This was no doubt so, in the sense, as some of the authors I have quoted in these two chapters believe, that the stage of development now reached by our societies could make it possible for everyone to enjoy life as only an elite could in the past, and also in the sense that access to 'culture', not at the educational level, but at that of creation, has been recognized as a fundamental aspiration. It was, however, a Movement – as shown in the tendency examined here – that was opposed to all assumption of authority, all hierarchy, and the place assigned to thought and to creation was, in principle, the most democratic that could be imagined, since everything must come from the base, outside all specialization, by a sort of *popularization* of decision-making and creative activity.

'A cultural revolution? Perhaps', wrote the author of a collection of mural quotations in a newspaper article. But it was certainly a very cultured revolution: one could read on all the walls of the Latin Quarter, side by side with innumerable original expressions of their authors' imagination and wit, quotations from or paraphrases of their illustrious predecessors in the field of political or artistic subversion. Fourier and Bakunin were placed immediately beside Breton and Tzara. If the May Movement does not seem, as I have said, to have taken its model from the thinking of any particular mind, it is obvious that certain parallels, whether historical or purely cultural, can be drawn. I have used the word 'parallel' advisedly, since I have no wish to give the impression in the next part of this work, in which I shall examine a number of literary and artistic tendencies, that these experiments were present in the minds of the participants. On the other hand, it might be claimed that the form of criticism directed at society and the form taken by revolts that try to overthrow that society are present in similar movements. There, too, the artist may, as he often hopes, in both the content and the form of his creation, prefigure the model of revolutions and societies of the future.

PART IV

Cultural Politicization:
Precedents and Parallels

CHAPTER 7

The Dada Explosion[1]

THE RUINS

'As long as we have not destroyed everything, there will remain ruins ...'[2]

One can hardly speak of Dada and Surrealism without taking account of the overwhelming fact of the 'Great War', in which almost all their members were involved and which, in any case, confronted them all.

However, although this experience was a decisive one, the explosion did not take place, and for very good reason, until after the war;[3] we should therefore direct our attention to the 'postwar landscape' if we are to discover some of the characteristic elements of the birth of a revolutionary situation in the 'ideological' sphere. The revolt could not break out immediately after the return from the Front, in a sudden explosion of the feelings accumulated and repressed during the massacre itself, but only later, when the postwar state was confronted by the image that had been formed of a new life. The break was provided by the war, but before refusal could burst out or acceptance wear thin, there had to be a period, of indeterminate length, of rest and readaptation, of a very human 'return to life' as it were.

One of the references most frequently used by the Dadaists and Surrealists themselves is to a society *in ruins*, a life against a background of ruins.[4] The same idea is applied by G. Ribemont-Dessaignes to Dada itself, which he calls (1931) 'a permanent state of ruin'.

The ruins, of course, are not only material ones. Although it might be thought that the entire superstructure of bourgeois society collapsed with World War I and that first the Dadaists, then the Surrealists, were confronted by its ruins, subsequent history has demonstrated that this

[1] By Pierre Gallissaires.
[2] Wall inscription, May 1968 (Sorbonne).
[3] Revolts, such as mutinies, etc., did occur during the war, but, in the intellectual sphere, only silence was possible in a country at war and it is obviously no coincidence that Dada was born in Switzerland.
[4] 'Soon we'll have charming ruins' – an inscription in May.

collapse was not enough, that capitalism was able to adapt itself to it and showed itself capable of inventing new methods of ensuring, through crises of all kinds, not only its survival, but its increasing prosperity.

Whatever the situation was in 1968, there was no question of Gaullist France being in ruins; nor did the economy show any signs of major crisis, such as widespread poverty or unemployment, at least for the overwhelming mass of opinion. On the other hand, the extent of the cultural ruin was steadily increasing: although the perfectly functioning, automatic, and now almost immediate tactic of absorption soon unprimed Dada and its radical negation, adopted and reapplied the most refined Surrealist techniques of subversion, and took over all later experiments of a similar kind so successfully that many of them now seem to have 'conformed' from their very inception, it is true none the less that every attack, whether in the form of a gradual disintegration or a sudden explosion, has had its effect and that bourgeois or post-bourgeois values as such now seem well and truly dead. A whole civilization, which no one will call 'Western' and 'Christian', survives only as a skeleton. Those who defend it often no longer believe in it themselves, and some do not hesitate to make the necessary adaptations for the safeguard of the only value that really interests them: its effectiveness as a means of justifying and preserving the established social order.

From an artistic point of view, the destructive seeds produced by Dada have grown vigorously. They have been so successful in disintegrating the ruins themselves that the expression that could be read so often on the walls of May – 'art . . . culture . . . has crumbled' – seems particularly apt. Apart from the historical fact that for a long time now there has been no major artistic school outside advertising, nor, since Surrealism, a movement of any scope, but only an ever more rapid succession of ephemeral 'groups', the disintegration is also to be found in the profusion, not to say confusion, of methods, techniques, and variations, including the multifarious but very sincere forms of artistic protest. The artist himself tends to disintegrate in a society that makes not only expression, but the formation of a whole personality, so difficult.

In the 1920s a new hope emerged from the ruins of capitalist society, from its values and outdated modes of expression: a new, socialist society was being built up. Although Dada took no note of the fact,[1] and although

[1] As it happens, Lenin lived not very far from the café in Zurich where Tzara and the first Dadaists met, but neither took the slightest notice of the other.

in its earliest stages Surrealism remained very far removed from the dialectical materialism that was to play so important a role in its development as a group and in that of its most influential members from 1925 onwards, the same cannot be said of the political consciousness of the present. The socialist 'system', too, has now collapsed. What remains is a scattering of the pieces, as seen in the existence of different 'models' now coexisting in greater or lesser harmony throughout the world. The historical evolution that has taken place within socialism in the last fifteen years has brought the whole edifice toppling down in ruins. In fact, as long as the reference image preserves some semblance of legitimacy, reduction and justification are widely accepted. A whole system for the transference of hopes and requirements may be put into operation, whether onto other spheres (the infrastructure: 'of course, literature and the arts have lost out completely, but look at the standard of living, the education of the masses, the economic and social side . . .') or in time (the future: 'our children . . . the next generation, etc.'). This is viable until the accumulation of external proof (various 'events', such as the 20th Congress, Berlin, Yugoslavia, Hungary, China, Warsaw, Prague, etc.) and internal doubt leads to the point at which the majority of the politically conscious of a period explode. In the case of French student youth, it might well be that such a point was reached in May 1968. By that time, the USSR and the French CP had emerged as 'bad reference-points' – a notion that was touched on in our group discussion (Chapter 3). Thus the appearances that held this political consciousness together now lay in ruins. What was left was first the feeling, then the admission, of general dishonour – all kings were now naked, not only de Gaulle, but also 'applied' socialism – and, above all, of an immense void.

'BOREDOM SWEATS'[1]

One fact seems clear: this consciousness is confronted by a substructure that is extraordinarily powerful and well organized.

It is not my purpose to describe either the content or the forms it has taken in its development, or, indeed, the radical character of the simultaneous process of the fetishization of goods and the alienation of man. It will be enough here to indicate its principal motive force, the permanent search for and accumulation of profit; this is why man is reduced to the state of a consumer. Everything tends to be organized, from the exploita-

[1] Inscription, May 1968 (Sorbonne).

tion of labour to the organization of leisure, with this object in view.[1] The form of society created by the bourgeoisie, with its triple pillars of hierarchy, specialization, and non-communication, has reached a point of considerable technical perfection. Within it, the mass of those who have adapted to it and are satisfied by it to a greater or lesser degree, and those who have not adapted to it, including the revolutionaries, must all live together – and they are all fragmented men in a situation that is 'blocked up' (bloqué).

Even the struggle against this 'order of things' is fragmented. In the consumer society, all the oppressive and repressive techniques are cleverly concealed under a veil of 'mildness'; within the revolutionary opposition itself, the fragmentation is geographical and ideological, but it also operates in the tactical sphere.

Ruins, crumbling, fragmentation: such a situation could not fail to produce feelings of powerlessness, emptiness, and hopelessness.

Two objectives, then, are necessary to a movement: to make people aware that the situation is 'blocked up', and to set out to 'unblock' it, with or without them in the first instance. Once a sufficient number of people have gained this awareness, in the very action of 'unblocking' the situation, it is likely that many more will follow, that everyone, in some way or another, will feel 'involved'. The same reasoning is to be found both in the activities of the Dadaists and in two of the key ideas of M 22, that of 'unlocking' (déverrouillage) and that of the 'exemplary action'. Two important consequences follow from this: the need to find the means, whether they are old – but redefined – ones or new ones, and the need to give first priority to 'unblocking' the situation on every front, without knowing a priori either whether it will succeed or where exactly it will lead if it does succeed. This explains the urgent, total, and indeterminate character that is to be found in various specific forms in Dada and in M 22 – and in the May Movement in general.[2]

In every sphere – whether that of ideology, the university, sex, language, art, etc. – both Movements have declared, and practised, this primacy of action. Thus, for example, this boredom, this fragmentation

---

[1] The eroticization of advertising, for example, is conducted not with the aim of enabling the individual to achieve an increase in his capacity for pleasure, but to stimulate sexuality just enough to make him manipulable by the economy. It is intended to create, and to maintain for as long as possible as a buyer, the perfect type of 'man-consumer', who has been described as a 'pre-genital' object fetishist. Is it surprising, then, that 'sexuality should now be part of revolution'!

[2] I have taken M 22 as a reference-point here for two reasons: for its political situation at the origin and spearhead of the May Movement as a whole, and for its theoretical precision, as expressed for example in Ce n'est qu'un début, continuons le combat (Mouvement du 22 Mars, 1968).

and this emptiness, which are said to be typical of social and cultural life,[1] were revealed in the action initiated at Nanterre, then taken up by an ever-increasing number of students: it is my belief that this also made possible the transition, in the consciousness of thousands of people, from the feeling of emptiness (vacancy) to that of the holiday (vacation). When the student minority – urging the majority, if not to follow them, at least to ask themselves a few questions – realized that this immense boredom of the 'capitalist landscape' existed at all perhaps only because there was the leisure to fill such a void, the transition was made. The void became 'holiday', that is, a 'void to be filled': this was a moment of sudden awareness and revelation, whatever means were used to reach it and whatever concrete political results ensued.

'PLUTÔT LA VIE'[2]

There are people who live from one day to the next, I live from one amusing idea to the next. But I also know that I shall get bored with this game before long. So much the better. I even work . . .

It might be said, without making too much of these lines written in 1919,[3] that 'the whole of Dada' (in the beginning, at least) is there, in the words of its founder: the game, cynicism, creation in spite of everything, and an admission of general boredom.

However, boredom – not to speak of its metaphysical variant 'total' boredom – the boredom of daily life cannot be experienced: it can only be 'outwitted', or combated, since to deny it is also a way of combating it. One effective method is to exteriorize it – when it is not sublimated in art. Dada did this in the particular form of *disgust*, expressed vehemently and repeatedly.[4] To discuss whether this was a purely negative emotion or not seems to me to be less interesting than to observe that this form of exteriorization did not imply death.[5] It was merely an indication of its seriousness, expressing, through just this obsessional character, the

[1] The French population as a whole scarcely, or, at most, confusedly, feels this.
[2] 'Rather life' – May inscription (Rue Mazet).
[3] Tristan Tzara, letter to Picabia, 19 March 1919.
[4] 'Dada was the materialization of my disgust' – Tristan Tzara, in 'L'arriviste Tzara va cultiver ses vices', interview, 1923.
[5] Very few Dadaists, to my knowledge, committed suicide. I have not made a statistical study of the question, but it would appear that the same cannot be said of the Surrealists, who were subject to a veritable 'wave of suicides' in their ranks. In my opinion, this should be seen as one more proof of the dazzling vitality of Dada, which, as its former member and historian, G. Ribemont-Dessaignes, has written (1931), and contrary to all the 'nihilistic' interpretations, had 'a taste . . . for happiness, if by that one means above all a taste for living one's life in all its fullness and freedom'.

certainty that if it is impossible to live such a 'disgusting' life, it is simply because it is not the *true life*. This fundamental affirmation, which, since it was first formulated by Rimbaud, has provided the point of departure for every revolutionary movement, at least in the sphere of the mind, and which the Surrealists sought desperately to combine with Marx's 'transformation of the world', and which is irresistibly exploding once more, was taken up word for word, if in different forms, in May.

In fact, 'the commitment to life is a political commitment. We do not want a world in which the guarantee of no longer dying of hunger is exchanged for the risk of dying of boredom', as the Situationists wrote on the walls.[1] The rejection of boredom always leads to a revolt against something else, namely, whatever implies it or, to put it another way, whatever is *there* in an established (too established) way. In both space and time, boredom is a result of repetition and ceremonial monotony; ordinary, 'always there', even in the apparent novelties of fashion and advertising, as in politics (stereotyped slogans, dogmas, etc.) or philosophy; variation, in fact, and not change, that is, the false unexpected, the false new. Order and boredom reign together: they reign with and through man.[2] 'The forest precedes man, the desert follows', said one apparently enigmatic inscription in May: the virgin forest, swarming with life, is followed by society, produced by man against nature, organized, ordered, concealing boredom.

If there is a general and striking similarity between Dadaist and Surrealist denunciations and demands and those of May 1968, it lies in the total character of the revolt, beyond the purely material, economico-social sphere, the rejection of compromises and abdications on this point. There is, of course, a difference of emphasis: Dada, which, as Tzara said, 'was never based on any theory and was nothing more than a protest', carried its rejection of *everything* to the point of declaring itself to be and wishing to be *nothing*. Denying both the economico-social and the 'spiritual', commerce and art, and so on, it threw itself into the immediate, the 'raw', the spontaneous, pure emotion,[3] and affirmed these 'values' only in living them, actively and without any preconceived notions, in the great current of contradictions.

'DADA, DADA, DADA', proclaimed the Manifesto of 1918, 'a howl

[1] Quoting from a work by one of their own members, R. Vaneigem (1968, Introduction).
[2] The expression 'boredom reigns' expresses very well the close link between this notion and that of power.
[3] The primacy of emotion over any other aesthetic criterion is also to be found in Surrealism: 'Only spontaneous forces interest me. The substition of one system for another leaves me totally indifferent . . . Only the whole system of the emotions is inalienable' (Breton, 1923).

of jarring colours, interweaving of contraries and all contradictions, grotesques, inconsequences: LIFE.' And, again, looping the loop, Tzara could declare:

> I'm not a professional writer and I've no literary ambitions. I would have become a magnificent adventurer, of great elegance, if I had had the physical strength and nervous energy to realize one single exploit: not to get bored . . .

EVERYTHING IS DADA

Sensational or quasi-mystical declarations such as those just quoted, provocations and continual scandals, cynicism and exhibitionism – all these were to be found in Dada. The same verbal and gestural violence, the same systematic practice of provocation,[1] are found again, in May 1968, combined with a certain audacity in the use of violence if necessary. A few quotations from Dadaist authors or direct references on the walls,[2] a tract of avowedly Dadaist inspiration, the same peremptory insolence: such similarities are obvious enough. But at this point perhaps we should take a look at the development of this movement, whose affinities with May 1968 are, in my opinion, as striking as those of Surrealism, though they have received less attention.

TO BE OR TO EXIST

'The revolution must cease to be if it is to exist.'[3]

The initial intuition, which seems a truism, is that the 'true life' is to be found *in* life. Although the Dadaists were no more lacking in 'culture' than the young revolutionary activists of May,[4] the fact is that many of them reached the conclusion that the salvation of Life, or of the Revolution, depended on a return to certain vital categories and on their re-activation. According to Arp,[5] these 'young dreamers' were also 'viveurs', if the pejorative undertones of the word can be removed. Their disgust could be expressed only in a vital rejection, above all in *Action*: '*A priori*, that is, with its eyes closed, Dada puts action first.'

[1] This time in the political sphere, though the 'cultural-spectacular' sphere was not neglected.
[2] 'Tout est Dada', for example (foyer of the Odéon theatre), which perplexed and disappointed the German journalist who set out one day to discover the ultimate meaning of the relations between 'the young French elite in revolt' and 'culture' (Günther Metken, *Frankfurter Rundschau*, 18 July 1968).
[3] Wall inscription, Hall A1, Nanterre.
[4] In any case, they do not make up the whole 'population' that is being studied here: everyone could express himself in May, on the walls or anywhere else, and in Paris at least (the Latin Quarter, with its various faculties and lycées, etc.) it could be said that 'everyone' did.
[5] 'The Dadaists were writers, painters, dancers, young dreamers' (Arp, *Gabrielle Buffet-Picabia*, 1925).

For the spectators, then, there were as many subjects to astonish them as there were for those who, last spring, were confronted by the literary 'group' that 'destroyed as it marched'. It had no declared leader[1] and no other apparent activity than the common practice of creating public scandal, in as absurd and violent a form as possible, and of provoking the public, for Dada always practised provocation, rather than contestation. Contestation implies, partly at least, a desire to convince, to win others over to the contesting cause; Dada rejected didacticism as lacking in real interest.[2] Provocation is also more physical and establishes more rapidly that *direct contact with the public* that the Dadaists sought by every possible means, like, for example, the reading of manifestos (a pre-eminently Dadaist form):

> From the very beginning in the Cabaret Voltaire we read and wrote manifestos. We not only read them, we declaimed them defiantly and with the maximum vocal intensity. The manifesto, as a literary form of expression, corresponded to our desire for direct contact. It was important to us not to waste time, we wanted to shock our enemy into opposition and, if necessary, create other enemies for ourselves. We hated nothing more than romantic calm and the search for a 'soul', which, we were convinced, could find expression only in our own activity . . . (Huelsenbeck, 1918).

The immediate aim was *to overcome passivity*[3] by cultivating in oneself, and with regard to others, intensity and spontaneity, and every kind of refusal – refusal to learn, to explain, to judge, to seek,[4] to order. Dada, 'the anti-philosophy of spontaneous acrobatics', has above all no wish to resolve contradictions, but to experience them and to act them out all together; no wish to define, but to create confusion.

The same wish was applied systematically in the particular use that Dada made of poetry, for example. Breaking with the tradition of an exclusively read poetry (by a reader, in a book), it revived and diversified the tradition of spoken poetry, addressed to an audience; wishing to break with another tradition, that of individual poetry, it presented poems written collectively, or recited by several people. It rejected all beauty, whether admitted or not, and any preconceived notions as to the 'noble',

[1] The slogan, 'Everyone is the director of the Dada movement' – which is recalled by that of the activists of M 22, 'We are all Cohn-Bendits' – was strictly applied in practice.
[2] 'I always speak of myself because I have no wish to convince others, I have no right to draw others into my current, no one has to follow me and everyone does his art in his own way' (Tzara, *Manifeste Dada 1918*).
[3] A similar reaction to D. Cohn-Bendit's denunciation of education as an 'initiation into passivity' (D. and G. Cohn-Bendit, 1968, p. 25).
[4] 'We seek *nothing*, we affirm the *vitality* of each *moment*' (Tzara).

'elevated', or any other character of poetry, and composed – or sometimes improvised on stage – classical or onomatopoeic, that is, 'lettrist' poems (before the school of that name was even heard of), to be declaimed, but also howled, spluttered, stammered, and even read while hopping, jumping, dancing, pedalling, etc. The range of these presentations[1] stretched from an experiment (a serious one) in what would now be called a 'total poetic spectacle' to the most provocatively absurd, by way of something more like the 'practical joke'. As a collective anti-aesthetic, confusionist practice, Dada can be seen as a form of 'poetry in action'.

Probably for the first time in French cultural history, art and poetry were, if not 'in the streets', at least on stage, in cafés, theatres, and all other public meeting-places, practised – in the full sense of the word – without distinction by each of these 'actors', thus showing, again for the first time perhaps, that they could be practised by 'anyone'. Creation was shown to be a natural, vital activity, within everyone's reach, provided one gives oneself up to the *play* of one's spontaneity.

It is enough to transgress the frontiers of logic, respect, seriousness, shame,[2] and traditions of all kinds, to realize that the main obstacle to all life and all creation is the *prohibition*, as the participants in May found as clearly and spontaneously as had the Dadaists. (Indeed, the discovery led the students to create one of their most justly famous slogans: 'Il est

---

[1] Here are details of a 'Dada evening' that could be regarded as typical, if somewhat 'official', since it was a 'Dada Festival' held on 26 May 1920:

1. *le sexe de Dada* – 2. *pugilat sans douleur*, by Paul Dermée – 3. *le célèbre illusioniste* Philippe Soupault – 4. *manière forte*, by Paul Éluard – 5. *le nombril interlope*, music by Georges Ribemont-Dessaignes, played by Mlle Marguerite Buffet – 6. *festival manifeste presbyte*, by Francis Picabia, interpreted by André Breton and Henri Houry – 7. *corridor*, by Dr Serner – 8. *le rastaqouère André Breton* – 9. *vaste opéra*, by Paul Draule – 10. *la deuxième aventure de Monsieur Aa l'antipyrine*, by Tristan Tzara, with Paul Éluard (M. Absorbtion), André Breton (Oreille), Mlle Marguerite Buffet (Mme Interruption), G. Ribemont-Dessaignes (Le cerveau désintéressé), Théodore Fraenkel (M. Saturne), Louis Aragon (M. Aa) – 11. *vous m'oublierez*, sketch by André Breton and Philippe Soupault: P. Soupault (Robe de Chambre), André Breton (Parapluie), Berthe Tessier (Machine à coudre) – 12. *la nourrice américaine*, par Francis Picabia, musique sodomiste, played by Marguerite Buffet – 13. *manifeste baccarat*, by Georges Ribemont-Dessaignes, with André Breton (Gauche), G. Ribemont-Dessaignes (Droite), Tristan Tzara (Milieu) and P. Soupault (M. Oxigénée) – 14. *jeu d'échecs*, by Céline Arnauld – 15. *danse frontière*, by G. Ribemont-Dessaignes – 16. *système DD*, by Louis Aragon – 17. *je suis des javanais*, by Francis Picabia – 18. *poids public*, by Paul Éluard, with P. Éluard (L'imbécile), Mme Éluard (L'idiote), P. Soupault (leur enfant) – 19. *vaseline symphonique*, by Tristan Tzara, played by 20 people.

It was also announced on the posters and invitation cards that all the Dadaists present would have their hair shaved off on stage.

[2] This theme of shame, then condemned as 'counter-revolutionary', is found again in May (Nanterre and Sorbonne: wall inscriptions); cf. the Censier Action Committee, *Nous sommes en marche*: 'Each individual should let himself be carried away by his own enthusiasm, without feeling guilty, and so relearn the meaning of what it is to be a human being' ('Preliminary propositions for a cultural revolution', 4).

interdit d'interdire' – 'Prohibition is prohibited'.) Dada poetry, which Arp called 'automatic poetry',

> emerges in direct line from the poet's entrails or from any other of his organs that have accumulated reserves. Neither the Postillon de Longjumau, nor the alexandrine, nor grammar, nor aesthetics, nor Buddha, nor the sixth commandment, can stop him. He crows, swears, moans, mumbles, yodels as the fancy takes him. His poems are like nature: they stink, laugh and rhyme like nature. Nonsense, or at least what most men call nonsense, is as precious to him as sublime rhetoric, for, in nature, a broken twig rivals the stars in beauty and importance, and it is men who decree what is beauty and what is ugliness (Arp, 1938a).[1]

One of the key terms necessary to any understanding of Dada is 'active simplicity'. This might be defined as a combination of dynamism, permanence, and collectivity. Thus, in May 1968, an inscription on the walls of the School of Oriental Languages that declared 'All that has been achieved is a result of *dynamism*, which flows from *spontaneity*', would apply perfectly to Dada. Another important characteristic of Dada was its determination, right to the end, to keep the movement *active* and *alive* by an uninterrupted series of 'action-manifestations' and their application in the most intense way possible to the greatest possible number of fields, regarded hitherto as *separate* and autonomous. A final characteristic of Dada, which was quite new at the time among people who were still regarded as 'writers', as *littérateurs*, was the practice of meeting not to 'talk shop' and recite poems to each other, but to organize together *actions* or theatrical events. The Dada 'manifestations', at which a series of 'expressions' were presented, either by individuals or by groups, were their real 'work', their creation, however ephemeral they may have been – and however indistinguishable they may have seemed from life itself. As Arp was later to say, 'at that time the action of opening a zip-fastener for a beautiful woman was called sculpture' (1957).

These, then, were a few of the rediscoveries made by Dada, together with the notion that things are proved by doing them, and can be done if one wants to do them. The aim of Dada was to proclaim, to show, and therefore to demonstrate that life (the *true* life) and art are simple things, that one has only to want them and to do them. The May Movement

---

[1] It should be noted that Arp represented a tendency in the Dada movement that was decidedly 'naturalistic' and mystical. But, as Tzara said, 'what interests a Dadaist is his own way of life'. Dada was one of the first of those 'action groups' that lie outside any precise ideology, bringing together, for that very reason, individuals with different points of view, yet avoiding the continual 'purges' that split the Surrealist group. Similarly, Dada advocated a policy of 'scuttling', and it might be said that it scuttled itself as a movement.

proclaimed, and hoped to show and demonstrate, that (true) politics –
indivisible from Revolution and Life[1] – are simple things, that one has
only to want and to do.

'LE N'IMPORTE QUOI ÉRIGÉ EN SYSTÈME'

'Anything built up into a system', proclaimed a wall inscription at
Nanterre. 'As the fancy takes him', said Arp of the poet, and he advocated *laisser pousser* in art, a belief whereby things must be 'allowed to
grow' of themselves.[2] Similarly, Hugo Ball spoke of 'spitting words'.
Dada was the first great 'liberator of expression' in this century, in its own
field, which, from the beginning, was wider than the merely literary or
artistic field; it was Dada, at least, that paved the way.

It was revolutionary – even if it did not practise revolution – because it
was the negation of everything that preceded it. It was compelled therefore to welcome the affirmation, which is to be found in both Marx and
the anarchists, that a new society can be built only on the ruins of the
old, after the destruction of the previous order.

The Dadaists, advocating a practising action, insisted on negative action
– and even seemed to many to be using and abusing only the negating
type of action. 'We must be pitiless', declared Tzara in one of his manifestos,

> after the carnage we will be left with the hope of a purified humanity . . . I
> am destroying the pigeon-holes of the brain and of society: demoralize
> wherever you go and plunge your hand from heaven into hell, re-establish
> the fecund wheel of a universal circus in the real powers and imagination of
> each individual.

'Destroy' and 'demoralize', first. Dada was the first to turn to its own
account, but in a plundering, distorting way, by means of the absurd and
the unconventional, the advanced arts and techniques in its field, such as
typography; the 'calligrams' inherited from Apollinaire in poetry, from
which it banished every aesthetic aspect in order to emphasize the dis-
location, the shock effects, and the disturbing aspects, which go well
beyond the mere surprise intended by their inventor; and, lastly, advertising, which was distorted, for example, by inserting false or libellous

[1] The theme of the unity of politics and life is theoretically developed in Surrealism, and was also
one of the principal themes in May.
[2] 'First the forms, the colours, the words, the sounds must be allowed to grow . . . First the legs,
the wings, the hands must be allowed to grow and then they must be allowed to fly, to sing, to
close, to manifest themselves . . .' (Arp, *Manifeste millimètre infini*, 1938b).

news[1] in newspapers, sometimes even concerning the 'literary person' or private life of its own members! Everywhere it put into practice – in everyday life too – that 'very subtle means' praised by Tzara for 'destroying the taste for literature . . . even while writing', namely to combat it 'by its own means, and in its own formulas'; even to the point of questioning itself and its existence as a movement. For,

> to disorder meaning – disorder the notions and all the tropical showers of demoralization, disorganization, destruction, disturbance, are guaranteed measures against thunder and recognized as being of public use.

'ASSEZ D'ACTES, DES MOTS'[2]

But the field in which Dada exercised its talents most vigorously was that of language. If, in fact, Dada placed active doubt 'above everything', it could hardly fail to cast doubt not only on the false images of the world in which it had to 'live', but also on the tools of this deception, in particular the most important of these, language. There too it wished to make a clean sweep, using, as its favourite weapons, humour, scorn, the absurd, negation, to establish first of all the necessary and salutary chaos that would sweep away by means of ridicule a language that was nothing but either idle chatter or 'discourse'. Discourse, or *a posteriori* speech, has a meaning – definition, justification, exposition, explanation, etc. – hence a construction and an order, by which it can be judged. Discourse is *made*. Chatter, on the other hand, speech that is immediate but still social in its use, can easily do without meaning: it need only be information, indication, or merely a means of relieving one's feelings, relaxing, or passing the time. So Dada accepts it as it is, whereas it employs discourse only derisively: 'Only chatter matters nowadays. The form in which it is most often presented is *Dada*.'[3] But Dada wants speech to be immediate, *raw*: the direct expression of the individual, an immediate translation of emotion, in which one is plunged, and sometimes drowns; that is not *made*, but *said*.[4]

In order to reach it and to set it flowing, it is necessary once again to crush prohibitions, all fear or 'shame', especially in the sphere of reason and logic. 'Words must be ploughed up', adds Tzara, after stating 'a

[1] One of the most famous being the announcement that Chaplin was to take part in a Dada 'manifestation'. The details are to be found in M. Sanouillet's *Dada à Paris* (1965).
[2] 'Enough of actions, let's have words', inscription, May 1968, Galerie des Sciences, Sorbonne.
[3] Tzara, *Dada manifeste sur l'amour faible et l'amour amer* (1930).
[4] Which does not mean, as we shall see later, Surrealist automatism.

great Dadaist secret: *Thought is produced in the mouth*' (1930, op. cit.). Thus, all means are valid, including the systematic use of chatter, on condition that it is emptied of all its social implications and, pushed to its limit, it rediscovers its immediate, raw character. Then, as we have seen with true life, true language will be attained, which will give us back the world in its truth, that is, above all, its density, its intensity, and its immediacy.

The way to this is through the 'anything', the clean sweep, or *tabula rasa* of language. In a sense, Dada may claim to work 'with all its might for the establishment everywhere of the silly . . . consciously'.[1] But this is because it 'wished to destroy the reasonable deceits of men and rediscover the natural, unreasonable order . . . replace the logical *nonsense* of men today by the illogical *senseless*', as Jean Arp put it,[2] establishing here an important distinction. All 'liberation of expression' can be achieved only at this risk and at this price. We are familiar with the criticisms directed at the innumerable assemblies, spontaneous or prearranged, that flourished in May 1968. These criticisms came not only from the political opponents of the Movement, but also from the traditional political activists, and included charges of 'idle chatter', slowness in arriving at decisions, and therefore inefficiency and uselessness, etc. Hence the explanations of Cohn-Bendit and others that it was only when people had 'said everything' and 'heard everything' that they would come to ask themselves the question, 'So what?',[3] that it was a necessary transition, and in no way a bad thing. Beyond this strictly political point of view is an idea that was equally central to May: that expression – verbal or otherwise – should be the most inalienable part of man,[4] and that everything should be done to preserve its purity and complexity.

---

[1] As an echo, here are two wall inscriptions from Nanterre: 'Contestation, mais con d'abord', and, written in capital letters, 'JE SUIS CON' (Room C 20). (The word *con*, which in force and social acceptability lies somewhere between 'stupid' and 'silly cunt', is as widespread in use as the English four-letter words – Translator's note.) Such statements should lead us to ask questions, I think, rather than to laugh (another inscription read: 'I dream of being a happy imbecile' – Music amphitheatre, Nanterre). One might also consider the wealth of possible meanings and applications in this 'simple' play on words. Faced with the general state of *blockage* in language, Dada could act positively only by 'unblocking' it.

[2] 'Dada is for the senseless, which is not to say nonsense. Dada is senseless as nature is senseless. Dada is for nature and against art. Dada is direct like nature. Dada is for infinite sense and finite means' (*On my way*, 1948).

[3] Cf. interview with J.-P. Sartre, *Le Nouvel Observateur*, 20 May 1968.

[4] 'For us, there was never any question of creating a new party, but rather of an objective situation giving birth to the possibility of self-expression at every level.' D. Cohn-Bendit and J.-P. Duteuil in Bourges (1968).

'WE'LL TAKE'[1]

So the essential problem, at the level of language, was to overcome the existing *blocage*. It might be said that Dada, following the main 'themes' of its activity – disgust, total rejection, and 'vitalist' (or vitalizing) action – proposed and practised, without in any way wishing to differentiate them or keep them apart, the three corresponding attitudes to language.

Disgust for an object as dead as it was accused of having become might lead one to express justified hostility: one uses language, then, quite simply, but in order to say, as well as possible, the *opposite* of what is usually said, thus showing up hypocrisy, ugliness, etc. Dada could not continue in this direction. To radical disgust corresponds, in a much more adequate way, the affirmation of incompatibility. Words are taken for something other than what they are in the eyes of everybody else: carried to its logical conclusion, one has to create one's *own* language, composed of one's *own* words[2] – not, to put it another way, an anti-language, but another language, which is more than a mere para-language, like slang, for example. It is a way of blowing up 'their' language and therefore of destroying the main bridge between 'them' and 'us', by incommunicability.

Although Dada sometimes launched a few missiles into this terrain, it made no great progress: perhaps it was too doubting, too much involved with life and too 'anti-art'[3] to succeed. Its favourite course was that dictated to it by rejection – which was no doubt also the one best adapted to rejection: destruction and plunder by the distortion and gratuitousness of the 'senseless'. To say neither the opposite nor anything else, but what I have called 'anything': a thing *and* its opposite, for example, if possible together and in the same breath (phrase or line), 'in a single fresh breath' (Tzara), or (why not?) immediately after each other,[4] not always systematically of course, but never holding anything

---

[1] 'We'll claim nothing, demand nothing, we'll take' – wall inscription, foyer of the great amphitheatre, Sorbonne.

[2] There have been several attempts of this kind, however, in contemporary literature: Henri Michaux, Lettrism, André Martel, J. Dubuffet, etc.

[3] Is not creating one's own language itself a work of art – even if it is neither beautiful nor successful? Tzara declared (1931): 'I write because it's natural, just as I piss, just as I'm ill' (*Proclamation sans prétention*).

[4] Or, again, to make up a Dada poem according to the famous recipe of the sack provided by Tzara (1930):

> To make a Dadaist poem, Take a newspaper / Take a pair of scissors / Select from the newspaper an article that has the length you wish to give your poem / Cut out the article / Then carefully cut out each of the words that make up the article and put them into a sack / Stir gently / Then take out each word one after another / Copy out the words conscientiously in the order in which they emerged from the sack / The poem will resemble you / And you will be a writer of infinite originality and charming sensibility, though misunderstood by the vulgar.

back – a confusion in which one can see, it seems to me, a means of 'anti-absorption'. Of course, 'since Dada burst on the scene, literature has never stopped absorbing it', as someone wrote in May at Nanterre: but it knew very well that everything was always interpreted. Moreover, it very skilfully played the double game of trying to carry absurdity to the limit of the non-interpretable and also of suggesting the greatest possible number of questions and interpretations, just for the sake of sowing confusion.

By means of this 'unconventional' practice and the pleasure it gave, the Dadaist authors found something of the 'true life' to which they aspired. Having brushed aside all obstacles, all justifications and all obligations – including that of explaining oneself[1] – they reached that vital level where joy, movement, spontaneity, and metamorphosis have their being; language is no longer a poor means, but a game, a celebration. Thus one passes from 'negative' qualities, as those that are merely negating are usually called, to all the positivity of pleasure and creation; thus language has become rich and full of promise.

'DISCOURSE IS COUNTER-REVOLUTIONARY'[2]

These lessons should not be forgotten in other fields: politics, to judge from the manifestations of the May Movement at the level of expression, was confronted by the problem of 'unblocking' a certain form of language,[3] of showing up its inadequacy and falseness, if not of destroying it completely, in order to seek and attain the new, or rejuvenated, language necessary for revolution – which itself consists, partly and immediately, of destroying, then, later, of beginning the organization of new construction.

First of all, it was necessary to shock, to provoke, hence the reproach that they 'refused to explain', a fact that surprised many people.[4] In order to bring people to awareness – and that was really what they were trying to do – it was necessary first to seize, as it were, the usual political language, and then bend it for use on a varying scale of means of expression,

---

[1] 'There are people who explain because there are others who learn. Remove them, and you're left with Dada,' declared Tzara. In fact, the immediate expression of the individual, which is what Dada was concerned with, is conveyed through emotion, never through explanation or reason.
[2] Inscription: Hall 13, Nanterre.
[3] 'Let us also reject the facilities of revolutionary language, an instrument for reducing and evading problems. Let us always ask what revolution we are talking about,' declared the Censier Action Committee, Nous sommes en marche ('Appeal to the population', thesis 24).
[4] And which, of course, had other causes than that referred to here.

'activation-techniques' such as visualization, gesturalization, theatricalization, occupation, and living multiplication by appealing for creative participation (posters, slogans, everyone being called on to 'write his own tract', etc.). The reader will no doubt have drawn other parallels with Dadaist activities than those noted here.

The initial shock administered and the 'detonation' obtained, the pursuit of revolutionary action necessitated the seizure of language. It was this that made possible the liberation of individual expression and the substitution of dialogue for discourse, the transition from the individual to the collective, the re-establishment of communication. It is remarkable how striking are the similarities here, despite differences in kind, with Dada language.

Having as its principal motive force a certain vitality of spirit, the dialogue, as practised in May, almost continuously, in the streets as well as in the Sorbonne and the Odéon, was remarkable for its freedom, its taste for the concrete and its immediacy of impact. It was as far removed from intellectual discussion as it was from everyday conversation or from the ceremonial of the political meeting or assembly. It often proceeded in a total absence of constraint,[1] by its own internal movement – not that of reasoning or reflection, but by association (of phrases, ideas, etc.), the guiding-thread being not a subject, a thesis, a programme to be expounded or demonstrated at the end of the exercise, but the immediate effect,[2] in a sort of joyful game. The aim was not so much to 'overcome', as, in the best cases, to arouse the widest possible participation in a collective game of searching for a 'truth': a provisional, fluctuating truth, quite the contrary of a dogma. Dogmas, which provided the subjects of earlier discussions, were now dead, for a time at least. Of course, speech, now liberated from the sermons of preachers of every tendency, sometimes floated towards 'metaphysical' shores, where it rediscovered a form of poetry, including that of Dada, an original language, a direct expression of man. The return to primary awareness, the source of all secondary affirmations, prior to any hypothesis, or even any formulation, in which everything meets and in which one finds all the revolutionary 'virtues', common to Dada and to May, of absoluteness, exactingness, urgency, immediacy, is achieved through the Dadaist practice of saying 'any-

[1] Whether intellectual (reflection or over-meticulous analysis), material (duration, place, such fixed frameworks as programmes, etc.), and, of course, physical, since everyone was free to express himself.
[2] Hence the abundance of repartee. Any attempts at lengthy exposition, which were more rare, were interrupted either 'seriously' or by noisy protest, experience having taught that such speakers were usually 'absorptionist' (*récupérateurs*) activists who had come to 'shoot their line'.

thing'. For, unlike strictly political language, it is not content to say something, that is, basically, to speak according to the object, but wishes to express (and therefore not depart from) the whole, undivided, 'total' human reality.

CHAPTER 8

The Surrealist Exploration[1]

'Drop everything. Drop Dada . . .' Thus, in 1922, André Breton openly acknowledged a break in the Dada movement.[2] Together with most of the other Dadaists, he broke violently with Tzara,[3] who retained only a few faithful followers, and devoted himself to organizing what was gradually to become known officially as the Surrealist group (*Premier manifeste*, 1924a).

All the themes so far examined concerning Dada and its relation with the May Movement can be found once more, and their developments followed, in the history of Surrealism, again from either a 'literary' or a 'political' angle. Thus, instead of the Dadaist initial disgust, one should speak, perhaps, in the case of the Surrealists, of a 'state of fury',[4] which put them at once into a general 'posture of aggression' (Breton). One also finds the same 'unlimited capacity for rejection'[5] as in Dada, and the practice of violent action, since Surrealism has 'no fear of making a dogma out of absolute revolt, total insubordination, regular sabotage', and expects 'nothing but violence' (*Second manifeste du surréalisme*, 1930). Even the value attributed to contradictions, or to culture, recurs frequently as a theme, though, theoretically, Surrealism was committed to their disappearance.[6]

[1] By Pierre Gallissaires.

[2] The most important indication of what was to ensue was the attitude of 'scuttling' adopted by Tzara on the occasion of the celebrated 'accusation of M. Barrès by Dada' (13 May 1921). It was confirmed by the refusal to take part in the 'International Conference for the determination of directives and the defence of the modern spirit', which Breton wanted to organize the following year and which, accordingly, was made impossible. Shortly afterwards, there were even a few 'scuffles' (the 'Cœur à gaz' evening, July 1923).

[3] Who pursued his own way alone, then later joined the Surrealist movement, at Breton's invitation (cf. *Second manifeste du surréalisme*, 1930).

[4] Cf. the text, dated 2 April 1925, quoted by M. Nadeau in his *Histoire du surréalisme* (1945), in which a number of Surrealists (A. Artaud, J.-A. Boiffard, M. Leiris, A. Masson, and P. Naville) declare that 'prior to any surrealist or revolutionary preoccupation, their minds are dominated by a certain state of fury'.

[5] 'That unlimited capacity for rejection that is the whole secret of human advance . . .' (Breton, *Position politique du surréalisme*, 1935).

[6] 'Our contradictions must be regarded as the sign of that sickness of the mind that is probably

Is this surprising, in view of the fact that the Surrealists, the founder-members at least, were ex-Dadaists? What had changed was not the feeling that action was necessary, nor the fact that one *did* act, nor the methods of action (they were diversified and enriched), but its *meaning* and its *aim*. To begin with, action now had one, open and declared, aim – which Dada had always been careful not to reveal. The application of certain *idées bouleversantes* (literally, 'overthrowing', that is, revolutionary ideas) and the use of the term *bouleversement* are typical. This, in fact, was the aim of Surrealism – and it implied revolution not only in the sphere of ideas, but in every sphere. This was certainly its starting-point and its favourite field of application, but its ultimate aim was to achieve a 'general revolution in sensibility', which would have 'incalculable social results'.[1]

ATTENTIVE RECEPTIVITY

I shall not pursue here all the questions that have so far been raised, but select a few of the themes in which Surrealism, if it did not introduce a total innovation in relation to Dada, at least contributed so much that they have since been regarded as its own, and which were also revived or rediscovered in May 1968. There is one such theme, for example, which was of such cardinal importance for Surrealism that Breton even went so far as to equate it with Surrealism itself,[2] and which was directly connected with Dadaist experiments with language – automatic writing, and automatism in general. It is this theme that I should like to examine first.

'Dictation of thought': this is obviously a long way from Dada, in respect of which it was also possible to speak, in a sense, of 'automatism', but in which everything – including thought – passed through and was produced in 'the mouth'. Dada gesticulated and spoke (spoke *while* gesticulating and vice versa), made a noise – and 'language' only incidentally – and listened to itself making a noise, the pleasure of listening reinforcing that of the generating activity. The Dadaist was well and truly conscious

---

our highest dignity. Let us repeat that we believe in the absolute power of contradiction' (*La Révolution surréaliste*, 1928). Dada would probably never have spoken of contradiction as a 'sickness of the mind'.

[1] Breton, in a crucial passage in *Position politique du surréalisme*, to which I shall return later.

[2] 'Surrealism: pure psychic automatism whereby it is intended to express, either verbally, by writing, or in any other way, the real functioning of thought. Dictation of thought, in the absence of any control exercised by reason and any aesthetic or moral preoccupation' (*Premier manifeste du surréalisme*). It should be noted that the first Surrealist texts of this kind – those that made up *Les Champs magnétiques*, by Breton and Soupault, were written in 1919, that is, before Tzara's arrival in Paris (January 1920).

– he enjoyed life and played his games wholeheartedly. The Surrealist, on the other hand, was a conscious dreamer;[1] he no longer believed in the naturalness and authenticity of Dadaist spontaneity. Moreover, he saw a danger in its character and its intentional practice of 'torpedoing the idea in the sentence that expresses it'.

> Dadaism wished to draw attention to this torpedoing. It is well known that Surrealism hoped, by its use of automatism, to save some edifice, some sort of phantom ship, from this torpedoing (Breton).

In fact, he had done far more than these words would imply: by going beyond the 'extraordinary and disturbing movement that takes place on the surface . . . of the content of the most unpremeditated activity of the mind'[2] – which was revealed in Dada by the emphasis on verbal automatism[3] – Breton had gained access to buried treasure.

Surrealism, on the other hand, abandoning pure delight for its *exploration*, was to produce most of the automatic writing.[4] The difference of attitude was a radical one: Dada *allowed itself* to follow any 'automatism', speaking as a tap flows, merely taking a wild, 'Bakuninian',[5] delight in the resulting linguistic chaos; for the Surrealist, however, 'automatism' is an *exercise* of a mental kind and sometimes quasi-mystical in its manifestations, and which, from the beginning, gives rise to various 'preoccupations' (of authenticity, interpretation, etc.). Although mediums, in whom the Surrealists always showed great interest, though carefully distinguishing between them and themselves, practised a kind of passive automatism and Dada an automatism of pure action, the Surrealist attitude to automatism can be summed up in the term *attentive receptivity*.[6]

[1] In *Nadja*, Breton regarded himself as his own ghost, and derived theoretical developments and conclusions from this notion.
[2] A criticism that expresses both attraction and mistrust: was this the 'vertigo' he experienced at Dada activities, which Tzara would have preferred to call 'intoxication'? Breton sought a different vertigo because, in his opinion, he was going farther: that of the 'vertiginous *descent* into ourselves', a means of 'total recovery of our psychic force', of which he speaks in his Second Manifesto.
[3] The 'Dada texts' that have survived are confined to the manifestos, a few slim volumes of verse, and a few rare plays (which were not collected and published until a few years ago). This paucity of material is not fortuitous: most of Tzara's manifestos were written to be declaimed, as were also the Dada poems. This was the only 'literature' that Dada allowed itself.
[4] Here, according to the Manifesto, is André Breton's recipe:

> Have writing materials brought to you, after settling in as favourable a place as possible for the concentration of your mind upon itself. Put yourself in the most passive or receptive state you can. Abstract your genius and your talent and that of others . . . Write quickly without any preconceived subject, so quickly that you cannot remember what you have written and don't be tempted to read it over. The first sentence will come of itself . . . It is rather difficult to say anything definite about the second . . . And it shouldn't matter to you. Continue as long as you wish. Put your trust in the inexhaustible character of the murmur . . .

[5] In the sense of this inscription-quotation from May (Sorbonne): 'The passion of destruction is a creative joy.'
[6] For a treatment of the whole complex of questions raised by Surrealist automatism, cf. M.

Not only is there a 'state of grace' – a sort of 'silencing' of the consciousness, in which the mind is ready to seize on the prey – but there are also certain conditions of listening and transmission, which, for Breton, are very close to being rules: do nothing that can break the unity of the verbal flow, resist any attempt either to intervene or to observe, with admiration or pleasure, the flow of images you are transcribing.[1] The consciousness does participate, therefore, observing in a sense what is taking place and even trying to make sense of the subconscious flow and to preserve the purity of the listening faculty, by means of certain modes of 'selection' that Breton not only allows it, but actually insists that it exercise on automatism.

At this stage, we should perhaps ask what Surrealism discovered in automatic writing that it should have become, at least at the beginning of the movement, its principal mode of creation. It can be said at once that it was not merely for the literary or aesthetic quality of the texts thus arrived at that the Surrealists took up this activity;[2] nor, really, for the immediate, tangible results on the sensibility of those who did take it up – which Aragon described somewhat lyrically in 1924 in his 'Une vague de rêves':

A power of which they had no knowledge, an incomparable ease, a liberation of the mind, an unprecedented production of images and the supernatural tone of their writings.

THE DREAM

'Forget all you have learnt, begin dreaming.'[3]

It is not a diversion to speak here of the dream: automatic writing is really a special form of 'waking dream', in so far as it makes possible a certain activity of the consciousness which, in dream as such, is impossible. It is quite normal, therefore, to find the same 'laws' and to draw

---

Carrouges (1967). Breton's description, in the First Manifesto, of the way in which he 'discovered' automatism (the sentence that 'knocked on the window') is very revealing about this state of attentiveness and receptivity.
[1] In spite of certain little 'tricks' that sometimes prove necessary, especially if the flow seems to be drying up or hesitating at a 'crossroads', it is first and foremost *dictation* – 'the illumination comes afterwards', wrote Breton, who is very clear and definite on this point. This remark shows how far removed he was from Dada.
[2] This is attested by a great many categorical statements, and by the historical fact that, after the dazzling initial period (1921–25 approximately), the production of automatic texts declined, while the practice of automatism, as such, extended to a number of other fields, in particular, to 'games', painting, and 'objects' in general (cf. below).
[3] Inscription, May 1968 (Sorbonne).

the same theoretical and practical conclusions from both. This Breton and his friends did not fail to do when they were seized by the great 'epidemic of sleep' described by Aragon,[1] and into which they never ceased to plunge.

Automatism revealed to the Surrealists the existence of a *permanent internal discourse*, which had previously manifested itself only in those few 'infiltrations to which one did not pay attention, such phrases as came to one "on waking" or while "half-asleep" '.[2] It also convinced them that this 'discourse' is available to everyone, which led them to the conclusion that 'inspiration' is merely the result of listening to it attentively and of recording what one hears.[3]

> The peculiarity of Surrealism is in having declared the total equality of all normal human beings before the subliminal message, in having constantly maintained that this message constitutes a common heritage of which everyone should claim his share and which must at all costs soon cease to be regarded as the prerogative of a few (Breton, 1934).

Moreover, through language and dream, automatism 'opened wide the gates of a world in which the liberated mind ran in joyful freedom'.[4] In fact, not only do dream and language break down our external behaviour by releasing us from *their* automatisms, but they *reveal* a new structure of the world: what we see, listen to, and transcribe is merely a dazzling series of verbal and visual transformations, a world in which 'all is possible', in which everything happens at a time and in a way that are marvellously unexpected.

> Boundaries were set up within which words could be put into contact with words, things with things. A principle of *perpetual mutation* seized hold of objects and ideas, with a view to their total deliverance, which implies that of man also.[5]

Man thus affirms himself to himself spontaneously, as it were, under the effect of this internal spectacle, he can see reality other than it is, he can take possession of the real other than rationally and logically. From this to a belief that it is possible to transform the world is but a step.[6]

---

[1] 'Une vague de rêves', *Commerce*, Autumn 1924.
[2] Breton, *Du surréalisme en ses œuvres vives*.
[3] Hence this definition of Surrealism by Aragon: 'Surrealism is recognized, accepted and practised inspiration. Not as an inexplicable visitation, but as a faculty to be exercised.'
[4] F. Gérard, *La Révolution surréaliste*, No. 1 (1924), thus, strange as it may seem at first sight, linking together the two words 'automatism' and 'freedom'.
[5] Breton, *Anthologie de l'humour noir* (texte de presentation de Lautréamont).
[6] One can also see how far Surrealism was from being a school, how far removed from any kind of 'literature', as such, and how close, in fact, to life, including the need for revolution.

From the reception and transcription of automatic texts and dreams, Surrealism moved on to their interpretation. In doing so, it discovered, with the help of Freud and psychoanalysis, the mainspring of that 'perpetual mutation'.

Although automatism led directly to 'the total psycho-physical field',[1] it found there the depths of the 'self' in which reign 'the absence of contradiction, the mobility of the emotive investments due to repression, intemporality, and the replacement of external reality by psychical reality, which is subject only to the pleasure principle'. This explains very clearly the conclusion of the author of *Nadja*:

> For the last fifteen years, the entire effort of Surrealism has been directed to the attainment by the poet of the instantaneous revelation of those verbal traces whose psychical charges may spread to the elements of the perception-consciousness system . . . I shall not tire of repeating that automatism alone can provide the elements on which the secondary work of emotional amalgamation and of the transition from the unconscious to the pre-conscious can be properly exercised (Breton, 1935).

Absence of contradictions, mobility, and association are terms that we must bear in mind. In this way, there emerged, and was justified theoretically, the principle, hitherto merely half-glimpsed by the poets,[2] of the *unlimited interrelation of all things*; the idea of the infinite possibilities to be found in the field of universal comparisons that made up man, the world, and the cosmos,[3] authorized by the presence, in the human consciousness, of those symbols that are charged with latent meaning and emotive power, heavy at once with past, present, and future, communicating at the point at which the two worlds of the unconscious and subconscious are joined.

It is from this source, by a process of association, that the visual and verbal flow is supplied; everything else has its source there, remembering, again, that it is 'that region in which unconstrained desire rises up . . . and that, too, in which the myths have their origin'.[4] It is there that Surrealist poetry originates, even the least 'automatic', such as that of

---

[1] Which, for Breton, was the essential criterion of 'surreality': 'A work may be regarded as Surrealist only in so far as the artist has tried to attain the total psycho-physical field (of which the field of consciousness is only a small part) . . .' (*Le Surréalisme et la peinture*, 1928a).
[2] In particular, the German romantics, whom the Surrealists admired, and Baudelaire.
[3] Cf., for example, Breton on esotericism:

> Whatever reservations one may have as to its principle, it at least offers the considerable interest of maintaining in its dynamic state the system of comparisons, that unlimited field at man's disposal that provides him with the means of relating apparently remote objects and partially reveals to him their universal symbolism (*Arcane 17*, 1947).

[4] Breton, *Du surréalisme en ses œuvres vives*.

Éluard, drawing life from that total freedom of universal interrelationship and nourishment for its finest images.[1] Without knowing, or seeking to know, 'who is speaking' through the mediation of the poet, a permanent and unlimited dialogue is established between the conscious man and that hitherto unknown part of him and, through it, between him and the universe as a whole; through automatism, at every moment and by every individual, that internal 'capillary tissue' may be revealed, which, according to Breton, 'makes possible the constant exchange that must be produced in thought between the external and the internal worlds' (Breton, 1932a

EVERYDAY ART

'Art is dead. Let us create our daily lives.'[2]

A permanent mutation originating on the association principle; this, then, was the nature of that universal and *permanent* language that the Surrealists sought, and they now knew where it was to be found. The immediate logical consequence that they drew from this was that it was decipherable, at all times and by all: 'It may be that life demands to be deciphered like a cryptogram', declared Breton in *Nadja*. Man must – and it is enough that he should do so – turn away from all acquired notions, all his habitual points of view,[3] and accept all the conditions necessary for the discovery and reactivation of the elements and values of this language; he must begin at once to practise that 'total liberation of the mind' demanded by the Surrealists.

Surrealism never succeeded, however, even in gaining recognition by

[1] The same must be said of Surrealist painting. Thus, in very characteristic terms, Éluard wrote of the work of his friend Max Ernst:

> In his *collages*, his *frottages* and his paintings, the artist constantly pursues his desire to confuse forms, events, colours, sensations, the futile and the serious, the evanescent and the permanent, the old and the new, contemplation and action, men and objects, time and duration, the part and the whole, night, dreams and light.

We are not far from Dada again, and it is quite natural that Tzara, writing as a Surrealist in 1938 (in *La Révolution surréaliste*), should celebrate *confusion* as the essence of poetry.

[2] Inscription, May 1968 (Sorbonne).

[3] Automatism, 'graphic as well as verbal', achieves in fact that 'rhythmic unity' which, for Breton, is 'the only structure that corresponds to the non-distinction . . . between sense-perceptible qualities and formal qualities, to the non-distinction . . . between sense functions and intellectual functions' (*Le Surréalisme et la peinture*), and may even 'resolve all antinomies outside the economic sphere'.

In this sense, it represents one of those 'points of the mind' in which all contradictions are resolved (cf. *Second manifeste du surréalisme*) – another important Surrealist theme that was to be rediscovered in May 1968 in that search for the *unity* of the human being that had been lost and should be reinstated:

> Revolutionary ideology is resolutely *unitary and totalizing*. It is neither 'democratic' nor 'totalitarian'. It rejects that opposition as it does all others and knows them not (Censier Action Committee, *Nous sommes en marche*: 'Advance-project for a social and cultural revolution', postulate 11).

the Communist Party, to which it offered its 'services' several times. Its activity remained isolated within the intellectual and artistic field and threatened with ineffectiveness both by this refusal of recognition and by bourgeois absorption. Except in the case of a handful of individuals, then, this desire was to remain unfulfilled. However, when a few revolutionary consciousnesses throw off the yoke of the absolute priority of economic emancipation and declare that they want everything at once, and, as in May 1968, succeed in directing a politico-social movement, the beginnings of a total revolutionary practice, such as the Surrealists 'dreamed' of, become possible. This may be summed up in the theoretical affirmation that the emancipation of artistic and literary forms is and must be indissolubly linked with that of the economic structures. If everything is not settled, as people have succeeded in convincing themselves since 1917, by the abolition of the private ownership of the means of production, it is because other spheres must be tackled and because 'there are no priorities, . . . no urgent problems. Everything is urgent and everything is to be done.'[1] The only problem that immediately presents itself is the practice of the ideas, the application of the means of the revolution that is both 'social and cultural, so that man may become himself and no longer be content with a humanizing ideology'.[2] A revolution that rejects 'all previous divisions and, in particular, the restriction of politics to the mere representation of the economic and social structures that are subjacent to it'.[3]

For the Surrealists, man must – and it is enough that he should do so – cease to regard art as a private terrain, a domain that is practised only by a few privileged individuals who have acquired the necessary tools, which are jealously preserved and sparingly distributed by nature and by society. Since its domain is now 'that of *pure mental representation*, as it extends beyond that of true perception, though not to be confused with the hallucinatory sphere',[4] the corresponding technical effort will consist of 'increasing the ways of penetrating to the deepest layers of the mental'. Far from remaining at the stage of dream and automatic writing, Surrealism increased the paths of exploration, from top to bottom of the scale of serious technique, on the basis, for example, of 'various experiments conceived in the form of party games', whose effectiveness seems

[1] Censier Action Committee, *Nous sommes en marche* ('Advance-project for a social and cultural revolution', postulate 25). Apart from the absolutist tone of the statement, this rejection of all priority, and of all specialization and categorization, is, as we know, one of the principal features of the May Movement. It is the theme of non-reduction: cf. Lefebvre, *L'Irruption: du Nanterre au sommet* (1968).
[2] *Nous sommes en marche* ('Appeal to the population', thesis 29).
[3] Ibid., 'Advance-project for a social and cultural revolution', postulate 9.
[4] The qualification is worth noting (Breton, 1935).

in no way to have been diminished by their unboring, not to say entertaining, character: Surrealist texts obtained simultaneously by several individuals writing at a given time in the same room, collaborations that led to the creation of a single sentence or drawing, of which one element (subject, verb, or object – head, belly, or legs) was supplied by each person . . .[1]

> In the definition of a non-given thing . . . in the prediction of events that the realization of a particular unimaginable condition would lead to . . . etc., we think that we have given rise to a curious possibility of thought – that of its *mise en commun* (Breton, 1930).

Thus poetry, among other things, becomes that 'activity of the mind', as Tzara defined it in 1934, adding:

> It is perfectly accepted today that one can be a poet without ever having written a line of verse, that a poetic quality exists in the street, in a commercial spectacle, anywhere, there is confusion everywhere, it is poetic . . .[2]

For confusion, like chance – 'Chance must be systematically explored', declared a wall inscription at Censier in May 1968 – is a meeting-place.[3] The whole history of the collage also tends to show that

> art has truly ceased to be individual . . . What is now being sustained is the negation of technique . . . and, with it, the technical personality; the painter, if we still have to call him that, is no longer linked to his picture by a mysterious, physical kinship analogous to generation (Aragon, 1930).

The incorporation in the 'work of art' of various elements and materials, of foreign bodies, even of living forms – in 1933 Picasso introduced a butterfly into one of his paintings – expresses both an opening of art onto life and the incorporation of the whole of nature in its creation.

Lastly, the application of tricks, techniques, and methods discovered by the Surrealists, individually or collectively,[4] was the result of two fundamental needs: to establish *contacts* between spheres that were hitherto regarded as foreign to one another, in order to create, from the resultant shock, the *overthrow* of sensibility.

[1] Examples of the various 'Surrealist games', with rules and results, are to be found in the appendices of Nadeau (1945) and in *La Révolution surréaliste*, Nos. 9–10.
[2] 'Essai sur la situation de la poésie', *Le Surréalisme au service de la Révolution*, No. 4.
[3] These wall hoardings, which were not all written, and to which anyone who happened to read them was invited to add his own opinion of the written text, or even to continue it as he wished, are obviously based on the same principle as the 'Surrealist games', even if the modes – and the field of application – are different: collective research, trust in immediacy and chance, etc.
[4] In addition to the collective 'games' and the collages, one might mention Max Ernst's 'frottages' (rubbings), Dali's 'paranoiac-critical' method, and Man Ray's discovery of various processes in photography.

PRIMORDIAL EMOTION

'Motions kill emotions.'[1]

For the Surrealist, life is a 'cryptogram' in the deciphering of which everyone may participate, there being many different ways and means of doing it: dream, automatic writing, humour, love, artistic expression, etc. There are no aesthetic norms, in fact, no such thing as beauty, separable from life, beauty that is or can be possessed, that can be presented and observed in the form of a spectacle. There are no walls between different fields, or at least those separations that still survive can be knocked down and the work of knocking them down must be started.

So the Surrealists wandered around Paris, with no other aim but to make, by placing themselves completely in the hands of 'chance', one of those contacts, to see one of those 'signals' light up, on one of those 'meeting-places' where decipherment takes place.[2] In addition to the essential and absolute trust placed in these two notions – the key of *waiting* and of *immediacy*[3] – whose illumination-revelation is awaited, it is interesting to note the nature of the 'click' by which the presence of the desired contact is made known to the consciousness. For the Surrealists, it takes the form of emotion: poetic, erotic, to mention only those which, for them, are virtually the same. This explains the statement made by André Breton in *Poisson soluble*: 'We shall reduce art to its simplest expression, which is love.' So love, too, provided one abandons oneself to it totally and experiences it as *amour fou* – to use Breton's words – as passion, is a permanent source of one of those 'points' which, human reason having lost its control, 'has every chance of producing the most profound emotion of the human being'; in other words, of attaining that 'region' in which the mind and desire have become one,[4] since the pleasure principle reigns there as master, and *allows the consciousness to be invaded by*

[1] Inscription, May 1968 (Censier) – 'motions' referred to the written resolutions submitted to the assemblies.
[2] 'Though one cannot say what signal exactly', wrote Breton in *Nadja*, a book devoted, as it were, to the description of these 'contacts'. Another, more 'literary', example of these 'magical wanderings' is to be found in Aragon's *Le Paysan de Paris* (1926).
[3] Only the waiting is 'magnificent', Breton was to say – which, logically, means more than the discovery, for example. This is not unlike that rejection of all determination that is a feature of all 'movements of revolt', up to and including that of May; only the absence of response would reveal the authentic man; all definition reduces, betrays, alienates. So, too, the idea that the essence, that is, the unity of man can be discovered only in the immediate is related to the 'immaturity' of the May revolutionaries (cf. the group discussion above).
[4] 'Anyone who regards emotion as foreign to logical thought should get himself killed on the field of that idealist vision' – Censier Action Committee, *Nous sommes en marche* ('Preliminary propositions for a cultural revolution', 20). Does this not reveal a similar search for the unity of these two normally dissociated principles?

this explosive charge. It is the source of an 'overthrow' which, if it were ever realized to the full, would transform man, the world, and life itself: a revolutionary faith, which, beyond all failures, temporary 'alliances', and compromises, Surrealism has always continued to proclaim.

'Spontaneity', which is so easily misunderstood either by excessive praise or in intellectualizing criticism, was always a part of the Surrealist 'game'. It was revealed both in the flow of 'automatic writing' and in the immediately recognizable illumination that took place when an 'idea' of desire found 'artistic' expression. It is hardly surprising that we should find in May those two characteristics of the free course of spontaneity, those two 'extremisms', that were *also somewhere other than in the words*, in Surrealism: the extreme pleasure of the game,[1] masking its extreme seriousness. Having brought about the 'unlocking of the ideological locks, violence, unexpectedness, frankness and the euphoria of the movement' will continue, by virtue of their own strength and that of the response encountered, thus defining their spontaneity. Opening onto that virgin ideological terrain, like one of those Surrealist 'regions', in which contradictions, as well as all barriers and obstacles, are swept aside, it means, for the whole or part of the working class (in the historical case of the spring of 1968) 'its ability to trigger off a movement and to invent its own structures of combat outside or against the "vanguards", whether large or small, that declare themselves to be the leadership of the workers' movement' (D. and G. Cohn-Bendit, 1968, pp. 171-172). I hope I have shown how short is the distance that separates this declaration from May 1968 and André Breton, 'I want people to keep silent when they no longer feel', or the fine expression 'innocence of desire', which, it seems to me, is probably one of the best definitions of spontaneity.[2]

DEREALIZATION: A MEANS OF OVERTHROW

'Down with socialist realism. Long live Surrealism.'[3]

The hoards of literally uncontrolled words with which Dada and Surrealism hoped to open the gates are not among those that can be withdrawn so vainly . . . One pretends not to have noticed too much that the logical mechanism

[1] Cf. D. and G. Cohn-Bendit (1968): 'Understand that the revolutionary struggle can only be a game in which everyone feels the need to play.' See also their description of the nature of the 'beauty' of the night of 10 to 11 May 1968 and of 'the festive atmosphere of the barricades'.
[2] It is to be found in a tract of the AGEN–UNEF of Nantes (Association Générale des Étudiants Nantais), written in 1967, and quoted by D. and G. Cohn-Bendit, 1968, pp. 28-29: 'Considering that the total rejection of psychology is unthinkable without an irresistible revelation of the *purity* of freedom that is expressed in the *innocence of desire*, in *creative serenity*, in *games, irony, festivity* . . .' (authors' italics).   [3] Inscription, May 1968 (Lycée Condorcet).

of the sentence is proving ever more powerless in man to set off the emotional shock that really gives some value to his life. On the other hand, the products of this spontaneous or *more* spontaneous, direct or *more* direct, activity, like those that are being increasingly offered to him by Surrealism in the form of books, pictures and films . . . he timidly leaves to them the task of over-throwing his way of feeling (Breton, 1930).

Not only does this quotation contain some of the key words with which we are concerned here, but it also leads us to recall the existence of what must be called, *post recuperationem*, 'Surrealist art', since it unleashed not only 'hoards of words', but also hoards of objects.

Elsewhere, Breton asks a question that is essential to the understanding of this passage: knowing from experience that 'to alter the order of words' is a means of attacking 'the apparent existence of things' (Breton, 1927), he is led to ask: 'Does not the mediocrity of our universe depend essentially on our power of enunciation?' Pure desire should be expressed in all its authenticity, by all means appropriate to its impatience, its violence, the strangeness of its laws; its perceived signals must be taken as such; the *donné*, the real, whether it is language or the 'world of objects', must be bent to the needs and laws of its spontaneous irruption, even at the price of an overthrow that is tantamount to their destruction and disintegration.[1]

Emotion can be expressed either from an object to us – 'we are seized with emotion at the sight of it' – or from us to the object – in which case, we 'seize hold' of it, in order to shape it (when it cannot be recreated totally) according to our 'emotion'. This, then, is the source of Surrealist artistic activity and of its different techniques, from surprise to the imitation of hallucination, by way of estrangement (*dépaysement*),[2] distortion,[3] etc. 'Surrealism will serve to alienate us from everything', said Breton of Max Ernst's collages, from which it follows that 'surprise must be sought for itself, unconditionally' (Breton, 1937). But the experiments carried out in the fields of language and painting, and the theoretical convictions acquired in their analysis, led Surrealism to go further, even to the point

[1] It is well known that the Surrealists had a particular interest in madness in all its forms. *L'Immaculée Conception* (Breton and Éluard, 1930) is an attempt to imitate and reproduce the language of different forms of madness – their defence of the 'insane' against psychiatry. It is in this sense, too, that Breton speaks of the 'negativist hand' of poetry.
[2] The French word – from *pays*, country – cannot be translated by a single word in all cases. The basic meaning is of being absent from one's own country, hence a feeling of strangeness in one's surroundings. It can mean the deliberate placing of something in an unusual context with the aim of disconcerting the observer, or it can approximate to the notion of alienation, though taken in a more neutral, less emotional sense. (Translator's note.)
[3] A desire that is also to be found on the strictly 'revolutionary' plane, since, according to the Second Manifesto, Surrealism proposes to pave the way for 'the definitive *distortion* of the intellectual forces now thriving in the interests of the inevitable revolution'.

of demanding and trying to provoke a 'fundamental crisis' (Breton, 1935), a 'total revolution of the object';[1] in particular, on the practical level, by the creation of strange 'Surrealist objects', poem-objects, Salvador Dali's 'soft watches', Marcel Duchamp's 'ready-mades', etc. The object becomes a field of speculation, capable as it is of a certain number of manipulations, which Breton defined as:

> distorting its true purpose by giving it a new name and signing it, which involves requalification by choice (Marcel Duchamp's 'ready-mades'); . . . showing it in the state in which it is sometimes placed by external agents, such as earthquakes, fire and water; . . . retaining it, for the very doubt that may be thrown on its previous use, for the ambiguity resulting from its totally or partially irrational conditioning, which involves significance through discovery (*objet trouvé*) and leaves an appreciable margin to interpretation, if necessary of the most active kind (Max Ernst's *objet-trouvé-interprété*); . . . lastly, reconstituting it as a whole from scattered elements, taken from the immediate datum (the Surrealist object, in the strict sense).[2]

One of the springs of the Surrealists' desire for derealization was already the struggle against the invasion of daily life by technology and its products. It was they who first gave expression to the theme of the rejection, and even the destruction, of 'merchandise' that was so much in evidence in May.[3]

> At all costs, we must strengthen whatever means of defence we can muster against the invasion of the sense world by things, which, out of habit rather than need, men use (Breton, 1928a).

By abstracting them from their usual context, putting them to other uses, or transforming their appearance by the subtraction or addition of one or several elements,[4] Surrealism 'undermined on every side' the world of 'concrete objects', which the writer of an inscription in the Sorbonne enjoined to 'hide themselves' from human gaze.[5]

If poetry and the theatre were in the streets in May and June 1968, it can be said that the most important collective creation of that time was

---

[1] An important passage in *Le Surréalisme et la peinture* (1928a).
[2] In *Le Surréalisme et la peinture* (1928a). To this list should probably be added the oneiric, or dream object (described by Breton, 1927) and the object with a symbolic function.
[3] A great many inscriptions, such as 'car-gadget', 'merchandise will be burnt', etc., and those advocating theft, revived, from an anti-consumer point of view, the old anarchist theme of 'individual appropriation'.
[4] Or, again, by deforming one or several of their own elements. Dali's soft objects – cf. the inscription found in the corridors of several métro stations: 'The walls are soft – write all over them', and the tract reproduced in Appendix III to this book (p. 313), 'Bite the soft machine' – are particularly interesting from this point of view, as is the link that he makes between desire-hunger and consumption-cannibalism. On this subject, cf. the chapter on *déréalisation* in F. Alquié's *The philosophy of surrealism*; for him, 'the soft object is the negation of all machinery and therefore of all physical technology'.   [5] 'Object, hide yourself!' (Amphithéâtre Richelieu).

the building of the barricades, whose reappearance and whose different and successive forms have already received a good deal of attention. Beyond their utilitarian purpose, they represented a series of symbolic values, as did a number of the manifestations of the May Movement, which is natural enough in such a total, and therefore also a cultural, revolution. Again, as with the 'Surrealist object', this is a case of the imagination in action. According to militants of M 22, what was exemplary about this action was not

> the building and defence of the barricade, but the sort of collective action in which everyone worked, and revealed such extraordinary inventiveness – this was far more important than the real effectiveness of the barricade as defence, which was fairly weak (Mouvement du 22 Mars, 1968, p. 68).

Similarly, the 'faculty of bringing two images together', which is at the basis of Surrealist activity, whether poetic or artistic, makes it possible, according to Breton (1928a), 'to rise above the consideration of the manifest life of the objects, which generally constitutes a limit' and make it turn back to 'an uninterrupted series of *latences* which are not peculiar to it and which demand its transformation'; thus its 'conventional value' is replaced by its 'value as representation' and an end is put to 'the prohibition resulting from the oppressive repetition of those that daily assail our senses and lead us to regard *all that may be outside them*[1] as illusory'.

What has been said of the barricade might also be said of those 'notions', so often regarded as impossible in an advanced capitalist country, of general strike, or revolution. The revolutionary imagination in action of May did not invent out of nothing, nor even realize, those objects of study of all realisms: simply reactivating the faculties that can bring them back to life, it has revealed the inhibiting character of the realisms and the inexhaustible vitality of reality. In this sense, the Surrealist group could then write:

> On 3 May 1968 realism was condemned to death. The objective of the Revolution, whose reality today remains intact, is to have it shot forthwith.[2]

THE IMAGINATION SEIZES POWER

Although it would be vain to try to discover what 'began it all', let us say, with Paul Éluard (1939), that at the beginning was hope: 'It is hope or despair that will determine for the awakened dreamer – for the poet – the action of his imagination.'

[1] My italics.   [2] In *L'Archibras* (1968), 'Le surréalisme le 18 juin 1968: Portrait de l'ennemi.'

Hope and its demands, for it was the same hope, the same desire, that animated the two approaches that Surrealism wished to bring together in a common struggle for the same Revolution: that of Marx and that of Rimbaud. Perhaps it was not until Surrealism – and, of course, the whole context in which it was born and to which it partly 'owes' its birth – that the Rimbaud approach could be established, in theory at least, outside the region of poetic 'illumination' in which it had been confined; it was no doubt necessary to experience the shattering of the hope placed in the achievements of the Marxist approach before this resurgence of 'dead' revolutionary ideas, this search for new modes of action, in short, this reactivation of the revolutionary imagination that we are now witnessing in the world, could be manifest.

This is hardly surprising. Image and imagination require distance. Thus, at the level of perception itself, we know that although visual and auditory images are more numerous than olfactory and tactile ones, etc., this is mainly because they inform the sensibility about objects situated at some distance.[1] Distance makes it possible to construct a spectacle – 're-presentation' – that is, the image, within sensation itself. From a philosophical point of view, Surrealism may be regarded as the desire to resolve this antinomy between desire and representation: man, having reached the stage of objective knowledge, is confronted by an *image* of the world, which he must take into account, whether he comes to terms with it or seeks to reappropriate it. By various means – automatism, the search for and construction of objects, delirium – the Surrealist hopes 'to place once again in the power of desire a number of images that have been formed only by a break with desire itself' (Alquié, 1965).[2]

It should be noted that the intention is always to allow the *irruption* of 'wild' images that will disturb the sensibility by shattering the coherence of those 'stable' images that make up, for each individual, the objective world. One can see at once the active side of the Surrealist *practice of the image*, or imagination: in fact, it is not merely a matter of being 'open to images', but of going towards them. In addition to the different approaches to the 'self', does not Breton speak of *organizing* those 'perceptions of an objective tendency', thus provoking 'imperiously, in external reality, something that responds to them' (Breton, 1935)?[3]

A practice tending to disturb and to overthrow is a revolutionary

[1] Cf. the chapter on imagination in Alquié (1965).
[2] Dali's famous saying – 'The culture of the mind will be identified with the culture of desire' – should be understood in this sense.
[3] This is the notion of *objectivation* – one of the most important in Surrealist practice.

practice, and once we have admitted that the field – let us call it the 'mental' field – explored by Surrealism is inseparable from the other domains of a total revolution, it is easy enough to draw a parallel with the revolutionary movement of May 1968.[1] When confronted by that movement, the whole of daily life opposed this practice with every means at its disposal, including that of the 'interiorization of repression'. As a result, there were only isolated groups of social non-conformists: madmen, artists, and revolutionaries. It is clear how much these two cases of rejection have in common: the first declaring in 1930 that it rejects 'without hesitation the idea that only those things that *are* are possible' and is able 'by a way that *is*' to attain 'what was claimed *not to be*',[2] the second declaring in May 1968:

> Workers, we must become ourselves. If we are told that it is a *utopia*, we must realize that *Revolution is necessary*. So *reality* will no longer be the privilege of those who exploit us and deprive us of our humanity.[3]

In this sense, the enemy is just that realism which must be destroyed if total reality, which for some is simply 'surreality', is to be built on its ruins – the realism that is so succinctly defined in the May slogans and by the present-day Surrealists in their review *L'Archibras:* 'All that is realistic is senile, all that is senile is realistic' ('Portrait de l'ennemi', 1968).

SURREALISM IS WHAT WILL BE[4]

'Our sclerotic and archaic psychical structures must be sabotaged to give way to the imagination of a new world', declared one of the 'propositions' put forward by the Censier Action Committee in May.[5]

Against utility, against reason, realism, logic, Breton affirmed[6] that the imagination 'alone *causes* real things'; Surrealism tried by every means to 'sabotage' rational and 'civilized' man, in order to deliver him up to desire,

---

[1] I shall not elaborate here, for example, the significant fact, admitted by the revolutionaries themselves, that their practice was in advance of their theory. To this should be added the view that the revolution was 'in advance of itself':

> The strength and weakness of a revolutionary movement lies in being in advance of itself. Whoever sees this only as a weakness is a reactionary. Whoever sees it only as a strength is a danger to the Revolution (Censier Action Committee, *Nous sommes en marche*, 'Advance-project for a social and cultural revolution', postulate 7).

[2] Breton (1930). He continues: 'How can we show tenderness, or even tolerance, towards any apparatus of social conservation? It would be the only truly inacceptable madness on our part.'
[3] *Nous sommes en marche* ('Activity–Work–Revolution', proposition 30).
[4] In *Cause*, a Surrealist manifesto of 1947.
[5] *Nous sommes en marche* ('Preliminary propositions for a cultural revolution', proposition 10).
[6] Preface of 1929 to the First Manifesto of Surrealism (1924).

that 'great bearer of keys' (Breton, 1952) and modeller of the imagination. The Surrealist life is characterized by the search for and the practice of an infinite series of psychical breaks of greater or lesser 'importance', if one dares to write such a thing – in this sense, by a permanent break. For desire precedes the consciousness that man may have of it and the determination to give it pre-eminence. The strength of imaginative realization is to be found in him who, when confronted by the real, acts upon it, transforming and creating it in his own way. For 'everything creates an image' in the real: 'the least object to which no particular symbolic role has been assigned is capable of representing anything' (Breton, 1932a); while once the mind is unleashed it turns out to be 'marvellously prompt to seize upon the slightest relation that may exist between two objects chosen at random' (ibid.). The Surrealist image, as we see once again, is neither presentation nor representation, but comparison – and, therefore, creative of the infinity of possible relations. The two sides of this active character are present in its dual direction: from the real to the image, the power of rejection, derealization, and imagination; from the image to the real, the realizing force by which forms are embodied.

It would be easy enough to draw a detailed parallel with the revolutionary activity of the May Movement in Surrealism's own politico-cultural field; to show, in particular, that although this active imagination, of which so much has been said, revealed, and for very good reason, only one of its sides, which resulted in its being regarded as wholly destructive, it also had a no less 'positive' or 'constructive' side. The two are not only indissolubly linked, but also determine each other, as emerges quite clearly, to take only two examples, in the demand for radical criticism and in the search for new means and solutions: total destruction is coupled with total reconstruction; new methods of struggle (exemplary actions, etc.) with new solutions for defence and organization (self-defence, self-management).[1] But I should like to concentrate attention on another characteristic, the *present*, immediate character of this image, which is undoubtedly a *sine qua non* of its possible realization, and therefore of its relation with the idea of action.

Against that 'cancer of the mind that resides in the fact of thinking

---

[1] Bakunin (*God and the state*) is particularly enlightening on this dialectical necessity:

> No one can wish to destroy without having at least a vague image, whether true or false, of the order of things that he believes should follow that which exists at present; and the more vivid his image, the more powerful his destructive force becomes . . . For destructive action is always determined, not only in its essence and its degree of intensity, but also in its methods, in the ways and means it uses, by the positive ideal that constitutes its initial inspiration, its soul.

much too sorrowfully that certain things *are*, while others, which could just as easily be, *are not*', Breton declared, in the Second Manifesto, that, not content to affirm theoretically 'that things must merge together, or be very closely interwoven', to the utmost limit, the Surrealists were under an obligation not to 'leave things there, *not to do less than strain desperately towards that limit*', and we have seen throughout this chapter the ways and means employed in this permanent struggle. Although this struggle was carried out from day to day – from break to break, one might say, at the individual, or even group, level – and in an apparently destructive manner, without a 'programme', this was merely because it took no account of the future. The fact that this notion is hardly developed at all in Surrealist writings, theoretical or otherwise, and that the word itself is hardly to be found, is symptomatic, in my opinion, of a total rejection, of the past, petrified in history books, as well as of the future, petrified in advance in programmes. Surrealism rose up against these two obstacles that blocked its way:

> Man must flee this ridiculous web that has been spun around him: so-called present reality with the prospect of a future reality that is hardly better.[1]

Like the May Movement, caught in the same pincer movement, Breton denies it all value and attacks it on both fronts, placing all his trust in a revitalized present, shaped, if not created, by the imagination in action. The imaginary is thus not only 'what tends to become real' (Breton, 1932b), but what becomes real every day when man becomes aware and takes possession of all his faculties, particularly those that have hitherto been repressed, and places them at the disposal of the creative imagination, which is now 'finally liberated'.

In this sense, Surrealism is totally opposed to utopias: for the Surrealists the task is not one of realizing abstract ideals, but of liberating man, beginning with a series of very concrete liberations: that of all the faculties, tendencies, or elements that have been repressed, concealed, or perverted. Desire, hope, and imagination are immanent in man and in his history, in time: they realize man and are realized in him to the extent that they 'have power'; the aim is to give them that power. Although Surrealism claimed to have found the means of placing creation at the disposal of everyone, it provided no formal description of it and offered no prescription or programme as to the use to which it was to be put. It knew

[1] Breton, 'Petit intermède prophétique', in *Prolégomène à un Troisième Manifeste du surréalisme ou non* (1942). In their definition of 'Leftism', D. and G. Cohn-Bendit also speak of the 'new' and the 'past', but not of the future (1968, p. 18).

only too well that its richness and power are such that it can only irrupt with the violence of joy; the same can be said of revolution, when the imagination is given free rein and recreates itself in an atmosphere which, however tragic it may be, cannot but be that of celebration. It cannot then claim to dictate the future, which would be putting the cart before the horse, since it exists in order to liberate not only man but itself, to be born and to grow with him.[1]

For this revolution – that of the imagination[2] – is a *permanent* revolution: it could not stop once an *a priori* programme had been applied. Such a prospect had as little sense for the Surrealist revolution as for that of May. The action of the Surrealist imagination is never *finished*, first of all because it is never exhausted, in so far as it can be regarded as a domain, a store of old images, but above all because it is always an image in the process of being created. Indeed, Surrealism talks of nothing but the imagination; it does not consider, as it were, the result of action, but action itself, any action capable of helping 'the thought to succumb at last to the thinkable' (Breton, 1930). This dialectical movement of mutual enrichment is not historical or chronological, with a before and an after: it is *immediate*, it takes place in the present moment. Every time the expression of a desire is made possible, man gains in power. Knowledge, pleasure, and imagination increase, and, in a continual, mutual, liberating process, become more and more flexible and open to expression. 'Man proposes and disposes. It belongs only to him to belong entirely to himself,' wrote Breton in the First Manifesto.

Against the idea of diversions and stages, the revolutionary movement of May 1968 also proclaimed this need to give back expression (or power, which, from this point of view, amounts to the same thing) to the imagination; proclaimed once again the demands of desire and its virtues: radicality, immediacy, efficacity. The authors of *Nous sommes en marche* wrote:

> The new society is not something to imagine and then to create. It is some-
> thing to be created and imagined at the same time in a single process of active
> disalienation, which must not be confused with passive deconditioning, the

---

[1] At most it can take on the character of an appeal to reality, as was seen in several texts published in May, as, for example, in the 'propositions' of the Censier Action Committee in *Nous sommes en marche*: 'All previous divisions of labour are abolished.' 'The whole of the traditional economy is revoked. The "laws" of the economy are abolished. All the old economists are called on to seek new techniques appropriate to man's new activity' ('Activity–Work–Revolution', propositions 12 and 13).

[2] 'The imagination does not possess the imitative instinct. It is the spring and torrent that drives one onward' (Éluard).

supreme alienation . . . The new society is already here with us, providing we do not give up the struggle, that is, providing we continue to be and to become ourselves.[1]

One can see to what extent the two attitudes are linked, if not identical. This is no doubt because they both place more emphasis on man (alienated, but capable of disalienating himself) and his power than on structures: these structures, whether substructures or superstructures, must certainly be replaced, but this is the work of man – a fact that has often been lost sight of. And if man has material weapons to accomplish this, it is a good thing that he be shown – whether in the 'political' or the 'artistic' field – that they are not the only ones. That there also exists that unknown factor, the imagination, which is the source of all for the man who has ever, as Breton shows, 'sat it on his knees':

> Listen to it. At first, you will think that it does not know what it is saying, that it knows nothing . . . You don't know what it wants. It makes you aware of several other worlds at once, to such an extent that you soon don't know whether you're in this one or not. At that point, the trial of everything opens, a trial that never ends.[2]

[1] 'Advance-project for a cultural and social revolution', postulate 30.
[2] 'Caractères de l'évolution moderne', in Les Pas perdus (1924b).

CHAPTER 9

Free Jazz

A parallel with a contemporary socio-musical movement will help us to complement this study of May, which is also the sketch of a prototype of a phenomenon with more general implications, with many different forms, but with one parental feature in common: cultural politicization.

The revolutionary activities of the students put the emphasis on the individual, who redefines his roles, invents others, and rejects the adaptation of a 'play' that he himself did not write. By practising collective improvisation, the students rediscovered procedures that had been practised at earlier times and in other places, and sometimes drew inspiration from those examples.

Improvisation has always played a large part in jazz. Whether collective or individual, improvisation presupposed the dialectical synthesis created by a group or an individual, redefining known elements, elements tha have just been played and experienced, while inventing new elements in the course of the activity itself. The parallel with jazz, such as it was until 1955, would have provided ample material for reflection, but I shall refer to this only in passing. There has appeared a variety of jazz, however – *free* jazz – which claims to be revolutionary, both politically and artistic-ally. This new departure should therefore provide a much closer parallel with a student movement that is also difficult to grasp as an entity, an *object* of projection on the part of the protagonists, and of its enemies and observers – though the politicization of a musical phenomenon, an abstract expression, does present problems.

It has been noted elsewhere that the term 'free jazz' is reminiscent of the 'Free Speech Movement' initiated by the students of Berkeley and taken over later by French students.[1] 'Free form jazz', as it is also called, which many regard as the expression of a revolutionary desire for social

[1] The politico-literary discussions of the relation between the FSM and poetic productions of a 'free-verse' type show that the extent of the phenomenon should be studied (cf., for example, D. Wesling, 'Free speech and free verse' (1965)).

emancipation, is also an artistic – or anti-artistic – school that seeks the emancipation of the non-formal. This is both a logical consequence and a questioning of the whole tradition of American Negro music (diffused and practised throughout the world, but rarely with any non-original admixture). But although we should avoid making close comparisons between the evolution of jazz, from its origins to its latest developments, and the evolution of Western, so-called 'classical', music, as has sometimes been done, we should note the *complexity* and the *rapidity* of this evolution. Jazz has changed at an ever-increasing rate; it has produced a great variety of musicians of different styles and schools. The collective improvisations of the first Armstrong quintet are today regarded as classical – as the 'preludes and fugues' of jazz – but the variety of the first bands or of the first musicians is perhaps as great as that of the European contemporaries of J. S. Bach; in any case, a great many of them can be identified without difficulty on the recordings that have survived. In short, the musical distance that separates the jazz of the pre-1930 period and the free jazz[1] of post-1960 is as great as that between a Bach cantata and the chorale of Michel Puig's 'Messe pour l'Arbresle'. There is not only a tradition in Jazz, but 'established' musicians and tendencies condemned by younger musicians, etc., which, however, does not prevent iconoclastic revolutionaries like Archie Shepp from quoting (though emphasizing that they are isolated exceptions) Don Redman, Fletcher Henderson, and Duke Ellington, side by side with such composers as Aaron Copland, Edgar Varèse, and John Cage, and insisting that the 'new music', in its American Negro branch, is simply a logical development of earlier preoccupations and the direct continuation of the efforts of such relatively recent innovators as Parker (who died in 1955) and Monk.[2]

To say that jazz has a history is more important at the strictly musical level than at the social level. In spite of a period of extreme commercialization, the tradition of the blues has continued throughout that history and most of the great musicians continue to express the same general social 'message' – this, at least, is the view expressed by LeRoi Jones and, less violently, by others (see Jones, 1963).

[1] The term appears to have been used for the first time on a record of the collective improvisation of a double quartet assembled by Ornette Coleman. The sleeve of this record was itself something of an event, being illustrated by an action-painting by Pollock.

[2] Cf. Archie Shepp, 'A view from the inside' (1966). My material is drawn largely from the writings of European critics. The 'free musicians' have almost all lived in Europe and various critics have visited New York to study the contemporary jazz avant-garde. The periodicals *Jazz Magazine*, *Cahiers du Jazz*, and *Jazz Hot* have published a number of studies, as has the German magazine *Jazz Podium*. These and other periodicals quoted often reproduce recorded interviews with musicians. I am also particularly grateful for the help of the Paris critics P. Carles and J.-L. Comolli.

As to the parallel with May, one misunderstanding should be cleared up at the outset. Various newspapers and commentators have talked of 'pianos on the barricades', of jazz in May, etc. A lot of people noted musical activities of a 'folk' kind. The fact is that on one of the first nights of the Sorbonne occupation, in the middle of a festive crowd, a concert piano, torn from its respectable, sedentary existence, was set up in the courtyard. But the common element between free jazz and the attempts of the four disparate musicians that I observed at one point can be no more than the need to express something and the absence of all arrangement, even of an oral kind – the 'happening' element. Even without the crowd, which invaded the platform to such an extent that it prevented the musicians from communicating, there could hardly have been any fusion between the girl student, who had a brilliant pianistic technique, beginning 'Night in Tunisia' (*à la* Bud Powell) and the 'rock' drummer or the plodding bass player. It was impossible for them to produce even an atmosphere of simple craziness, by abandoning known forms and the learnt use of the instruments – which is usually not without a certain effectiveness of its own, provided there is *enough* motivation and *enough* freedom. In fact, the essential thing about this group was not the way it functioned but its setting. The crowd was amused by the idea that one could *give oneself permission* to play jazz in such a place, on a concert grand that the occupiers had themselves decided to take outside, and to make this noise under the eyes of Marx and Mao looking down on them from posters near the statue of Victor Hugo, on the plinth of which was written: 'Liberate expression.'[1]

What I am offering here is a sketch of the socio-musical phenomenon of American Negro free jazz; whatever parallels can be drawn with May, as a non-musical movement, will be the result of a general kinship on major points.

I shall pass from the formal and organizational aspects to the discussions on politicization, though it is not always possible to make such divisions in a phenomenon that is obviously so fusionist and so varied – as we shall see when we try to arrive at a general definition of the 'movement'.

NO DEFINITION: PRACTICE

The term 'new thing' is a pejorative one, even though it has been adopted by the defenders of the movement. It is obviously no coincidence that it

---

[1] True free jazz improvisations do appear to have taken place in May, but I have been unable to collect any precise information on the subject. It might be noted, however, that the high spirits of the members of the Beaux Arts brass band often created an atmosphere of fierce hilarity that was closer to free jazz than anything produced in the Sorbonne by the means described.

was used for the first time by a professional avant-garde musician, Don Ellis, a white, and an intellectual, who preferred his music to be ordered and structured.[1] Commentators – and musicians – have continued to use the term. In its positive sense, the word implies opening, a form of embodiment of a phenomenon that is both varied and elusive when one tries to reduce it to a formula, and concretely apprehensible when reduced to its physical appearance, as sound material, when one believes that the objectivation makes it possible to apprehend the spirit. This problem indicates from the outset one of the characteristics that has been observed elsewhere in this study: opening, the ever-incomplete definition of the 'thing' that leaves a freedom of appreciation and active, constructive participation, not only to the individual who is most obviously partici-pating, but to the observer, and – a fact that is even less often recognized – to whoever the movement is addressing, whether the audience or society. But, to begin with, let us remain within the more strictly musical field. One of the reasons why the protagonists themselves may accept the term is their determination not to be confined within a label – 'new thing' and 'free' are anti-labels.

How can this 'thing' be described except in relation to the development of jazz, and, more widely, by reference to the practice of the men who 'live' it, as they themselves describe it?[2]

It has always been difficult to express in the abstract what are regarded as the two most important aspects of jazz or the blues, *feeling* and *swing*. The writer and engineer Boris Vian, who was no less remarkable as a jazz musician and journalist, stated the need for interiority in this way:

> I have never presumed to explain jazz to anyone . . . In my view, the main thing is to listen and to love – the word 'understand' means nothing in this field; you don't understand a piece, you understand the man who played it.[3]

Alain Gerber, the psychologist and jazz critic, expresses a similar view of free jazz. The pleasure principle implies two polarities. From now on, 'displeasure' is part of the experience.

It is right to say (of free jazz) that it is a *thing*, for it is precisely this ineluctable

[1] Cf. Postif and Kopelowicz, *Jazz Hot*, No. 210, 1965.
[2] Another method of analysis consists in objectifying the music by means of codified notation: Casser (on Armstrong), Papparelli (on Parker and Gillespie), Heckman (on Ornette Coleman), and Schuller (on Cecil Taylor) have shown that the transcription of individual, if not collective, improvisations is practicable. It is true that what eludes codification is particularly important in free jazz, since more importance is given to variations of sound.
[3] Written in 1953, reproduced in *Chroniques du jazz* (1967, pp. 142–143).

facticity: it is presence, matter almost, defying all ingestion. One doesn't *like* free jazz, one realizes one fine day . . . that it *is*.[1]

And he reminds one that the intellectualism that 'makes conceptual understanding not the instrument, but the criterion of truth' prevents the honest man from receiving this form of music, from recognizing that giving displeasure to the audience does not preclude the beautiful. He makes an existential psychoanalysis, interpreting not only musical data but observations of the personal behaviour of the musicians (behaviour on stage, relations between the musicians, etc.). One must understand the man in order to have a better appreciation of the music, and appreciate the music in order to deepen one's knowledge of the man. For the musicians themselves, this reversal is not new, but it is perhaps adopted more completely than ever before. Jazz musicians have always practised expressionism at least, if not 'intensity of life', to increase creativity and vice versa.

Parker, the uncontested leader of a whole generation of musicians,[2] practised this two-way movement, or rather fusion. Reisner has described this extraordinary *liver*, who sought with great intensity all imaginable kinds of experience. 'He put more life into his brief period of existence (1920–55) than any other human being.' And he recalls one of Parker's most famous statements:

> Music is your own experience, your thoughts, your wisdom. If you don't live it, it won't come out of your horn. They teach you there's a boundary line to music. But, man, there's no boundary line to art (Reisner, 1962).

One of the most important aspects of free jazz lies in the fact that it is above all an ever-changing, *immediate exteriorization* of life; it is therefore what, at a particular moment, those who are creating it (musicians and audience, in their reciprocal relations) *are*. But first let us return to the conceptions of jazz and above all to its radicalization in free jazz.

The development of musical techniques must be retraced, though I do not believe that each phase can be explained as a negation of the preceding one, any more than a few exceptional innovators embody the principles of each stage. It will be seen how one passes from internal criticism of a procedure to its reversal.

---

[1] *Jazz Magazine*, No. 133, 1966, p. 43; author's italics.
[2] And more generally, with Dylan Thomas and James Dean, one of the gods of the Beat Generation.

FROM STRUCTURE TO ACTION

Before anything else, one should speak of *rhythm*: the rhythm of marches has always struck an ear habituated to New Orleans jazz as 'rigid', though it sprang from the same tradition that the Negroes interpreted. The articulation of Armstrong's 'phrasing' went beyond this school and consisted of superimposing a ternary scheme (for example, a crotchet and a quaver in a triplet) on the bass of the binary rhythm, of seeking rhythmic independence, of freeing himself from the tyranny of metronomic tempo.

> Armstrong developed this principle of interplay in relation to several tempi or several bars . . . He was content to place over the tempi certain notes of his phrases, certain tempi being marked, others not, the internal beat remaining constant, hence the great freedom that the attentive listener senses in his music (Guérin, 1960, pp. 51–52).

Two other leading musicians made radical innovations in rhythm. Lester Young – apathetic, 'cool'[1] – introduced and carried very far the timing behind the tempo, and Parker – intense – alternated the timing ahead of and behind the tempo.

Whereas in the march and in early jazz, there was a strict rhythmic alignment between the wind instruments and the 'rhythm section', the soloists began more and more to move away from the rest, first by playing with strong and weak accents, then by abandoning even the rhythmic articulation *within* the units of the beat. From the time when the practice of the off-beat in relation to the rhythm section gave it the role of a reference-point, it was logical that the emancipation of the soloist, which was carried very far indeed in bop, with its dialectical interplay of off-beats on the tempo, should be followed by a corresponding emancipation of the rhythm section. The development of the playing of the three instruments traditionally called the rhythm section is very clear in this respect.

The development can be expressed schematically in this way: at stage A, percussion, bass, and piano beat out a rhythm on the tempo, in unison; at stage B, the bass-playing became more complicated, the piano began to free itself from the rhythm and move towards a more harmonic role, and

---

[1] Cf. A. Gerber (1967), who diagnoses abulic neurasthenia, one of the characteristics of which is a rejection of the present, of action, of social time, etc. It should be added that although the psychological explanation accounts for an individual's behaviour, the *diffusion* of a pattern presents a sociological problem. A whole generation – that which called Young 'the President' – adopted rhythmic non-involvement, elegant detachment. It was *cool*.

It defined an attitude that actually existed. To be *cool* was, in its most accessible meaning, to be calm, even unimpressed, by what horror the world might daily propose (LeRoi Jones, 1963, p. 213).

the percussion retained the task of accompanying steadily on the beat; then, in stage C, the regularity, the 'guiding-thread', subtly exteriorized by the bass and cymbals, is constantly attacked by the rhythmic challenges from every side, from the piano, the bass drum, the side-drum, and the so-called melodic soloist or soloists, fusing their action on the basis of the now 'interiorized tempo', the whole process amounting to a sort of dialectical interactiogram.

Free jazz is not only situated beyond, after a declining stage C, but in *extension*, since the principle of the dialectical interplay between integration and non-integration into an existing order is completely abandoned. There is no longer any attempt to interiorize an external rhythmic reference, which, in the last resort, was still marked *explicitly*, and less and less completely, only by the cymbals and bass, all the other musical sources being placed flexibly around, in free variation. Metrical regularity was now abandoned, and with it even the interiorized metronome, with its scarcely perceptible rhythmic articulation, which still made it possible to count clearly, for example, the length of a solo (one or several *choruses* of 32 bars).

In stage D, the rhythmic unity is broken up into rhythm-sounds[1] and long periods, for example, of great calm, then of excitement, of extreme rapidity, through decelerations and accelerations – procedures that were traditionally excluded from jazz. We are now beyond the rhythmic conflict over the metronome – a rhythm regarded as constrictive even though, in practice, it was totally abandoned, leaving the musician to 'fly'. All that remains is a collective definition, in action, of periodization, of cadence, not the subjective interpretation of an experienced *external* regularity, but the ever-developing definition of a reference that is now merely *internal* to the group that is playing, with some regard perhaps for the audience.

This development of schemas, which passes through the progressive interiorization of an external order[2] and ends in their reversal – a revolution in the literal sense – seems clearer as far as rhythm is concerned than

---

[1] Or vibrations, which is shown by the growing interest of free jazz musicians in sound climates. K. Stockhausen (1963) replies to those who complain that contemporary European music 'has no rhythm' that 'it is all rhythm, but there is no metrical regularity', since the rhythm is now to be found in the oscillations, etc. The same argument is also valid for free jazz.

[2] In a sense, one is still within the schema when the external reference is no longer materialized even by the bass (cf. the study of Scott La Faro – G. Kopel, *Cahiers du jazz*, No. 8 – the bass soloist who abandoned the role of rhythmic support) as long as the implicit metric is respected. John Cage (1967) claims to be troubled by the metrical regularity of jazz, even when expressed in so subtle a way, that is, in a latent way, beneath a torrent of effects that conceal it, as by the percussionist Elvin Jones in 'A love supreme'. For him, this is still the constraint of the clock, of ordered time.

for the other musical aspects. Yet major transformations have taken place in the use of the instruments, in harmony, etc.

A complex development has taken place in harmonic structures that is also worth schematizing.

Quite apart from the big bands, for which jazz composers or arrangers have written scores that often repeat simple themes or phrases in fairly complicated harmonic variations, superimposing various chords, the harmonic structure of jazz in the small groups, which are the more numerous, has become increasingly complex.

Whereas initially, as in the rhythmic relations between musicians, everything was 'in line', the chords of the accompanying instruments being the same as the harmonic 'grid'[1] that was followed by a soloist, breaks were now introduced. The accompanying musicians, pianists and guitarists, were supposed to supply not only a support, a bass, but also a continuity throughout the piece. More than the soloists, they developed a differentiated harmonic skill. In addition to the relatively simple harmonic grid, they were able to decorate the chords of this grid, during an accompaniment, and so avoid monotony and boredom: apart from 'transition chords', they used additional notes, sometimes chords that were out of step with the grid and the soloist.

When the bop school introduced complex schemas, sometimes on standard themes – and redefined them, by introducing many more harmonic changes – the soloists were led to improvise in an increasingly complex way. In the end, soloists and accompanists followed highly systematic harmonic itineraries. Pushed to the limit, each important note of a theme, each phrase of an improvisation, led to chords of different accompaniments.

Once they had got over their initial surprise at the harmonically complex methods of the bop school, musicians became so used to every imaginable chord within each piece that it was inevitable that a growing process of liberation should be established. Respecting certain reference-points – tonic, dominant, etc. – they played notes belonging to chords that the accompaniment exteriorized only occasionally. Solo and accompanying instruments became more and more content with simple grids: more complex chords were then *suggested* by the soloist, a series of notes played melodically, or even isolated notes, recalling, by the interval that separated them from the basic chords, a whole series of interiorized chords.

[1] A succession of chords on which the melodic line of a piece is built up and which serves as a guide to the improviser, at least in traditional jazz.

Miles Davis and John Coltrane carried this free play in relation to the basic chords very far indeed.[1]

Various musicians have sought more and more desperately to escape from the *current system* (invented very largely by musicians like Bud Powell). The clarinettist and flautist E. Dolphy is among those who constantly give the impression of a struggle 'to get out': through sound, but also in the actual choice of notes, he tries constantly to destroy the norms that he transgresses with ever greater frequency. The breaking-point is reached both in terms of the rules of musical procedure and with regard to the socio-political content expressed in this struggle in the music.

All these 'habits' that have been erected into a sort of harmonic grammar have become intolerable. Whereas the bop school imposed complex basic grids, introducing musicians to the reference to ever more varied chords, these basic grids were capable of becoming more and more simple again. The soloists continued 'automatically' to meander off on their own, and even to execute very 'curious' changes, as in the most difficult modern themes (like 'Giant steps'), at least, to the furthest extremes of basic chords of 'logical' themes.

After this period of interiorization of simple structures as the complex scaffolding of superimposed additions, the *break* came from various solutions.

Coltrane introduced 'modes', drawing inspiration from the traditional music of other cultures. Instead of playing 'on the chords', in arpeggios, he played in *series of notes*, following fairly scrupulously not always their order, but the notes that they posited. It might well be asked what advantage was brought by the liberation from a system (of grids of chords) that made it necessary to accept the norms of another, even more constrictive system.[2] It seems to me that what is interesting about this system is its combination of two contrary principles: the static nature of the mode, creating a *single* atmosphere for each piece, and *movement*, upon which the improviser, freed from the constraints of a grid of chords, was able to concentrate. He is no longer obliged, as in bop, to change direction often, as if the harmonic grid forced him to run about as though trying to escape from a labyrinth. Now he can run along one or two corridors only. The 'energetic' school, as it was called, concentrated its attention on the

---

[1] The specialists are not in agreement as to which of the two musicians made the first step towards this liberation, by improvisation on suggested chords; as J. Berendt observes (1967), 'it was in the air' – which again shows the logic of the development.

[2] 'You say that Coltrane broke the chains. No doubt he did, but what good was that if it was only to place himself under the yoke of modes?' (A. Hodeir, 1968, p. 34).

intensity to be found along a particular path; in a sense, there is a great deal of freedom, the musician may enunciate notes, in series of varying lengths, rising or descending, he may 'liberate' energy.

The entirely 'free' variety of this school adds less articulation of the notes, the rising and descending emissions of sounds acting sometimes as gestures, represented in photography by *flous de bougé*, the blurring caused by the movement of the object.

The second variety, after the break with chords, proceeds from another kind of radicalization. Whereas there have always existed, among jazz improvisers, musicians who have preferred to follow *ideas*, that is, an itinerary, rather than the *harmonic grid* of a theme, the improviser could never, until now, go outside the established system of a piece; the basic melody of the theme, as well as the harmonic grid, were unchangeable and inseparable.

Having the temperament of a melodic improviser, Ornette Coleman effected a dual break, not only by abandoning the established theme, in order to improvise *another* melody on the prescribed harmonies, but by inventing melodic itineraries *without* a pre-existing harmonic schema. While it usually starts from a theme in its raw state – which, played by all the musicians present, gives the piece its particular character – the improvisation takes place entirely in action, in melodic action, but without following a theme, being obliged neither to keep to nor to depart from any *a priori* reference: the harmonies remaining subjacent, in the sense that a certain succession of chords might be played when a fellow-player has a good knowledge of the improviser's favourite itineraries (but this type of musician plays without the accompaniment of chords).

At most, if there are any norms,[1] they are worked out in the course of the action – they are ephemeral – both rhythmically and melodically, or from the point of view of the overall atmosphere of the piece. We are as far removed as possible from pre-established *structures* – they are constantly being developed.

This leaves the most spectacular, if not the most important development: that concerning *sound*, or instrumental technique.

It is no longer possible to consider the playing of the musicians in relation to one another, as could be done when examining rhythm and harmony. Although the intensity of the felt rhythm could, for example, be expressed in the conflict and interplay of a soloist and the rhythm

---

In fact, every musician establishes a particular *manner*, at least for a time, but the fact remains that he may change it according to his partners or his mood.

section, the nature of the sound produced by an instrumentalist must be appreciated above all in terms of expression. The general process of actionalization is even more spectacular here: the individual player and the instrument are inseparable,[1] as in the case of the blues singer – the blues *is* entirely in his voice. At most, the fusion reduces the whole process to this felt 'thing' known as sound – creator, creative process, product offered and received (for the audience is obviously in the circuit and can appreciate the sound only by 'feeling' it).

Again, of course, the radicalization that has taken place in the development of jazz can be related to an external norm.

Jazz players have always produced *rich*, that is, impure, sounds, by conservatoire norms.

> The purity of the tone that the European trumpet-player desired was put aside by the Negro trumpeter for the more humanly expressive sound of the voice (Jones, 1963, p. 79).

Even if the adoption of a sound is not the result of a decision implying a desire for orientation and first of all political consciousness, the fact remains that academic purity of sound corresponded neither to the social personality of the Negro instrumentalists nor to their culture, quite apart from any question of learning techniques. Indeed, it could well be that this quite puritan purity corresponded, even in Europe, to the ideas of only a section of the population. Jazz musicians, then, developed new and often very high standards of instrumental technique, with the accent on melodic and harmonic invention, and an expressiveness of sound that was closer to vocal traditions.[2]

It is obviously difficult to describe in words aspects of sound that are further removed from notions of structure than rhythm or harmony.[3] Once again, I must have recourse to a writer's transposition.

What Boris Vian says of a singer's voice is all the more interesting in that the way the audience experiences the sound is part of his description, which, moreover, reveals a phenomenon that is very closely related to the equally provocative sound of the more hostile free jazz musicians, even though in the case of the latter the desire to please may be entirely absent.

[1] An indication of this is that some instrumentalists play with hard reeds in order to increase the effort involved in producing the sound, which, since it is expressed through the playing, is evidence of this identification (means and end).

[2] Only the ethnocentrism of so many European observers can explain why the nature of these developments should have remained unknown for so long; for some time, however, the practice of jazz musicians, who 'provide the instrument with new possibilities of development', has become increasingly recognized; cf., for example, C. Orieux, 'Jazz et conservatoire', 1965.

[3] It is true that it is now possible to materialize sound structures or even ways of 'phrasing' in graphs.

The voice of Billie Holliday, which is a sort of subtle philtre, *surprises* at first hearing. It is the voice of a provocative cat, audacious in its inflexions, striking in its flexibility, its animal suppleness . . . or to use a terribly brilliant comparison, an octopus. Billie sings like an octopus. It's not always very reassuring at first; but when it gets you, it gets you with eight arms. And it doesn't let go (Vian, 1967 edn, p. 105).

The free jazz musicians belong to this craft tradition of self-taught instrumentalists and inventors of new ways of using existing instruments. They accentuate even more than previous schools the proximity with the voice, with the cry.

Whereas the players of reed instruments use growling and high-pitched whistling to reach a climax, the bass clarinettist E. Dolphy goes so far as to use almost permanently squeaking, strident, whistling sounds. During the period immediately before the break, some musicians (such as, for example, the multi-instrumentalist R. Kirk) made people aware of the importance of timbre, by changing instruments,[1] and stretched the sound by combining vocal techniques with blowing (into a flute) or playing without a reed, etc. After the break, what had been *one* of the elements of instrumental expression became, more generally, the centre of personal experimentation.

This is a dual and apparently paradoxical concern. Although the aim is to acquire a greater freedom of sound, both with regard to academic practices and in relation to the habits of particular schools, by distorting the original use of instruments, the frequent changes of manner,[2] according to partners, mood, or instrument, should not conceal the search for the same, underlying truth. Among many different musicians, one constantly meets with the idea that a certain sound (or instrument) corresponds to the type of personality of a particular musician. 'Every musician, every human being, has his own sound and rhythm.'[3]

The paradox disappears as soon as one recognizes that this desire to get back to 'nature' – of which more later – can reach to only a certain depth

[1] Even going so far as to use oriental instruments, or instruments not usually used in jazz, like the bassoon ('It's not enough for me to express all I want on one instrument, I choose them according to the timbre of the composition,' said the musician Y. Lateef, cf. *Jazz Podium*, October 1967).

[2] S. Rollins is an example of a musician who changes from one night, sometimes from one piece, to another (cf. *Jazz Magazine*, No. 163, 1969). One of his partners even explains how Rollins and he, in the middle of recording a structured piece, freed themselves from the harmonic grid and ended up by producing sounds on the mouthpieces only. Some musicians, such as B. Wilen, who has recorded improvisations on the saxophone against a background of noise produced by racing-cars, now call themselves 'sound-makers' (interview with P. Carles).

[3] Says the vibraphone-player K. Berger (cf. *Jazz Magazine*, No. 159, 1968), who explains how carefully he set about, with the instrument-maker, to discover *the* type of alloy that would give the metal strips the exact sound he sought.

of a personality that remains inevitably social (or 'cultural'). The individual changes, so the successful attainment of a 'match' between the player and his playing is never a definitive one. Finally, the individual himself derives from a created musical environment: the musician becomes what he plays – this is another (neglected) aspect of this movement of actionalization; there exists a relation of interdependence between the life of the music and the music-life.

According to temperament and the moment, musicians give greater or lesser importance of rhythmic, melodic, or sound actionalization. Let us say that an improvisation that is entirely action would combine, in a search without any prearrangement, a group of musicians and an audience with particular affinities, or with differences to settle.[1] They live a particular tempo, variable in intensity, determined as they go along, that can go through moments of lethargy and failure, and then of frenetic excitement, communion, and inspiration, some having followed a melodic itinerary, while others – or the same ones – exteriorize a whole potential of energy, since expression in sound is no longer inhibited by any taboos.[2] The common feature of all these tendencies is the abandonment of *a priori* structures; in extreme cases, they are not even present as interiorized references, or as foils.

Are we any nearer to solving the problem of the political meaning of this 'new thing'? More specifically, what do the musicians themselves say of the socio-political content of their activities? What can be read into their stage behaviour and perhaps even into the music itself?

INEVITABLE POLITICIZATION

'. . . the music of Archie Shepp is the great black beauty of black power'.[3]

In 1968, on his return from Sweden, where he had attended the meetings of the Russell Tribunal, the black political leader Stokeley Carmichael met some free jazz musicians in Paris. At the time, Archie Shepp and his band were on a European tour. The American Negro poet Ted Joans, who describes their meeting in a Paris club, recalls a passage from the Surrealist Manifesto – 'there is no mode of action that we cannot use, if necessary' – and quotes some of the things that Carmichael said to these musicians,

[1] It is now possible to play against a fellow-musician, or against some adversary, symbolically or actually present.
[2] Except perhaps that of a new routine, as D. Ellis, a musician of the 'civilized' school, has the wit to observe (cf. 'The avant-garde is not avant-garde', 1966).
[3] Stokeley Carmichael, Paris, 1968, quoted in *Jazz Magazine*, No. 150, 1968.

whom he refers to as revolutionaries: 'Look after this Black Power music; we need all our strength in this struggle to transform the evil of white power' (ibid.).

I shall speak first of the *politicizing tendency* of the free jazz musicians. Without being an organized group, and without belonging directly to any political movement, as far as one knows, a number of musicians have expressed their political views in the most overt way. My description of this tendency, to which the black writer LeRoi Jones belongs, will be centred on the work of the militant musician Archie Shepp.

LeRoi Jones writes regularly on jazz, in record reviews and books on the history of jazz.[1] This virulent militant, whose formulations are obviously interpretative, is becoming increasingly recognized as the spokesman of the political intentions of certain black musicians, and perhaps partly their inspirer, or catalyst. Archie Shepp is close to him not only in his political position, but also by the fact that he too has attended university and expresses himself in writing[2] – he has written a play, *The Communist* – and by speaking at public meetings, which is rare for a jazz musician.

Neither of these men is content to belong to the most conscious elite of a political generation, but each places himself above, and not merely beyond, a liberal political position – and even a white left radical position. It is in this sense, it seems to me, that we should interpret what, in them, appears as counter-terrorism, an anti-white racialism, which, above all, is a determination to do something about the lot of the blacks, by forming themselves into an independent elite, whose exclusively black character would be a guarantee of legitimacy.

Shepp sometimes abuses audiences who have come to attend discussions (cf. *Jazz Hot*, No. 211, 1965), or addresses concert audiences, which is bordering on a particular kind of provocation, since such audiences are largely composed of whites who sympathize with the black cause. As a musician, Shepp is searching for a musical practice and a form of stage behaviour that will exasperate and alienate his audience. He often produces, without interruption, a particularly exacerbated sound, pointing his saxophone aggressively at the hall – the instrument, being, as he says, many things, notably a Freudian symbol and a machine-gun.[3] He was one

[1] Up to now, said one musician (Cecil Taylor, *Jazz Magazine*, No. 125, 1965), with a touch of irony, the blacks have provided the best musicians and the whites the best critics in jazz. LeRoi Jones has become not so much a critic as a politico-musical interpreter of jazz; cf. his *Blues people* (1963) and *Black music* (1967), a collection of various writings.
[2] The writer, as LeRoi Jones himself recognizes (in *Blues people*, p. 133), enjoys a special prestige in the black community.
[3] Shepp (1966). One is reminded of 'the simplest Surrealist act', firing a revolver into a crowd (Breton).

of the first to adopt African dress,[1] and when he ends his long number he never acknowledges applause – inverted Uncle Tomism – and leaves the stage with all his musicians in Indian file, in an almost 'tribal' manner.

In the audience one feels that between stage and auditorium there is more than a break, a frontier and a symbol; one is in the presence of a 'feedback' of the alienation suffered by the blacks; the musicians make the 'non-African' spectators feel this.

This type of free jazz musician goes as far as to reject consciously any attempt to please, which he replaces by exasperation; he aims to awaken rather than intoxicate, and perhaps at times – following the logic of Dada – to produce an intentionally incomprehensible music, in order to ridicule the audience's search for a meaning. The violent, impenetrable musical 'object' resists aesthetic absorption.

Though this type of musician does not always go to such nihilistic lengths, he seems in any case to take great care in building up his relation with the audience. Indeed, the very nature of the music is suited to such a *mise-en-scène*, as the French critic who places most emphasis on the political intentions of free jazz describes it:[2]

> [Free jazz) requires of the listener acute attention, an awareness of every moment, which he must not allow to lapse into day-dreaming, nor try to hold in a state of semi-consciousness. On the contrary, in an often very brutal way, by strident, aggressive sound effects, by tonal breaks, the musician creates in the listener a state of irritation, of expectancy that is never satisfied. If 'traditional' jazz may be defined as a pleasure-giving act . . . in which everything combines to give satisfaction . . . free jazz proceeds by *frustration*. By skilful gradations in the untenable, or the chaotic, it forces the listener to hope more and more desperately for an aesthetic solution, an ecstasy after anger, desires that it stimulates, but deliberately fails to satisfy, rejecting the satisfactions of balance as much as the graces of perfection.

The books of LeRoi Jones contain a specific social objectivity, that of the committed witness, particularly in the sense that his definition of the meaning of jazz history is that of a radical black minority. G. Schuller, a composer and practising instrumentalist, takes up a position at the exact opposite end of the spectrum, in an objective analysis of the 'specifically musical'. He observes the musical expression of a period and 'proposes nothing in the order of musical structures that is not perfectly defined'.[3]

[1] Since then, the wearing of 'African'-type clothes has become widespread among free jazz musicians.
[2] Cf. J.-L. Comolli (1966b). For a critique of his 'aesthetic Leftist' interpretation, cf. E. Plaisance, *Cahiers du jazz*, No. 15.
[3] L. Malson, *Le Monde*, 3 January 1969. Gunther Schuller (1968) compares the positions of an 'old critique' and of a too exclusively socio-political 'new critique'.

For him, the blues 'is not and never has been a purely social phenomenon'; it appears 'in the first place as a poetic form and a way of making music'.[1]

I have been unable to find specifically musical analyses of the work of Shepp and those closest to him (R. Rudd, for example). It is as if, for the time being, their work was regarded as being entirely political. This is how Shepp himself defines one of the aims of the free jazz musician: 'It is a denial of technological precision and a reaffirmation of *das Volk*' (1966).[2]

Even the signing of a photograph is for him an opportunity to take up a position (cf. *Jazz Hot*, No. 211, 1965): 'The liberation of the aesthetic is merely a prelude to the liberation of man – the ennobling of culture.' This musician is too orthodox to mean by this that culture must be transformed before the economy; on the contrary, he has spoken elsewhere of the economic constraints that weigh upon music:

> Some people find it odd that the word jazz should appear side by side with such cold, harsh realities as society or economics; but it cannot be denied that the origins of music and its later developments are rooted in social structures.[3]

Music, then, must challenge not so much culture as society – it must express demands, a state of mind.[4] The message of the new jazz

> tells of the suffering of a whole mass of people. It speaks of emancipation, of the destruction of the ghettoes and of fascism. I'm a black jazz musician, a black father, a black American, an anti-fascist; I am outraged by war, Vietnam, the exploitation of my brothers, and my music talks about all that. That's the New Thing.[5]

It is impossible to say how many musicians should be included in this first tendency, whose main characteristic is an attitude of political 'voluntarism', of maximum explicitation of social intentions. Moreover, there is a kinship between most free jazz musicians, in spite of their diversity, and, sometimes, considerable conflict between them. Curiously enough, one of these conflicts concerns the audience. To mention it at all is tantamount to relativizing political interpretations.

[1] This is also the opinion of the black writer Ralph Ellison, who criticizes LeRoi Jones for his political preconceptions, which, although understandable as 'commitment', lead him to misunderstand even the poetry of the blues or to deny that a slave, as a musician, can be a man (cf. Ellison, 1964, pp. 247–258).
[2] Like LeRoi Jones, he makes frequent use of terms borrowed from other languages, especially German (?) – cf., for example, the title of Jones's poem 'Black Dada Nihilismus', etc.
[3] Quoted in *Jazz Magazine*, No. 131, 1966.
[4] One of the theses of his article (Shepp, 1966) is that free jazz is not a movement, but a state of mind.
[5] Interviewed by J.-L. Noames in *Jazz Magazine*, No. 125, 1965.

Generally speaking, the 'new music' is presented to largely white audiences. The interpretation of the behaviour of musicians like Shepp is built up therefore at least as much on the basis of the symbolic black–white relation, both inside and outside the auditorium, as on the basis of the music or the on-stage behaviour. Although the pointing of the instrument at the white audience may represent the brandishing of a machine-gun, this way of playing is only the *redefinition, in situ*, of a widespread practice on the part of black musicians, playing, 'swinging', to the maximum, in black dance halls (rhythm and blues). When musicians like Shepp play, in their African shirts, to the children of Harlem, musicians who adopt their way of playing, including the habit of pointing at the audience, certainly rediscover their music in an original *definition*.[1]

In fact, several free jazz musicians speak enthusiastically of positive experiments made with audiences of children, in schools and in the street. The following characteristics of the music–audience relation – they are valid for jazz in general, but are even more central for recent tendencies – emerge: the active participation of the listener, both physical and projective, at least as an observer who follows and 'lives' what is being done, is necessary; the successful hearing is a naïve reception; the most vital music is closest to the street, to the *everyday*.[2]

Jazz should be played in stadiums, on base-ball fields, in the street . . . Children love the new music . . . Children have the imagination you need for the music we play; you can do what you like with it.[3]

Jazz should go out into the street, musicians should take their instruments with them and when they meet others play with them . . . in the parks, and in the schools . . . [4]

A second tendency, one of *cultural affirmation*, can be differentiated fairly clearly by the absence of political declarations and by the fact that it does not put much emphasis on what it *denies*, but reveals, on the contrary, a total commitment – the term 'total music' has also been used – in a

---

[1] There is no lack of illustrations of the relativity of judgement where public performances are concerned; at one concert, Armstrong, who was recovering from an illness, was musically somewhat 'alarming', but, as J. R. Masson notes (*Cahiers du jazz*, No. 3) 'the powerful impression of shoddy work was sublimated by the circumstances of the situation and by the sympathy that was established between the musicians and the crowd'.
[2] Shepp speaks of experiments made by musicians giving free concerts in the streets of Harlem, perched on a lorry: 'You should have seen it . . . the kids surrounded the truck and adored this music, which is really made for them.' Cf. G. Kopelowicz, *Jazz Hot*, No. 211; cf. also *Jazz Hot*, No. 216, 1966.
[3] Marion Brown, interviewed by A. Corneau, *Jazz Magazine*, No. 133, 1966.
[4] Clifford Jordan, *Jazz Podium*, No. 6, 1967. Other musicians have played in schools, for example K. Berger (cf. *Jazz Magazine*, No. 159, 1968).

music that affirms a 'beyond' (cultural, social, and political, by implication). This tendency is perhaps best represented by J. Coltrane, 'the father of a generation':

> I know there are bad forces, forces that bring suffering to others and misery to the world, but I want to be the opposite force. I want to be the force which is truly for good.[1]

One can see why this musician has been called the Martin Luther King of modern jazz, but such a label throws a false light on the musically revolutionary action of someone who really was 'a beautiful person'.[2] He had the ability not only to explode earlier schemas, but to pursue, with the greatest possible seriousness, slowly but surely, an exploration that was never content with any stage of achievement. His was an exemplary career, one of permanent change and fundamental questioning, pursued with such seriousness and single-mindedness that it led to exhaustion and a premature death. 'I want to go as far as I can' was one of the general explanations he often gave. The *unexpected* was the only thing one had any right to expect at every stage in the development of this musician.[3]

Few of Coltrane's statements touch on political problems; he speaks most often of *love*, in the sense of love of God and one's fellow-men – 'religion is everything for me, my music is a thanksgiving to God'.[4] It was after the recording of the piece called 'Alabama' that the producer, Bob Thiele, asked Coltrane if the title 'had any significance for today's problems':[5]

> COLTRANE: It represents, musically, something I saw down there, then translated into music from inside me.

> LEROI JONES: Which is to say, Listen. And what we're given is a slow, delicate, introspective sadness, almost hopelessness . . . The whole thing is a frightening emotional portrait of some place . . .

As well as by goodness, beauty, and innovation, his music is characterized, as I have remarked, by a curious conflict between the static (the modes) and movement (the rapid succession of notes). More precisely, it

---

[1] J. Coltrane, 1967, in a sleeve-note for the record 'Expression', recorded just before his death.
[2] This was said of him by many of his fellow-musicians, cf., for example, *Down Beat*, No. 7, 1967.
[3] Cf. Berendt (1967), who notes to what extent, in Coltrane's music, transformations are the result of maturity, unlike the changes of manner adopted from one day to the next by others, or a simultaneous game, in various different styles, according to the commitment of the moment; though it is true that M. Mantler (1969) seems to be saying that musicians can be validly avant-garde while practising various other styles.
[4] Cf. *Jazz Hot*, No. 212, 1965. Cf. also his poem on the record 'A love supreme'.
[5] Cf. the sleeve of the record Impulse A(S)50: 'Coltrane live at Birdland', text by LeRoi Jones.

is movement 'towards´ an idea that is expressed in the title of one of his records, 'Ascension'.

Although like many others, before and after him, he chose elements from other cultures, it was to enrich his creation with elements that he experienced and used positively, as an affirmation to put in the place and position of an established culture, which, at no time, did he wish to attack.

He was an explorer in a triple sense. He was a musical explorer, who discovered, and knew how to combine and vitalize, elements from various cultures. The choice of the modal was, as well as a means of escaping from established musical routines, an ideological preference: the international language of the music of the coloured peoples.[1] He was a Surrealist exploring content and boundaries, in a musically active introspection that must provide knowledge about the individual man and about man in general, offering the audience a universe in which the beautiful is close to 'nature', and therefore 'true', which leads to a third way, that of spiritual exploration, towards an 'elsewhere'. It is at this point that his career takes on the dual appearance of a hopeless search for a sort of paradise – of mystical life – and of a marathon, which is human in its urgency, and in the circumstances of an unbearable social reality, and very far from the serenity of religious initiation.

One must, it seems, interpret the combination of static elements (the use of modes and establishment in a 'sound') and dynamic elements (movement, both physical and emotional), as the meeting of a religious search and a social pursuit, the second being as real as the first, though unconscious. The normal mystical career is too obviously a process of passive discovery for this inventive search, with all its movement and intensity, to claim such an interpretation.

We are reminded that the term *Beat* Generation means both 'beaten' by society and a search for *beatitude* and rhythm (beats), the latter symbolizing vitality. Coltrane, whose mysticism I have no desire to deny, probably lived all three dimensions of this definition; without denying through hate earlier ways of life or creation, he replaced them by a *new culture*, a search for truth, even more than for beauty.[2]

In a very divided profession, Coltrane was always ready to help young musicians or fellow-players.[3] Indeed, he was more 'social' than political

[1] J. Clouzet and M. Delorme, interview with J. Coltrane, in *Cahiers du jazz*, No. 8.
[2] Which he produced in abundance; the beauty of Coltrane's music is evident 'in spite of or perhaps because of the essentially vile profile of America', wrote LeRoi Jones, whose own methods are very different (record mentioned above). [3] Cf. description by B. Thiele in *Coda*, May 1968.

and even declared himself, in a very clear way, to be apolitical on the most burning issue:

> I don't know by what criteria you can differentiate a black musician from a white musician; in fact, I don't think there are such criteria.[1]

Many free jazz musicians, and not only whites, share this position, including one of Shepp's partners, the black trumpeter B. Dixon:[2]

> I don't know whether you can say that [the new music] is black, white, or colourless. Which is obvious when I play (and if I am black), I play from so-called black experience . . .

Either on purely professional grounds, or because of a certain sort of humanism, many musicians have declared themselves to be against conscious politicization.

The musician and musical analyst, Don Heckman, says that 'the conscious insertion of political, religious, philosophical or ideological content into a work of art adds a useless and often specious burden' (cf. *Jazz Magazine*, No. 125, 1965). K. Berger, a free jazz musician of German origin, defines latent politicization thus:

> If there is a chance of finding a form of human union in the world, our music is the beginning of it. Music is my politics, my religion, my philosophy (ibid.).

Others go so far as to admit religious commitments (among many others, Steve Lacy, in this respect a very moderate man, claims to have adopted the *Tao Teh Ching* ('The way of life') by Lao-Tseu as his Bible and guide for everyday living – cf. *Jazz Magazine*, No. 121, 1965).

From a musical point of view, Coltrane, who is regarded as a free jazz musician only from his final period, was above all an innovator, a solitary soloist, pursuing his own ways of improvisation without responding to or expecting musical responses from his fellow-players. Those players created an atmosphere by following parallel itineraries of improvisation. They have each, in their own way, developed a type of improvisation that is largely autonomous, very 'free' in this sense.

On stage, the musician behaved with introspective concentration, playing until he was exhausted; the result was spectacular, but in no way

---

[1] Clouzet and Delorme (op. cit.). This can be compared with a statement made by Shepp. When an interviewer remarked: 'You seem to think that jazz is only music for blacks . . .', Shepp replied: 'There are very few whites. As far as I know, there are no white jazz musicians. No. I take that back, I know a few' (Noames, *Jazz Magazine*, No. 125, 1965).

[2] Cf. *Coda*, quoted in *Jazz Magazine*, No. 152, 1968.

contrived. Much has been said of the hypnotic fascination that developed, through the energy projected into the music and by the repetitive aspects of the music. A record can never recreate to the same extent the hypnotic quality achieved by a long, live session.

Although Coltrane sometimes shocked his audiences by leaving the stage abruptly, without acknowledging applause, or by a certain lack of organization at the end of pieces,[1] he does not seem to have behaved in a hostile way.

Unlike the politically oriented musicians, Coltrane and those like him, although, musically, extremely radical, were concerned not so much to destroy as to develop. The hypnotic fascination that he himself felt and wanted to communicate is not strictly of an artistic order, but he provides no further information as to what is expressed in a search that has been described, somewhat over-hastily, as purely mystical. Like a whole series of other musicians – and in particular the founder of a musico-religious sect, Sun Ra[2] – he wished to create a sort of living utopia, a deep study of which should explain with precision the factors linked with a given social situation.

Sun Ra is an extravagant character whose exotico-mystic theatricality goes well beyond anything else of that kind one has ever seen. It may be difficult to take him entirely seriously, but a great many musicians have expressed their great esteem for him, in particular for the training they have received in his 'Arkestra', which is one of the few new orchestras of any size and permanence. It might well be that this training is primarily a *deconditioning*, and secondarily an awakening to new sounds; Sun Ra dresses his musicians in exotic clothes, and arranges them in a semi-circle, each one complementing his modern instrument with fundamentally different, traditional ones (African, Middle Eastern, Far Eastern).[3]

Sun Ra, who believes that the creation of a new form of jazz is 'necessary to the realization of his prophecies' about the world (cf. *Jazz Magazine*, No. 159, 1968), wishes 'to resolve cosmic equations on a musical plane'.

QUESTION: Has your music anything in common with that of the 'new thing' musicians?

SUN RA: Not really, because what I'm doing is based on the natural, while

Cf. *Jazz Hot*, No. 212, 1965, Antibes Festival.
[2] A pianist, composer, and conductor.
[3] Western musicians, like those of the Groupe de Recherches Musicales, in Paris, have recognized the need for a process of deconditioning, and this liberation takes the form of contact with so-called 'primitive' music.

what they're doing is probably based on what they learnt at school (*Jazz Magazine*, No. 125, 1965).

This musician, who is certainly idiosyncratic in his ritualism and messianism, has no monopoly in the search for the *natural*.[1] The theme of nature opposed to culture is one of the major concerns of this second tendency in free jazz: the rediscovery of 'childhood' and 'long-lost innocence'.

A man cannot become a child once again without becoming puerile. But does he not rejoice in the naïveté of the child, and must he not himself strive, at a higher level, to reproduce his truth? Does not the nature of childhood relive the character of each period in its natural truth?[2]

Of course, professional musicians are usually more distant from, and amateurs closer to, this innocence. This is one of the reasons for the success and fairly widespread appeal of free jazz: anyone, providing he lets himself go, in a sporadic search and experiment, can *practise* free improvisation, and with a good deal of success.

After listening to a record, one professional musician passed this judgement on the music of one of his fellow-players:

The sound produced by the man is a developed, organized, civilized sound. When someone plays at random, the music takes the musicians on a trip, the music makes itself. That's what 'free' playing, without structures, is. I give two stars to this record because it's a good little sound landscape, but to a bird singing in the country I'd give three stars.[3]

Ornette Coleman, the first free jazz musician to achieve fame, has this in common with Coltrane, that he 'leads to an aesthetic that is not entirely negative, that is not only the rejection of what the others do', but the *affirmation* of something else, which is also to be found beneath the eccentricities of Sun Ra.[4]

Coleman hardly says anything about politics; 'he hasn't read Trotsky and draws the crowds'.[5] There is nothing special about his behaviour on stage, but his desire to remain pure, to guard himself against routine, even at the price of deprivation and trouble,[6] is well known. This attitude

---

[1] This new jazz is also referred to as 'native music' (*Jazz Magazine*, No. 125).
[2] These are not the words of an unknown eccentric, but one of Marx's rare comments on art (at the end of the Introduction to the *Critique of political economy*, 1857).
[3] D. Pike, *Jazz Magazine*, No. 158, 1968.   [4] M. C. Jalard, *Cahiers du jazz*, No. 16/17, p. 18.
[5] P. Carles, *Jazz Magazine*, No. 130, 1966.
[6] 'Once I played . . . for a conference of the American Architects' Association – it was for a discussion entitled "Beauty and Ugliness" . . . they told me that I represented ugliness' (comments reproduced by M. Van Peebles, *Jazz Magazine*, No. 125, 1965).

is also illustrated by the fact that, although a saxophonist, he has chosen to use instruments of a very different kind.

> I see in this use of the violin, or the trumpet, a cold determination to keep his art outside the grasp of our aesthetic criteria, not to allow his music to be accepted without question, and not to allow us to confuse it with those beautiful things that raise no problems that we're so fond of (Comolli, 1966b).

Whether or not this musician has a conscious intention to 'distance' is perhaps less important than the fact that such a distancing effect is felt by the audience. There is, however, another justification for this process of permanent renewal. It is easier for the beginner to achieve that state of innocence on an instrument, to discover an *emotional* mode of expression, than for someone whose years of practice have led not always to mastery, but often to mere routine.

If the 'professional' attitude of a musician is defined by the use of established techniques and more generally by specialization, Coleman represents an anti-professional tendency. He sometimes illustrates the sleeves of his records with his own paintings and poems; and does not hesitate to get his ten-year-old son to accompany him on the drums.[1] For him the essential thing is to create, to experience a group atmosphere that is favourable for creation.

Marion Brown, another saxophonist, sees action in a similar way, as existing through and in creation:

> I don't think that a revolution has to be based on anger. Your behaviour or your words don't matter. What does are acts. In life, the great revolutionaries don't raise their voices.[2]

This musician is influenced by Sun Ra and lives according to principles of experiment, non-specialization, and the combination of elements of diverse cultural origin; he practises yoga, as do a great many avant-garde musicians. He insists, however, on the importance of the *everyday*: 'this music is not the expression of exceptional events . . . it expresses a daily struggle'. Musicians are no longer looking for artificial paradises, as was often the case with the preceding generation (alcohol and drugs).

> When I become one with my instrument, it's then that I lose myself and really start playing. Music is my real drug (ibid.).

Brown wants to create a musical novel:

> I'd like to juxtapose my pictorial, musical and literary preoccupations . . . [with] the text of the Constitution, documents . . . on the history of the

[1] As on the record 'Empty fox-hole'.   [2] Interviewed by A. Corneau, *Jazz Magazine*, No. 133, 1966.

black people . . . The music would be the result of a dramatization of all the elements together: the speeded-up voice of Kennedy, a passage from a record by Coltrane, the slowed-down voice of Malcolm (ibid.).

While various jazz players have often tried to amuse by using musical quotations (old refrains, traditional themes, etc.), the montage envisaged by Brown, or the collages produced by another important practitioner of free jazz – Albert Ayler – are now becoming a major technique.

The quotations of the theme itself begin to sound like alien elements, or rather are taken to be parts of the collage, which has the effect of placing on the same footing the themes and other quotations, references, and clichés that nourish free jazz, as if all these odds and ends, which, nevertheless, are intimately concerned with jazz, with the nature and history of jazz, etc. . . . should be put in inverted commas and, out of either prudence or *irony*, be quoted as a reminder, in order to make one feel the distance that separates free jazz from its pre-history (Comolli, op. cit.).

But there does not seem to be any element of derision, of a desire to be free of a tradition that has become oppressive. Ayler,[1] like those from whom I have already quoted, wishes to recapture a sort of innocence and freshness: his irony is tinged with admiration for the big tunes of military marches and circus music, which he mixes with a modern way of playing; he seeks 'joy' as well as 'purification'. 'Like Coltrane, I'm trying to play the beauty of the future . . .'[2]

We are the music we play. Our commitment is to peace, to greater under-standing. We are continually trying to purify our music, to purify ourselves, and those who listen to us . . . in a way we are trying to do again what Armstrong did at the beginning. It was joy at the beauty to come.[3]

Ayler, who is musically exceptionally violent, pleads for 'joy and peace on earth' and adds that he believes 'that music is capable of making this truth come to pass, because music really is the universal language' (ibid.). Among all these musicians there is a great diversity in the relations with the audience. Ayler seems neither to adopt Shepp's hostile or provocative behaviour, nor to seek to 'hypnotize'; just as Sun Ra's musicians play 'in a circle, as in an Arab orchestra', without thinking of the audience, Ayler's group does not seem to be concerned with the audience either:

What gives the impression of a provocation of the audience is a struggle over

[1] A saxophonist.
[2] Cf. N. Hentoff, text and interview accompanying the record 'Ayler in Greenwich Village, 1967'.
[3] Ayler, on the title of the record 'Truth is marching in', which recalls the old theme 'When the saints go marching in' (Armstrong).

the sounds. In fact, there's a glass wall between the stage and the audience. The musicians simply throw sounds at one another. When we heard Ayler's group in a cellar, it was impossible to hear properly, they played much too loud, we had to submit to it as one submits to a storm.[1]

Although the second tendency I have described, whose principal dimension is the affirmation of a *religious*, but also a cultural and social, beyond, is close to Surrealism (Coltrane) and Dada (Ayler), the same cannot be said, despite the characteristics shared by almost all the avant-garde musicians, of a third tendency. Although it does not pursue explicit political aims, and is not particularly concerned with implicit socio-political contents, though it does not deny them, the tendency of *'culti-vated' affirmation* creates, in a sense, a synthesis of the political voluntarism, modern in its negation, of the first tendency and the cultural affirmation, at least partly a-historical, of the second tendency. Cecil Taylor, who is its most typical representative, is both modern and affirmative:

> In society, musicians are not only art objects. They *are* society, even if they are only on the edge of it (*Jazz Magazine*, No. 125, 1965).

Taylor, who is opposed to militancy among musicians, is conscious both of the constraints imposed upon the artist in contemporary society and of the creative contribution of the artist, who expresses not only the world of today, but also the society of the future.

> When you want to go in for politics you don't stay in New York. I've no great admiration for people – white or black – who take up positions here. The people I respect are the young blacks of Mississippi or Alabama who don't hesitate to get themselves clubbed by the police in order to win the case.[2]

> Commitment, in music, is a luxury. If you really look, you can find in it a whole lot of social comment that is much deeper than the provisional character of a political option . . .[3]

For this pianist, the political meaning and significance of a piece of music do not depend on the intentions of its creator: it is when he strives to *construct*[4] an original work that the whole of his personality is expressed, almost unknown to himself, in what he creates. He is quite clear on this point:

[1] Interview with P. Carles and J.-L. Comolli.
[2] Interviewed by G. Kopelowicz, *Jazz Hot*, No. 216, 1966.
[3] Interviewed by J.-L. Noames, *Jazz Magazine*, No. 125, 1965.
[4] It is in this sense, it seems, that one may interpret the label of 'constructivist' music that this musician suggests to describe his work.

It seems to me that in the long run your art becomes the reflection of a consciousness which, if it is powerful enough, may change the social consciousness of the people who listen to you. Great music implies a challenge to the existing order (op. cit., 1965).

He has shown, however, in critical analyses of society, especially American society, that he is under no illusions as to the conditions in which the new art is diffused.

The structure of the consumption of works [which the dominant forces] have determined is not the result of chance. The separation of the artist from his public, the ideology of art as something separate from everyday realities . . . pure of any social, sexual implication, etc., is all connected. What is done is to canalize subversion and contestation, and at the same time to censor it, into the modes of consumption.[1]

Taylor showed that he is perfectly well aware that black musicians produce a necessary contribution to American cultural life in a discussion between a club-owner and fellow-musicians, who were also divided among themselves. He proposed a *general boycott*: all black musicians would refuse to play in public, or in a studio, they would oppose the musicians' union and any kind of association concerned with music, and cease – together with white musicians who 'have a social conscience' – to answer questions put to them by jazz magazines.[2]

And it is typical that he can pass from an analysis of the extremely hard living conditions of the blacks that is full of sordid details to *affirmation* where artistic creation is concerned:[3]

. . . my responsibility as an artist is to see, to absorb, to observe and to use whatever is beautiful in this society, regardless of who gave impetus to its creative form . . . and to merge it with what I am, a black man (ibid.).

Indeed, this musician has a keen interest in all the arts, visits art galleries and museums, and knows the works of Godard, Antonioni, Béjart, Genet, etc. The black artist of today belongs to an international culture, while affirming new forms of a culture that remains his own.

[1] Interviewed by M. Le Bris, *Jazz Hot*, No. 248, 1969.
[2] Cf. 'Point of contact: a discussion', in *Down Beat* (Yearbook, 1966, p. 21). It was also Taylor who insisted that musicians being interviewed should be remunerated for the information they supplied to the specialist magazines. *Down Beat* (a widely distributed American magazine) 'exists because there are musicians to write about. And these irresponsible, ignorant and malevolent editors live in California and have swimming pools, whereas I live on the East Side.'
[3] 'The greed of the whites is such that they prefer to count their money rather than repair the defective pipes of the heating so that black babies can reach adulthood, or at least have some heating while they die' (*Down Beat*, op. cit., p. 31).

Whereas Taylor's method of treating the piano (the agglomeration of bundles of notes, etc.) reminds one, for example, of the works of Stockhausen, the spirit, the sound, and the rhythm of his music are different.[1]

> I say that Stockhausen does not belong to my community; the aesthetic that he proclaims loudest, or that he could proclaim, is totally divorced from mine.[2]

EXTENSION AND AUTONOMIZATION

The desire to avoid being confined within a particular school, within pre-existing rhythmic patterns, to reject harmonic sequences that have become rigid frameworks, and to get away as completely as possible from the usual way of playing the usual instruments – these are all expressions, at the level most obviously proper to the musician, of a desire for liberation and already, among many musicians, of a way of asserting their freedom, at least at that level.

I have tried to show that the jazz that calls itself 'free' has done more than merely add further variations to earlier schools. Although it is caught up in the logic of a development that I have been forced to schematize, it is more than a mere supplementary stage. In its most complete manifestations – when several of the developments described above come together – this 'new thing' is the most complete 'overthrow' imaginable, a revolution in earlier ways of thinking.

The more explicitly political forms of behaviour are close to the relations that an actor, or a militant orator, might have with his audience – which does not mean that the purely 'musical' choices, for example the sounds expressing and becoming exasperation, are not directly subversive, both in intention and in effect.

For the moment, the *free*, in jazz as in other spheres, is even more varied and incoherent than the nature of the phenomenon requires. I have tried to produce as consistently as possible references to musicians or observers who describe it and interpret it, while remaining perfectly well aware that in this field the objectivation of the phenomenon lies in action, and that I would have to mention, and first know, many other events of this type before offering an interpretation or explanation. My aim in this study was not, however, to relate the world of the phenomenon to an

---

[1] As can be seen in a comparison of Stockhausen's *Klavierstücke* and Taylor's playing in the record 'Unit structures'.
[2] Interviewed by F. Pinguet, *Jazz Hot*, No. 248, 1969.

'exteriority', to provide an account of its socio-historical genesis. It goes without saying that the climate of oppression and therefore of revolt that reigns in the United States, that the relations between the dominant culture (white) and the culture of the dominated (black), that many economic aspects should be examined in relation to such 'free' tendencies: to free oneself from, to free something, to assert freedom in a particular sphere, even to express the suffering involved in non-freedom – these are the principal synonyms of the only label acceptable to musicians who wish to plead for freedom, at the same time as they seize it.

Rather than draw one by one the parallels to be found with May, and more particularly with the views expressed in this study – though the parallels do stand out of their own accord – it would be profitable perhaps to reflect on the more general tendencies of the phenomenon, in which the significance of this libertarian politicization is embodied: autonomization, as expressed in the musician's relations with other cultures, with the various aspects of established musical practice, with the audience, or with the most symbolic of the relations, society, in a spirit of extension and not of contraction.

The relation with other *cultures* enables us to understand this movement in its two apparently contradictory tendencies: the search for an identity and concern for the identity of others. Everything takes place, we must remember, in the *here* and *now*. 'Freedom now suite' was the title of a well-known work by the drummer Max Roach. The insistence on the present moment has always been relatively important in jazz, but it has become an absolute requirement – a need to feel the rhythm, a mood, a movement,[1] in the present, by autonomizing a brief period. How can this often very introspective concentration be reconciled with the extension of the cultural field of reference?

It is apparent that this search involves not only liberation but liberty, for it is not a question of continuing to reject the dominant 'classical' culture (Western, white American culture, in both the artistic sense and the general sense of 'way of life') in order to establish another domination.[2] Neither is it possible to reject the oppositional culture of the established schools of jazz, which, if they have not always been 'absorbed', end up, like all systems, with the aim of establishing a new orthodoxy.

If one now considers the practice of this opening to cultures that are

---

[1] One of the methods of the two great exponents, J. Coltrane and C. Taylor, consisted of running in a circle, then beginning another at once.
[2] Except perhaps for what I have called the 'politicizing' tendency – though even there it is far from certain.

equally 'classical', but in a different way – the African cultures, legitimized by the black's return to his own identity, by his realization that he was transported to the United States, then de-Africanized, by his desire to find himself; the Middle or Far Eastern cultures, which are justified by reference to their age-old wisdom, purity, and truth, which are so badly needed when one is trying to escape from a world that one feels is corrupt – one realizes that it involves a number of new possibilities rather than submission to a new domination. Contact with these cultures contributes towards liberation, through their 'deconditioning' effect, by a return to the emotional life, they provide elements that can be incorporated into work and techniques of self-development (yoga). The borrowed elements are 'lived', that is, redefined, merged in a personality that contains similar motivations to those of the individuals, in those different cultures, who produced them.

Finally, what might be called the *cultivated culture* of present-day artists, in various fields, provides yet another ground on which one can breathe. 'Avant-garde' artists – by which is often meant artists who are socially in revolt – practise the assertion of a sort of *beyond* on earth.

Autonomization, then, involves leaving the dominant culture and the culture of the established opposition, with the help of quite *different* cultures, without becoming enslaved to them, by techniques of adaptation and distortion (collage, montage). At a more general level, it is the affirmation of a new, modern, and primarily subversive culture, a black culture, that of the young black 'American', which links up, of course, with other manifestations that cannot be defined by a colour, but by a certain type of consciousness.

The relation to *music* was always, in jazz, that of the improviser, mixing his own personality with a certain dose of known structures. Now one finds musicians improvising according to a personal itinerary, without referring, even implicitly, to an external order. This liberation through a very advanced autonomization is a movement towards individuality. Everyone has his own rhythm, his own harmony, his own *sound*. Looked at more closely, this is not a particularization, for many of the dimensions experienced are experienced in common, by a whole generation for example. Without wishing to get too involved in dialectical formulations, one might say that it is in trying to reach *nature* – or, as was so often said in May, spontaneity – that the individual finds his *own* nature, and also that of many other individuals. The solution is not individualism, but the discovery through a process of creation – of the work and of oneself –

of a *cultural*, and not a natural, personality, made up of rejections and affirmations. It is by seeking the maximum autonomy that the authentic common characteristics emerge, which implies, it is true, the image of a society in which great diversity and permanent change will be accepted. This new type of personality, opposed to rules, demands the non-fixation, even the diversity, of individuals, thus leading to constant redefinitions of what is ever only provisionally attained. The abandonment of a style that one has developed oneself (Coltrane), of an instrument that one knows very well (Coleman), and many other procedures reveal what, in May, was called 'scuttling'.

The relation with the *audience* reveals that it is the verbal and gestural behaviour, rather than the actual sound produced, which, according to the situation, provides material for a political projection of this 'new thing'. It is true, however, that in so far as the music requires in any case, by virtue of its indefinite character, an important projective activity, it leads the audience, or the listener, to an autonomous interpretation, necessarily different from those made at other times (on the basis of recordings). And this applies quite apart from the fact that the musicians, more obviously than ever before, will play only once in any particular way – which does not mean, of course, that they are any the less authentic for that. For, apart from the fact that they have changed from one concert to the next, and despite differences of detail in the playing, it can be said, without paradox, that they are audibly the *same* at the next concert, *through* their music, if not in the form that it takes.

A number of specialists have discussed the relation of 'free jazz' with *politics* and have failed to dispose completely of the problems involved. This, it seems to me, is because the notion of politics may be understood in at least two senses: (*a*) institutional/organizational, or explicit; and (*b*) cultural, a latent force of conservation or transformation.[1] Observers and musicians should be classified according to this distinction.

To distinguish between different tendencies within a movement which, according to Shepp, is no more than a state of mind is certainly hazardous. The phenomenon is not only varied, but partly contradictory, and certainly too insufficiently developed as yet for the subdivisions to be regarded as socio-historical categories. Nevertheless, one must reflect upon the significance of the various tendencies. The first of these, the *politicizing* tendency, at least has the merit of being clearly defined. Although it

---

[1] One of the reasons why the political role of cultural aspects is often unrecognized is that 'the' culture is traditionally that of the dominators, and therefore conservative.

resembles the other two tendencies in many respects, it differs from them in its evidently militant approach and in its emphasis upon negation.

Throughout this book, the other two tendencies – to be found also in other chapters – are not regarded as being less important, quite the contrary. The current of *cultural affirmation* and that, further removed from the contemplation of ancient cultures or of a 'beyond', which one might hesitantly call the current of 'cultivated' affirmation, and which is inspired by an ideal, that of the artist, of professional creators, are both some distance from what is traditionally meant by the term 'political'.[1] It is characteristic that Cecil Taylor, a musician who rejects both explicit politicization and any resort to the exotic or to mysticism, can extend his horizon to a number of avant-garde experiments, and at the same time remain a black American whose socio-economic analysis of the situation seems harsher yet less dogmatic than that of Shepp.

One question arises that I shall answer in the affirmative: is the explicit politicization of culture, approximating to organized militant activity, less subversive in fact than the affirmation of a culture, which, while apparently less 'political', has an inherent capacity for self-renewal?

In any case, it can hardly be denied that this free jazz presents, in a general way, not only the problem of the present oppression of the blacks and of the search for an identity that the young blacks share with many others, of different origin, but also that of the alternative – too often dismissed as utopian in the pejorative sense – of future non-oppression, of the absence of an imposed order. This utopia, in the sense of a living project, is certainly present in free jazz, at least up to now – it is to be hoped that the explosive, exploratory, energetic qualities of these musicians do not become commercialized, absorbed into a fashion that is only too successful, and thus lose contact with the musicians who produced it.

Even musicologists who, in the past, usually considered themselves above making a comprehensive appreciation of jazz, have been led, in speaking of contemporary music in general, to the theoretical conclusions that underlie the search for freedom in free jazz, and even invoke the social problem that it presents:

> In music, too, one should ask why men, as soon as they are free, get the feeling that *things must be put into good order* . . . They imagine that order must be imposed on freedom from the outside, that it must be restrained rather than allowed to organize itself, without obeying any heteronome criterion, which would mutilate what demands to develop itself freely (Adorno, 1967).

[1] These two currents, each in its own way linked with culture, should be given more systematic study.

CHAPTER 10

The Avant-garde Overtaken[1]

In the last few chapters we have dealt with literary and musical move-ments that were prior to or parallel with May 1968 but outside that event. It is in the field of the theatre and the cinema, however, that in many respects the relation between certain forms of action originating in May and the avant-garde experiments being carried out by certain artists is most in evidence. Not, it seems to me, that these parallels are more justi-fiable, in substance, than those already made. But, being nearer in time than Dada and Surrealism, and more widely known than free jazz, these experiments in the cinema and the theatre are more readily identifiable with the explosion of spring 1968.

Of all the work done in these two fields, I have chosen, for closer examination, that of Jean-Luc Godard and that of the Living Theatre. The choice is admittedly a questionable one and requires some explana-tion. It is also a rather obvious one. Other work would certainly have merited more attention: unfortunately such work is not very well known, since it has not yet enjoyed the doubtful privilege of being absorbed by the system, to use the vocabulary of May. In a field where financial considerations all too often govern creation, it takes no little courage to attack the prevailing taboos. And those who, despite that fact, achieve a certain commercial success, like Godard, or a certain renown, like the Living Theatre, run the risk of being suspected by those for whom one does not validly combat an enemy by leaving the choice of weapons to him. But I have no wish to pursue an argument along these lines.

While remaining fully aware of the limitations of such a study, I shall complete this account with the particularly apparent culmination of this juncture of the cultural and political: the theatrical experiments observed in May, and again in the summer of 1968 at the Festival of Avignon, experiments in collective creation such as the poster studio of the École

[1] By Paul Beaud.

des Beaux-Arts, etc. These phenomena would obviously have to be studied at greater length than is possible here. There is some hope that all that was done in this field during the May events will not fall into oblivion for lack of observers, since, to my knowledge, certain performances at least were recorded or filmed.

'LA CHINOISE'

It is said that when the first serious incidents broke out at Nanterre certain journalists, unfamiliar with student politics, went back to the film section of their documentary departments for information on the mysterious Marxist–Leninist students. As a result, the revolt at Nanterre was described by a section of the press as 'typically Chinese'.

The film *La Chinoise* was shot in March 1967, a year before the May explosion, and revealed, to a public for whom such problems were still very remote, the existence of a new form of politicization among the students.[1] Whether a mere coincidence or a demonstration of Godard's intuition, *La Chinoise* contained a number of elements that were to be found twelve months later in the Movement that began at that same Nanterre. It is not my intention to examine to what extent the director was content to produce a piece of ethnography – he readily admits to having been trained as an ethnographer and to having a particular liking for the subject, while, at the same time, showing a certain flair for socio-political developments – or whether he skilfully exploited what existed at the time in order to sell a subject that could well meet with a certain success (the little red book was selling like hot cakes in the fashionable bookshops), or whether it was merely pure chance. However, I am inclined to think that Godard could be described as a talented non-professional sociologist.

In short sequences pieced together in an editing technique peculiar to Godard, *La Chinoise* recounts the life of a small group of Marxist–Leninist militants who are spending their summer vacation in a flat lent by a girl whose parents are away: this 'cell' life, with its internal ideological conflicts, its extra-political problems, and its decisions to exclude certain individuals, is illustrated in periods of discussion, self-education, and criticism, and in a theatrical representation of the Vietnam conflict, etc. Only two scenes are shot outside. One is of a terrorist expedition aimed at

[1] One of the protagonists of the film is a philosophy student at Nanterre, the others are a science student, an ex-prostitute, a young actor, and a painter.

the assassination of an important Soviet figure. The other is a discussion, on the suburban train to Nanterre, between the main heroine of the film and Francis Jeanson, a writer best known in France for his work for the FLN[1] during the Algerian war – a discussion that deals with a number of the subjects to be found in the assemblies in May, such as the treason of the Communist Party, the need for illegality, violence, action, and culture.

Nevertheless, it is not at the level of subject-matter that I wish to determine Godard's original contribution to the cinema and the basis for the parallels with the May Movement. As we have seen, the Marxist–Leninist tendency hardly belongs to the broad current that we have chosen to describe in this book – though this does not mean that we have any wish to deny its role and its influence during the events.[2] At this level, other films by Godard, such as *Weekend*, are certainly closer than *La Chinoise* to the ideas discussed in May.

What concerns me here is not so much what Godard thinks of this or that particular problem as the motives of his interest in these problems and the way in which he approaches them and deals with them, for Godard deals with a subject rather than tells a story in the traditional way.

It might be said that Godard's work is situated at the intersection of two 'disciplines', the cinema proper and reportage, the first being generally regarded as a noble form, the other as a mere technique, as 'journalism', an eminently vulgar form for those for whom 'Art is Art'. In this respect, he is not far removed from the experiments developed by the socio-ethnographical school of *cinéma vérité* (cf. in particular, J. Rouch).

Godard has repeated on several occasions that what would interest him most would be to work as the director of a television news service, whose role would be the dissemination of information, in a very wide sense, operating in a number of different directions at once, including information on current events, politics, finance, advertising, and also on science and the arts.[3] For him, there is no subject that cannot be dealt with in the cinema, especially in a consciously political cinema, for everything is politics, beginning with the things of everyday life. With few exceptions, his films lose their interest a relatively short time after being made. Godard accepts the *ephemeral* since, as he says himself (1967), his ambition is to observe change. Thus, *La Chinoise* attempts to capture a particular

[1] Front de Libération Nationale, the politico-military organization fighting for Algerian independence. (Translator's note.)
[2] It is worth mentioning that, according to one film critic, the young Marxist–Leninist militants with whom Godard had long discussions before starting the film were far from satisfied with it, and did not recognize themselves in the characters of the story.
[3] Interview that appeared in *Public*, No. 2.

form of student politics, *2 ou 3 choses que je sais d'elle* was inspired by an inquiry made by the weekly magazine *Le Nouvel Observateur* on prostitution, the plot of *Made in USA* is a fictitious ending of the Ben Barka affair, etc.

A cinema of this kind, in which fiction and documentary are mixed, in which the intentions of the author/director go well beyond anything that could be expressed in his usually very summary plots – Godard's films, his more recent ones at least, are not enclosed within the beginning and end recounted by the author, but are rather 'slices' cut from the lives of the characters represented – a cinema of this kind is not well suited to traditional discursive continuity. Indeed, Godard rejects such continuity from the outset – rejects the hypnotic *fascination* of the film that plunges the spectator into a world from which he re-emerges only when the words 'The End' appears on the screen. Neither *La Chinoise* nor *2 ou 3 choses que je sais d'elle* contains a single sequence that allows more than a few seconds' passive reception. The incoherence with which Godard has been reproached, even if it may sometimes seem excessive even to his admirers, is often the result of a desire to prevent the audience from being lulled into torpor, to force it to participate in some way, if only by means of irritation. Just as Godard, he tells us, watches himself making his films as he is shooting them, the spectator is forced to watch himself seeing the film. Because he participates in the actual shooting, he must, in a sense, follow the same itinerary as the director. In *La Chinoise* particularly – a cartoon, presented at the beginning of the first reel, warns us that it is 'a film that is still in the making' – all continuity is dispensed with: the clapperboy and camera crew appear on the screen, the actors are sometimes 'in the film' and sometimes outside it, sometimes they speak directly to the spectator (which may give one the impression that one is the director with whom the actor is speaking), sometimes they answer questions put to them by an interviewer who appears on the set. The film operates constantly on several levels. Indeed, it is quite striking to see, in discussions afterwards, how very different certain sequences appeared to different spectators, each one placing particular emphasis on one of the levels offered by the director. In this sense, Godard's films are not, as is often said, slapdash from a technical point of view, but on the contrary highly planned. In Godard's films, none of those 'alien', unintentional sights and sounds, which are usually excluded from studio shooting, and whose exclusion is responsible for the hypnotic fascination mentioned earlier, are eliminated. It may be irritating when part of a dialogue is drowned by the noise of a motor-cycle or a pneumatic drill, but Godard does not claim to have made a finished work, but rather a *sketch* of a piece of a reality that one does not have to be a film director to see. The Godard method is based on a desire to 'demythify' the art and technique of the cinema. As François Truffaut puts it (1967, p. 45), Godard has 'fichu la pagaille'[1] in the cinema and made it possible for France 'to become a country of forty-five million film directors'. Not, of course, that all technical limitations are eliminated. Godard has simply introduced, into a field where they did not previously exist, as much for financial as for artistic reasons, improvisation and the 'unfinished'.[2]

As Godard has frequently explained, his method does not involve total improvisation at the time of shooting; it necessitates a great deal of preparation and a thorough soaking in the subject. 'I make my films', he says (1967, p. 6) 'when I'm dreaming, having lunch, reading, talking to you now.' This preparation is not intended to preclude the unexpected, but, on the contrary, to allow greater freedom during the actual shooting. And neither this shooting nor the film presented to the public is regarded as the culmination of a creative process, but rather as a stage in that process. In this respect, Godard represents the antithesis of a certain aesthetic of the French cinema whose prototype might be said to be the work of René Clair, who is reported to have said: 'My film is almost finished – all I have to do now is to shoot it.' It would be interesting – but difficult – to know how much each participant contributed, not to the making, but to the actual shaping of the film. Without going so far as to speak of collective work, it could be said that *2 ou 3 choses que je sais d'elle*, for example, is a case in which a large degree of autonomy was left to the actor (for this film, the principal actress had no script to learn in advance and sometimes had to reply, during the shooting, to unexpected questions put to her by the director through a miniature ear-phone).

In an article on *Une femme mariée*, made in 1964, J. Doniol-Valcroze wrote (1965) that it would be possible to assemble all Godard's films to form a *film-fleuve* lasting several hours, in which each character could intervene in a story to which he did not belong, and wander in and out of the re-edited whole without any sense of incongruity. The spectator of a Godard film is in a similar situation. He wanders in and out of the film rather than observes it. He can see one sequence from the inside, another from the outside, without losing anything of the essential experience,

[1] Slang meaning 'turned everything upside down', 'caused chaos', etc. (Translator's note.)
[2] I am speaking here of the French cinema. There are a few 'off-beat' directors in the United States who might be compared with him.

dwell on a particular scene, then 'skip' others. The editing, which is never discursive, and in which speed alternates with slowness, 'interesting' moments with 'boring' ones (which need not be the same for every spectator), helps him to do this by presenting him with choices: to select, to see, to listen, or to see and to listen. This produces what might be called an aleatory participation that often goes beyond the intentions of the creator. Each sequence becomes an object, as J. Doniol-Valcroze remarks, independent of the rest of the film, which may be looked at 'from many different points of view' and experienced 'in an autonomous duration'. The meaning of these objects is not imposed at the outset; it is built up by projection onto a body of information supplied by the director.

It is obviously not my intention to make Godard the precursor of new forms of culture that were to emerge in May. And one can readily accept certain criticisms that have been made of his work. It cannot be denied that it is often ambiguous. Some (including himself?) see him as a Maoist, others as a left-wing or right-wing anarchist, or perhaps even as an 'ambidextrous' anarchist – in any case, he cannot easily be labelled. Is he naïve and pretentious, a genius and mediocre, sincere and cunning? Godard may be all these at once. Nevertheless, his films represent a break with the conformism of an art that is as rich in possibilities as it is unimaginative and, according to some, subjected to an aesthetic terrorism. Godard's main contribution is perhaps in having inverted the terms of a rule that subjected the mind to the form by tending to put the form entirely at the service of the idea to be conveyed, without regard to the 'beautiful' and the 'logical'. Even if, for reasons that cannot be attributed entirely to him, he has only partly succeeded, his work has challenged the notion of cinema spectacle,[1] and therefore a certain image of culture, the relations between the creator and his public.

LIVING THEATRE AND ANTI-THEATRE

Neither the cinema nor the theatre escaped the great wave of fundamental questioning that occurred in May. At Cannes, directors and actors, both French and foreign, brought the Festival to a halt. At a meeting in the premises of the École Nationale de Photographie et de Cinéma, the 'Estates General of the French Cinema' laid the foundations for a new status for the profession. 'The cinema must belong to the public', they

[1] Godard rejects the terms *cinéaste* and 'artist' and would like to be regarded simply as a *chercheur*; cf. *Le Monde*, 27 January 1967. (The word *chercheur* usually refers to a 'research worker' or 'research scientist', though without the specialist connotations of the English equivalents – Translator's note.)

declared, hence the need for 'a complete restructuring of its means of production and distribution'.[1] The Estates General was then transferred to the Paris suburbs, where, at the beginning of June, it drew up a statement condemning the purely commercial structures of the cinema:

> Films, which are works, are treated as commodities. The manufacture, distribution and consumption of this merchandise takes account only incidentally of its artistic, critical and cultural value . . . At the four stages of its existence – production, distribution, programming and exploitation – the system is subjected to the degradations of commerce.[2]

At the same time, camera crews were formed to film the demonstrations, the occupations of the factories, etc. The sequences that were shot were put together by a commission and projected 'whenever possible outside the normal circuits, even in the streets' (*Le Cinéma s'insurge*, p. 37). The work was entirely anonymous of course. The cinema abandoned fiction and took part in action. A new genre emerged, the *ciné-tract*.[3]

The revolt in the theatre was even more 'spectacular', and far from petering out in June continued throughout the summer at the Avignon Festival. The tone was set at the Odéon theatre by the Committee of Revolutionary Action, which, in a tract, advocated

> the systematic sabotage of the cultural industry and in particular of 'show business', and its replacement by true collective creation . . . The only theatre is a guerrilla theatre. Revolutionary art takes place on the street.

The Odéon *enragés* met again in July at Avignon, where they denounced the Festival as a 'cultural supermarket' (see Lebel, 1968). Ranged against them were the municipality, the police, the director of the Festival, Jean Vilar, and a section of the theatre companies invited. With them were a few young authors and the actors of the Living Theatre, who, in the end, withdrew from the Festival proper when forbidden to play in the streets.

Is it an anti-theatre? The term has often been used of the Living Theatre by its detractors. But it could also be used, without any pejorative implications, by its defenders. By wishing to go out into the streets to act – if the word still has any meaning in this context – free of charge, Julian

---

[1] Quoted in *Le Cinéma s'insurge* (1968, p. 1).
[2] Quoted in Zegel (1968, pp. 233–235).
[3] A short sequence, lasting two or three minutes, that could be inserted in any programme, and that illustrated some slogan or demand, etc.

Beck, Judith Malina, and their company made a definitive break with The Theatre, with its play, stage, actors, and spectators.[1]

Was it a sudden revelation, the shock produced by the great contestation of May, or the logical culmination of a new conception of the theatre? The attitude of the Living Theatre at Avignon can perhaps be explained by both reasons. The declaration made by Julian Beck when the company left the Festival, and to which I shall return later, is sufficient proof of the influence of the May events on the Living Theatre. But there is also an obvious kinship between the ideas previously professed by its members and the redefinitions of art, and of culture in general, that appeared in May, both in discussion and in practice.

To begin with, there is one obvious similarity, which I have no wish to insist on, but which is suggested by the politico-cultural tendency described in Chapters 5 and 6. From its inception, the Living Theatre has not only taken a stand with the anarchists, but striven to apply within itself the libertarian and egalitarian principles it has tried to express on the stage.[2] It would be an easy matter to find in the plays presented by the Living Theatre some of the major themes with which we have been concerned throughout this book, notably in *The Brig*,[3] *Frankenstein*, a parable about man perverted by society, which robs his actions of their true nature, and, of course, *Paradise now*, which I have already mentioned.

As with the films of Jean-Luc Godard, however, the relation with May is to be found not so much in the content of the plays as in the way in which the Living Theatre conceives of theatrical 'representation' and in the fusion it achieves, or seeks to achieve, between life, culture, and politics.

Can one conceive of a theatre without a script, without a stage, even perhaps without actors and spectators, in which everyone becomes a participant? When the Living Theatre was founded in New York, it seems that Judith Malina and Julian Beck did not think so. They wanted to change the theatre, but not by following in the footsteps of the Federal Theater, which had been set up by the American government during the Great Depression as a means of giving work to out-of-work actors, and which, in a more or less improvised way, presented experimental plays

---

[1] Speaking of *Paradise now* in the film, itself 'contested', on the 'contestation' of the Avignon Festival, *Être libre*, one of the members of the Living Theatre said: 'It's not a play, it's a *thing* that tries to show our state of mind, our way of living, of solving the problem.'
[2] The anarchism of the Living Theatre, however, with its archaic and sometimes mystical tendencies, is very different from that of the young militants whose writings were examined in earlier chapters.
[3] In the description of life in a prison for American Marines, it is 'a world dominated by money, authority, and dedicated to death, unless the man reacts' that is accused (cf. P. Biner, 1968).

throughout the United States dealing with problems of the moment.[1] Such an enterprise seemed to them to be impossible. At that time, their ambition – itself bordering on the impossible – was to attack the 'show business' monopoly symbolized by Broadway. If the earliest productions of the Living Theatre broke with theatrical tradition it was no doubt due as much to necessity as to the wishes of Julian Beck and Judith Malina. First an apartment, then an attic, served as a theatre. Admission was free; the voluntary contributions of the spectators – most of them friends – were collected in a basket.

At first, the Living Theatre's repertoire (Brecht, Jarry, Strindberg, Cocteau, Pirandello, Racine, etc.) and its working methods were hardly off the beaten track. The first real innovation took place in 1959, with the production of *The Connection*, a play by an unknown young writer, Jack Gelber, which combined fiction and reality, both on the stage and in the auditorium: a group of drug addicts, four of whom are jazz musicians, are in a flat, awaiting the arrival of their pusher. In the meantime, a camera crew is filming them, thus giving the illusion that the drug addicts are real drug addicts, really waiting for their 'fix'.

For the Living Theatre, however, the real interest of the play lies not in the subject, but in the discovery, through the jazz musicians who play themselves on the stage, of the possibility of new relations between the actors and the audience. As Judith Malina explains, a jazz musician

> comes into personal contact with the audience; when he goes down into the auditorium, he is known for what he is, there's no difference between what he was on stage and what he is (Biner, 1968, p. 44).

It was as a result of the experience of *The Connection* that the actors of the Living Theatre tried 'to play *themselves*'.

At the same time, Julian Beck and Judith Malina discovered the work of Artaud and his writings on the theatre, which confirmed them in their conviction that they must escape from the theatre-as-spectacle, the theatre-as-dream cut off from reality, a game that the spectator 'does not really feel, but experiences mentally' (ibid., p. 46). The spectator must be reached physically, by presenting him not a sweetened dream world, but the world as it is, absurd, cruel, and barbarous. It is not in escaping from reality, but on the contrary by accepting it, that man is able to change it. This theme was particularly important in *Frankenstein*:

Frankenstein, a powerless spectator of violence and injustice, decides to go

[1] Much of the information used here is taken from Biner (1968).

269

back to the beginning and start again, so that the world might be different, more habitable. All his actions, which originate in a sincere desire to do good, are inverted. Against his will, he creates evil (ibid., p. 127).

The working methods of the Living Theatre underwent a corresponding change. Production became less strict, and the actor played a greater role in the creation of the whole. The texts of the plays were often heavily altered (*Frankenstein* underwent several versions) and the company tried out certain experimental, quasi-Surrealist plays, in which the roles, situations, and dialogue were distributed at random. Julian Beck says:

> We let the sets and production emerge from the play . . . She [Judith Malina] made the action flow for the actor, then the actor could move around and invent things as soon as rehearsals began, when he knew more about his character than the director did (ibid., p. 71).[1]

This autonomy of each participant – the test of a genuine community – became increasingly important after the European exile of the Living Theatre: after being prosecuted several times for their activities in the cause of peace, and for the non-payment of fines and taxes, and after a particularly heavy sentence on Julian Beck and Judith Malina, the actors left the United States in 1964. The subject of the play they were then presenting, *The Brig*, a violent polemic about the Marines, was no doubt not unconnected with the severity of the sentence.

The Brig, and the events connected with it, marked a turning-point for the Living Theatre. As Julian Beck says (ibid., p. 71), it was as a result of that experience that the company adopted different political positions, began to turn itself into an anarchist-type community, and hence altered its acting style: 'because before we didn't know what to change in the acting'. The author's theatre was practically abandoned, to the benefit of collective creation on simple themes. With the exception of a play by Genet, *The Maids* (*Les Bonnes*), and an adaptation of *Antigone*, the Living Theatre confined itself in Europe mainly to *Frankenstein* and *Mysteries and smaller pieces*, a show in nine largely improvised parts, in which all the company's favourite themes are brought together: death, money, the dehumanization of the world, freedom, communication.[2] Their first

---

[1] These ideas are comparable with experiments being carried out in free jazz or contemporary music. Certain 'open' works recently produced in France (*Archipel I*, by Boucourechliev, for example) are made up of separate sequences that can be put together as the actors wish, which gives every performance a different character. This relative self-effacement of the creator – playwright, composer, director, etc. – to the benefit of the interpreter, or group of interpreters, even to the benefit of the message of the work, is one of the important points to be found in May.

[2] Communication is the major obsession of the Living Theatre. The communication between the

experiment in 'free theatre', in which a large number of spectators participated, took place in Paris in 1964.

The Living Theatre's experience of 'free theatre' was not a happy one. The first performance, in Paris, disappointed many members of the company; they were even frightened by the ambiguity of the reactions of certain members of the audience. Another performance was more successful – at least from the point of view of the actors, less so for much of the audience. The members of the company remained in the middle of the audience, silent and motionless, as if at a party, expecting something to happen. The audience felt frustrated because the 'actors' had not 'acted'. The 'actors', on the other hand, claimed the reverse: 'We transformed a particular atmosphere into a quite different atmosphere.'[1]

There is, in this kind of experiment, a contradiction that the detractors of the Living Theatre have not failed to point out: that of a community wishing to be open to the outside world, but whose growing internal cohesion may also lead to sectarianism and to a growing incomprehension of everything outside itself. Has the company escaped this danger? It may not have done, as the description in Chapter 3 of its visit to Nanterre perhaps shows.

What is certain, however, is that one can find in the work of the Living Theatre, sometimes clumsily expressed or applied perhaps, the seeds of some of the key ideas of those who, in May, sought to redefine not only a new society but also a *new culture*, by living and experiencing them both. Moreover, the Living Theatre found in May, as can be seen in Julian Beck's statement at Avignon, an encouragement to carry its own convictions further than it had so far done.

The 20th Avignon Festival provided the last act of the 'iconoclastic festival' of May, to use the phrase already borrowed from J. Starobinski by R. Jean (1968, p. 83). This Festival was to see the often brutal confrontation of two conceptions of the theatre, art and culture. That of Jean Vilar, the Festival director, reputedly 'a man of the Left', and his supporters, for whom 'the servitude of an actor is to act, however he may be affected by events'.[2] And that of the 'Leftists', who were to be joined by the Living Theatre, for whom the playing of Brecht or Genet on the stages of theatres that one knows perfectly well are scarcely frequented at

---

actors and between actors and spectators is symbolized in different ways in its productions. A symbol that is often used is electricity (*The Connection, Frankenstein*), transmittable *energy*, seen under its two aspects as a generator of life or death, according to how it is used.

[1] Judith Malina, in Biner (1968, p. 148).
[2] J. Vilar, in *Le Nouvel Observateur*, 29 July 1968.

all by the 'ordinary people' who are supposed to be one's audience is either sheer hypocrisy or a means of assuaging one's conscience – especially when this theatre is subsidized by the state, which proves that the state has nothing to fear from such productions.

But no more than two months before, at the occupied Odéon, the argument concerned more than statistics on the social composition of audiences. There were those who wanted to denounce a culture that had become a commodity, an object of speculation, 'a product of mass consumption' (Lebel, 1968, p. 12) in the hands of the few, and therefore to denounce the production stage also, to use the same vocabulary. For art, like science, is contaminated as soon as it ceases to be totally independent of the system. No art is neutral, and no art can be revolutionary when it bows to the norms of official culture.

And what is to replace the overthrown idols, Art, Culture, the Artist? 'Our artistic creation', replies one of the Living Theatre actors, 'is life . . . it's something everyone can do.'[1]

For the Living Theatre realized at Avignon that if only 1 per cent of the Festival audience were workers,[2] it was not a question of money, but of culture:

> The workers refuse to consume cultural values whose class content is flagrant. Created for and by an elite, the theatrical industry remains a thing of the bourgeoisie, a thing of 'educated people' (Lebel, op. cit., p. 15).

ART IN LIFE

Although it has not always drawn the consequences for a new conception of acting, the Living Theatre has always opposed the 'Method', which derives from the teaching of Stanislavski[3] and has been developed in the United States principally by Lee Strasberg. It seemed to Julian Beck and Judith Malina that this search for perfection in interpretation, this attempt on the actor's part to immerse himself totally in another personality, in his role, was in some way false and artificial.

> People don't have to speak better than other people. Nothing is better than people . . . I want actors to stop posing. I'm speaking here also of Method

---

From an interview in *Être libre*.

[2] A figure quoted by J.-J. Lebel (op. cit., p. 25) and taken from an inquiry carried out at the request of the Festival authorities. This same inquiry is also used, by its defenders, to prove the democratic character of the Festival: apparently only 2 per cent of the audiences were composed of heads of commercial and industrial concerns! The audiences were made up for the most part of students, teachers, and artists.

[3] Cf. *The formation of the actor*; *My life in art*, etc.

actors. They must stop trying to create effects and violating the honest representation of life.

To the reconstituted realism of Stanislavski, the Living Theatre prefers realism itself, the realism that Brecht spoke of when he said 'it's not how real things are, but as things really are'. After looking for it on the stage, the Living Theatre discovered it in May, then in July, in the streets of Paris and Avignon, where the *enragés* debaptized art and called it *life*:

> Today it is life, minute by minute, that is creation and art. It is life itself that has taken over the task of entertaining and stimulating the emotions. It is life that draws people out of their houses to communicate. It is life that is the best teacher. And which makes one want to live and struggle.[1]

By going out into the streets to play *Paradise now*, the actors of the Living Theatre were merely extending the experiments made in May by a few young actors and directors, together with amateurs, in an attempt to escape from the ghetto of the theatres in search not of an audience, but of participants wherever they happened to be, whether in the streets or in the factories.

This new theatre has scarcely any points in common with the old: it need be no more, for example, than miming a scene in the street (a demonstrator chased by the police, etc.), parodying a sequence from the television news, or feigning a political argument in order to get the passers-by to join in, and then moving on to another place. Other experiments were carried out in real theatres (mainly the Théâtre de l'Épée de Bois), in which actors and audience presented poems, songs, and sketches that were then re-enacted at crossroads, *métro* stations, etc. The content of these texts was often regarded as of only secondary importance: 'the discussion with the audience about what has just been presented is more important than the representation itself' (*Au joli mai*, 1968, p. 42). The fact that the authorities agreed to a play like *Paradise now* being played in a theatre but not in the streets strengthens the conviction that

> what is dangerous for the bourgeois system is not so much the political content of the play as the transformation of that content into direct political action ... The Avignon Festival has shown that only theatre performed in the streets is dangerous for the bourgeoisie (*Action*, No. 24, 4 September 1968).

Culture–life, action–culture, and therefore culture in movement. The

---

[1] A. Benedetto, in *Bulletin de la Nouvelle Compagnie d'Avignon*, 20 May 1968, quoted by J.-J. Lebe (1968, p. 56).

ephemeral establishes itself where the desire for immortality prevailed.[1] The beautiful is no longer what will be admired tomorrow, the beautiful is what is being done, what everyone is doing, what others are doing and through which everyone learns and recognizes himself. People are imagining a culture

> which would have neither the same function nor the same character, . . . individual or collective activities which, instead of being shut up in museums, would take place permanently, in everyday life, in direct contact with the constant transformation of human relationships . . . These activities will be meaningful only if they are the privilege of no one individual, no caste and above all no class (Lebel, 1948, p. 28).

It was also the ambition of those who worked in the poster studio of the École des Beaux-Arts – undoubtedly the most successful experiment in this field to emerge in May – to remain in direct contact with daily life and to break down the temporal isolation of the artist. In their first platform of action, voted on 16 May in a general assembly, one reads:

> Privilege encloses the artist in an invisible prison. The fundamental concepts that underlie the isolation imposed by culture are:
>   the idea that art has 'conquered its autonomy' (Malraux) . . .
>   the defence of 'creative freedom'. Culture enables the artist to live in the illusion of freedom . . . He is a 'creator', which means that he invents something out of nothing, something unique and of permanent value, above historical reality. He is not a worker at grips with historical reality. The idea of creation deprives his work of reality.
> By according him this privileged status, culture prevents the artist from doing any harm.[2]

As in the case of the experiments carried out at the Théâtre de l'Épée de Bois, the conception and production of the posters was a common, absolutely anonymous process:

> Two workers came and suggested slogans, discussed things with the artists and students, criticized the posters that had been made or distributed them outside (ibid., p. 10).

Traditional criteria of judgement disappeared,[3] with the exception of effectiveness. 'Professionals' saw their projects rejected in favour of the

---

[1] 'We want a music that is wild and ephemeral' – slogan on the walls of the Conservatoire de Musique.
[2] Quoted in *Atelier populaire présenté par lui-même* – 87 posters of May–June 1968, pp. 8–9.
[3] Indeed, this seems to me to be the case in the various parallel cultures discussed in this part of the book. The absence of objective criteria of judgement – in the sense in which artistic production becomes an object that lends itself to comparison – is an essential characteristic of such attempts

harder-hitting work of amateurs. Suggestions for posters were discussed in the assembly, after an analysis of the day's events, and were sometimes altered, not from some aesthetic point of view, but in relation to the opportunity of the slogan illustrated:

If you have nothing to say, you can't do anything interesting, even if you've got a perfect mastery of the technique. If you don't have the technique, but want to say something, the means used cannot but be spontaneous, new and profitable.[1]

The work was carried out almost entirely collectively, as can be seen on some of the posters, where different parts have quite obviously not been drawn by the same person. As J. Michel observes, collective creation plays a role as mutual instruction:

'Non-directive' instruction, which replaces the 'vertical' structures of instruction handed down from master to pupil by a 'horizontal' structure in which everyone is undergoing a continual apprenticeship in creation with everyone else (Le Monde, 13 June 1968).

This mutual instruction benefits those who possessed some mastery of the rudiments of design as much as, if not more than, complete novices. The former were able to rediscover their spontaneity through the latter:

People who couldn't draw at all, started producing designs: very often their posters were the best, for their inspiration had not been stifled by any definite criterion of beauty. I remember one in particular, one of the finest designs we produced, but unfortunately it didn't get printed (we had more urgent slogans to send out). One of the comrades sketched it in a moment of anger (Partisans, op. cit., p. 170).

Other experiments were attempted: a wall newspaper was started (five issues were distributed); a marionette studio gave performances in the streets, factories, and universities. Again, there was a single aim in mind – to arouse discussion,[2] to get everyone to participate. For the collective

---

to go beyond accepted cultural norms. As Julian Beck and Judith Malina remarked at a 'free theatre' performance, 'if you play "free theatre", you can't say this is bad, that is good' (Biner, 1968, p. 91). Judgement is now entirely subjective, since the creative act has value only in the immediate meaning projected onto it by the actors.

[1] Comment by one of the participants in the studio, in the review Partisans, No. 43, July–September 1968, p. 171.

[2] At the beginning of June, I witnessed the following scene: on a long hoarding a student was sticking a series of posters denouncing the general secretary of the CGT – 'Séguy has sold out the working class' – watched by a group of people talking on the pavement. A man in his fifties, who had been watching the posters go up, took out a pen and altered one of the posters, replacing the words 'sold out' by 'given away'. The student came back, spoke a few words with the group, then corrected the other posters himself.

does not exclude the individual, but on the contrary enables him to realize himself:

> A new kind of aristocracy is being born here, accessible to all, in which only the intrinsic value of the individual counts (*Partisans*, op. cit., p. 170).

'THE SACRED, THAT IS THE ENEMY'[1]

In the article mentioned above, J. Michel tells how, at the Salon de la Jeune Peinture, which should have opened on 1 June 1968,

> twenty-five artists, who wanted their paintings to be in contact with current events, came together and painted a collection of fifty pictures, in which each painter could intervene in anyone else's work, on a single theme – the Vietnam war. . . . After having raised to a mythical level the individuality of the artist, and his arbitrary rule within the bounds of the canvas, where he reigns as absolute master, the ceremonies of collective creation appear to have been intended to abolish individuality at man's most individual level, the artistic.

Other 'coincidences' of this kind, both in France and elsewhere, may be adduced, which reveal a link between a certain artistic avant-garde and ideas that were developed in May. A new trend is emerging in the cinema, the theatre, music, and painting that we have been able to illustrate with only a few examples. The May Movement is probably no more than the most spectacular expression of the juncture between the cultural and the political, of the merging of art and action. The experiments in street theatre had their equivalent in Germany, where students organized parodies of official events; in the United States, where groups improvised in public sketches against the Vietnam War. In fact, the last student drama festival at Nancy (April 1969) was a perfect illustration of the trends outlined here. B. Poirot-Delpech wrote of this festival:

> Not only have they forbidden any prearranged site for the performance, any price of admission, any author's play and any notion of 'leading roles', but these collectively created street shows are becoming increasingly reduced to mime or to the use of puppets, with a minimum of text and on current themes, simplified in the extreme (*Le Monde*, 22 April 1969).

Less obvious, on account of the conditions of distribution, the same trend is no less important in the cinema. In France, Great Britain, Canada, the United States, and Latin America, a 'free cinema' is developing out-

[1] A slogan in May.

side the usual production channels and outside their norms and conformism. Describing this new 'underground' cinema, L. Marcorelles says:

> From being pure entertainment, the film is becoming an instrument of com-
> bat, a tool for knowledge and communication . . . It personalizes in the
> extreme the relations between the work and the creator, while breaking down
> the barriers that held the spectator prisoner in a magic enclosure. Sometimes,
> the protagonists of the film, and even the spectators, become co-creators of
> the work.[1]

Curiously enough, it would appear that it was those who had gone
furthest in this direction who, in May, felt confused about what was
happening in the streets and in the faculties.[2] As Julian Beck declared at
Avignon: 'Today, we're at rock bottom . . . our action began only three
or four days ago.' The sacred notions of Art and Culture that they had
wanted to overthrow, without always escaping the ambiguities of a
rejection that can be expressed only by the very means that they are
rejecting, were suddenly volatilized, art having become subversion and
subversion art.

'The students', say the detractors of the May Movement, 'don't really
want revolution. They're quite content to play at it.' I don't think all the
students referred to here would totally reject this statement. A certain
theatrical element was often present in the more serious as well as in
lighter moments. To borrow a sociological vocabulary that is particularly
well adapted to these circumstances, the social actors suddenly discovered
that the author of the play in which they were acting had disappeared.
Society had stopped handing out roles. Some of them, like wretched
musicians suddenly without a score, took fright. Others chose to become
their own authors.

P. Labro (1968, p. 158) relates the following incident. In a large Paris
store a journalist was questioning a girl employee, a member of a strike
picket, who answered:

> I don't know what to say . . . I'm not a very cultured person.

A fellow-striker, a girl of about the same age, interrupted:

> You mustn't say that. There's no such thing as knowledge any more. Culture
> is just talking now.

---

[1] Cf. 'Les nouveaux cinéastes', Le Monde, 4 April 1969.
[2] The others took refuge in a sulky wait-and-see policy or signed innumerable petitions and collective declarations, which in France is often regarded as the greatest proof of commitment and
political courage that an intellectual can offer.

PART V

Conclusions

Methods of Overthrow,
the Overthrowing of Methods

We have worked like craftsmen, plunging into the material we are seeking to understand. Although it is true that the structure of a sociological study emerges in the course of the work – that the data are not simply 'there', ready to be collected – and that problems of selection and presentation are present throughout the work, we have noticed much more clearly than in other studies to what extent the phenomena selected themselves, rather than we selected them. Our work was craft-like in character, that is, isolated, and limited by the resources and help available.[1] At the quasi-manual stage in the development of research work, the craftsman has to be able to turn his hand to anything. This approach is less archaic and more satisfactory than might appear, because of the constant presence of all aspects of the question at once; it is also limiting, and one runs the risk of never crossing the river. We should perhaps examine the epistemology of our study, in order to present it in its true perspective, and, at the same time, to reveal the problems of general interest that it raises.

Research workers have repeatedly suggested[2] that research teams should be set up for 'emergencies', but when I began this project I had no budget, no assistants, and not even a minimum of 'technical' equipment. And the almost total involvement of most Parisian sociologists created its own barriers to any informal arrangements. Only a small team could function, on an almost 'family' basis, during May and June (interviews, collection of documents). The fact that I had previously worked on the study of images of society enabled me to draw up a questionnaire rapidly. For all these reasons, this study was qualitative and intensive, rather than quantitative and extensive, and it remained so throughout.

---

[1] It should be mentioned that P. Gallissaires, who helped us in our work, is a poet; a number of the poems he wrote in May were published in the review *Les Temps modernes*, No. 271, January 1969.
[2] Cf. Pagès (1963). Others have made similar suggestions, as, for example, at the time of the great Belgian strike.

The study gradually emerged as an *exploration* of a particular type, carried out in the heat of the moment, as it were: it consisted of the collection of data in the middle of a social crisis, and in the middle of a methodological crisis in the pursuit of understanding. The method is perhaps a modern variety of hermeneutics. It is not particularly historical – at most, it retraces a process over a certain period – it is above all the sketch of a *socio-logic*; it tries to discover the meaning of various documents, by comparison with similar phenomena. A 'historical' characteristic could be found, perhaps, in the attention given to the specificity of the particular event, which, of course, does not exclude, but, on the contrary, demands, subsequent reflection on the significance of this prototype in relation to the evolution of 'industrial' societies. On the basis of the naïve and 'informed' intuition of the kinship of various phenomena (past and present), we began to 'construct' our study: to read, classify, discuss, and relate various aspects that selected each other.

It may be that this constitutes a 'hermeneutic circle' or a culturalist circle, but I know of no other method that could take account, from the inside, of a movement that is characterized by its very interiority. In any case, to place oneself inside such a movement does not exclude a sociological awareness of the problems presented in and by the phenomenon. Our objects of study are also *subjects*, capable of awareness – at least before and after an 'action', and at least partially. Moreover, like the participants of the movement he is studying, the sociologist is himself an object–subject of his society, which makes it less surprising that he can be sufficiently 'inside' and 'outside' at the same time, contrary to normal practice in ethnography.[1]

In my experience, moreover, the project of studying revolutionary movements leads to the adoption of a strategy that is the reverse of the traditional approach. Instead of relating so-called 'subjective' and 'objective' data, or an established society and a counter- or anti-society, we should replace these approaches, at least at the initial stage, with the study, from the inside, of a *new culture* in its relations with a *society* that is *projected* and partly lived. In this approach the aim was to reveal a new type of affirmation, beyond both negation and non-integration; by practising not even the sociology of a subculture, but that of a new culture. Such a

[1] Cf. the discussion between C. Lévi-Strauss and P. Ricœur on 'Structure et herméneutique' (Ricœur, 1963). For Ricœur, 'hermeneutics is a stage in the appropriation of meaning', and he insists on the need to grasp the 'content' quite apart from the structural 'arrangement' – 'hermeneutics speaks in terms of tradition, inheritance, the revival (or "rebirth") of a decaying meaning in a new meaning, etc.' And, on the subject of certain symbols, he lays particular stress on the 'reserve of meaning ready for use in other structures'.

project is utopian in Mannheim's, as well as in Marcuse's,[1] sense of the term, hence its importance; once the phenomenon is revealed, or *displayed*, there is no reason why one should not keep one's distance and explain its origin, dynamism, and evolution in the traditional way; that is a different matter. At that stage, the participants in the phenomenon present us with the problems that confronted them. In fact, it is useless to attempt to understand the student revolt in terms of the students' careers, families, etc.; the fact remains that the students themselves are questioning the present and the future of society, and their questions cannot be contained within a sociology that treats such questioning as deviance; it is 'normality' itself that is in question.

The principal stages of the inverted approach, on the basis of the experience acquired in this study, may be as follows:

Since the 'design' of the study cannot be planned, nor the tools prepared over a long period of time, one loses in initial clarity what one gains on another level: being further removed from sociological research and closer to the experimental work carried out in laboratory conditions mainly by social psychologists, 'hot' sociology describes a 'wild' experiment in the course of which certain fundamental 'variables' are manipulated *socially*.[2] The difficulty of circumscribing the object of one's study, which is always so important in sociology, arises of course at the analytical stage. Throughout this study, we have insisted on the fact that we do not regard 'May' as a simple totality. We have tried to discover part at least of its 'nature', but from the beginning we decided to concern ourselves with *one* current of ideas – that which seemed to us to be linked with other phenomena involving a juncture of the political and the cultural.

If one sets out with an initial, formal definition, the various chapters must all progress at the same time; the exposition cannot then be truly linear, it takes into account what might – hypothetically at least – be termed as the common nature of different phenomena (May, Dada, Surrealism, Free Jazz, certain trends in the cinema and theatre) or as the

[1] Mannheim 'emphasizes the power of "utopian" thought which (like ideology) produces a distorted image of reality, but which (unlike ideology) contains the necessary dynamism to transform this reality, so that it will resemble this image' (Berger and Luckmann, 1966, p. 10). Marcuse proposes to define utopian as 'that which the power of established societies forbids to see the light of day' (Marcuse, 1969, p. 12).

[2] Notably the *pressure* of the established society, and police *repression*. But whereas the first is, in a sense, 'lifted', the second is omnipresent as an objectivation of the first, experienced both more directly – materially – and as more provisional, in so far as the participants in the action believe in their own ultimate victory.

common nature of a single phenomenon apprehended through various methods (qualitative interviews, opinion polls, discussion between specialists, published documents, parallels). The inevitable consequence, which is connected with the procedure followed, but also with the nature of the phenomena – such, at least, is our thesis – is obviously that one finds in the different chapters sketches of the same model.

From the moment the research worker is confronted by a phenomenon that commands his attention, rather than his preparing a controlled description of it, the definition of what is instrumental changes fundamentally. Instead of defining the object of study on the basis of the instruments for the collection and analysis of data, as has often been done, or in the interaction of instruments and data, which is better, instead of concerning oneself with phenomena that can be assimilated in terms of economic and social management, a form of action of the type we are considering is itself the *instrument* of change that the observer records. In so far as he wishes to understand, the researcher passes through an initial stage of immersion in the material, before emerging into a second stage of consciousness, of analytic description.[1] As a subject who is aware of meaning, first from the inside then from the outside, the researcher himself becomes the principal instrument of the study: he is both 'questioner' and 'questioned' (to use Sartre's terms) and must also answer questions; lastly, since his own emancipation is not independent of that of others, he has as much interest as the subjects he is observing in not confining himself to an instrumental role.

Finally, the separation between explanation and description is even less plausible than usual, since the traditional connection between subjective data and an external, 'objectivated' world is suspended for a time. Although it is always true that the subjective has its own objectivity seen from both the inside and outside, it is as if the *instituant* (the new, or emergent power) has only the most tenuous links with the *institué* (the established power), at least in a period of great upheaval. That is an extreme case, but it seems that the phenomenon we are trying to present must be placed in that perspective: first, from the fact of its 'interiorism', which is partly justified by possible revolution, whether a reality or merely a belief; then from the fact of the radical change of perspective, to which we have referred several times (notably in

---

[1] 'We cannot, at one and the same time, try to understand things from the outside and the inside; and we can understand them from the inside only if we are born on the inside, if we in fact are inside' (Lévi-Strauss, see Ricœur, 1963, p. 637).

Chapter 4) – 'revolutionary' change at the level of 'surreality', in the very sphere that one is trying to understand. In other words, the explanation of the phenomenon is, more than ever, to be found already in its description, the description implying on our part a hermeneutic effort to deploy all its aspects, which have never been brought together by a single participant.

The establishment of relations with other elements (the social origin of the students, the labour market, technocracy) is certainly necessary, but it follows a different logic: it is not because it can and must be practised that 'immanent' understanding – to use a term that has fallen into disuse – would provide only a description with explanatory content.

Moreover, the emergence of a prototype does not amount to the conceptual definition of an ideal type, or to a 'positive' description of the distribution of various characteristics throughout a given population. We have presented the results of a 'minimum' opinion poll in order to draw attention to the diversity of the student population, which would have been shown to be even greater had a much larger sample been taken of students who were not present when and where the poll was carried out. The prototype or phenomenon with which we are concerned is of another kind, modal rather than median. It involves the *meaning* of a phenomenon over and above the precise consciousness of it achieved by individual participants. To reveal this meaning, we have carried the internal logic of one of the currents to the limits of its own field of meaning.[1]

The fact that certain critical minds, observing the situation from the outside – from a point of view supposedly closer to 'reality'[2] – may choose to condemn this current as utopian, in the pejorative sense, is both legitimate and trite; the questions presented by the 'irruption' of 'surreality' are in no way disposed of by such an attitude.

[1] P. Bourdieu (in a postscript to Panofsky, *Architecture gothique*, 1967) proposes 'to relate a style to its own norms of perfection' (p. 163) and suggests that 'the ultimate truth of a style is not inherent in the original inspiration, but is defined and redefined continually in accordance with a constantly evolving meaning' (p. 161).
[2] Or, rather, 'subreality', that is, a point of view that confines itself to what happens, at the time, to be 'objectivated' and generally accepted as 'reality'.

Imaginaction

There can hardly be any doubt that the phenomenon presented here is too rich and too mobile to be embraced by a single, simple, definitive synthesis; a reductive interpretation would be particularly inappropriate to this 'bushy' phenomenon.[1] However, the current outlined here is also too limited to represent the *whole* of the May events of 1968. Our conclusions, then – quite apart from the *questions* posed by the emergence of this current and the way in which we have described it – will never be anything more than the essential characteristics, brought together for the first time, by fusion or combination, of normally separate elements. In fact, our contribution stops short of such a conclusion. A systematic analysis would not be impracticable; a new conceptualization, which would not consist of a mere reordering of the notions to be found in the sociology of established systems, must be developed. 'Affirmative' sociology, that is, the analysis of unrepressed sociological phenomena, is only in its infancy (social psychology, which is able to create micro-climates of freedom in laboratory conditions, seems more advanced in this respect).

A series of questions will help us, at the outset, to clear up certain misunderstandings and to place our work in its proper perspective, and also in that of the Movement itself.

SOCIOLOGY OF THE LATENT?

To begin with, a double hypothesis must be made.

The anarcho-Marxist, politico-cultural, affirmative and libertarian, Surrealist current was far from being representative of the participants in the May Movement as a whole, or of the whole period covered by the events. It was difficult, in May, not to notice the presence among the participants of many individuals whose attitudes were not only authoritarian and violent, but also elitist and terrorist, and whose words were anything

[1] A term used by E. Morin during a conference of the Société française de sociologie (March 1969); sociologists are too concerned with large-scale structures (trees) and tend unfortunately to regard images, which are the first steps towards a new conceptualization, as unworthy of their attention.

but in accordance with their practice. Even when taking into account, as is often done, and rightly so, the fact that this practice was conditioned by the nature and action of the established system, the contradiction was often a flagrant one: the anti-authoritarian objective of the action and the authoritarian beginnings[1] of a revolutionary process created serious doubts as to the future. Moreover, the period of 'free-wheeling' and of affirmation of a non-authoritarian, fusionist society was short-lived; since then, the return to the old sectarianisms, divisions, condemnations, and absolutist solutions has been so marked that many of the participants relegate the experience that they really did live through, and help to create, to the domain of 'myth'. The term we have suggested would describe, therefore, only a dream reality – imaginaction would be only a dream (seen from the inside) or a nightmare (seen from the outside): an imaginary action.

On the other hand, the sketch of the current presented here, which was valid for a section of the participants and for a limited period, documents reality of a type that is sociologically fairly rare, but that clearly goes beyond the *mental sphere*. Even if it is true, and we would not wish to deny it, that fairly considerable discrepancies existed between written or spoken declarations and behaviour in the streets, in the assemblies, in direct contact with the workers, in day-to-day interaction and creation, the description offered here contains many elements relating to reality. On several occasions we have remarked that the analysis of behaviour must, of course, be carried further; nevertheless, written and spoken behaviour is sufficient evidence of what took place at the level of consciousness; according to many reports, according to the projects that can be read in the sphere of education, as elaborated by the students, and, last but not least, if we consider the extension of the action to the national level – though this was not, of course, entirely the work of the students – we are able to judge the degree of 'reality' of the phenomenon.

The Gaullist electoral victory that followed May gave added support to the pejorative interpretation of the term 'revolutionary psychodrama', used by Raymond Aron of the May 'revolutionaries' in general. In fact, the term does not exclude the expression of profound content by the participants[2] – one has only to recall its origin in Moreno's use of

[1] To this internal contradiction, which was present in certain minds, must be added, of course, the conflict between two political currents: the totalitarianism of the methods used by some, which were seen as foreshadowing a so-called 'provisional' period of totalitarianism in society, and what might be called the totalism of others, whose objective was the retotalization of the individual.
[2] Though this does not perhaps apply to the first term, 'pseudo-psychodrama', which R. Aron used in a broadcast on Radio Luxembourg; subsequently, in *La Révolution introuvable*, he repeats

psychodrama or sociodrama. With the opposite political outcome (the overthrow of the regime, a shift in the power relations, civil war, etc.), the same behaviour, preceding the final phase, would have been seen in a different light. But since things are much what they were before, many observers stress the idea of imaginary action rather than that of imagination in action, which was, in fact, so important.

Among the disturbing questions that may arise concerning the current of ideas and behaviour outlined here, the following are perhaps of particular relevance to the sociologist:

What do so-called representative samples represent? Do they not contain a quantitatively balanced selection of many social categories that are relatively integrated in established society, side by side with a sub-category of individuals, in normal conditions not very numerous, who are integrated into a 'latent' society?[1] In other words, how can one assess the importance of a new phenomenon: is it true that reflection on an exceptional period that saw the irruption of the 'latent' has led to a questioning of the mechanical quantitative methods that attribute too much reality to what is simply more widespread?

Why is it that only experimental social psychologists and a small number of industrial consultants (in the field of *action research*)[2] can practise social experiment? Such ideas as the avoidance of *a priori* solutions and crystallized schemas as soon as they are adapted were expressed repeatedly in May – but they are still relatively new in Europe. There are very few social experiments in which sociologists participate in any other way than as external specialists with *a priori* or *a posteriori* ideas. In May, young sociologists, notably at Nanterre, filled this professional gap in their own way. 'Why were so many young sociologists so passionately involved in May?' The question can and must be turned upside down: 'Why are so many professional sociologists so far from demanding sociological experiment, or at least a study of the "latent"?'[3]

several times the words 'psychodrama that might have ended in drama', thus recognizing the phenomenon of expression as well as the reality of the process initiated (1968, pp. 35–40).

[1] It should be remembered that few of them are capable of expressing really extreme positions; this is the problem of *realized consciousness* and of *possible consciousness* referred to by L. Goldmann (in, for example, 'Projet d'enquête sociologique sur les nouvelles structures mentales, apparues en Mai–Juin 68', a paper presented at a conference of the International Council of the Social Sciences, December 1968: 'Our work has shown that the maximum possible consciousness . . . sometimes resulted in expression from the pens of great creators . . .', since many individuals in a group are not capable of expressing it; this maximum constitutes however an index of the 'tendencies of the consciousness of the groups . . . and possible modifications of that consciousness'.)

[2] Such as the Tavistock Institute, London; E. Thorsrud, in Oslo; H. Van Beinum, in Amsterdam; and E. Rhenman, in Stockholm.

[3] There are a great many social resistances to such a course, but is this a sufficient explanation?

Should we develop different approaches and methods for periods of relative calm and for periods of relative upheaval? Should the methods used in times of peace be applied to 'hot' phenomena, in order to avoid excessive enthusiasm on the part of the observers? Should the methods used in the understanding of upheavals be applied to apparently 'cold' phenomena, in order to prevent the systems from being regarded as more definitively established than they are? There is more here than the problem of a possible combination of a phase of intuition and understanding and a phase of 'cold' analysis. The 'hot' method, applicable in times of upheaval, is characterized as they study of the universe of one or several social participants in action, rather than the study of a system. This is to some extent inevitably the case when the changes seem so great to the participants – and indeed are, for a time at least, as in the spring of 1968 in France – that action is taken 'as if' the established social structures no longer existed. If the same method were more systematically applied to societies in their 'normal' state, it is possible that the established systems would appear, not only to sociologists, but also to intellectuals generally and, in the end, perhaps, to the population as a whole, as less established than they appear to be today.[1]

EXPLAINING ONE PHENOMENON BY ANOTHER

Although it is true that we do not claim to have described, completely or independently, either the phenomena of May or the cultural parallels outlined here – a fact that is inherent in the method advocated – it should be made clear that their common elements are seldom as *visible* in each case taken separately. This is the first reason why one cannot really deny oneself the revealing power of the parallel. On the other hand, apart from these parallels, a number of aspects would seem fortuitous and ephemeral, or merely superficial – as many observers have remarked, while admiring, quite apart from any snobbish motives, the works, for example, of the Surrealist painters, and vigorously denying that *they* were superficial. Lastly, the parallel phenomena (anterior or contemporary) provide the image of an entity part of which at least bears the same features. Although it would certainly be a gross exaggeration to claim that May, or even one of the currents present in May, is the exact homologue, in either content

---

[1] This was the problem, in May, of 'bureaucratic' and 'capitalist' thought for many a young Marxist whose critical analyses scarcely concealed his faith in the extraordinary rigidity and solidity of the established systems.

or structure, of Dada, Surrealism, etc., certain elements may well preserve a similar significance, in themselves and in their relation to the participant and to society.

In all these ways, one thing explains another more adequately than the *a priori* concepts of a certain mode of analysis.

Why, then, are cultural movements anterior? Artistic creation is more protected from social, or state, control; it has probably benefited from a margin of tolerance, and 'subversion' is able to develop more easily – stimulated at some periods more than others, as Dada was stimulated by World War I – and artists, often less integrated into society than most, have acted as the seismographs of the inhuman tendencies of modern society, even before the intellectuals. Artists, who are non-conformists by trade, or by choice, have dared to state, and above all develop, what others have not even imagined. Lastly, to a much greater degree than pure thinkers, who may attain the maximum possible consciousness mentioned by Goldmann, artists, who are 'existentialists' without knowing it, have practised and lived out their conceptions. The ideas of profession, as a separate area of life, and of specialization and segmentation have been more easily rejected by them.

Some of them gave public expression to their desire to destroy or go beyond a form of 'culture' that seemed to them to be as ossified, as alien to 'life' and to themselves, as the society in which they had to live, but they created new forms of culture, in micro-societies that became their permanent reference-points.

It is perhaps this schema that is the broadest common denominator between the various phenomena that have been brought together in this study, the desire for liberation (freedom from) and for emancipation (freedom for), or self-development.[1] It is found over and over again: one is led to think that an ossified culture or society cannot be maintained without recourse to social domination.

ACTION AND IMAGINATION

Did the partisans of the current described really act? Did they possess imagination? We believe that we have answered these questions by means of description and we shall content ourselves with returning to one or two of the major characteristics.

It has been said that the students were imitating movements abroad and

[1] The terms in parentheses are Erich Fromm's.

above all that their ideas were heteroclite and archaic and that, consequently, there was little room for the imagination.

Although it would be quite useless to deny the similarities between their
Movement and a number of others, both earlier and contemporary, it
seems to us to be important to show that they made their own *collage*,
whatever materials went into its making.

Some of the students knew other movements (Marxism, Bakuninism,
Dada, Surrealism, etc.) from which they derived one or more elements.
Others saw only the elements proposed by their comrades without themselves knowing these movements, or, at most, knowing them only in the
personal presentation of them given by someone who happened to be on
the spot. This collage, which can be distinguished from *bricolage*, in
Lévi-Strauss's well-known usage, is characterized thus, the arrangement of elements drawn from various contexts is constantly altered; if the
elements take on a new meaning, it is because they are placed, temporarily, beside other elements, in a structural arrangement; it is above all
because the meaning of the element is defined more by the individual
who 'senses' it, now, than by its original context; in other words, the
element acquires, through many discussions, something of a life of its
own, autonomous, but new.

But apart from that, the 'old' elements, which were known above all
at the abstract level of principles, preserve a 'real' novelty, since they have
never been applied, outside the artistic field, for example, outside small
communities and exceptional periods (the same can be said for certain
forms of socialism), or never perhaps in a way that measures up to the
ideal advocated (self-management, for example).

The imagination, then, comes into play in the activity of the collage: it
requires a constant *personal* understanding of the elements, a reflection that
is not 'impersonalized' – i.e. scientific, according to the usual positivist
canons – without any attempt to respect the contexts in which a certain
social, intellectual, or artistic solution had been conceived.[1]

This at first sight barbarous, egocentric, and subjective point of view is,
it seems to us, the one that has always been practised by most creators. It
refers the creative activity and the resultant work to the individual who
works (acts) and to his own objectives, without involving established
norms and systems of interaction, which are regarded as alien.

---

[1] The notions, for which no exact equivalents exist in French and English, of *Verwissenschaftlichung*
and *Versachlichung*, being often taken as synonymous ('scientification' and 'technicization'). A
refusal is implied here of science and technology considered as something outside man, as natural
or mechanical laws.

This conception of *Homo faber* in action, which is so different from that of *Homo oeconomicus* (or *politicus*) does produce, of course, a certain blindness and deafness to the outside world that may be disastrous. The development of movements of this type tends to show up their fragility, but such movements are no less effective for that; what seems to fail as an immediate revolution may succeed as a new culture, revolutionizing the standing models of life and action.

We must return for a moment to the socio-logic of the phenomenon, or, more precisely, to its voluntarism, its opposition to historical or social determinism. Whether a movement expresses indirectly what it wishes to affirm, in an action of negation, or begins to live, here and now, a new affirmation, it comes up against the possibilities of absorption (*récupération*) possessed by the system, which the enemies of the movement may use in their own interest.

This is doubtless a serious danger. All the movements, in May, came up against this problem. The word *récupération* was on everyone's lips and was often used as if it was a sort of fatality. The least-recognized mechanism, in this respect, was perhaps that related to the fear of absorption itself; this and confidence in the self-regulating processes of the accursed system were one of the strongest factors in an effective absorption. Many convinced structuralists do not attribute so much weight to structural determinism. In this respect, the imagination has proved to be most inhibited, perhaps by the kind of undialectical interpretation of Marx that is still so common.

Another tendency, however, proved more imaginative, especially in the student circles described here. It presents the possibility of *distortion* (*détournement*) or *autonomous development*: negation by redefinition of an existing context and therefore indirectly affirmation, or new definition by collage, as we have said. What this amounts to is that a conscious social group is always able to give *another* meaning to a reality that appears to impinge on the individual, ready made, but which is nothing outside the perception that men have of it, since it must act upon them. *Distortion* is therefore an *absorption* performed not by the system, but by a social group in opposition. Similarly, the affirmation of a new world can survive, for those who belong to it, can extend, even if the 'system' or those who dominate it try to digest it – as long, at least, as this definition of a new world remains in action, in movement, for then its adherents can go on believing in it. Moreover, both processes are perfectly capable of transforming the system, or eroding it, possibly by weakening it at strategic points (in the educational field, for example). This, then, would be the logic of a conception of re-creation or creation of a new social world, whose inward-looking character is a strength or a weakness, according to circumstances; its different phases of growth could, hypothetically, lead it to a stage at which it would embrace 'society' itself.

It should be added that this form of lived action, in which the element of imagination, the invention of new meanings, plays so great a part, must contain an element of the *imaginary*, of projects in which one does not hesitate to go beyond, in imagination – the word is used in a different sense here – one's own limitations. It is here that we come very close to traditional phenomena of the image in society. A social category not only represents to itself its own position in present-day society, but also identifies the future society with a conception of contemporary society. It extends its present image of society to the whole of the society of the future.[1]

IMAGINATION AND IMAGES OF SOCIETY

Ten years after World War II, in a Europe that had found a new equilibrium, one found images of society relatively well established and logically distributed over a whole population, despite more confused areas, notably in the middle strata, where different views of society were to be found side by side.[2] The theory of reflection could be applied here with some success: the image reflected the knowledge of an apparently *stable* society; it differed according to the social positions of those questioned.

The doubts that arose about the affirmation of an absence of hope and utopias[3] in the vision of society led either to a desire that crises would shake up the whole somnolent world, or to a conclusion that we had seen the 'end of ideology', that men would now work rationally, without sterile ideological conflicts, for the success of economic growth.

In France, as M. Crozier, an observer who has proved very sensitive to cultural changes,[4] said, a 'new form of rationality' has been spreading for about ten years. Whereas the intellectuals of the literary and artistic world

[1] This idea was suggested to me by P. Naville, in the discussion of my contribution to a seminar, in which I examined the use of the image of society in studying change (cf. Willener, 1968).
[2] This is not the place for an account of all the work done on this subject: Dahrendorf, in *Class and class conflict in industrial society* (1959) presents some of this work, and interprets it in relation to the domination/subordination dichotomy. Since then, new studies have appeared: cf., in particular, two volumes on *The Affluent Worker* by Goldthorpe *et al.* (1968 and 1969), and Lockwood (1966).
[3] Cf. for example, Andrieux and Lignon, *L'Ouvrier d'aujourd'hui* (1960), which presents the working class as being without hope.
[4] Cf. 'The cultural revolution' (Crozier, 1964b).

continued to reflect abstractly on action, on the basis of an image of an ideal society – in terms of value judgements – a new model was beginning to prove more effective in action. The 'vital forces of the nation', students, young peasants and young employers, together with specialists in the social sciences, were looking for concrete commitment, contact through participation, and even responsibility (ibid., p. 536).

Among the characteristics of this model, the first, at least – and it is not a negligible one – coincides with the options of the current in the May Movement described here; a horror of formulas and *a priori* systems.

The model outlined by Crozier in 1964, suggested and foreseen by him well before,[1] constitutes the prototype of the *technocratic* phenomenon, which was challenged in 1968 by the *prototype of the action–image* of society.[2]

Although both reject *a priori* formulas and attempt to escape the ends/means dilemma – the option between whether to act or whether to preserve the image of an ideal society – a dilemma in which the adherents of the old model were and are still caught, the comparison hardly goes any further.

In fact, the technocratic solution is based on a *consciousness of the possible*, which amounts to defining the ends to be pursued according to the resources available – human, social, and cultural resources defined in statistics. Technicians of the possible, including applied sociologists, working on sociographic studies or on studies of 'how the system works', must offer practicable solutions, which does not exclude, however, but on the contrary includes, a certain voluntarism, based on the established trends of society.[3] In their concern to take into account the resources, and possibly the social aspirations, within the system, they define, in fact, not only 'functional requirements', but also their own image of the future of society. It is not our purpose here to examine if it is true that no one,

[1] Cf. articles published by the Club Jean-Moulin; it should be noted to what extent the various political clubs that began to spread at this time met this need for participation and effective construction, filling a gap left by a parliament and parties that were devoid of vitality or plunged in sterile dispute.

[2] The whole student movement expressed views on the problem of technocracy, often in a rather confused way; we are dealing here with the fundamental rejection of it by the current that is the subject of this study.

[3] Cf. *Tendances et volontés de la société française* (edited by J.-D. Reynaud, 1965) – a collective work comprising the public contributions of those who took part in a discussion organized by the Société française de sociologie in the presence of senior officials of the National Plan. One of the few contributions that could not be presented and discussed during the meeting, but which is included in the published proceedings, is that of E. Morin ('L'Avenir dans la société française'). He describes technocratism thus: 'Its viewpoint leads it to accommodate on the basis of the present, and as rationally as possible, processes already in operation, but not to question the direction or the roots of the existing social order.'

in a process of democratic development, can really express an opinion on the options of the technologists, the fact is that the question presents itself.

The *action–image* is an exactly opposite mode. It rejects technocrats and balance-sheets, which it opposes with invention. The ends/means dilemma is also resolved in action, but by the identification of the objects and subjects of action, by an *initial telescoping* that identifies ends and means. Men are the means of action, but at the same time they are the ends of action and not resources to be used in a system, man-agents and man-objects simultaneously. The image of society develops in and through the process of projection and action. Only those who live this process – and the implication is obviously that this will soon include all the social categories dominated at present – *are* society. In so far as action brings about upheaval (radical, rapid, constant change), the image can no longer refer to an established society, and therefore to a society that is stable or slowly changing, whose 'trends' express above all the 'established' aspects of a system that is felt to be alien, despite reform (the partial expression of as yet non-established aspects). Nor will the image refer to an abstract table, drawn up on the basis of traditional, *a priori* principles or arguments.

Change itself, rather than the stability of a system (embodied or abstract), the whole *process* of the development of a new society, will be the base, or, better still, the moving *itinerary*, of this new type of image of society, which would evolve through permanent discussion and activation.

Of course, questions of functioning do arise. But they are regarded as being only of minor importance (in the conception outlined here), which is logical enough so long as a *second telescoping*, of the ends of action and action itself, is achieved. In the new culture envisaged, and, for a time, lived, the act of creating is as important as, in fact more important than, the product that results. It is, in other words, the inversion of the instrumentalism that is to be observed in the thinking of many modern specialists: instead of sacrificing to the admiration of technology, which one runs for its own sake, for the repressed satisfaction of seeing something function efficiently, without concerning oneself with the ends that an apparently pure 'technicity' implies, the aim here is to give preeminence to any (a-technological) attempt to express creativity, independently – again – of the (external) objectives actually achieved, the true ends being the retotalization of man, a way of living in directly creative activity.

It is obvious that there is a movement away from the respect traditionally accorded to technology and more generally to established culture, all the more so as neither is becoming a mere means, accepted as such.

M. Crozier discussed the place of culture in the new pragmatic model. Contemporary Europe still seems to be paralysed by its former glories. In the new mode of action, which aims above all at efficiency and economic development, culture must be 'a means, a resource and not a treasure to be piled up and hidden away' (Crozier, 1964b, p. 54).

Throughout this study, we have seen how virulent were the criticisms of culture in the artistic sense – as a distinct sphere and therefore to be respected – and how they were connected with the redefinition of culture as everyday, 'lived' creation (which brings it close to culture in the sense of 'social mode of life', indeed, of civilization). Having emerged from the sphere reserved for treasures, it did not, however, become a *means*, a *resource*, but, on the contrary, *an end*, which was no longer the preserve of creators and privileged consumers, but open to all, without any frontiers to be crossed, and without any need for special training.

CULTURAL VITALIZATION

It has often been remarked that in wartime people feel – for once – that they are really living, living intensely. In France, in May 1968, the same observation was made; many people, and not only students, discovered a degree of self-expression that went well beyond anything that life, even private life – a life, therefore, relatively free from pressures – would normally permit.

When, in normal times, one speaks of an image of society – both terms in the singular – one thinks that one is referring to something fixed, external, to a double objectivation. Society, it would appear, is an *object*, a whole formed by interactions, normal and deviant, but *habitualized*, established once and for all. The social image appears to be, in fact, a direct relation of the photographic image, objectivating directly a simple perception. But, of course, we cannot remain at this stage of reflection, either in general, or as a conclusion to this study.

On the one hand, attentive sociology reveals that if society has an objective and objectivated existence, that existence is never entirely independent of the subjective worlds of the various populations: the concept of a society without men-subjects is precisely what is usually stigmatized by the term reification (or ossification). What is more, even if it were possible for a man to 'take' an image of such an entirely external reality, he would not really succeed in doing so. His mind cannot be reduced to the passivity of a photographic lens; there is more to it than the selection of an angle of vision, or the choice of the right moment. Indeed, even in photography, as P. Bourdieu has shown, the image is more than an image in the flat sense of the term.[1] And it is the sociologist's task to 'grasp a constituted truth, the objectivation of subjectivity, which is never given immediately either to those who live it, or to those who observe it' (ibid., p. 20).

On the other hand, the very particular phenomenon that we have tried to 'grasp' reveals, on the part of the students, a profound concern with the non-human content of the objectivation of society and of the stereotyped image. It is as if the objectivation implied not only distance and exteriorization – as the original German word, *Vergegenständlichung*,[2] suggests – but the idea of an inert, meaningless object ('thingification') to which one is subordinated, and of which one is no more than a *consumer* (and, by implication, from which one is alienated).

Hence the desire for permanent, rapid movement, for non-objectivation, the only accepted form of exteriorization being that which excludes distance: the image becomes what one *is* and *does*, in action. It will constantly change, therefore, like the society and culture that one is, in creating them.

There is an overthrow of perspectives here that plunges everyone, immediately and permanently, into a process of endless redefinition. It is a *vitalization* by and for culture.[3] The adherents of this phenomenon wish to depart as far as possible from the idea of culture–civilization, or culture–art. These two 'sacred' ideas seem to them to be ossified. On the other hand, culture as a redescent to the act of daily 'lived' creation is vital and vitalizing. Whether it is suffering or joy, it cannot leave one indifferent: it is based on the internal pleasure principle, and not on the external laws of nature.

It should be added – the students possess the 'capital of knowledge'[4] – that this overthrow of perspectives particularly concerns man's relation with *science*.

Just as they tend to reject objectivation, the students do not hesitate to question the normal canons of objectification (*Versachlichung*). The form of this *scientification*, which is presented as a purely technological

---

[1] Cf. Bourdieu (1965, p. 291): 'a symbol as well as an image, that is, an image that also acts as a symbol, through the mode of its presentation, that which is not its intention to express'.
[2] Becoming an object.
[3] E. Goffman explains the passion experienced by roulette-players by the fact that between each bet, hurried and insecure, but able to re-intervene directly, they redefine what has passed and what is to come (in the course of a lecture given at Edinburgh in 1968).
[4] 'Capital connaissance' – a phrase used by Touraine.

discipline, seeking to discover the 'natural' laws of life in society, without taking into account the (considerable) social and cultural relativity of the so-called human sciences, meets with a good deal of scepticism.

Neither 'society' nor 'culture', nor even 'science', conceived as objects, are accepted and pursued as external truths whose meaning has to be *discovered*. They must be put back inside a process, a simple action, becoming an *object* on which a *meaning* is projected, as it is being created.

To the vitalization that comes from movement, or rhythm, explaining, eventually, movement by movement, should be added the central aspect, what might be termed self-determination. If the movement were other-determined, suffering would prevail.

This study makes no claim to be anything more than an exploration that leaves the way open to different interpretations, but it does seem worth remarking that in any overall explanation we believe the axis of *anti-authoritarianism* would be central. With their aims of liberation and emancipation, of man's fuller self-realization, the current of thought and action presented here, and the other 'parallel' cultural movements, are libertarian phenomena. What requires to be done is 'the social construction of reality' (Berger), by permanently creating it and re-creating it ourselves in a positive way.

The practice of this conception would lead, not only to the creation of an external world that would remain in intersection with the internal world, but also to a greater intensity of life and to a broader consciousness: 'If meaning is not a segment of self-understanding, I don't know what it is' (Ricœur, 1963, p. 636).

Appendices

Questionnaire: Images of Society

PRELIMINARY STUDY

This study is the first part of a wider inquiry, to be carried out in several countries, concerning students, intellectuals, young workers, technologists, etc. An important movement of reflection has been initiated here and we particularly value the free, perfectly frank opinion of others. Our aim is not to study the student movement or recent events as a whole, but only certain aspects of that experience in relation to the image of society present and future. One may, of course, discuss the questions and add whatever one may consider to be important.

1. *New society*
   In discussions that have taken place recently throughout the country, an image of a new society has emerged; what features of this new society are important to you personally?

   Present-day society
   We should like to ask you four brief questions about present-day society (of the last few years):

2. *The country:* When you think of France, how do you classify people? (*a*) or (*b*)?

(*a*) the liberal professions	(*b*) the ruling class
tradesmen	the middle class
technicians	the working class
office-workers	
workers	

   2a. Is your chosen list satisfactory: yes or no?
   What other list would you prefer?

3. *The city:* When you think of an average French city, how do you classify people? (*a*) or (*b*)?

(*a*) doctors and lawyers	(*b*) self-employed professions
bankers	salary-earners
artists	wage-earners
managerial staff	
office-workers	
workers	

3a. Is your chosen list satisfactory: yes or no?
What other list would you prefer?

4. *The factory:* When you think of a factory, which of the following two classifications seems to you to be the more natural?

(*a*) the managing director	(*b*) the boss and his collaborators
the engineers	the workers
the office staff	
skilled workers	
unskilled workers	

4a. Is your chosen list satisfactory: yes or no?
What other list would you prefer?

5. *The university:* How would you define the university in France prior to the events created by the students? (Ask for a list of categories; state if there is a regrouping of categories.)

6. *Structures/process:* All these lists (questions 2–5) express a particular form of society; now state your long-term and short-term views:

(a) Would you say that in the long term, between 1948 and 1968, for example,
  – the *structures* have not basically altered?
  – the structures are changing and the *process* of change is slow, but constant?

(b) Would you say that events in the short term, in May 1968, for example, demonstrated
  – the possibility of *overthrowing* the structures?
  – the possibility of *transforming* the structures?
  – the *impossibility* of altering the structures?

Comments:

7. *Change:* Should change depend
    – on *spontaneous*, new, but unoriginal forces?
    – on *organized*, established, but older forces?
    – on *new* forces, in the process of being *organized*?

Comments:

8. *Profession:* Three professions for which you have particular respect (in order of preference):

Three professions for which you have particular contempt (in order):

9. Do you see your future career as:
    – a path (to be followed whether one likes it or not)?
    – a zig-zag (with mobility between various activities, and adjustment)?
    – a labyrinth (representing the unknown)?

(Differentiate between (*a*) and (*b*)):

    (*a*) before the students' action
    (*b*) after the students' action

10. *Science:* Everyone admits that science plays a role in industrial societies – but in what way? Who or what, in your opinion, benefits? (Arrange in order of preference.)

    – all social categories benefit
    – certain social categories benefit more than others (which ones?)
    – the 'system' benefits (science helps it to maintain itself).

Comments:

General identification
Interviewee: Anonymous   Student in:
Interviewer: Age: Social background:

Are you a *member* of an organization (group, union, party) etc.: yes or no?

Are you an active *sympathizer* with an organization: yes or no?

INSTRUCTIONS TO THE INTERVIEWER

1. Hold the questionnaire in front of the interviewee: if he can read the lists or alternatives himself, the interview will not take so long and will leave more time for comments.

2. You may abbreviate the answers; when there are alternatives, ask the interviewee if he prefers (*a*) or (*b*), etc.

Quote key phrases or expressions *word for word*, in inverted commas.

3. Write in any way you like, even using abbreviations, but *legibly*. If necessary go over what you have already written.

4. If someone wants to write for himself, alone or with you, that too will be all right.

5. If possible add a personal comment on the last blank page.

Thank you

Note on the Sample

In view of the circumstances, and the resources at our disposal, it was hardly possible to carry out a poll over a broad sample, or even, confining ourselves to a limited number of interviews, to reflect, in proportion, the exact characteristics of the population of the French universities.

We had no alternative, therefore, but to limit our scope – and chance, it must be admitted, came to our aid – to a selection of interviewees, which, if not the most representative, at least did not go beyond the approximate bounds of probability that a rapid examination of the statistics concerning the university lays down.

On this basis, then, we took a sample in which the two broad groups of Arts subjects (including art itself) and Science subjects (including medicine) were almost equally represented (30 interviewees out of 77 and 31 out of 77 respectively), the remainder being divided between 'Law' and a 'Miscellaneous' category. Six questionnaires were reserved for final-year pupils in lycées, who were among the most active participants in the May events.

We followed a similar course with respect to the age of the respondents. We tried to represent in the sample the whole spectrum of the principal age-groups of the students by dividing them, almost evenly, into those over and those under 21 (38 out of 77 against 31 out of 77), a large majority being between 20 and 24.

It was much more difficult, on the other hand, to select the interviewees in proportion to the representation of the different social categories in the universities. We were very agreeably surprised, therefore, to find later that our sample corresponded almost exactly to the official figures: we found, for example, that our sample contained 7 interviewees of working-class origin out of 77, while the statistics show on average that 9 per cent of students are from working-class backgrounds.

Nevertheless, such a sample can hardly be taken as the basis for a quantitative analysis. The figures and tables derived from this sample are intended only as an indication that may enable us to reveal some of the principal trends.

It should be noted that we encountered no major obstacles in carrying out these interviews, despite the mistrust that this kind of approach usually arouses, which one might have expected to be even greater in this period (end of May, beginning of June), when events were at their most critical stage.

Although we had to overcome the usual reticence of those interviewed, we did benefit from the neutrality, and even the cooperation, of the *de facto* university authorities of the time. The Occupation Committee of the Science Faculty, for example, gave us the use of a lecture-room for our interviews and even offered us the use of the sound equipment. Apart from movement, the main difficulty was to persuade these students to spare half an hour or so of their already fully occupied time.

IDENTIFICATION OF THE SAMPLE

I. Faculties

Arts	25
Law	6
Fine Arts	5
Sciences	21
Medicine	10
Miscellaneous	4
Lycée pupils	6
Total	**77**

2. Age

	17–19	20–24	25 and over	No reply
Arts	—	16	6	3
Law	—	5	1	—
Fine Arts	—	—	4	1
Sciences	3	15	—	3
Medicine	2	6	2	—
Miscellaneous	—	3	—	1
Lycée pupils	5	1	—	—
Totals ($N = 77$)	10	46	13	8

3. Social background[1]

	Upper-middle class	Lower-middle class	Working class	No reply
Arts	11	6	4	4
Law	2	2	1	1
Fine Arts	—	4	—	1
Sciences	9	5	2	5
Medicine	6	4	—	—
Miscellaneous	1	1	—	2
Lycée pupils	6	—	—	—
Totals (N = 77)	35	22	7	13

[1] The original terms were suggested by the interviewees themselves – no alternative categories were offered by the interviewer. The answers were then regrouped into the following: upper-middle class (*bourgeoisie*, liberal professions or upper managerial); lower-middle class (including lower managerial and tradesmen); and working class.

4. Political or union membership

	Member			Sympathizer		
	yes	no	n.r.	yes	no	n.r.
Arts	8	15	2	8	12	5
Law	1	4	1	2	3	1
Fine Arts	1	4	—	1	4	—
Sciences	6	13	2	—	18	3
Medicine	2	8	—	4	6	—
Miscellaneous	1	2	1	1	2	1
Lycée pupils	—	5	1	4	2	—
Totals (N = 77)	19	51	7	20	47	10

5. Background and political or union membership

	Member			Sympathizer		
	yes	no	n.r.	yes	no	n.r.
	%	%	%	%	%	%
Upper-middle class (35)	23	66	11	28·5	63	8·5
Lower-middle class (22)	27	68·5	4·5	36·5	59	4·5
Working class (7)	43	57	—	—	71·5	28·5

APPENDIX III[1]

Documents

Probably the richest source – and the most immediately accessible, since the publication of several collections[2] – is to be found in the inscriptions and graffiti that flourished in May 1968 over the city's walls, inside and outside occupied buildings, in the streets, in the corridors of *métro* stations, etc.

In them can be found, and studied in detail, from a formal point of view, a whole range of literary techniques, including most of the methods developed by twentieth-century French literature. Here are a few of them, by way of example:

From plays with words ('Sot-Sceaux-Seaux-Ceaux-Sot-So' – Nanterre; the signature 'Moa' – a way of transliterating 'Moi' pronounced exaggeratedly, opposed to Mao) to fairly simple plays on words ('Le veau d'or est toujours de boue' – 'The golden calf is always made of mud', with the implication 'The golden calf is still standing' (*debout*) – Odéon).

From antithetical statements ('Crier la mort, c'est crier la vie' – Nanterre; 'Quand l'assemblée nationale devient un théâtre bourgeois, tous les théâtres bourgeois doivent devenir des assemblées nationales' – Odéon) to inverted slogans ('Tout le pouvoir aux conseils ouvriers: un enragé – Tout le pouvoir aux conseils enragés' – Censier).

From the distorted saying or proverb ('Les murs ont des oreilles: vos oreilles ont des murs' – Censier; 'Aimez-vous les uns sur les autres' – Censier; 'Voir Nanterre et vivre' – Nanterre) to neologisms ('Que les doyens doyennent, les flics flicaillent et que les révolutionnaires fassent la révolution' – Censier), popular speech ('Quand j's'rai grand, j's'rai flic' – Censier) and phonetic writing ('Jem ekrir en fonetik' – Censier).

We have divided the following texts into two parts. The first consists of a few tracts (I, II, and III), in which, it seems to us, certain of the demands that make

---

[1] This Appendix was compiled by Pierre Gallissaires. In this English edition the prose documents have been presented in English only and the poems in French and English. One exception is tract I (p. 310), which is untranslatable in the sense that its whole point would be lost in translation, and it is therefore presented in French only.
[2] For example, *Les Murs ont la parole* (Besançon, 1968).

the May events a 'cultural revolution' are expressed particularly clearly: sexual revolution (tract I, which is also remarkable for its 'Dadaist' character, in attitude, language, orthography, typography, not to mention the direct reference to Picabia); 'socio-psychological' liberation (II); and appeal to spontaneous, permanent creativity (III).

The poems (IV to VII), which make up the second part, are all anonymous, born of the ground-swell of expression aroused by the May events: we found the first (IV), for example, in the roadway of the Rue Mouffetard (Paris 6e), where it had been written in chalk a short time before, on 9 July 1968. Like much of the satirical verse of this kind, which flourishes at every period of revolt or revolution (1789, the Paris Commune, etc.), it shows what a 'modern' popular poetry could be;[1] it is, it seems to me, one of the rare examples collected of this particularly spontaneous and ephemeral *genre* of 'street poetry'.

The last three poems,[2] which are fairly 'direct' or imbued with 'cultural' elements, in the broad sense of the term, reflect in different ways some of the feelings – rancour, disgust, satiety, exigency, or hope – some of the themes that formed the face, physical and moral, of this 'faceless Revolution'.[3]

---

[1] As opposed, for example, to most of the poems written at the time by *lycéens*, which, naturally enough, reflect their classical education. The poem given here shows, it seems to me, the influence, indirectly at least, of Prévert, the only truly 'popular' French poet of the twentieth century.
[2] Extracts from the collection *Poèmes de la révolution: mai 1968* (edited by Bruno Durocher, 1968).
[3] In particular, the conception of the revolution as a vital, total pleasure (V), libertarian demands (VI), anti-authoritarianism (VII).

I

SOP, SOP, SOP, . . .
SOP, SOP, SOP, . . .
SOP, SOP, SOP, . . .

TouTe RÉVOLtE bue touT paVÉ éjaCULlé toute ProCCoxie dénoncée toute inCUba-
tion entamée⁰ toute PonTe Z'eu le CRAS ORGANE authentiquement révolutionNaire
SanS peur et SanS défroQue s'insURGE devant LA MASturBAtion inteLLectueLLe devant
l'OOOrgasme verbeux devant l'utilisation inCONsidérée de CONtraceptifs visant à
sTRanguler la révoluTION le comité D'AGITATION SURSEXUELLE n'a pas PEUR de
se déNUder afin de créer chez d'autres une CUriosité EXcitatrice.

Les forces populaireS se sont ÉBRANLÉES PROVOquant LA déBAND – ade de la
bourgeoisie, laquelle est acCULée à son dernier DERRIÈRE:

LA CÉHAIRESSERIE¹

Le capitalisme est CONtesté il faut en déTRUire l'arrière garde le FONDEMENT
capital du Kapitall à morale chrétienne, celle qui accouche de la

PSYchose et de la THALYDOMIDE

Le CRAS CHARCUTERA ET CHATRERA les deux.

Les moyens: Le CRAS doit féCONder d'autres CRAS
Nous comité révolutionnaire d'AGITAT-
-TION SURSEXUELLE appelons à la CO-
-PULATION collective et révolutionnaire

à savoir: secrétion à un
éCHElon interna-
-tional au ventre
de toute SOciété
du VENIN CRASISTIQUE
Élaboration d'un gigantesque livre opaQue.

Réunion mardi à 20 HEURES
3 rue Michelet
Institut d'art
Bureau du CRAS
3 ème étage   'à mon dernier manifeste cannibal, je vous ai dit que le cul, le cul
représente la vie comme les pommes frites'

Francis Picabia

CRAS²

⁰ Les FLICS sont parmi nous, l'un d'eux a substitué 'dénon cée' à entamée'   rectifiez!!

¹ Abstract noun from the initials of the riot police, CRS.
² CRAS: Comité Révolutionnaire d'Agitation Sursexuelle.

310

II

THE REVOLUTION GOES ON...

Comrades,

Government propaganda, the attitude of the CGT,[1] the wait-and-see policy of those who are reorganizing their political groups, are shaking the confidence of some of us in the future of the movement of revolt that began on 3 May.

The revolution must continue, for its nature is not challenged by these acts of sabotage. The analysis of the themes of our revolt, the courage of the demonstrators and their nature demonstrate that only the traditional character of our analyses can make us doubt the Revolution.

This is why the Revolution goes on.

In the week from 3 to 10 May, we saw the formation of the FRONT OF THE EXCLUDED from the system: the workless, the young workers, *lycéens* and students, intellectuals crushed by the consumer society, rebellious Beatniks, graduates discovering their role as 'watchdogs', the young unemployed . . .

It is to reconstitute this front that we must continue the Revolution that was begun, and that is NOW BEING DROWNED by those who are provided with a function by the system: sclerotic union officials, 'absorptionist' professors, established political parties, ex-warrior-workers of the social struggle, now peace-loving family men . . .

In the struggle against the established economic and socio-psychological struggle, we must abandon the idea that only the workers are revolutionary: that way lies the policy of wait and see.

We must forge ahead with the allies that we made during the police repression.

It is not the students themselves, some illusory 'student class', nor the workers, all too often stuck in the habits of petty comfort, and hypnotized by the mirages of consumption, who are revolutionary.

IT IS ALL THOSE WHO ARE CRUSHED OR EXCLUDED BY AN INHUMAN SYSTEM.

The struggle must have as its FINAL OBJECTIVE the establishment of a socialist system in which, through the destruction of barriers, the creativity of each individual will be set free. This objective implies a revolution not only in the relations of production, but in the mode of life, in ways of thought, in human relations, and in the concept of the sexual life of all.

The struggle must have as TACTICAL OBJECTIVES for the student movement in the present situation revolutionary action that will revitalize the contestation of the state:

To protest against the polluted atmosphere of the city of Paris and sexual

[1] Confédération Genérale du Travail, the Communist-led labour organization.

repression: the liberation of the Luxembourg Gardens, which will be open 24 hours a day to young people and workers. From the Sorbonne to the Rue d'Assas, let us organize a permanent campus with revolutionary vigils at night.

To ape and ridicule government censorship: let us forbid the sale in the Latin Quarter of those newspapers that refuse to publish the communiqués of the revolutionary movement.

To struggle against the conditioning of people's minds: by booing and shouting get the adverts and news in cinemas replaced by demystifying short films that have not previously passed through the government censor.

To improve solidarity with the workers: offer our help to workers occupying their factories with a view to starting work in the service of the workers themselves. In a more symbolic way, students might offer to decorate a factory notice-board; the workers will, of course, have the right to choose their decorator.

As the sum of all accumulated discontent, the revolution must necessarily provide an outlet for them. There is a risk that fascism would be the only alternative.

'FREUD–CHE GUEVARA' ACTION COMMITTEE

III

THE COMMITTEE OF PERMANENT CREATION has just been formed.

We reject:

The dominant ideology of our society:
the ideology of consumption.

We denounce the paralysis and torpor of criticism and creation.

This society is based on economism and reduces man to the single dimension of a half-witted consumer.

It is characterized by constant repression, accepted, demanded, voted for.

The political opposition, culture, and contestation are integrated, absorbed: they have become elements of equilibrium and social cohesion.

The only weapon of the individual, and of the group, is creation, permanent contesting spontaneity at every level. Only pure creation is subversive, and cannot be absorbed. Creation is dangerous for all systems of repression, whether avowed or hypocritical.

We invite you to come and join us. Let us re-create, on the basis of our revolutionary experience, a permanent critique of daily life. Let us reply to the kicks in the backside that advertising (among other things) inflicts on us daily by giving free rein to our aggressivity.

BITE THE SOFT MACHINE, IT WILL CRACK UP IN THE
END

IV

Repas présidentiel

Des larmes sont tombées dans son potage
il a jeté le potage
Des pavés sont tombés dans la viande
lui ont cassés une dent
il a jeté la viande
Un mort est tombé dans ses frites
et les a refroidies
il a jeté ses frites
Une Sorbonne de fromage est bientôt arrivée
alors il l'a mangé
Quand la glace est arrivée
il l'a renversée comme l'université d'été[1]
Maintenant l'est bien content l'a presque rien mangé
mais on n'est pas tous morts
car reste le café

Presidential meal

Tears fell into his soup
he threw the soup away
Cobble-stones fell into the meat
and broke one of his teeth
he threw the meat away
A dead man fell into his chips
and made them cold
he threw his chips away
A Sorbonne of cheese came next
and he ate it
When the ice-cream arrived
he overturned it like the summer university[1]
And though he's hardly eaten anything, he's happy
but we aren't all dead
there's still the coffee

[1] The summer university was a 'free university', open to all, which the students proposed to hold during the summer of 1968 in the faculties or teaching establishments that they occupied.

V

Barricade

Nourrir le feu
du moindre de mes os
du collier de mes plaies
de mes rêves en sang
Se jeter tout entier
dans cette joie nouvelle
et faire de son corps même
Une Barricade.

Let me feed the fire
with my every bone
with my necklace of wounds
my bleeding dreams
Let us throw ourselves heart and soul
into this new joy
and make of our bodies
A Barricade.

VI

Pauvres flics habitués aux feux rouges.
Rouge signifie 'Stop' danger!
Danger de mort pour qui
Dépasse ce feu rouge qui signifie 'Stop' danger!
Danger de mort pour qui?
Pour les colonisés du BHV[1]
Pour les cocus de l'an 36
Pour ceux qui refusent la paille humide des lits trop chauds
Et prennent le métro pour le Styx
Départ: Bastille tous les 30 ans.
Pour ceux qui aiment tellement leurs femmes
Qu'ils ne peuvent plus leur faire l'amour
Honteux de n'offrir qu'un sexe d'exploité
Entre deux chaines de cadences infernales.
Pour ceux qui vont la faire
Cette salope de révolution,
Pour mieux boire après, toujours.
Pour ceux qui ignorent point les problèmes
De la planification accelérée en économie socialiste.
Pour ceux qui en ignorent tout, s'en foutent,
Mais veulent bouffer.
Pour ceux qui lient anarchie et communisme,
Enfants de bakounine et de la cinémathèque,
Enfants de Mao, enfants de Bogart,
Pour les lanceurs de boulons
Qui donnent des grands coups de crâne sur les matraques
    des CRS
Et n'appartiennent pas au Parti
Et n'appartiennent pas au CA Montreuil.
Pour ceux-là
Le rouge signifie liberté bien sûr,
Mais la couche de peinture doit être appliquée
de bas en haut.
Les papes meurent, les Battista se décomposent,
Les Staline meurent, les Johnson se lézardent,
Les Fascistes crèvent, Ubu va suivre,
Malcolm X sera vengé.
Rappellons-nous toujours des sanglots longs des violons de
    Beaujon.[2]

[1] BHV: Bazar de l'Hôtel de Ville, a Paris department store.
[2] Beaujon: the centre for the checking of identity of the Paris Prefecture of Police, where every arrested person was taken.

Poor cops with their red lights.
Red means 'stop, danger!'
Danger of death for whoever
Goes beyond this red light that means 'stop, danger!'
Danger of death for whom?
For the slaves of the BHV[1]
For the cuckolds of 1936
For those who reject the damp straw of over-warm
  beds
And take the *métro* for the Styx
Departure: Bastille every thirty years.
For those who so love their wives
That they can no longer make love to them
Ashamed of having no more to offer but the sex of an
  exploited man
Between two rattling chains.
For those who are going to make
This bitch of a revolution,
In order to drink more soundly, afterwards and forever.
For those who are not ignorant of the problems
Of increasing planification in a socialist economy.
For those who know nothing, and couldn't care less,
But want to eat.
For those who link anarchy and communism,
Children of Bakunin and the cinema club,
Children of Mao, children of Bogart,
For those who fling bolts at the truncheon heads of the
  CRS
And don't belong to the Party
And don't belong to the Montreuil Action Committee.
For all those
Red means liberty of course,
But the layer of paint must be applied
from bottom to top.
The Popes are dying, the Battistas are decomposing,
The Stalins are dying, the Johnsons are cracking,
The fascists are dying, Ubu will follow them,
Malcolm X will be revenged.
Let us not forget the long wails of the violins of
  Beaujon.[2]

VII

Cher papa,
Tu n'auras jamais
Ce que j'ai
Enlève de moi le pain
La viande, les manteaux
Je m'en fous, même des
Cigarettes presque.
Le Vent
La faim
Me dit constamment
Que je suis libre
Libre de toi
    Mon Général.

Dear Dad,
You will never have
What I have
Take from me bread
Meat, clothes
I don't care, even
Cigarettes almost.
The wind
And hunger
Tell me constantly
That I am free
Free from you
    Mon Général.

Photographic Illustrations

The theme that this selection of photographs[1] is intended to express in concrete terms is above all the important technique of distortion (*détournement*), so difficult to present verbally. Some of the posters left *gaps* that attracted, almost irresistibly, the addition of inscriptions, political initials, and names (Mendès; *cocos* – the slang name for the Communists; PSU, etc.). For instance, in example 5, the inscription simply disturbs the original system of reference. Example 11 is a case of the reply. The inscription 'Neutral science – crap' was written on a wall of the Science Faculty, and expresses suspicion of a science that is distorted at its foundations, or distorted in its development or transmission, or contaminated by the society that surrounds it and uses it. The comment that follows the inscription, 'Ah ha!', emphasized by the drawing of a grimacing head, sets up a counter-suspicion.

Strictly speaking, the technique of distortion is a skilful alteration of the meaning of a drawing or inscription by the strategically placed addition of a single element (4: addition of the fingers making the 'V' sign (victory) of the Gaullists); or, less typically, by a correction (7).

The element added may succeed in distorting the original power possessed by the poster to the benefit of another cause. As we have seen, the technique was used, in particular, against insults.

Often, the distortion takes advantage of the power of the original images or of altered expressions: thus in example 9, in which 'Faculté des lettres et sciences humaines', a name that might be regarded as pretentious, became 'Faculté des illettrés (illiterates) et sciences inhumaines'.

Many posters were placed in such a way that they took on significance in relation to the posters that were already there (3). There were a great many witticisms – the context often providing a note of 'contrast' or humour – that were certainly not the result of mere chance.

The symbol of the *factory* became the central figure of a number of posters (for example, 2, 6, and 8): the factory struggling, the capitalist factory, the factory crushed by repression. It became the principal axis of the students' image

[1] Taken in May and autumn 1968 by A. Willener.

of society. There is no need to illustrate the posters directed against police, state, and political repression. Policemen's heads were to be found mixed in with everything – the threat of fascism was referred to in many different ways (3, for example). The existence of private police forces in certain factories (12), or even the word factory (*usine*) itself (10), provided a concrete index of that community of problems that was often said to exist between students and workers (and students and citizens generally: posters showing a policeman talking into a microphone, or on a television screen – the state-controlled mass-media became more and more the target of anti-repressive criticism as the elections approached).

Lastly, the example of the factory managed directly by the workers (2) – the worker does not need the boss – with its classic portrait of the capitalist as the only one who is filling his pockets, without contributing anything to the creation of wealth, and the poster on the rejection of negotiations (8), which is also based on industrial symbolism (the machine), provide a complement to the image of society, in both the graphic and the sociological meaning of the term, to be found (cf. our opinion poll) among a large section of the students, and probably of the strikers.

Whereas in May the distortion technique was often used by the opponents of the 'revolutionaries', it is obviously the students who have now seized upon the, to them, central symbol of the execrable consumer society – advertising (1) – which enables them to recall their analyses.

The last illustration (13) shows that the notion of distortion can be extended beyond a purely political meaning. We are now seeing more and more cars personalized in this way by the addition of various decorations on the body (geometrical motifs, flowers, inscriptions, etc.). It seems to us that this is more than a passing fashion, a desire to 'appropriate' articles which, for commercial reasons, one tries artificially to diversify, but without succeeding in disguising their uniformity.

A Contrasting Interview

We could not end this study without at least mentioning the problem to which some people would like to reduce the May Movement, by taking refuge behind the all-purpose argument of the 'conflict of the generations'. Not that we would deny all value to this explanation; we would simply like those who use the term to explain exactly what they mean.

In an attempt to do just this, we interviewed, at the beginning of November 1968, a retired engineer who expressed interest in the work that we were doing, and who, it must be said, offered to give us the benefit of his opinion.

We present this interview[1] without comment, since it seems to us to speak for itself. The Chinese Cultural Revolution, we are told, is a conflict between the young Red Guards and the old leaders of the state, economic, and educational apparatus. Although it did not take the same forms, the May revolution seems, in this sense too, to have been a cultural revolution.

A RETIRED ENGINEER

I'm going to show you some photographs . . . I'd like your opinion of them. Tell me exactly what you think . . .

It's very kind of you to show me all this. I suppose any kind of document is interesting for people in your profession.[2]

You recognize this – the Boulevard Saint-Michel? What I wanted to show you was first this . . . It shows cars, barricades, flowers, and then, a second photograph, showing Victor Hugo, with a student standing in front, and they've written on the statue: Liberate expression!

It's just a cliché – a uselessly complicated cliché. 'Liberate expression'! The word liberty . . . The same words are used each time. Instead of saying 'Give us the chance of expressing ourselves', they say 'Liberate expression'. It's really an enslavement to whatever words happen to be fashionable at the

---

[1] Interview recorded by W.
[2] A double page from a newspaper on the barricades of the night of 10–11 May.

moment. They talk about 'dialogue', 'structures', 'liberation'. Once someone has said that, it becomes a term you can't 'liberate' yourself from. Liberation from slogans and clichés . . .

Another word that was often to be found on the walls: imagination. 'Imagination seizes power!' for example.

Imagination is only a motive force, a means – it has no value in itself. Anyone can imagine anything. It's got to fit in with practical possibilities. If you're not careful it might have the opposite of the effect you want. (He reads a sentence from *Les murs ont la parole* that is shown to him.) 'Be realistic, ask for the impossible!' Who's that addressed to? The students?

It was written on the walls at Censier.

Yes, but was it written for the students?

Yes, for the students and . . .

But they didn't write it . . . Did it apply to the students who were asked, 'Don't ask for the impossible', or to the workers who were told, 'Don't ask for things that will have the opposite result of the one you want'? You know, I'm delighted to have this talk with you, because really I want to educate myself a lot more. So if someone asks my opinion, I tell him what I think . . . For example, I'm horrified that in a world that calls itself Christian, in religious circles, young people are bombarded systematically by demagogues, who encourage by their words action that could be terribly dangerous and could lead to war, civil and external. Violence is a terribly dangerous thing.

As a Christian, I can't accept the phrase 'forced to use violence', because it's far too dangerous. Someone in prison for murder might say, 'I had to kill him'. Well, I can't accept that. He has committed a very dangerous act and I've every admiration for a government that managed to avoid shedding blood when confronted by a riot that was quite unexpected and so couldn't be nipped in the bud. These young people are just children – they are children because they despise what is called experience, which is more than a mere accumulation of isolated memories, but a formation of the mind – anyway, they're only children and don't see the problems involved. And they think the problems are simple, because they haven't got all the data you need to understand them – the problems are too big for them. Violence is a terribly dangerous thing. And, anyway, can one really say that Ben-Cohit[1] and all those violent extremists were really an expression of the students, really

[1] Cohn-Bendit. There can hardly be any doubt that this slip of the tongue – *Ben coit* – is 'significant.' At the end of the conversation, the interviewee's wife intervened to remark that it all boiled down to a *volonté de jouir* (a desire to enjoy themselves, with, in French, the ambiguous meaning, obviously unconscious in this case, of sexual pleasure – Translator), and that these young people did not want to work.

represented what they thought? You follow your leader and I think . . . Would sociology exist without the great principle of Panurge's sheep?

Maybe not, but . . .

Was Lamartine, who was a peace-loving man, right when he said: 'The people is only an element.' The group soul belongs to the great people of this world; nothing is more dangerous than a group leader, nothing is more dangerous than collective action.

But Gaullism is also based on collective action.

Gaullism? And what is Gaullism? I don't know.

It's this, for example.[1] You see the Gaullists marching in procession. That's a mass movement too.

They were the counter-weight to a violent movement, they were saying 'We want order' and wanted to encourage the man who also wanted order, to prevent him from getting disheartened, to show him that there was a mass of people who didn't agree with violence. It was a question of proving that *France* [emphasizing the word] did not agree with it. And the elections proved it, in a quite astonishing way. I think de Gaulle was really thinking of retiring and that he was extraordinarily courageous.

The really *terrifying* thing is that these children did not realize that they were opening the door to violence and to the workers' movement, which took advantage of this open door, and did something that was certainly the opposite of the students' interest.

What were the students afraid of? They are being educated, they feel they are being educated in a particular way – perhaps I'm talking nonsense now, correct me if I am – and that at the end of it all, after all that education, they won't find a proper place in society. But they were incapable of realizing that their action would lead to the madness of workers' action, which in turn would create unemployment.

I've got a nephew who says he's PSU and all that. He works for a cultural organization in Morocco – they employ a lot of Moroccan labour. He said: 'The workers' movement couldn't have taken place without the movement of those young people, who did not realize that behind the immediate goal, in a particular field, there could be more distant consequences that they did not foresee.'

What do you think of the problem of the Odéon? You know that the students went to the Odéon, the theatre. They presented the problem of culture, that is, 'Have we the theatres we need, the literature we need, etc.?' What do you think of that?

[1] Photograph taken on 30 May, showing the demonstration in support of General de Gaulle marching up the Champs-Élysées.

Of what?

Of the problem of culture. They criticized not only society or the economy, but also literature, the theatre, painting . . .

They criticized painting and yet they're the ones who follow it, like sheep – I may shock you now, but modern painting . . . is an expression of *utter madness*, bluff, lies, a mentality . . . It's a terribly serious matter when such crazy things can survive.

Have you looked at this book, 'Les murs ont la parole'?

Scrawl filth all over those walls in that way! It's cost a terrible lot of money to clean it off, I can tell you that. It would have been better to send the 30 million francs it has cost France to people who really are hungry and dying of hunger, to increase our cooperation with the under-developed countries – for if we don't, there'll be war. Perhaps we won't avoid it anyway. All the same, there are more serious problems.

They're just a lot of complaining children . . . I can't help but compare them with my father. My grandfather was a wheelwright, because his father, who was a building contractor, used to undercharge for religious buildings, and his children suffered as a result. My father had a religious ideal, a faith – there still are people like that, you know – he wanted to be a pastor, and became one. But he could only study by earning enough money as a *pion* [a *surveillant*, a student employed in *lycées* in a supervisory capacity – Tr.]. In the end he became quite a highly esteemed pastor – well, when I compare his situation with these people who have everything they want [his wife added: 'It's true! It's true!'], and have huge sums of money spent on them . . .

Well, I think it's shocking. When they set out to reform the whole educational system, they didn't give a thought to the handicapped and to the blind, who are just as important as they are, and who haven't even got free education yet. So, you see, you can't present them as people who have really got an ideal. No, they thought of absolutely nothing but themselves. They were afraid! They were afraid of not finding jobs, because, they said, of the way they were taught. They won't find jobs for another reason, and that's because the movement that has battened onto them has made it practically . . . and machinism is much more advanced than it used to be.

And I'm convinced – it mustn't be forgotten that that is the point of machinism, especially in the intellectual sphere – that those poor idiots, thinking-machines, can replace them to a large extent.

They did a terrible thing from the point of view of the real risk they were running, the risk that they'd find no jobs. Personally, I think the young have the great advantage of having new ideas, but they try to solve problems that are quite outside their comprehension without having what I, as an engineer, call all the *data* of the calculation. What is terrifying in the present state of democracy . . . And yet I'm as social-minded as anyone . . . Since I retired, I've devoted all my time and money, as a consultant engineer, to helping the blind and handicapped to get jobs just like anyone else. I think Christians that go in for demagogy, thinking they can get young people into the churches that way, by behaving in a way that is the exact opposite of Christian . . .

Let's go back to what you said about the young having ideas, but not the data of the problem.

No, and what's more, they haven't even got the intellectual training of someone who doubts himself, because the problems are quite outside our comprehension. At the present time, we're confronted by young *madmen*. Anyone can have an opinion on foreign policy. Now, if there is something that is outside our comprehension, if the search for immediate advantage is madness, or, at least, can lead to the opposite of what we want, it's in this field.

Yes, but if you'll go back to what you said just now about the data of the problem, you agree – you were an engineer – that technology, for example, changes, and society changes. Then, the difficult problem is that those who have the competence refer to the past, and those who refer to the future lack the competence, but . . .

It's a pity they don't refer to the past enough, and that the discoveries, which, *basically*, have come from the older generation, should have developed machinism in such a way that they have got ahead too fast, and that's what's dangerous. It's on the basis of an experience of the past that one can have new ideas that are worth having. You showed me an inscription on a wall that said 'Don't ask for the impossible . . .' er . . . no . . . 'Be realistic, ask for the impossible'. Was it a joke, or what?

No. I think what it meant is this: the things that are possible, that are realistic today, are things that are not human, therefore, if one wishes to be human, one must ask for the impossible, in order to go beyond the reality of today.

We don't speak the same language as those people. I can worry my brains out over a statement like that. To me, it just seems crazy. 'To go beyond reality' – doesn't mean anything.

I'll give you an example that I found in a book on painting to explain what I mean; tell me what you think of it. If one takes a portrait of a man with a camera, one obtains a so-called 'realistic' picture of him. A painter's image, on the other hand, may express a deeper reality, something that one does not notice at first glance. For example, I'll show you a picture . . .[1]

[1] A reproduction of a painting by Magritte, showing a man whose face is largely hidden by an apple.

325

It's an interesting symbol, I suppose, but it's quite silly really, because you can't see the man. You can see his ear vaguely, but one would like to see more of him.

It's a Surrealist work, and, in a way, what the young people were doing was a form of Surrealism.

Yes, it's a form of Surrealism. I understand that. It's a parable, and it means that this man's view is blocked by an apple. But the apple might represent any number of things. Consequently, it doesn't say what it set out to say. It could be the search for immediate satisfaction . . . and yet . . . he's not trying to eat the fruit. I think it's very badly expressed, because when one wants to say something, one has to be clear. That's just bluff.

You began just now to talk about art, about painting . . . You were saying 'some of them are mad . . .'

I think that they're either mad or very clever. Take Picasso, who can draw so well (and that's his excuse), well, he's just exploiting the public. He had to do that to get on, human stupidity being what it is. What he does is incomprehensible and stupid. It's hateful! It's terrifying. How can one spend fantastic sums of money to buy things that bring you nothing? I may be very materialistic, but when faced with anything, I want to know what it's for. But I think I'm right. My aim is much more spiritual than materialistic, but, from a practical point of view, when you do a thing, it has to serve some purpose when there are people dying of hunger, and when the danger of war is all around us.

What's the purpose of religion then?

Religion means, in fact, the Church – it's a shameful thing that must be destroyed. It's the reflection of something that is infinitely beautiful, the fossilization of something. It's an image; it can be a cage. I'm terribly fond of this saying of Jaurès's . . . something to the effect that 'We have carried off the flame and left the ashes'. It is the image all the same, the temporal framework that holds people together and perhaps places them all the same in a situation, an atmosphere that leads them, whether out of pride or hypocrisy, it doesn't matter – God uses every means – to seek the profound humility that consists of saying, 'I must not act alone, I do not possess the data of the calculation.' Men were incapable of inventing Jesus Christ, what's more, they rejected him. It is impossible to find him, and I find him in myself, in my heart. The proof is that it is impossible for there to be anything superior to ourselves if it is not the God of Love revealed by Jesus, who is a miracle.

I'd like to link what you say with what you said before. If it is true that in the religious sphere there is something that is not immediately apparent, something behind it all that is more subtle, the same is true when one looks at society today. One could say, in a way, that all the present data of the problem are there, but one can still construct something that goes beyond that . . .

Beyond? For each individual it won't go beyond death.

But while one is still alive one can imagine a society that is different from the imperfect one we have.

It's imperfect because of all the violence and crime, including religious wars and religious intransigence. It's violence that creates evil, an absence of love, egotism. The students are materialists and egotists. Their souls have been killed . . . I'm appalled . . .

When you say 'their souls have been killed', are you thinking of anyone in particular who is responsible?

I'm thinking of the Church in the first place.

And then?

Others who are not responsible, who have not had the extraordinary privilege of being guided perhaps by their hearts, their hopes, by an ideal, by a thirst for self-improvement, on a way where proof is to be found. I'm talking as if I was a Salvationist . . . I'm a Salvationist[Salvation Army] who would really like to proselytize . . .

You said 'young people have no heart . . .' How do you explain that?

Really, you know, they have every excuse, because . . . they're afraid. They're afraid of not being a success in life, afraid of finding obstacles. From a practical point of view, I think the Bible throws light on one thing: 'Honour thy father and thy mother.' Everything is based on the family. Everything based on *segregation*: segregation between young and old, any form of segregation, can only lead to an exaggeration of the tendencies of each group, which seeks only its own interest and therefore meets opposition. You end up with unavoidable conflicts between young and old, parents and children, with a few exceptions. And these exceptions are to be found in Christian backgrounds. I didn't say religious backgrounds.

I can see what you mean about the family, but I'd like to remind you that during these events they showed their solidarity by shouting 'We are all German Jews'. They also used the phrase 'Union of workers and students'. They went into the factories because they said 'We are against segregation between those who are students and those who are factory workers'. So you see, there isn't that much difference between you . . .

I was thinking above all of the segregation that comes about when the *natural* family is broken up, that is, above all, the segregation that the young

327

practise towards the old. It all started when Christians allowed young people to talk, automatically, of *croulants*, then later of *croulés* . . . [from *crouler*, to collapse, totter, crumble: pejorative terms used by young people of the old – Tr.]. It is written: 'Honour thy father and thy mother.' Why? For a profound reason, for a higher, spiritual reason, but it's true. It's madness to cut yourself off! I'm appalled by this basic segregation.

How can they talk of union between students and workers? Perhaps they're after contacts? Yes. They're afraid of not finding jobs, and what do they do? Like the children they are, they do the very thing most calculated to bar the way for themselves.

Now, does this union of the students and workers really come from themselves or from a few isolated ringleaders? You know, one talks about 'the students', but the group spirit obeys a core of one or two ringleaders who aren't really students at all.

One really must distinguish between the ringleader and the children who *follow* him. They aren't able to judge these people that flatter them.

How do you think these ringleaders come about?

They come about . . . as a result of an evolution, a technique adapted to all the poor devils who are incapable of doing anything for themselves. So they choose the easy way out – they become leaders of movements. Personally, I think they're people who are incapable of doing anything else. They don't become leaders for idealistic reasons. It's a way of getting a living, or satisfying their pride. You're not going to tell me they're idealists. Personally, I think any idea of changing 'structures' is crazy – it's the human heart you've got to change.

To conclude, would you like to say something about your professional life, in a very general way?

When I was young, my father had attained a very good position in the world, but he had seven children, so his means were limited. This is why I chose the first opening that came my way – I went to the École des Ponts et Chaussées, as an external student. I was extraordinarily lucky to get a job straight away, while I was still at the beginning of my studies, in a good company. It so happened that, in this company, Monsieur L. was a man of action and his partner, a fellow-student at the École Polytechnique, was the brains of the business. It was a family concern and they tried to make their employees feel part of the business, and you can say what you like about *paternalism*, I was very happy in that company. I liked my bosses and played fair by them. And it worked both ways – and this was particularly true before the workers started putting in demands. I'd always been a salaried engineer in that company. I began as a student-engineer in 1910. When the war was over, I had no alternative but to go back to the same company. [The interviewee's wife interjected: 'My husband was in the army for seven years.'] The extraordinary thing about that company was that everyone, engineers, office staff, the workers on the sites, we all felt we had a common interest. There was no break inside the family. This came out in an extraordinary way at the time of the . . . the events . . . [A long silence. His wife suggested 1936, the occupation of the factories.] At the time, everyone, the office staff, the draughtsmen, the tracers and the workers who were in contact with us went to the engineers and said: 'It's silly for us to fight one another.' You see, my company was inspired, you might say, by corporative ideas . . . It was an example, at the time, of a business syndicate that from a moral point of view was a marvellous thing. But of course the whole thing changed as people for whom the company meant nothing started making their demands. My best friend is an engineer I took on. The whole atmosphere was against segregation inside a natural family.

The firm has often been compared to a family.

I think it's true – it's not a series of horizontal grades, in which you create a class . . . It's quite *shameful* [he emphasized this word more than any other in the interview] to use the word 'class'. I apologize for speaking fast, or raising my voice rather, it pains me when people use the word 'class'. There's no need for it. My father went without necessities in order to study. And he made a success of his life through hard work, through going without things, through strength of character, which meant that in spite of difficulties at the outset and not being able to choose which engineering school I was to go to – I went to Ponts et Chaussées as a civil engineer, because my parents couldn't afford to pay the fees for the Polytechnique . . . One of my higher maths teachers was furious that I didn't go to Polytechnique. We couldn't even afford the École Centrale, which was also fee-paying. So I went to Ponts et Chaussées, which was free. I really can't see where the class division takes place if it's not between those with guts and the others. People like that have to carry the others.

Socialism has done something that I consider to be very regrettable. It may have been necessary, but it's responsible for introducing the group spirit among employers.

In the old days, one could be a free man – and that's a marvellous thing! Is a wage-earner really free? Is even a trained engineer arriving in a relatively high post, with several assistants working under him, as I was . . . It was to be free that I started a business of my own, perhaps even against my own best interests . . . I think it's absurd to say that there's a barrier between the students and what they might be tomorrow if they have no ability. That's not where the division comes. Unfortunately, some of them will now be forced into joining a group. For a long time now the young, like their leaders, or rather the leaders of the young and the leaders of the workers, have created segregation.

The most horrible segregation was what Hitler did with the Nazi youth, by completely dividing young people from their parents and getting them to spy on their parents. This segregation is a terrible thing. The word *class* is a *shameful thing*.

They certainly tried to break down the segregation between the students and the workers. But why? Because the workers' movement that had battened onto them did them a *terrible* lot of harm, in the very field that concerned them most, that is, getting a job, these students, who, in the present set-up can't be free men, but are forced to work for someone else. They have no other thought but to be dependent on someone who will tell them what to do . . . and if that someone is socialism, it becomes more and more a matter for the state, or something just as bad, at least . . .

Bibliography

ADORNO, T. W. (1967). Vers une musique informelle. In *La Musique et ses problèmes contemporains*. Paris: Julliard.

ALQUIÉ, F. (1965). *The philosophy of surrealism*. Ann Arbor, Mich.: University of Michigan Press.

ANDRIEUX, A. & LIGNON, J. (1960). *L'Ouvrier d'aujourd'hui: sur les changements dans la condition et la conscience ouvrière*. Paris: Rivière.

ARAGON, L. (1926). *Le Paysan de Paris*. Paris: Gallimard.

— (1930). *La Peinture au défi*. Paris: Galerie Goemans.

(L')*Archibras*, No. 4 (out of series), 1968. Le Surréalisme le 18 juin 1968. Portrait de l'ennemi.

ARON, R. (1968). *La Révolution introuvable*. Paris: Fayard.

ARP, J. (1925). *Gabrielle Buffet-Picabia*.

— (1938a). *Dadaland*.

— (1938b). *Manifeste millimètre infini*.

— (1948). *On my way: poetry and essays*. New York: Wittenborn.

— (1957). *Petits poèmes à l'intention de Viani*.

— (1966). *Jours effeuillés: poèmes, essais, souvenirs 1920–1965*. Paris: Gallimard.

Atelier populaire présenté par lui-même (1968). 87 posters of May–June 1968. Paris: Usines, Universités, Union.

Au joli mai (1968). Mai–juin 1968: directives d'action. Paris: UNEF (Union Nationale des Étudiants de France). (Limited circulation.)

BARJONET, A. (1968a). *La Révolution trahie de 1968*. Paris: John Didier.

— (1968b). CGT 1968: Le subjectivisme au secours de l'ordre établi. *Les Temps modernes*, No. 265, July, pp. 94–103.

BENSAÏD, D. & WEBER, H. (1968). *Mai 1968: une répétition générale*. Collection 'Cahiers libres' No. 133. Paris: Maspero.

BERENDT, J. (1967). In memoriam: J. Coltrane. *Jazz Podium*, August.

BERGER, P. & LUCKMANN, T. (1966). *The social construction of reality*. New York: Doubleday.

BESANÇON, J. (1968). *Les Murs ont la parole*. Paris: Tchou.

BILANDZIC, D. (1967). *Gestion de l'economie Yougoslavé*. Belgrade.

BINER, P. (1968). *Le Living Theatre*. Lausanne: La Cité.

BLOCH-MICHEL, J. (1968). *Les Journées de mai 1968*. Paris: Laffont.

BON, F. & BURNIER, M.-A. (1968). *Si Mai avait gagné*. Collection 'enragée'. Paris: J.-J. Pauvert.

BOULDING, K. E. (1956). *The image: knowledge in life and society*. Ann Arbor, Mich.: University of Michigan Press; London: Oxford University Press, 1957.

BOURDIEU, P. (1965). *Un Art moyen: essai sur les usages sociaux de la photographie*. Paris: Minuit.

— & DARBEL, A. (1966). *L'Amour de l'art*. Paris: Minuit.

— & PASSERON, J.-C. (1965). *Les Héritiers*. Second edition 1967. Paris: Minuit.

BOURGES, H. (1968). *La Révolte étudiante: les animateurs parlent*. J. Sauvageot, A. Geismar, D. Cohn-Bendit, J.-P. Duteuil. Paris: Le Seuil.

BRAU, E. (1968). *Le Situationnisme ou la nouvelle internationale*. Collection 'Révolte'. Paris: Nouvelles Éditions Debresse.

BRETON, A. (1923). Clair de terre. *Littérature*.

— (1924a). *Premier manifeste du surréalisme*. Paris: KRA.

— (1924b). *Les Pas perdus*.

— (1924c). *Poisson soluble*.

— (1927). *Introduction au discours sur le peu de réalité*.

— (1928a). *Le Surréalisme et la peinture*. Paris: Gallimard; New York: Brentano, 1945.

— (1928b). *Nadja*. Paris: Gallimard. (English trans. Gloucester, Mass.: Peter Smith.)

— (1930). *Second manifeste du surréalisme*. Paris: KRA.

— (1932a). *Les Vases communicants*. Paris: Cahiers Libres.

— (1932b). *Le Revolver à cheveux blancs*. Paris: Cahiers Libres.

— (1934). *Point du jour*.

— (1935). *Position politique du surréalisme*.

— (1937). *L'Amour fou*. Paris: Gallimard.

— (ed.) (1940). *Anthologie de l'humour noir*. Paris: Sagittaire.

— (1942). *Prolégomène à un Troisième Manifeste du surréalisme ou non*.

— (1947). *Arcane 17*. Paris: Sagittaire.

— (1952). *Entretiens, 1913–1952*.

— (1962). *Manifestes du surréalisme*. New edition. Paris: J.-J. Pauvert.

— & ÉLUARD, P. (1930). *L'Immaculée Conception*. Paris: Surréalistes.

— & SOUPAULT, P. (1920). *Les Champs magnétiques*. Paris: Sans Pareil.

CAGE, JOHN (1967). Das tödliche Mass. *Jazz Podium*, September.

CARROUGES, M. (1967). *André Breton et les donnés fondamentales du surréalisme*. Collection 'Idées' No. 121. Paris: Gallimard.

CENSIER ACTION COMMITTEE (1968). *Nous sommes en marche*. Pamphlet by the Student Action Committee of the Censier Annexe of the Sorbonne. (Limited circulation.) Reproduced in *Quelle Université? Quelle Société?*

(*Le*) *Cinéma s'insurge* (1968). Paris: Losfeld–Le terrain vague.

COHN-BENDIT, D. & G. (1968). *Le Gauchisme: remède à la maladie sénile du communisme*. Collection 'Combats'. Paris: Le Seuil.

COHN-BENDIT, G. (1968). Pourquoi je suis anarchiste. *Magazine littéraire*, No. 19, July.

COMOLLI, J.-L. (1966a). Voyage au bout de la new thing. *Jazz Magazine*, No. 129.

— (1966b). Les conquérants du Nouveau Monde. *Jazz Magazine*, No. 131.

COOPER, D. G. (1967). *Psychiatry and anti-psychiatry*. London: Tavistock.

COUDRAY, J.-M. (1968). La Révolution anticipée. Pp. 91–142 in *Mai 1968: la Brèche*. Paris: Fayard.

CROZIER, M. (1964a). *The bureaucratic phenomenon*. Chicago: University of Chicago Press; London: Tavistock. (First published in French, *Le Phénomène bureaucratique*, Paris: Le Seuil, 1963.)

— (1964b). The cultural revolution: notes on the changes in the intellectual climate of France. *Daedalus*, pp. 514–542 (Special issue: 'A new Europe?').

DAHRENDORF, R. (1959). *Class and class conflict in industrial society*. London: Routledge.

DEBORD, G. (1967). *La Société du spectacle*. Paris: Buchet-Chastel.

DEJACQUES, C. (1968). *À toi l'angoisse, à moi la rage: les fresques de Nanterre*. 65 photographs. Paris: E. Nalis.

DONIOL-VALCROZE, J. (1965). Jean-Luc Godard, cinéaste masqué. *L'Avant-Scène du cinéma*, No. 46.

DURANDEAUX, J. (1968). *Les Journées de mai 68*. Paris: Desclée de Brouwer.

DUROCHER, B. (ed.) (1968). *Poèmes de la revolution: mai 1968*. Paris.

ELLIS, D. (1966). The avant-garde is not avant-garde. *Down Beat*, June.

ELLISON, R. (1964). *Shadow and art*. New York: Random House.

ÉLUARD, P. (1939). *Donner à voir*. Paris: Gallimard.

ÉPISTÉMON (1968). *Ces idées qui ont ebranlé la France*. Paris: Fayard.

FROMM, E. (1949). *Man for himself*. London: Routledge.

GABEL, J. (1962). *La Fausse Conscience*. Paris: Minuit.

GALLISSAIRES, P. (1969). Poèmes. *Les Temps modernes*, No. 271, January.

GERBER, A. (1967). Le Président était-il fou? *Cahiers du jazz*, No. 15.

GLUCKSMANN, A. (1968). *Stratégie et révolution en France 1968*. Paris: Christian Bourgois.

GODARD, J.-L. (1967). On doit tout mettre dans un film. *L'Avant-Scène du cinéma*, No. 70.

GOLDMANN, L. (1968). Projet d'enquête sociologique sur les nouvelles structures mentales, apparues en mai–juin. (Paper presented at a conference of the International Council of the Social Sciences, December.)

GOLDTHORPE, J. H., LOCKWOOD, D., BECHHOFER, F. & PLATT, J. (1968). *The affluent worker: industrial attitudes and behaviour*. Cambridge: Cambridge University Press.

GOLDTHORPE, J. H., LOCKWOOD, D., BECHHOFER, F. & PLATT, J. (1969). *The affluent worker: political attitudes and behaviour*. Cambridge: Cambridge University Press.

GUÉRIN, R. (1960). Le Style d'Armstrong. *Cahiers du jazz*, No. 1.

HODEIR, A. (1968). In L. Malson, Neufs entretiens sur le jazz neuf. *Cahiers du jazz*, No. 16/17 (Special issue: 'New thing').

HUELSENBECK, R. (1918). *Erste Dada-Rede in Deutschland*. Berlin.

(Les) Idées de l'anarchie étudiante (1968). Interview in *Magazine littéraire*, No. 19, July.

JEAN, R. (1968). La Fête iconoclaste. *La Pensée*, No. 140/141, August/October.

JONES, LEROI (1963). *Blues people: Negro music and white America*. New York: Morrow; London: McGibbon & Kee, 1965.

— (1967). *Black music*. New York: Morrow.

LABRO, P. (ed.) (1968). *Ce n'est qu'un début*. Collection 'Édition spéciale'. Paris: Éditions et publications premières.

LEBEL, J.-J. (1968). *Procès du festival d'Avignon: supermarché de la culture*. Collection 'J'accuse'. Paris: Pierre Belfond.

LEFEBVRE, H. (1967). *Position: contre les technocrates*. Paris: Gonthier.

— (1968). *L'Irruption: du Nanterre au sommet*. Paris: Anthropos.

LEFORT, C. (1968). Le Désordre nouveau. Pp. 35–62 in *Mai 1968: la Brèche*. Paris: Fayard.

LINBAUM, R. (1968). Prendre Mai au sérieux. *Kadima*, November. (Limited circulation.)

LOCKWOOD, D. (1966). Sources of variation in working class images of society. *Sociological Review*, **14** (3): 249–267.

LOURAU, R. (1967). L'Autogestion et les managers. *Autogestion*, No. 2.

— (1968a). L'Instituant contre l'institué. *Les Temps modernes*, October, pp. 681–697.

— (1968b). Penser l'autogestion. *Combat*, 31 May.

MCLUHAN, M. (1966). *Understanding media: the extensions of man*. New York: McGraw-Hill.

MALSON, L. (1968). Neuf entretiens sur le jazz neuf. *Cahiers du jazz*, No. 16/17 (Special issue: 'New thing').

MANTLER, M. (1969). Living orchestra. *Jazz Podium*, No. 3.

MARCUSE H. (1968). *La fin de l'utopie*. Collection 'Combats'. Paris: Le Seuil.

— (1969). *Vers la libération*. Paris: Minuit.

MORIN, E. (1965). L'Avenir dans la société francaise. In J.-D. Reynaud (ed.), *Tendances et volontés de la société française*. Paris: SEDEIS.

— (1968a). La Commune étudiante. Pp. 13–33 in *Mai 1968: la Brèche*. Paris: Fayard.

— (1968b). Une Révolution sans visage. Pp. 63–87 in *Mai 1968: la Brèche*. Paris: Fayard.

MOUVEMENT DU 22 MARS (1968). *Ce n'est qu'un début: continuons le combat.* Collection 'Cahiers libres' No. 124. Paris: Maspero.

NADEAU, M. (1945). *Histoire du surréalisme.* Collection 'Pierres vives'. Paris: Le Seuil. (English trans., *History of surrealism*, New York: Macmillan, 1965; London: Cape, 1968.)

NAVILLE, P. (1957). *Le Nouveau Léviathan: 1, De l'aliénation à la jouissance.* Paris: Rivière.

— (1960). Vers l'automatisme social. *Revue française de sociologie*, **1** (3): 275–285.

— (1962). *Trotsky vivant.* Paris: Julliard.

— (1963). *Vers l'automatisme social? Problèmes du travail et de l'automation.* Paris: Gallimard.

Noir et Rouge (Cahiers d'études anarchistes-communistes). Special issue, No. 72, 1968: La Grève généralisée en France, mai–juin 1968. (Limited edition.)

Nous sommes en marche (1968). See under Censier Action Committee.

ORIEUX, C. (1965). Jazz et conservatoire. *Jazz Hot*, No. 213.

PAGÈS, R. (1963). Du reportage psycho-sociologique et du racisme: à propos de la marche civique sur Washington. *Revue française de sociologie*, **4** (4): 424–437.

PANOFSKY, E. (1967). *Architecture gothique et pensée scolastique.* Postscript by P. Bourdieu. Paris: Minuit.

Quelle université? Quelle société? (1968). Texts collected by the Centre de regroupement des informations universitaires. Collection 'Combats'. Paris: Le Seuil.

REISNER, R. G. (1962). *Bird: the legend of Charlie Parker.* New York: Citadel Press.

RIBEMONT-DESSAIGNES, G. (1931). *Histoire de dada.* Paris: Gallimard.

RICŒUR, P. (1963). Structure et herméneutique. *Esprit*, November. The article is followed by a discussion with C. Lévi-Strauss.

ROLLE, P. (1962). Normes et chronométrages dans le salaire au rendement. *Cahiers de l'automation*, **4:** 9–38.

SANOUILLET, M. (1965). *Dada à Paris.* Paris: J.-J. Pauvert.

SARTRE, J.-P. (1960). *Critique de la raison dialectique.* Paris: Gallimard.

SCHULLER, G. (1968). *Early jazz: its roots and musical development.* Basic History of Jazz Series, Vol. 1. London: Oxford University Press.

Servir le peuple. Special issue, 21 May 1968.

SHEPP, A. (1966). A view from the inside. *Down Beat* (Yearbook).

STANISLAVSKI, C. (1956). *My life in art.* London: Bles.

— (1957). *The formation of the actor.*

STOCKHAUSEN, K. (1963). Die Einheit der musikalischen Zeit. In *Zeugnisse.* Frankfurt: EVA.

STÜCK, H. (1968). Französischer Mai. *Blätter für deutsche u. int. Politik*, **8**: 840–851.

TONKA, H. (1968). *Fiction de la contestation aliénée.* Paris: J.-J. Pauvert.

TOURAINE, A. (1965). *Sociologie de l'action*. Paris: Le Seuil.

— (1968). *Le Mouvement de Mai ou le communisme utopique*. Collection 'L'Histoire immédiate'. Paris: Le Seuil.

TRUFFAUT, F. (1967). La Savate et la finance, ou deux ou trois choses que je sais de lui. *L'Avant-Scène du cinéma*, No. 70.

TZARA, T. (1927). *Manifeste dada 1918*.

— (1930). *Dada manifeste sur l'amour faible et l'amour amer*.

— (1931). *Proclamation sans prétention*.

— (1968). *Les Manifestes dada*. Collection 'Libertés nouvelles'. Paris: J.-J. Pauvert.

VANEIGEM, R. (1968). *Traité de savoir-vivre à l'usage des jeunes générations*. Paris: Gallimard.

VEDEL, G. (ed.) (1962). *La Dépolitisation, mythe ou réalité?* Cahiers de la Fondation nationale des sciences politiques. Paris: A. Colin.

VIAN, B. (1953). In *Chroniques du jazz*. Paris: La Jeune Parque, 1967.

VIÉNET, R. (1967). Les situationnistes et les nouvelles formes d'action contre la politique et l'art. *Revue de l'Internationale situationniste*, No. 11.

— (1968). *Enragés et situationnistes dans le mouvement des occupations*. Collection 'Temoins'. Paris: Gallimard.

WALDBERG, P. (1965). *Chemins du surréalisme*. Bruxelles: La Connaissance.

WESLING, D. (1965). Free speech and free verse. *Nation*, 8 November.

WILLENER, A. (1957). *Images de la société et des classes sociales*. Berne.

— (1967). *Interprétation de l'organisation dans l'industrie*. Paris: Mouton.

— (1968). Intérêt et difficulté de l'étude des conflits industriels. *Epistémologie sociologique*, pp. 55–64. Paris: Anthropos.

— *et al.* (1969). *Les Cadres en mouvement*. Fondation Royaumont. Paris: EPI.

ZEGEL, S. (1968). *Les Idées de Mai*. Collection 'Idées actuelles' No. 166. Paris: Gallimard.